Essentials of Assessing, Preventing, and Overcoming Reading Difficulties

Essentials of **Psychological Assessment** Series

Everything you need to know to administer, score, and interpret the major psychological tests

I'd like to order the following *Essentials of Psychological Assessment:*

- ❑ WAIS®-IV Assessment, Second Edition (w/CD-ROM)
  978-1-118-27188-9 • $50.00
- ❑ WJ® IV Tests of Achievement
  978-1-118-79915-4 • $40.00
- ❑ Cross-Battery Assessment, Third Edition (w/CD-ROM)
  978-0-470-62195-0 • $50.00
- ❑ Executive Functions Assessment (w/CD-ROM)
  978-0-470-42202-1 • $50.00
- ❑ WPPSI™-IV Assessment (w/CD-ROM)
  978-1-11838062-8 • $50.00
- ❑ Specific Learning Disability Identification
  978-0-470-58760-7 • $40.00
- ❑ IDEA for Assessment Professionals (w/CD-ROM)
  978-0-470-87392-2 • $50.00
- ❑ Dyslexia Assessment and Intervention
  978-0-470-92760-1 • $40.00
- ❑ Autism Spectrum Disorders Evaluation and Assessment
  978-0-470-62194-3 • $40.00
- ❑ Planning, Selecting, and Tailoring Interventions for Unique Learners (w/CD-ROM)
  978-1-118-36821-3 • $50.00
- ❑ Processing Assessment, Second Edition (w/CD-ROM)
  978-1-118-36820-6 • $50.00
- ❑ School Neuropsychological Assessment, Second Edition (w/CD-ROM)
  978-1-118-17584-2 • $50.00
- ❑ Gifted Assessment
  978-1-118-58920-5 • $40.00
- ❑ Working Memory Assessment and Intervention
  978-1-118-63813-2 • $50.00
- ❑ Assessing, Preventing, and Overcoming Reading Difficulties
  978-1-118-84524-0 • $50.00

- ❑ Evidence-Based Academic Interventions
  978-0-470-20632-4 • $40.00
- ❑ Nonverbal Assessment
  978-0-471-38318-5 • $40.00
- ❑ PAI® Assessment
  978-0-471-08463-1 • $40.00
- ❑ CAS Assessment
  978-0-471-29015-5 • $40.00
- ❑ MMPI®-2 Assessment, Second Edition
  978-0-470-92323-8 • $40.00
- ❑ Myers-Briggs Type Indicator® Assessment, Second Edition
  978-0-470-34390-6 • $40.00
- ❑ Rorschach® Assessment
  978-0-471-33146-9 • $40.00
- ❑ Millon™ Inventories Assessment, Third Edition
  978-0-470-16862-2 • $40.00
- ❑ TAT and Other Storytelling Assessments, Second Edition
  978-0-470-28192-5 • $40.00
- ❑ MMPI-A™ Assessment
  978-0-471-39815-8 • $40.00
- ❑ NEPSY®-II Assessment
  978-0-470-43691-2 • $40.00
- ❑ Neuropsychological Assessment, Second Edition
  978-0-470-43747-6 • $40.00
- ❑ WJ III™ Cognitive Abilities Assessment, Second Edition
  978-0-470-56664-0 • $40.00
- ❑ WRAML2 and TOMAL-2 Assessment
  978-0-470-17911-6 • $40.00
- ❑ WMS®-IV Assessment
  978-0-470-62196-7 • $40.00
- ❑ Behavioral Assessment
  978-0-471-35367-6 • $40.00
- ❑ Forensic Psychological Assessment, Second Edition
  978-0-470-55168-4 • $40.00

- ❑ Bayley Scales of Infant Development II Assessment
  978-0-471-32651-9 • $40.00
- ❑ Career Interest Assessment
  978-0-471-35365-2 • $40.00
- ❑ 16PF® Assessment
  978-0-471-23424-1 • $40.00
- ❑ Assessment Report Writing
  978-0-471-39487-7 • $40.00
- ❑ Stanford-Binet Intelligence Scales (SB5) Assessment
  978-0-471-22404-4 • $40.00
- ❑ WISC®-IV Assessment, Second Edition (w/CD-ROM)
  978-0-470-18915-3 • $50.00
- ❑ KABC-II Assessment
  978-0-471-66733-9 • $40.00
- ❑ WIAT®-III and KTEA-II Assessment (w/CD-ROM)
  978-0-470-55169-1 • $50.00
- ❑ Cognitive Assessment with KAIT & Other Kaufman Measures
  978-0-471-38317-8 • $40.00
- ❑ Assessment with Brief Intelligence Tests
  978-0-471-26412-5 • $40.00
- ❑ Creativity Assessment
  978-0-470-13742-0 • $40.00
- ❑ WNV™ Assessment
  978-0-470-28467-4 • $40.00
- ❑ DAS-II® Assessment (w/CD-ROM)
  978-0-470-22520-2 • $50.00
- ❑ Conners Behavior Assessments™
  978-0-470-34633-4 • $40.00
- ❑ Temperament Assessment
  978-0-470-44447-4 • $40.00
- ❑ Response to Intervention
  978-0-470-56663-3 • $40.00
- ❑ ADHD Assessment for Children and Adolescents
  978-1-118-11270-0 • $40.00

Please complete the order form on the back. • To order by phone, call toll free 1-877-762-2974
To order online: www.wiley.com/essentials • To order by mail: refer to order form on next page

Essentials

of **Psychological Assessment** Series

ORDER FORM

Please send this order form with your payment (credit card or check) to:
Wiley, Attn: Customer Care, 10475 Crosspoint Blvd., Indianapolis, IN 46256

QUANTITY	TITLE	ISBN	PRICE
_____	_____	_____	_____
_____	_____	_____	_____
_____	_____	_____	_____
_____	_____	_____	_____
_____	_____	_____	_____

Shipping Charges:	Surface	2-Day	1-Day
First item	$5.00	$10.50	$17.50
Each additional item	$3.00	$3.00	$4.00
For orders greater than 15 items, please contact Customer Care at 1-877-762-2974.			

ORDER AMOUNT _____

SHIPPING CHARGES _____

SALES TAX _____

TOTAL ENCLOSED _____

NAME_____

AFFILIATION_____

ADDRESS_____

CITY/STATE/ZIP_____

TELEPHONE_____

EMAIL_____

❑ Please add me to your e-mailing list

PAYMENT METHOD:

❑ Check/Money Order   ❑ Visa   ❑ Mastercard   ❑ AmEx

Card Number _____ Exp. Date _____

Cardholder Name (Please print) _____

Signature _____

Make checks payable to **John Wiley & Sons.** Credit card orders invalid if not signed.
All orders subject to credit approval. • Prices subject to change.

To order by phone, call toll free 1-877-762-2974
To order online: www.wiley.com/essentials

WILEY

Essentials of Psychological Assessment Series

Series Editors, Alan S. Kaufman and Nadeen L. Kaufman

Essentials of 16 PF® Assessment
by Heather E.-P. Cattell and James M. Schuerger

Essentials of ADHD Assessment for Children and Adolescents
by Elizabeth P. Sparrow and Drew Erhardt

Essentials of Assessment Report Writing
by Elizabeth O. Lichtenberger, Nancy Mather, Nadeen L. Kaufman, and Alan S. Kaufman

Essentials of Assessment with Brief Intelligence Tests
by Susan R. Homack and Cecil R. Reynolds

Essentials of Autism Spectrum Disorders Evaluation and Assessment
by Celine A. Saulnier and Pamela E. Ventola

Essentials of Bayley Scales of Infant Development–II Assessment
by Maureen M. Black and Kathleen Matula

Essentials of Behavioral Assessment
by Michael C. Ramsay, Cecil R. Reynolds, and R. W. Kamphaus

Essentials of Career Interest Assessment
by Jeffrey P. Prince and Lisa J. Heiser

Essentials of CAS Assessment
by Jack A. Naglieri

Essentials of Cognitive Assessment with KAIT and Other Kaufman Measures
by Elizabeth O. Lichtenberger, Debra Broadbooks, and Alan S. Kaufman

Essentials of Conners Behavior Assessments™
by Elizabeth P. Sparrow

Essentials of Creativity Assessment
by James C. Kaufman, Jonathan A. Plucker, and John Baer

Essentials of Cross-Battery Assessment, Third Edition
by Dawn P. Flanagan, Samuel O. Ortiz, and Vincent C. Alfonso

Essentials of DAS-II® Assessment
by Ron Dumont, John O. Willis, and Colin D. Elliot

Essentials of Dyslexia Assessment and Intervention
by Nancy Mather and Barbara J. Wendling

Essentials of Evidence-Based Academic Interventions
by Barbara J. Wendling and Nancy Mather

Essentials of Executive Functions Assessment
by George McCloskey and Lisa A. Perkins

Essentials of Forensic Psychological Assessment, Second Edition
by Marc J. Ackerman

Essentials of IDEA for Assessment Professionals
by Guy McBride, Ron Dumont, and John O. Willis

Essentials of Individual Achievement Assessment
by Douglas K. Smith

Essentials of KABC-II Assessment
by Alan S. Kaufman, Elizabeth O. Lichtenberger, Elaine Fletcher-Janzen, and Nadeen L. Kaufman

Essentials of Millon™ Inventories Assessment, Third Edition
by Stephen Strack

Essentials of MMPI-A™ Assessment
by Robert P. Archer and Radhika Krishnamurthy

Essentials of MMPI-2® Assessment, Second Edition
by David S. Nichols

Essentials of Myers-Briggs Type Indicator® Assessment, Second Edition
by Naomi Quenk

Essentials of NEPSY®-II Assessment
by Sally L. Kemp and Marit Korkman

Essentials of Neuropsychological Assessment, Second Edition
by Nancy Hebben and William Milberg

Essentials of Nonverbal Assessment
by Steve McCallum, Bruce Bracken, and John Wasserman

Essentials of PAI® Assessment
by Leslie C. Morey

Essentials of Planning, Selecting, and Tailoring Interventions for Unique Learners
edited by Jennifer T. Mascolo, Vincent C. Alfonso, and Dawn P. Flanagan

Essentials of Processing Assessment, Second Edition
by Milton J. Dehn

Essentials of Response to Intervention
by Amanda M. VanDerHeyden and Matthew K. Burns

Essentials of Rorschach® Assessment
by Tara Rose, Nancy Kaser-Boyd, and Michael P. Maloney

Essentials of School Neuropsychological Assessment, Second Edition
by Daniel C. Miller

Essentials of Specific Learning Disability Identification
by Dawn Flanagan and Vincent C. Alfonso

Essentials of Stanford-Binet Intelligence Scales (SB5) Assessment
by Gale H. Roid and R. Andrew Barram

Essentials of TAT and Other Storytelling Assessments, Second Edition
by Hedwig Teglasi

Essentials of Temperament Assessment
by Diana Joyce

Essentials of WAIS®-IV Assessment, Second Edition
by Elizabeth O. Lichtenberger and Alan S. Kaufman

Essentials of WIAT®-III and KTEA-II Assessment
by Elizabeth O. Lichtenberger and Kristina C. Breaux

Essentials of WISC®-IV Assessment, Second Edition
by Dawn P. Flanagan and Alan S. Kaufman

Essentials of WJ III™ Cognitive Abilities Assessment, Second Edition
by Fredrick A. Schrank, Daniel C. Miller, Barbara J. Wendling, and Richard W. Woodcock

Essentials of WJ IV™ Tests of Achievement Assessment
by Nancy Mather and Barbara J. Wendling

Essentials of WMS®-IV Assessment
by Lisa Whipple Drozdick, James A. Holdnack, and Robin C. Hilsabeck

Essentials of WNV™ Assessment
by Kimberly A. Brunnert, Jack A. Naglieri, and Steven T. Hardy-Braz

Essentials of WPPSI®-IV Assessment
by Susan Engi Raiford and Diane Coalson

Essentials of WRAML2 and TOMAL-2 Assessment
by Wayne Adams and Cecil R. Reynolds

Essentials

of Assessing, Preventing, and Overcoming Reading Difficulties

David A. Kilpatrick

WILEY

Published by John Wiley & Sons, Inc., Hoboken, New Jersey.
Published simultaneously in Canada.

For general information on our other products and services please contact our Customer Care Department within the United States at (800) 762-2974, outside the United States at (317) 572-3993 or fax (317) 572-4002.

Wiley publishes in a variety of print and electronic formats and by print-on-demand. Some material included with standard print versions of this book may not be included in e-books or in print-on-demand. If this book refers to media such as a CD or DVD that is not included in the version you purchased, you may download this material at http://booksupport.wiley.com. For more information about Wiley products, visit www.wiley.com.

Library of Congress Cataloging-in-Publication Data:

Kilpatrick, David A.
    Essentials of assessing, preventing, and overcoming reading difficulties / David A. Kilpatrick.
        pages cm. – (Essentials of psychological assessment)
    Includes index.
        ISBN 978-1-118-84524-0 (paperback) – ISBN 978-1-118-84540-0 (epdf) –
ISBN 978-1-118-84528-8 (epub)
1. Reading. 2. Language and languages. I. Title.
LB1050.K493 2015
372.41–dc23

2015013485

Cover image: © Greg Kuchik/Getty Images
Cover design: Wiley

This book is printed on acid-free paper. ∞

Printed in the United States of America

10 9 8 7 6 5

To Dr. Philip J. McInnis, Sr., In Memoriam
A pioneer in applying research findings to classroom practice

and

To Carol Byrnes-Troendle, In Memoriam
A resource teacher whose energy, enthusiasm, and dedication were an inspiration to all who knew her

CONTENTS

SERIES PREFACE

In the *Essentials of Psychological Assessment* series, we have attempted to provide the reader with books that will deliver key practical information in the most efficient and accessible style. Many books in the series feature specific instruments in a variety of domains, such as cognition, personality, education, and neuropsychology. Other books, such as *Essentials of Assessing, Preventing, and Overcoming Reading Difficulties*, focus on crucial topics for professionals who are involved with assessment in any way—topics such as specific reading disabilities, evidence-based interventions, or ADHD assessment. For the experienced professional, books in the series offer a concise yet thorough review of a test instrument or a specific area of expertise, including numerous tips for best practices. Students can turn to series books for a clear and concise overview of the important assessment tools and key topics in which they must become proficient to practice skillfully, efficiently, and ethically in their chosen fields.

Wherever feasible, visual cues highlighting key points are utilized alongside systematic, step-by-step guidelines. Chapters are focused and succinct. Topics are organized for an easy understanding of the essential material related to a particular test or topic. Theory and research are continually woven into the fabric of each book, but always to enhance the practical application of the material, rather than to sidetrack or overwhelm readers. With this series, we aim to challenge and assist readers interested in psychological assessment to aspire to the highest level of competency by arming them with the tools they need for knowledgeable, informed practice. We have long been advocates of "intelligent" testing—the notion that numbers are meaningless unless they are brought to life by the clinical acumen and expertise of examiners. Assessment must be used to make a difference in the child's or adult's life, or why bother to test? All books in the series—whether devoted to specific tests or general topics—are consistent with this credo. We want this series to help our readers, novice and veteran alike, to benefit from the intelligent assessment approaches of the authors of each book.

In the present volume, David Kilpatrick, an expert and experienced clinician who excels in reading assessment and intervention, provides a window into the vast world of research into reading acquisition and reading disabilities. Research reports in this area number in the thousands. Rather than a global survey, this volume presents information that is directly relevant for understanding and assessing students who present with various types of reading difficulties. With the material in this volume as a guide, practitioners can use standard psychoeducational assessment tools and approaches to more precisely determine the reasons why these students struggle in reading. The author shows how such assessment information can lead directly to well-targeted and highly effective reading interventions.

Alan S. Kaufman, PhD, and Nadeen L. Kaufman, EdD, Series Editors
Yale Child Study Center, Yale University School of Medicine

PREFACE

Reading difficulties represent one of the most common referral issues in schools. School psychologists, literacy specialists, special education teachers, and other educational professionals are routinely called upon to evaluate students with reading problems and to generate intervention plans. The present volume is designed to assist such professionals by opening up a vast and largely untapped body of empirical research on reading acquisition and reading difficulties. There have been literally thousands of research studies in the last four decades on all aspects of reading, but only small bits and pieces seem to make their way out of the scientific journals and into our K–12 classrooms.

To illustrate this, studies of the most common intervention practices used for struggling readers show that those interventions result in an average improvement of 2 to 5 standard score points. By contrast, some of the research coming from federal intervention grant initiatives indicate average improvements of 12 to 25 standard score points that are maintained at 2-, 3-, or 4-year follow-ups (see Chapters 10 and 11). The fact that we are not seeing average gains like these in our schools demonstrates why I referred to this research as "largely untapped."

In 1997, after I had been a practicing school psychologist for nearly a decade, Dr. Philip J. McInnis, a former president of the New York Association of School Psychologists, introduced me to the top scientific journals publishing research on reading. Being an adjunct lecturer in psychology at the time, I had access to these journals, which allowed me to vigorously pursue this area. In addition, McInnis asked me to travel with him for a few summers to his workshops in school districts around the northeastern United States. These districts had been using his Assured Readiness for Learning program. McInnis's program simply involved translating the research with the best-available outcomes into a practical curriculum for teachers. I got to meet administrators and teachers who were very excited to share how they had dramatically reduced the number of struggling readers in their schools. McInnis used to publicly claim that his program would reduce the number of struggling readers by 50%. Privately he said it was closer to 75%. I asked why he did not say this publicly. He replied that educators had a hard enough time believing his 50% claims so he felt he would lose all credibility if he publicized the actual results! Although McInnis's claims may sound outlandish to the average educator, they are not. Some of the most successful studies reported in the literature have demonstrated across-the-board reductions in the number of struggling readers by 70%–80% or more (e.g., Shapiro & Solity, 2008; Vellutino et al., 1996). McInnis had such good results because was applying approaches from research studies that had displayed similar impressive results. McInnis passed away in March of 2002, and his highly effective program has been largely inactive and not promoted since that time.

Since 1997 I have also endeavored to integrate the reading research into my assessment practices. I developed what I call *intervention-oriented assessment,* which involves determining *why* a student struggles in reading. The reading research field has fairly well-established knowledge about the component skills needed for success in reading, and I have tried to align my assessment practices with those findings. Chapters 6 through 9 are a reflection of those efforts.

What I believe to be the most important contribution of this book is the presentation of *orthographic mapping* in Chapter 4. Orthographic mapping refers to the mental process readers use to store written words for later, instant retrieval. Orthographic mapping explains how students turn unfamiliar words into instantly accessible sight words, with no sounding out or guessing. This is something that weak readers do very poorly, and as a result, they have limited sight vocabularies and limited reading fluency. Now in its third decade of empirical validation, orthographic mapping is the "holy grail" of reading education. Students who are good at remembering the words they read (i.e., orthographic mapping) develop skilled word-level reading, whereas those who do not, become weak or "disabled" readers. Orthographic mapping represents a very large part of reading acquisition and should guide curricular decisions, evaluation practices, and intervention approaches. Indeed, the highly successful research results described above came from studies whose interventions were consistent with our understanding of orthographic mapping.

Many folks reading this volume will simply want the "bottom line" in terms of what needs to be done for assessing and remediating reading. I understand this kind of thinking, given our busy professional lives. However, our educational system has many long-held beliefs about reading that are fully entrenched in our curricula, textbooks, and general thinking. Simply presenting the "bottom line" will not likely promote change.

It is for this reason that I have decided to "pull back the curtain" to reveal not only what we know, but also the science behind how we know it. Nonetheless, this volume contains much practical information related to assessment and intervention, so those looking for the bottom line should find precisely the kind of information they are looking for.

ACKNOWLEDGMENTS

Many people assisted me in some way or another in writing this book, and I owe them a debt of gratitude. First, I would like to thank Drs. Alan and Nadeen Kaufman for including this volume in their celebrated *Essentials* series. It is an honor for me to be a contributor to this excellent collection of resources.

Next, my thanks go to Marquita Flemming, Senior Editor at John Wiley & Sons, Inc., who has been a great source of encouragement and patience during these last 21 months. She made the experience a very positive one. Thanks also to Elisha Benjamin and Melinda Noack for their assistance during the production process.

I would like to thank Dr. Dawn Flanagan for suggesting I submit a proposal to this series and for recommending me to the editors. Her role was pivotal.

Numerous people read parts of this manuscript and offered comments and suggestions. My thanks go to Dr. Larry Lewandowski, Dr. Benjamin Lovett, Dr. Joann Baumgardner, Beth DeWolf, and Cheri Panek. Luqman Michel, a reading tutor in Malaysia, read nearly the entire manuscript and contributed countless improvements. I would like to thank Sue Alongi and Dr. Cara Smith, both school psychologists who provided me with tests to review that I did not otherwise have available.

My wife Andrea provided feedback on portions of the manuscript and helped free up time for me to work on the book. I greatly appreciate her support.

I would like to thank the interlibrary loan staff at SUNY Cortland who provided me with dozens of hard-to-access resources, always in a timely fashion. Thanks also go to Edward Copenhagen, the special collections librarian at the Monroe C. Gutman Library, Harvard Graduate School of Education, who was incredibly accommodating during the three days I spent there while preparing this volume (and thanks to the Dacey family for letting me stay with them for those three days). My research assistants Meaghan Stadtlander and Deniz (Ecem) Cabas helped download hundreds of journal articles from our library site and scanned many of my books, so almost all of the resources I needed were always accessible on my computer.

I extend a very special thanks to fellow school psychologist Dr. Shawn O'Brien. She graciously read the entire manuscript and provided extensive feedback on multiple levels. Had she done any more work on this, I would have had to list her as a coauthor!

One

INTRODUCTION

THE UNFAIR RACE

Picture yourself attending a high school track meet. The athletes are lining up for the 1,600-meter race, which requires four laps around the track. There are six lanes on the track, and you notice that in one lane is a set of high hurdles and in another lane is a set of low hurdles. The other four lanes have no hurdles. When the gun sounds, the runners in the two lanes with the hurdles are soon behind the other runners and continue to get farther behind as the race progresses. The runner in the lane with the high hurdles is the farthest behind. As the race goes on, the gap widens. There is almost no likelihood that either of these runners will catch up with the others. The whole event seems surreal and quite unfair—even painful to watch.

This scenario has close parallels to the development of reading skills among our K–12 students. The top two-thirds of students, as represented by the four lanes without hurdles, take off down the track and have nothing hindering them from running. The bottom third has differing degrees of hindrance based upon how high their hurdles are. Just as one-third of the runners had hurdles, the National Assessment of Educational Progress indicates that each year, about 30% to 34% of fourth graders in the United States read below a basic level.

Efforts to help these weaker readers have been geared toward teaching them how to jump more efficiently over their hurdles. This volume is not about helping children become better and more efficient hurdlers. It is about removing the hurdles from the track before the race even starts. It is also about removing hurdles still ahead of the runners once the race has begun.

> **DON'T FORGET**
>
> This volume is not about helping children become more efficient hurdlers. It is about removing the hurdles from the track.

DON'T FORGET

···

The goal of this book is to open up the vast and extensive world of empirical research into reading acquisition and reading disabilities in order to capitalize on the most useful findings for assessing reading difficulties and for designing highly effective interventions.

The goal of this book is to open up the vast and extensive world of empirical research into reading acquisition and reading disabilities. Surprisingly, this large and heavily grant-funded scientific endeavor has not had sufficient impact on the fields of general education, literacy education, special education, and school psychology (see more on this later in the chapter). Yet school psychologists, literacy specialists, and special educators play a large role in evaluating children with reading difficulties. They are called upon to make recommendations about how to best address the learning needs of poor readers. This volume will provide educational professionals with the tools and knowledge they need to pinpoint the reasons why a given student is struggling in reading. It will also provide recommendations that result in highly successful interventions.

THE IMPORTANCE OF READING

It is difficult to overestimate the importance of reading for success in school and in life. Reading is essential for all academic subjects. Science and social studies require textbook reading. Many math tests, including state-level assessments, require students to read word problems. Poor reading virtually guarantees poor writing skills. Art, music, health, and physical education classes sometimes require background reading and written projects. As a result, reading affects a student's entire academic experience. How well children succeed in school affects their future endeavors in life (Miller, McCardle, & Hernandez, 2010). While we all know of cases to the contrary, it is normally the students who do well in school who are more likely to go to college and have greater career opportunities.

Poor reading can also affect school behavior (McGee, Prior, Williams, Smart, & Sanson, 2002; Morgan, Farkas, Tufis, & Sperling, 2008; Tomblin, Zhang, Buckwalter, & Catts, 2000; Willcutt et al., 2007). Many children who are poor readers display behavior problems. There appears to be a two-way relationship between poor reading and at least some of the behavior problems we see in schools (Morgan et al., 2008). Significant reading difficulties appear to put students in later elementary school at a higher risk for depression (Maughan, Rowe, Loeber, & Stouthamer-Loeber, 2003). Students who are poor readers in third grade are 4 times more likely to become high school dropouts compared to skilled readers (Hernandez, 2012). At a 30-year follow-up of over 1,300 adults who had been diagnosed with a reading disability at age 7, McLaughlin and colleagues found that these adults were less likely to have obtained post–high school degrees and were more likely to attain lower levels of income than those who were average or better readers at age 7 (McLaughlin, Speirs, & Shenassa, 2014).

School districts are fully aware of the impact reading has on students. Millions of dollars are spent every year on general educational and special educational reading remediation. Despite this, poor readers generally remain poor readers (Jacobson, 1999; Maughan, Hagell, Rutter, & Yule, 1994; Morgan et al., 2008; Protopapas, Sideridis, Mouzaki, & Simos, 2011; Short, Feagans, McKinney, & Appelbaum, 1986; Sparks, Patton, & Murdoch, 2014). Studies of both general and special educational remedial reading indicate that these efforts have not been effective at normalizing reading performance (Bentum & Aaron, 2003; Jacobson, 1999; Moody, Vaughn, Hughes, & Fischer, 2000; Rashotte, McPhee, & Torgesen, 2001; Swanson & Vaughn, 2010; Torgesen, Rashotte, Alexander, Alexander, & MacPhee, 2003).

It would be easy to conclude from this that there is a substantial portion of students, perhaps due to neurodevelopmentally based reading disabilities, who are simply unable to develop normal reading skills, regardless of the nature of the remediation. However, there is ample empirical evidence to challenge such an assumption. For example, in a large study funded by the National Institute of Child Health and Development (NICHD), researchers were able to reduce the number of children who require ongoing general or special educational remediation from the national average of about 30% down to 3% (Vellutino et al., 1996). In another NICHD-funded study, researchers showed that a large percentage of third through fifth graders with severe reading disabilities could reach an average reading level, and stay there (Torgesen et al., 2001). In fact, it has been shown in multiple empirical studies that a large proportion of students at risk for reading difficulties, as well as students with severe reading disabilities, can develop and maintain normalized reading skills when provided with the right kind of intervention (Alexander, Andersen, Heilman, Voeller, & Torgesen, 1991; Lennon & Slesinski, 1999; Rashotte et al., 2001; Shapiro & Solity, 2008; Simos et al., 2002; Torgesen, 2004a; Torgesen et al., 2001, 2003; Torgesen, Wagner, Rashotte, Herron, & Lindamood, 2010; Truch, 1994, 2003, 2004; Vellutino et al., 1996).

If this is the case, why are we not capitalizing on these findings?

THE GAP BETWEEN READING RESEARCH AND CLASSROOM PRACTICE

There are several reasons why our K–12 schools are not making use of the kinds of encouraging findings described above. In what follows, some of the most important ones are presented.

An Illustration of the Gap Between Research and Practice

Since the release of the Report of the National Reading Panel in 2000, phonological awareness has gained popularity in the literacy-teaching repertoire of early elementary school teachers. *Phonological awareness* refers to an awareness of the sound structure (syllables, phonemes) of spoken language. There has been an explosion of materials, programs, and opportunities available regarding phonological awareness. One might even consider phonological awareness to be an educational fad. Consider the following quote by Nancy Lewkowicz in the *Journal of Educational Psychology*:

> The ability to perceive a spoken word as a sequence of individual sounds, which has been referred to recently as phonemic awareness, phonological awareness, and auditory analysis skill, is attracting increasing attention among reading researchers. The high correlation between this ability and success in reading is by now well established. (p. 686)

This quote appears to support the emerging interest in phonological awareness in recent years. In reality, this quote does no such thing—the quote is from 1980! It seems there was a lag time of about 20 years from when the scientific findings regarding phonological awareness became "well established" and when it became popular in schools. Actually, phonological awareness training *was* popular in the 1970s and early 1980s, but ironically it began to decline not long after Lewkowicz's comment just quoted. It fell out of use, apparently as a result of changes in reading philosophies in the 1980s and 1990s, even though researchers continued to study the role of phonological awareness in reading. This example serves to illustrate just how large the gap between research and practice can be. It was well established by 1980 that phonemic awareness was an essential element for successful reading, but there were nearly two decades in which it was not being incorporated into literacy instruction.

THE UNFORTUNATE REALITY ABOUT READING RESEARCH: NOBODY KNOWS ABOUT IT!

In 1999, the American Federation of Teachers (AFT), the second-largest teachers' union in the United States, published *Teaching Reading IS Rocket Science*

(American Federation of Teachers, 1999). This book stated that a "chasm exists" between the scientific research into literacy and classroom practice.

Fast-forward 10 years to July 2009 at the international conference for the Society for the Scientific Study of Reading. R. M. Joshi, a professor of literacy from Texas A&M, was presenting to about 40 researchers in a breakout session I attended. Joshi displayed results from a survey of college literacy instructors who teach and train public school teachers to teach children to read. His data showed that, as a group, these literacy instructors were unfamiliar with the scientifically oriented research on reading. For example, 80% confused phonemic awareness with phonics. The reaction in the room was astonishing and uncharacteristic of a room full of scientists. There were audible gasps and moans, as if Joshi had announced that a beloved member of the society had passed away. The reactions suggest that the researchers in the room were confronting the reality that their life's work was not making its way out of the scientific journals and into our K–12 classrooms.

Other studies have shown that K–3 general education teachers (Cunningham, Perry, Stanovich, & Stanovich, 2004), reading teachers/literacy specialists (Moats, 1994, 2009), special education teachers (Boardman, Argüelles, Vaughn, Tejero Hughes, & Klingner, 2005), teachers-in-training (Ness & Southall, 2010), Head Start teachers (Hindman & Wasik, 2008; O'Leary, Cockburn, Powell, & Diamond, 2010), and English as a second language (ESL)/English language learner (ELL) teachers (Goldfus, 2012) are generally unfamiliar with the scientific findings regarding reading acquisition and reading difficulties. Sally Shaywitz, a neuroscientist and reading researcher who heads the Yale Center for Dyslexia and Creativity, expressed frustration over "the relative lack of dissemination and practical application of these remarkable advances" (2003, p. 4).

Joshi's study appeared later that year in a special issue of the *Journal of Learning Disabilities* that was devoted to addressing the gap between reading research and classroom practice (Joshi, Binks, Hougen, et al., 2009). Another study in that special issue found that undergraduate and graduate textbooks on literacy that were designed to prepare teachers drew very little from the empirical findings on reading (Joshi, Binks, Graham, et al., 2009).

It would be easy to conclude that college professors and textbook authors are to blame for this gap between research and practice. However, such finger-pointing would be overly simplistic, unfair, and quite unproductive. The problem is that the fields of early childhood education, literacy, and special education all have their own journals and textbooks. Most of the scientific research on reading is outside the journals in those fields. In an article about dyslexia for reading specialists, Erika Gray laments: "Unfortunately, many of the articles and studies on this disorder are published in journals teachers rarely read" (2008, p. 116).

An example that is closer to home for school psychologists may bring the issue into focus. In a report in *School Psychology Review*, Nelson and Machek (2007) surveyed 497 school psychologists' knowledge and graduate training regarding the research related to reading acquisition and reading difficulties. Their results indicated that knowledge about the scientific findings on reading is quite limited within our field. This raises the question as to why there is such limited knowledge of reading research among those who need it the most.

WHY IS THERE A GAP BETWEEN RESEARCH AND CLASSROOM PRACTICE?

There are several reasons that reading research is not well known to educational professionals. One is the fact that scientific journals are inaccessible unless one lives near a university library. Once educators get their degrees, they lose access to the journals. Second, even if the journals were accessible, where would one begin? There have been thousands of research reports on reading acquisition and reading difficulties in the last 40 years, spread across over 100 journals (see Rapid Reference 1.1). It would be the proverbial needle in a haystack problem trying to find the most relevant information. While preparing this chapter, a search on the term "dyslexia" in the PsycINFO database, which is comprised primarily of scientific research journals like those in Rapid Reference 1.1, yielded 6,875 articles. The term "phonics" returned 1,309 results and "phonological aware-ness" and "phonemic awareness" combined to yield 3,659. The terms "visual word recognition" and "visual word identification" had 1,471 hits and "reading comprehension" returned 12,731 articles! The needle in a haystack analogy is no exaggeration.

Every year, there are hundreds of newly published, scientifically oriented research reports on reading. Even the researchers themselves struggle to remain current in their niche areas within the broader field of reading research. Books are more accessible than journals, and there are dozens of books written by reading researchers that cover many facets of the scientific study of reading. Most of these books, however, are technical books written for others in the field and presume much prior understanding on the part of the reader. Also, they are not typically available in catalogs or on websites aimed at teachers, administrators, and school psychologists. Books that accurately review reading research written for educational professionals are surprisingly scarce. A list of such books is provided in the "Further Reading" section at the end of this volume.

≡ *Rapid Reference 1.1 Journals That Report Empirical Research on Reading*

Reading/literacy journals that publish only empirical studies on reading acquisition and/or reading difficulties

Annals of Dyslexia

Dyslexia

Journal of Research in Reading

Reading and Writing: An Interdisciplinary Journal

Scientific Studies of Reading

Written Language and Literacy

Reading/literacy journals that routinely publish empirical studies on reading acquisition and/or reading difficulties

Journal of Literacy Research

Literacy Research and Instruction

Reading Psychology

Reading Research Quarterly

Non-literacy-related journals that regularly include empirical studies on reading

American Educational Research Journal

Applied Psycholinguistics

Assessment for Effective Intervention

Australian Journal of Learning Difficulties

Brain and Language

British Journal of Educational Psychology

Cognition

Cognitive Psychology

Cortex

Journal of Child Psychology and Psychiatry

Journal of Educational Psychology

Journal of Experimental Child Psychology

Journal of Experimental Psychology: Human Perception and Performance

Journal of Experimental Psychology: Learning, Memory, and Cognition

Journal of Learning Disabilities

Journal of Memory and Language

Journal of Research on Educational Effectiveness

Language, Speech, and Hearing Services in Schools

Learning and Instruction

Learning Disabilities: A Contemporary Journal

Learning Disabilities: A Multidisciplinary Journal

Learning Disabilities Quarterly

Learning Disabilities: Research and Practice

Memory and Cognition

Psychonomic Bulletin and Review

Quarterly Journal of Experimental Psychology

A sampling of journals that occasionally include empirical research on reading acquisition and/or reading disabilities

Applied Neuropsychology

Australian Journal of Language and Literacy

Australian Journal of Psychology

Behavior and Brain Function

Behavior Research Methods, Instruments and Computers

Biological Psychiatry

Biological Psychology

Brain

Brain Research

British Educational Research Journal

British Journal of Developmental Psychology

British Journal of Psychology

Canadian Journal of Experimental Psychology

Child Development

Cognitive Brain Research

Cognitive Neuropsychology

Cognitive Science

Contemporary Educational Psychology

Developmental Neuropsychology

Developmental Psychology

Developmental Science

Early Childhood Research Quarterly

Educational and Child Psychology

Educational Psychology Review

European Journal of Cognitive Psychology

Exceptional Children

Exceptionality

International Journal of Disability, Development and Education

International Journal of Language and Communication Disorders

Journal of Behavioral Education

Journal of Child Neurology

Journal of Cognitive Neuroscience

Journal of Communication Disorders

Journal of Deaf Studies and Deaf Education

Journal of Educational and Developmental Psychology

Journal of Educational Research

Journal of Psychoeducational Assessment

Journal of Research in Childhood Education

Journal of School Psychology

Journal of Special Education

Journal of Speech, Language, and Hearing Research

Journal of Vision

Language and Cognitive Processes
Learning and Individual Differences
NeuroImage
Neurology
Neuron
NeuroReport
Neuropsychologia
Neuropsychology
Proceedings of the National Academy of
  Sciences
Psychological Bulletin
Psychological Review

Psychological Science
Psychology in the Schools
Remedial and Special Education
Review of Educational Research
Scandinavian Journal of Educational
  Research
Scandinavian Journal of Psychology
School Psychology Quarterly
School Psychology Review
Trends in Cognitive Science
Vision Research

The Most Important Scientific Discovery You Have Never Heard Of

Another problem with translating research into practice is that one of the most significant discoveries about reading is absent from nearly every presentation of reading research to those outside the research community. This is the discovery and empirical validation of *orthographic mapping*, which is the process students use to turn unfamiliar written words into instantly accessible "sight words" (Ehri, 1998a, 2005a, 2014; Kilpatrick, 2014a; see Chapter 4). How does an unfamiliar word become a familiar sight word? Why do poor readers have limited sight vocabularies? Orthographic mapping

> **CAUTION**
> ....
> The term *sight word* has at least three different definitions in education: (1) an alternative term for the classic *whole-word*, Dick-and-Jane-style reading approach; (2) an irregular word that cannot be adequately sounded out, such as *sign, one, from, said*; and (3) a word that is instantly recognized. This third definition of sight word refers to a known or familiar word as opposed to an unfamiliar word that has to be sounded out or guessed. In this book, *only the third definition* of sight word is used.

answers these questions. When reading research is presented, whether in books or other documents such as the National Reading Panel (NICHD, 2000), the focus is on phonemic awareness, phonics, fluency, and reading comprehension. Absent from such presentations is information on (a) *how* a student develops a large and instantly accessible pool of sight words, and (b) *why* some students have such limited sight vocabularies (see the Caution regarding the term *sight word*).

> ## DON'T FORGET
> ....
> In this book, a *sight word* refers to a word that is instantly recognized regardless of whether it is phonically regular or irregular. Thus, a sight word is a known or familiar written word as opposed to a word that is unfamiliar and needs to be sounded out or guessed. A *sight vocabulary* refers to the pool of words that an individual can instantly and effortlessly recognize.

In a sense, orthographic mapping represents the "holy grail" of reading education. This skill determines whether students easily remember the words they see. Students who are poor at remembering the words they read must rely heavily on phonic decoding and/or guessing words from context. Students with reading problems are very inefficient at orthographic mapping, whereas typically developing readers acquire this skill quite naturally. Chapter 4 of this book covers orthographic mapping in detail.

Questioning a Scientific Approach to Reading

An additional factor that has hindered the adoption of reading research findings is the apparent distrust of the scientific study of reading by some prominent authors in the literacy field (Goodman, 1989, 2005; Smith, 1999). They are advocates of the three-cueing systems model of reading. The three-cueing systems model represents the foundation of the approach to reading that has gone by various names such as the *literacy-based approach, whole language,* and *balanced instruction* (Goodman, 2005). This philosophy of literacy has had an enormous impact on reading instruction since the 1980s. Some high-profile proponents of this approach argue against most of the methods used in the current enterprise of reading research (Goodman, 1989, 2005; Smith, 1999). Various scientists (e.g., Ehri, 1998b; Stanovich, 1993) have catalogued the vociferous efforts by some advocates of whole language to steer teachers away from the scientific findings on reading. The point here is not to malign proponents of the whole language approach to literacy. They have clearly dedicated their careers to helping children develop a love of literacy. Rather, the point is to recognize one of the significant reasons why there exists such a gap between reading research and classroom literacy instruction.

The Contentious Environment of the "Reading Wars"

In 1955, Rudolph Flesch published *Why Johnny Can't Read* and made a presentation at a large reading conference claiming that phonics was superior to the classic whole word type of instruction. He concluded his presentation by saying that teachers who did not use phonics were communists! In 1955, McCarthyism was in full swing.

History repeated itself around 1990 at an International Reading Association conference. M. J. Adams read a report from a research review that indicated that phonics and phonemic awareness were essential for skilled reading. A whole-language advocate was the next speaker, and he was visibly upset by Adams's presentation. He said to the crowd: "Someone get a silver bullet and shoot this woman, she's a vampire!" Dr. Philip McInnis was in the audience and recounted the story (personal communication, July, 1998). Reading researcher Linnea Ehri (1998b) and a reporter for the *Atlantic Monthly* (Levine, 1994) also chronicled the incident. McInnis indicated that he was puzzled that an educated person would say something so bizarre; everyone knows a silver bullet is for a werewolf and a stake through the heart is required for a vampire (McInnis, personal communication, July, 1998).

Humorous anecdotes aside, such outlandish comments illustrate the heated debates about reading over the last few decades. Yet, we have a way of resolving such debates: the scientific method. Matters of importance should be "settled by research rather than by proclamation" (Ehri, 1998b, p. 100). However, scientific findings are not always met with enthusiasm in the atmosphere of the Reading Wars, which has fostered defensiveness rather than an openness to new findings.

Summarizing the Causes of the Gap Between Research and Practice

We have identified several reasons why reading research is not making its way into K–12 contexts: inadequate training of teachers and school psychologists, inaccessibility of the research journals, the sheer volume of the research, limited available books summarizing the research for teachers, the efforts by some to dissuade educators from paying attention to the research, and the limited openness resulting from the Reading Wars. There are likely other reasons, but these seem sufficient to account for much of the problem.

THE POWERFUL RESEARCH RESULTS WE HAVE BEEN MISSING

The most encouraging findings from the research are not about small improvements in struggling readers. They are about a revolution in how we understand literacy development and reading difficulties. The following are descriptions of studies with highly successful outcomes in at-risk readers and students with reading disabilities.

Prevention in At-Risk Students

The National Reading Panel (NICHD, 2000) reviewed numerous studies regarding kindergarten instruction that substantially reduced the number of struggling readers. The basic gist is that if you provide kindergarteners with (a) direct and explicit phonological awareness training, (b) ample letter-sound instruction, and (c) if you teach the connections between those two, you will substantially reduce the number of students struggling in reading at the end of first, second, and even later grades. To illustrate, Shapiro and Solity (2008) did explicit and systematic phonological awareness training and letter-sound instruction with low socioeconomic status (SES) students and compared their findings to a school matched for SES and beginning skills that was doing "business as usual" kindergarten instruction. They found that by the end of first grade, the number of struggling readers in the school that represented the experimental condition was 75% lower than in the comparison school.

Early Intervention

Vellutino et al. (1996) intervened in the spring of first grade with 74 students who were at risk for reading difficulties. They represented the lowest 9% of students who did poorly on letter names, letter sounds, and basic phonological awareness in a kindergarten screening the year before. The intervention consisted of intensive phonemic awareness training, systematic instruction in phonics, and the opportunity to read connected text. By the end of the 15-week intervention, 67% of these most severely at-risk students scored at or above average on tests of word-level reading (above the 30th percentile), and these results were maintained 3 years later (Vellutino, Scanlon, & Lyon, 2000). For those not up to an average level, an additional 8 weeks of tutoring was provided in the fall of second grade, resulting in only 15% of the original at-risk students continuing to score below the 30th percentile at the end of second grade. Vellutino et al. (1996) projected their results across the original population of students screened in kindergarten from which these at-risk students were drawn. Assuming their intervention would work with less involved cases (and research suggests it would, e.g., Fletcher et al., 1994; Stanovich & Siegel, 1994), they indicated that with such an intervention available, only 3% of the total population they drew from would score below the 30th percentile and of those, only half (1.5%) would score below the 16th percentile.

Intervention With Older Students

Torgesen et al. (2001) intervened with 60 third through fifth graders with average IQ scores and very severe reading disabilities. Their mean standard score for word-level reading on the Woodcock Reading Mastery Test–Revised (WRMT-R) was in the bottom 2% nationally. Following intensive instruction in phonemic awareness and phonics and the opportunity to read connected text, these students made average gains of 14 standard score points on the WRMT-R Word Identification subtest and 20 to 27 points on the Word Attack subtest. These results were maintained at 1- and 2-year follow-ups. Most startling was that nearly 40% of these students with severe reading disabilities required no ongoing special educational reading help after the intervention.

Some of the most common approaches used with poor readers (e.g., repeated readings, READ 180, Reading Recovery; see Chapter 11) tend to display improvements that range from 3 to 5 standard score points. With such small gains, these children rarely catch up. However, there is ample research to show that weak readers can progress far beyond that, with a fairly large percentage developing normalized reading skills, even for students who previously scored in the bottom 2% to 3% of the population. There is no suggestion here that reading problems can be eliminated entirely. However, based on the studies with the most successful outcomes, it seems that a large majority of reading difficulties/disabilities can be prevented or corrected, and for those not normalized, reading performance can be much higher than traditionally thought.

Vellutino, Scanlon, Zhang, and Schatschneider (2008) pointed out that the entire enterprise of Response to Intervention (RTI) was the result of trying to capture the incredible results from the Vellutino et al. (1996) and Torgesen et al. (2001) studies previously

> **DON'T FORGET**
>
> RTI was prompted by the tremendous results from the studies previously described. Yet, when RTI was translated into a process and a framework, the instructional techniques that produced these great results were left behind. Chapters 10 and 11 describe these techniques in detail.

described. However, in developing the framework and process of RTI, the highly effective intervention methods that provided such outstanding results were left behind. Teachers and school psychologists now struggle to figure out those elusive researched-based approaches needed for effective RTI. Chapters 10 and 11 present those approaches.

ACKNOWLEDGING AND RESPONDING TO THE GAP BETWEEN RESEARCH AND PRACTICE

Millions of our tax dollars are spent each year on reading-related research. On one level, these research grants have been a huge success because researchers now have a very good understanding of the nature of reading acquisition and of reading disabilities. However, on another level, the whole enterprise has been a failure because children are not benefitting from these important findings.

Although this situation may be difficult to believe, it is nonetheless a fact that desperately needs to be addressed. Reading research has had minimal impact on professional fields that could benefit from its findings, such as education, literacy, special education, and school psychology. This is despite the fact that the reading research field is comprised of scientists from many different fields (see Rapid Reference 1.2, list C), including each of those just mentioned. These researchers are not part of some academic "fringe." They come from Harvard, Yale, Oxford, Cambridge, and dozens of top universities around the world. To illustrate, three different colleges at Harvard University—the Medical School, the School of Arts and Sciences (Department of Psychology), and the School of Education—have all made tremendous contributions to the scientific research on reading. The same can be said of other institutions. Reading researchers are awarded countless millions of dollars in research grants each year. One would expect a field comprised of scientists from many disciplines, top universities, and many countries would be more widely known and have a greater influence on educational practices. However, studies show that this research has been having limited impact on our K–12 students. Based upon U.S. government statistics, the finding that nearly one-third of fourth graders read below a basic level has been stable for decades. While it is true there will always be a "bottom third" of a distribution, the reality is that the status of being "bottom third" does not presume a functional level. For example, the bottom third of NBA players are still excellent basketball players.

≣ *Rapid Reference 1.2 Where Does Our Scientific Knowledge of Reading Come From?*

Note: All lists are alphabetical.

A. Languages

The following is a sample of languages for which there are hundreds of scientific research studies related to reading acquisition and reading difficulties.

Arabic[1]	Greek
Chinese[2]	Hebrew[1]
Dutch	Italian
English[3]	Japanese[4]
Finnish	Korean[4]
French	Norwegian
German	Portuguese
Russian	Spanish
Serbo-Croatian[5]	Turkish

Notes:

1. Arabic and Hebrew writing are often studied because they are halfway between an alphabetic and a syllabic form of writing (in syllabic scripts, characters represent syllables, not individual sounds). Those writing systems only represent the consonants of spoken words and typically not the vowels. Wrds r wrttn lk ths.
2. Chinese written language is *logographic* not *alphabetic*. That means, roughly speaking, that Chinese characters represent whole words, whereas the characters in an alphabetic script (i.e., letters) represent sounds within words.
3. By a wide margin, English is the most commonly studied written language.
4. Japanese and Korean are of interest to researchers because they each use two different writing systems. Japanese uses *syllabic* and *logographic* scripts, and Korean uses *alphabetic* and *logographic* scripts.
5. Serbo-Croatian is of interest because it is a language that uses two different alphabets that do not completely overlap. Some of the letters that are the same in both alphabets represent the same sound in the spoken language. Other letters between the two alphabets look the same but represent different oral

sounds. Finally, some letters are unique to each alphabetic script. This situation provides scientists with interesting controls on the relationships between letters and sounds.

B. Countries

The following list is a sampling of countries that routinely contribute to the scientific research into reading acquisition and reading difficulties.

Australia	Italy
Belgium	Japan
Brazil	Korea
Canada	The Netherlands
China	Norway
Finland	Spain
France	Sweden
Germany	United Kingdom
Greece	United States
Israel	

C. Disciplines

The following are academic disciplines represented among reading researchers.

Deaf education	Psychology—cognitive
Education	Psychology—developmental/child
Linguistics	Psychology—educational
Literacy/reading education	Psychology—experimental
Medicine—neurology	Psychology—neuropsychology
Medicine—pediatrics	Psychology—psycholinguistics
Medicine—ophthalmology	Psychology—school
Optometry	Special education
Psychology—behavioral	Speech/language pathology

Note:

Worldwide, more scientific research on reading comes out of departments of psychology than any other discipline.

≡ Rapid Reference 1.3 A Sampling of Common Types of Methods Used to Study Reading

General Research Designs

Experimental

Quasi-experimental

Cross-sectional

Longitudinal

Correlational

ABAB and lag designs

Case study

Multiple case study

Statistical Analyses Commonly Used

Correlational analysis

Latent growth curve modeling

Factor analysis

Multiple regression

Structural equation modeling

Principal components analysis

ANOVA/ANCOVA/MANOVA

ROC curve

Path analysis

Types of Research Participants

- Children who are typical readers
- Pre-readers
- Students at risk (pre-K to grade 1)
- Students at every elementary grade level
- Middle school readers
- High school readers
- ELL students
- Adult skilled readers
- Adult ELL readers
- Adult literacy participants
- Adults with head injury or stroke

- Dyslexics
- Hyperlexics
- Individuals with mixed reading difficulties
- Individuals with speech or language impairment
- Individuals who are deaf or hard of hearing
- Individuals with intellectual disabilities
- Individuals with emotional disturbance
- Individuals with autism or other syndromes (e.g., Williams syndrome)

Specific Experimental Methodologies

Methods Used Primarily in Reading Comprehension Research

Sentence Reading The participant reads sentences with certain semantic and syntactic structures.

Paragraph Reading This is similar to sentence reading, but with more opportunity for reading extended text, and can include a greater number of comprehension-related elements.

Open-Ended Responses The participant reads a single sentence or a lengthy passage and the experimenter asks open-ended questions requiring a verbal response from the participant.

Multiple Choice The participant reads a sentence or paragraph then reads and answers multiple-choice questions.

Cloze Questions A sentence or brief paragraph is read in which there is a blank space indicating a missing word. The participant must supply a reasonable word to indicate comprehension of the sentence or paragraph.

Literal and Inferential Questions Different types of questions are asked to determine various levels of understanding of a passage.

Garden Path Passages A sentence or passage is read that leads the individual to expect something in the final sentence, and there is a twist in that final sentence that tends to catch weaker readers unaware, but does not catch stronger readers.

Methods Used in Both Reading Comprehension Research and Word-Level Reading Research

Eye Movements This technique measures the precise timing and tracking of eye fixations during reading. An advantage is that with many eye-movement studies, individuals read connected text, which directly parallels normal reading behavior. A special issue of *School Psychology Review* (2013, vol. 42[2]) provides an introduction to eye-movement research in reading.

Reaction Time This tests how quickly a student responds to a stimulus, typically reading a word or pressing a button indicating yes/no response. This is commonly used with lexical decision and masked priming tasks (see below).

Homograph/Homophone Reading Homographs are words with different meanings that are spelled the same (e.g., *dove/dove; bass/bass*) and homophones are words pronounced the same but with different spellings (*I'll/aisle; their/there*). Such words are sometimes used in comprehension research to add ambiguity to sentences. Also, such words are used to test their effects on word-level learning and retrieval.

Morphological Tasks The participant interacts with morphological elements in words, such as the root, prefixes, suffixes, indicators of verb tense, and so forth.

Semantically Ambiguous Words Semantically ambiguous words (e.g., *ring, match*) can be used to assess sentence comprehension.

ERP Event-related potentials (ERP) are electrophysiological responses in the brain that follow a particular stimulus. These are used to help determine the timing and location of responses in various areas of the brain during reading.

Brain Scanning (fMRI, MEG/MSI, PET) Unlike traditional static MRI or CT scans, there are techniques that can look at the brain in action as individuals perform basic cognitive tasks, such as listening, speaking, or reading. These include functional magnetic resonance imaging (fMRI); magnetoencephalography (MEG), which is combined with an MRI to produce magnetic source imaging (MSI); and positron emission tomography (PET). These have been used to evaluate different aspects of the reading process among skilled readers, beginning readers, average readers, and struggling readers.

Neurological Studies These involve examining individuals, typically adults, who had been competent readers but who lost some or most of their reading skill as a result of a stroke or head injury.

Genetic Studies These can range from family studies of the incidences of various types of reading and reading-related problems to a direct examination of the human genome. Multiple large-scale twin studies in multiple countries have contributed to understanding the genetic bases of reading difficulties.

Methods Used Primarily in Word-Level Reading Research

Context-Free Word Identification The participant is asked to read words from a list, either timed or untimed. Or, words are flashed on a computer screen one at a time.

Nonsense Word Reading Pronounceable nonsense words (e.g., *prute, spreng*) are read either from a list or one word at a time on a computer screen. This is designed to determine an individual's phonic decoding ability.

Passage Reading Fluency Students read normal, connected text, and the evaluator makes note of reading speed, reading accuracy, and prosody (i.e., intonation, emphasis).

Lexical Decision A participant responds as quickly and accurately as possible to yes/no response keys indicating whether a string of letters is a word, or whether a word belongs in a semantic or phonological category (e.g., Is *pair* a fruit? Is *splanch* a word? Does *been* rhyme with *seen*?).

Masked Priming A target word is flashed on the screen for a fraction of a second and is preceded and/or followed by another stimulus, which is called a *mask*. The mask could be a set of characters following the word (e.g., #####) to cancel out any after image on the retina to ensure a very precise exposure time. The mask could also be another word or set of letters that will either facilitate or hinder the speed or accuracy of the participant's recognition of the target word (e.g., *pear* flashed quickly before *pair* vs. *zqrm* flashed before *pair*).

Homophone and Pseudohomophone Reading Words are used that sound the same (homophone) but are spelled differently (e.g., *right/write*, *close/clothes*) to evaluate orthographic knowledge during reaction time or masked priming tasks. Pseudohomophone tasks involve nonsense words that are spelled to sound like real words (e.g., *brain/brane*, *wait/wate*) and are commonly found in lexical decision tasks (e.g., Is *brane* a body part?).

Orthographic Choice Task The participant is asked to determine which alternative spelling is correct (e.g., Which of the following is a fruit: *pair, pare, or pear?*).

Wordlikeness Task The participant is asked to indicate which of the following nonsense words displays a spelling pattern most like real words (*plmk* vs. *bock, rrin* vs. *rinn*).

Use of Different Fonts, Mixed Case, or Degraded Appearance Words are printed in very different fonts (e.g., avenue, **avenue**), mixed case (hApPiLy), or with degraded visual appearance (e.g., only parts of the letters show through a screen or mask).

SUMMARY

There is a vast amount of empirical research on literacy acquisition and reading disabilities that has been largely untapped by those working in schools. This is due, in part, to the sheer volume of this research and its inaccessibility. Many educational professionals in general and special education can benefit tremendously from this information, not to mention developers of reading series and intervention materials. This book is designed to communicate the most important findings from that vast research. The focus will be on applying the most relevant research findings to assessing, preventing, and correcting reading problems.

🖋 TEST YOURSELF 🖋

1. **According to the National Assessment of Educational Progress, approximately what percentage of fourth graders read below a basic level?**
   (a) 3%–5%
   (b) 8%–10%
   (c) 13%–15%
   (d) 30%–34%

2. **Since _____, it has been well established that phonological awareness is critical for reading.**
   (a) 2000
   (b) 1995
   (c) 1990
   (d) 1980 or earlier

3. **Professors of literacy routinely make use of the empirical reading research when training future teachers.**
   (a) True
   (b) False

4. **School psychologists generally have a good working knowledge regarding empirical reading research.**
   (a) True
   (b) False

5. **Which one of the following is *not* a likely reason why there is a gap between reading research and classroom instruction?**
   (a) Teachers' unwillingness to change the way they teach
   (b) Lack of easy access to the research
   (c) The overwhelming amount of research available to sift through
   (d) Attempts by some high-profile literacy experts to discourage teachers from incorporating practices based on scientifically oriented research findings

6. **What appears to be "the most important scientific discovery that educators have not heard about"?**
   (a) The research findings about phonics
   (b) The research findings about reading comprehension
   (c) The research findings about how readers build a sight vocabulary
   (d) The research findings about English language learners

7. **What is *orthographic mapping*?**
   (a) Making sure all letter-sound relationships are systematically introduced in a developmentally appropriate fashion in a kindergarten curriculum
   (b) A strategy for enhancing spelling instruction in younger students
   (c) A strategy for enhancing spelling instruction in older students
   (d) In reading, the mental process used to store words for later, instant retrieval

8. **Prevention research indicates that we can reduce the number of struggling readers by:**
   (a) 10%–12%
   (b) 15%–18%
   (c) 20%–25%
   (d) 50%–80%

9. **What does the best intervention research suggest about the most severely reading-disabled students (i.e., the bottom first to third percentiles)?**

   (a) While milder cases of reading difficulties can be corrected, the amount of growth potential among the most severely reading disabled is quite limited.

   (b) With the right kind of intervention, we can expect that these individuals make 4 to 6 standard score point gains on nationally normed reading tests.

   (c) These students can make an average of about a standard deviation of improvement based on nationally normed reading tests.

   (d) The outcomes are so variable that no estimate can be made.

10. **What was the major problem with the origin of RTI highlighted in this chapter?**

    (a) The original developers of RTI could not decide on whether RTI should represent a three- or four-tier service delivery model.

    (b) There was no real scientific foundation for the development of RTI; it was just a clever idea.

    (c) RTI was inspired based on very strong research outcomes, but during the development of the RTI service delivery model, the instructional and intervention approaches that produced such successful results did not get widely disseminated.

    (d) The developers could not agree on whether to capitalize the *t* in the middle (i.e., RTI vs. RtI).

Answers: 1. d; 2. d; 3. False; 4. False; 5. a; 6. c; 7. d; 8. d; 9. c; 10. c

Two

HOW WE TEACH READING AND WHY IT DOES NOT WORK WITH STRUGGLING READERS

Federal statistics show that about 30% of fourth graders score below a basic level in reading. This chapter will examine the common instructional practices we have been using to see if this will help us understand why we have so many weak readers. However, factors other than instruction can affect reading outcomes. Indeed, if 30% of students struggle in reading, that means approximately 70% learn to read without any great difficulty using our current approaches. One might suggest that the instructional methods are not the issue; rather, the problem is that many reading difficulties have a neurogenetic basis, which is a well-established finding (Fletcher, Lyon, Fuchs, & Barnes, 2007; Hulme & Snowling, 2009; Pennington & Olson, 2005; Vellutino, Fletcher, Snowling, & Scanlon, 2004). How can we expect to teach students to read proficiently if the reasons they struggle in reading are neurogenetic?

Or, perhaps parents are not doing enough, given the extensive evidence to show how important early language and preliteracy skills are for the development of reading (Maclean, Bryant, & Bradley, 1987; Metsala, 2011; Nicholson, 1997; Snow, Burns, & Griffin, 1998). Between the neurogenetic and early environmental factors, we could easily conclude that our reading methods are not the problem, especially since the majority of children learn to read with our current reading instruction.

The problem with this assumption is that we have ample research to show that by making changes in our instructional approaches, we can prevent many reading difficulties as well as substantially accelerate the reading growth of most students with reading difficulties (see Chapters 10 and 11). If instructional methodology can make such a difference, we should carefully consider how we teach reading. First, let us examine *why* our current approaches do not seem to address the needs of struggling readers.

A VERY BRIEF HISTORY OF READING INSTRUCTION

The Mesopotamians first developed word reading about 3500 BC, and alphabet-based writing was developed by the Phoenicians about 1700 BC. Thus, reading instruction has been going on for a very long time. Yet, approaches to teaching reading in the United States did not become formalized or systematized until the late 1600s to early 1800s (Crowder & Wagner, 1992; Smith, 1965). One of the earliest approaches taught children syllables and letter combinations (e.g., *ib, id, ic, em, in, mi, mo, mu*). Another was an early form of phonics, called the *alphabet method* or *ABC method*. Unlike modern phonics, the child had to say each letter name before pronouncing the word. Then the whole-word method gained popularity, which has also gone by the names *look-say approach*, *sight-word approach*, and *basal reading approach* (because it was so commonly incorporated into basal reading series). This approach downplayed individual letters and sounds and encouraged children to look at words and simply say them. What is now called *whole language* was developed around the 1870s and was called the *sentence method*. It focused on the sentence as the unit of study rather than letters or individual words.

Various concepts and specific strategies drawn from these three classic approaches form the basis of our current reading instruction. Yet it seems that these traditional approaches have not been effective in addressing the needs of weak readers. While phonics appears to have important benefits in addressing the needs of struggling readers when compared to the other two approaches, for a large percentage of struggling readers, it is still insufficient to close the gap with their typically developing peers (see more in Chapters 4 and 11).

What We Can Learn From the Wright Brothers

Most of us have seen old movie clips of early attempts at flight. While some of the contraptions in those old clips look outlandish, others look like they *should* have flown. There is a little-known fact that explains why the Wright brothers were successful while all the others were not. When considering designs for their flying machine, the Wright brothers made use of a wind tunnel. The Wright brothers' competitors designed and built machines that *seemed* like they should fly, but their intuitions were incorrect and they were unsuccessful. By contrast, the Wright brothers constructed many different designs in miniature and tested them in the wind tunnel. Once they found a design that flew in the wind tunnel, they built a full-scale version and they became the first to fly.

Historically, reading education has functioned more like the Wright brothers' competitors. The three classic approaches (whole word, phonics, and whole language) all originated long before there was any scientific research on reading development and reading difficulties. Our current approaches to teaching reading represent a repackaging of assumptions and methodologies from those three classic approaches. Yet, we have extensive "wind tunnel" data that could be used as the basis of our educational practices.

There have been multiple attempts to take a wind tunnel approach and thus encourage reading practices based on research rather than on tradition or intuition. An early attempt was funded by the U.S. government (Bond & Dykstra, 1967) and has been referred to by later researchers as the *first grade studies* (Adams, 1990). This was a large-scale longitudinal set of studies that found that teaching students phonics yielded better results than the classic whole-word approach. Then, *Becoming a Nation of Readers* (Anderson, Hiebert, Scott, & Wilkinson, 1985) reviewed the research at the time and, like the first grade studies, concluded that instruction in phonics had superior results over the classic whole-word approach.

Five years later, Adams (1990) published *Beginning to Read: Thinking and Learning About Print*. This was an extensive review of reading research sponsored by the U.S. government's Office of Educational Research and Improvement. Adams's review went beyond previous efforts because she described how various characteristics of learners contribute to which students easily learn to read and which students struggle. One of the individual differences she highlighted from studies in the 1970s and 1980s was phonological awareness.

In 1998, the National Research Council published *Preventing Reading Difficulties in Young Children* (Snow et al., 1998). This review of research stressed the importance of children developing phonics and phonemic awareness early in their reading careers to prevent later reading difficulties. Two years later, the National Reading Panel (NICHD, 2000) published a research review stressing the benefits of phonics over the other two classic approaches and also identified phonological awareness as a critical element in developing reading skills. In 2008, the National Early Literacy Panel (NELP, 2008) produced a meta-analytic review of early reading acquisition that confirmed and refined the National Reading Panel's basic findings. Also, the governments of Australia (Australian Government, 2005), Great Britain (Department for Education and Skills, 2006), and Canada (Ontario Ministry of Education, 2003) have each produced reviews of the scientific research on reading. The findings from all of these reports are parallel to those from the United States. Early, explicit, and systematic instruction in phonics, along with direct instruction in phonological awareness, can prevent reading difficulties and can also remediate reading difficulties.

The Problem With the Term *Research Based*

The reading panels from various countries all encourage educators to use practices that research has demonstrated to be effective—that is, *research-based* practices. However, some major problems have already emerged regarding the term *research based*.

The first problem is that there is no protection for the term *research based*. Anyone can develop a program and call it research based. Given the push for research-based approaches and the absence of any protection for the term, all publishing companies marketing to schools automatically use the term *research based* to describe their reading programs, whether they are research based or not. Unfortunately, the term *research based* has simply come to mean nothing more than "please buy our program."

The second problem is, what constitutes a research-based program? The No Child Left Behind Act of 2001 says it applies to "education activities and programs." If you develop a program that happens to include some activities, principles, or techniques that have been shown by research to work, can your program be legitimately called research based? What if the program also includes approaches that do not work? Should the whole program be shown to be effective in a carefully done independent study and reported in a peer-reviewed journal before it can be called research based? Or, can simply incorporating research-based methods or techniques into the program qualify it for that term?

Third, odd as it may sound, *research based* does not necessarily mean a program is effective. There are programs that have been studied and reported to have "statistically significant" results in peer-reviewed journals. However, the program may have generated only a 3 standard score point improvement, and that 3 standard score point improvement was *statistically* significant. Teachers would have a difficult time noticing the difference if a student went from an 80 standard score to an 83 on a reading test! So statistical significance should not be assumed to mean educational effectiveness. The very small gains in these statistically significant studies are not even close to the degree of improvement struggling readers will need to close the achievement gap. More importantly, since there are approaches that consistently yield 12 to 20 standard score point improvements, schools should not be investing in programs that yield substantially less. These highly effective approaches will be described in Chapters 10 and 11.

WHY OUR CURRENT APPROACHES TO READING INSTRUCTION ARE INEFFECTIVE WITH STRUGGLING READERS

In what follows, the assumptions and methods of the classic whole-word, phonics, and whole language approaches will be examined. For at least two reasons, it is important to understand *why* these approaches are inadequate. First, because they have been around so long, these traditional approaches involve assumptions that seem to be deeply embedded in our collective beliefs about reading. Because they are so deeply ingrained, we can easily default to them—they now seem intuitive. Second, when interacting with teachers and administrators, it will be important to be cognizant of the kinds of assumptions that go into our current teaching practices and why they have not been successful with children who struggle in reading.

Word Identification Versus Word Recognition

For clarity in terminology in what follows, it will be important to define key terms. In Chapter 1, *sight word* and *sight vocabulary* were defined. These refer to words that students can instantly and effortlessly recognize from memory. Two other key terms are *word identification* and *word recognition*.

DON'T FORGET

In this volume, the term *sight word* refers to a word that is instantly and effortlessly recognized from memory, regardless of whether it is phonically regular or irregular. A *sight vocabulary* refers to a student's pool of words that are instantly and effortlessly recognized.

Illustrating Identification Versus Recognition

Let's say you were asked to give a note to a man you have never seen before who was in a meeting with 30 people. You are told that he is a tall man with red hair and glasses. Those clues allow you to *identify* him. Thus, identification does not require recall from memory. Yet if you were asked to hand a note to your best friend in that same meeting, no clues would be necessary. You would instantly *recognize* your friend because you have a memory of him or her. This illustrates a distinction between the terms *identification* and *recognition*. Recognition requires memory and identification does not. Of course, you may still speak of identifying your friend as well, so *identification* appears to be a broader term than *recognition*.

For precision, in this volume the term *word recognition* will refer to the instant recall of familiar words. This is sometimes referred to as "reading words by sight" from a person's sight-word vocabulary (Ehri, 1998a, 2005a). By contrast, the term *word identification* will be generally avoided because it is imprecise. It can refer to identifying a word via any manner, such as instant recognition, phonetic analysis, guessing, or any combination of these. There is no specific term in the research literature that refers to identifying an unfamiliar word without reference to the manner in which that identification occurs. The term *decoding* is

CAUTION

The terms *word identification* and *word recognition* are often used interchangeably. This imprecision can be problematic. In this volume, *recognition* presumes drawing from memory (*cf.* Webster's and American Heritage dictionaries), and thus *word recognition* refers to instant access to known words. The term *word identification* will be avoided and replaced with *word-level reading* or *word reading*. This generic terminology will include real-word reading (familiar or unfamiliar words) or nonsense word reading.

often used, but its usage is broad and inconsistent, sometimes referring generically to word reading (including instant recognition, phonetic analysis, and/or guessing) (e.g., Gough & Tunmer, 1986), but it often refers to figuring out an unfamiliar word (Scarborough & Brady, 2002). Thus, the generic term *decoding* will also be avoided. To address the idea of figuring out an unfamiliar word, more precise terminology will be used throughout this volume, such as *phonic decoding* and *contextual guessing*. The generic term for reading words, regardless of familiarity, will be *word-level reading* or simply *word reading*. This broad term includes reading familiar words and unfamiliar words (see Figure 2.1 for the relationships between these terms).

Word Recognition in the Classic Reading Approaches

None of the classic approaches to teaching reading focuses attention on both identifying new words and recognizing familiar words. The whole-word approach directs its attention to recognizing familiar words. It does not have much to say about encountering unfamiliar words. This approach assumes that words are stored as visual wholes, and that multiple encounters with words are needed to encode words into visual long-term memory.

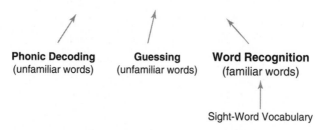

WORD-LEVEL READING/WORD READING

Phonic Decoding
(unfamiliar words)

Guessing
(unfamiliar words)

Word Recognition
(familiar words)

Sight-Word Vocabulary

Figure 2.1 Terminology Related to Word-Level Reading

By contrast, phonics and whole language both focus on children encountering unfamiliar words. Neither of these approaches has much to say on how words become familiar. Phonics emphasizes using knowledge of the letter-sound code of written English to correctly identify unfamiliar words. There seems to be an implicit assumption among phonics advocates, however, that after multiple opportunities to sound out a given word, the reader finally stores the word in some sort of visual memory bank, much like the whole-word approach suggests. Whole language intertwines word-level reading and reading comprehension to such a large degree that it is very difficult to even talk about concepts that are specifically related to word-level reading. From the whole-language perspective, word reading results from comprehending, and comprehending results from word reading—it is an interactive two-way street (Goodman, 1996).

Inadequate Attempts at Understanding Word-Level Reading

There are some foundational assumptions about reading that form the basis of our current reading approaches. These assumptions derive from the three classic reading approaches. An examination of these assumptions will help us understand why struggling readers have not fared well with the methods we have been using, despite our well-intentioned efforts.

To understand an alphabet-based written language, one must obviously be able to read the words. Skilled readers have instant, effortless access to all, or almost all, of the words they read. This allows them to focus on comprehension (Fletcher et al., 2007; LaBerge & Samuels, 1974). The three classic approaches were developed long before researchers began studying reading scientifically. None of these classic approaches has a well-developed hypothesis about reading both familiar words and unfamiliar words. They each focus on one or the other. Table 2.1 displays the basic differences among the theories in terms of their perspectives on unfamiliar word reading versus reading familiar words.

The classic whole-word approach assumes that words are stored as visual wholes based upon visual memory. This will be referred to below as the *visual memory hypothesis*. The whole language approach understands reading to be the product of three interactive cueing systems: (1) semantic–contextual, (2) linguistic–syntactic, and (3) grapho–phonic. This has been referred to as the *three cueing systems* approach. The phonics approach proposes that unfamiliar words are best determined by applying knowledge of the code of written English to sound out words. It does not, however, explain how students remember words so that they no longer have to sound them out.

Table 2.1 What the Three Classic Reading Approaches Have to Say (or Not Say) About Word Identification Versus Word Recognition

Traditional Reading Approach	Assumptions About Word Identification (Encountering Unfamiliar Words)	Assumptions About Word Recognition (Encountering Familiar Words)
Whole word	Not made explicit. When stuck on an unfamiliar word, students can ask someone to tell them the word, or perhaps guess based upon context; use the visual "look" of the word or some of its letters.	Words are recognized based on visual memory. The process of naming words is like naming objects or people, presumably based upon visual–verbal paired-associate learning.
Phonics	Sound out letters and blend those sounds to activate the spoken word. Use context to help with phonically irregular words.	Not made explicit. The assumption seems to be that after successfully sounding out words multiple times, visual memory takes over, like the whole-word approach.
Whole language	Three systems of cues work together to make sense of print: (1) semantic–contextual, (2) linguistic–syntactic, and (3) grapho–phonic.	Any notion about this is not emphasized or made explicit. The idea of a sight vocabulary of instantly recognizable words appears to be downplayed or ignored.

THE VISUAL MEMORY HYPOTHESIS OF WORD READING

We can instantly name familiar objects or people when we see them, such as a door, a chair, a stapler, or a family member. Undoubtedly, visual memory is responsible for this. We get visual input, we activate an associated verbal memory, and we name the item. When we look at printed words, much the same appears to be happening. We look at words and we correctly name them. However, research has shown quite convincingly that the process of naming a chair or a stapler is cognitively quite different than reading the words *chair* or *stapler*.

James Cattell published a paper in 1886 demonstrating a newly developed timing mechanism that could measure reaction times to within 1 millisecond (i.e., 1/1,000th of a second). With this level of precision, he discovered that the reaction times for reading printed words like *chair* or *tree* were faster than reaction times for naming a chair or a tree when shown a picture of those items. Thus, over 125 years ago, there was evidence that naming objects and naming written words were not the same skills, contrary to our intuitions.

In the 1960s and 1970s (Adams, 1979, 1990; McClelland, 1976), scientists used mixed-case studies to better understand word-level reading. WoRdS wErE pRiNtEd LiKe ThIs. Researchers discovered that college students responded more quickly to words printed normally than to mixed-case words (McClelland, 1976). However, when readers were given prior opportunity to get accustomed to seeing words in mixed case, they were able to read any new words printed in mixed case as quickly as they read normally printed words, even though they had not previously seen those test words in mixed case (Adams, 1990). We have all received a wedding invitation or graduation announcement printed in an ornate font. While difficult to read at first, we mentally adjust and can read it just fine. Similarly, we effortlessly recognize words in multiple fonts, in various types of handwriting, and even when they are curved or rotated (see Figure 2.2). The visual memory hypothesis would imply that we have dozens of visual memories for each of the words we can instantly identify.

In some of the mixed-case studies, words were flashed on a screen very quickly (between 1/10th and 1/20th of a second) and the college students were not told they would be mixed case. Their speed and accuracy in naming these very briefly presented words were the same as with normally printed words. During the debriefing, many students said they never noticed that the words were in mixed case, while some insisted the experimenter was incorrect and that they were normally printed words (Adams, 1990)! These individuals were able to instantly recognize words printed in mixed type that they had never seen presented that way, without noticing they were mixed type. These findings are highly inconsistent with the visual memory hypothesis, given that mixed case versions of words differ dramatically in visual form from their normal, lowercase versions. In Figure, 2.2, note how all the uppercase and lowercase letters in "reading" look different (e.g., R/r, E/e).

Another problem with the visual memory hypothesis surfaced in the 1960s and 1970s (see Vellutino, 1979). It was demonstrated that there is little or no

Figure 2.2 A Sampling of Some of the Many Possible Visual Forms of "Reading"

correlation between visual memory skills and word-level reading. This is inconsistent with the idea that word reading is based on visual memory. Add to this, from the early 1970s onward, there was growing evidence that phonological awareness correlated quite strongly with word-level reading (Wagner & Torgesen, 1987). Thus, despite its strong intuitive appeal, it became nearly impossible for scientists to maintain the visual memory hypothesis.

CAUTION

The terms *auditory, phonological, and phonemic* are sometimes used interchangeably. There are important distinctions between them.

Auditory refers to all of the sound input we perceive, like a knock on the door, a baby crying, music, an airplane flying over head, or a person speaking.

Phonological is a subcategory of auditory. It refers exclusively to the sounds of spoken language. Students with reading problems do not have general, non-phonological auditory issues (Share, Jorm, MacLean, & Matthews, 2002). Their difficulties are primarily phonological in nature. The term *phonological* can refer to the sounds of words, syllables, or phonemes.

Phonemic is a subcategory of phonological. The phoneme is the smallest perceptual unit of spoken language. Letters are designed to represent phonemes in alphabetic languages (though English is inconsistent in this regard). Most phonemes are represented by single letters (e.g., *h-a-t, b-e-s-t*), but some are represented by multiple letters (e.g., *sh-e, th-e-n, b-ee*). So *Tom, bike,* and *said* have three phonemes, while *shoe* and *though* have two, and *test, stop, breathe,* and *box* all have four (*x* is the only letter that represents two phonemes concurrently: /k/ /s/). It is phoneme-level skills that are needed for proficient reading.

With the onset of brain scanning techniques to study reading, the visual memory hypothesis has become even more untenable. Neuroimaging studies demonstrate that the areas of the brain that activate during visual memory tasks (e.g., naming objects) are not the same as those areas that activate during word-reading tasks (Dehaene & Cohen, 2011; Forster, 2012; Simos, Rezaie, Fletcher, & Papanicolaou, 2013; van den Broeck & Geudens, 2012). This finding provides an explanation for Cattell's discovery over 125 years ago. The difference in reaction times between reading the word *tree* and naming a picture of a tree is likely due to the fact that different areas of the brain mediated those two tasks. This implies that different cognitive processes are involved. Based upon all of this evidence, it seems clear that our intuition fails us when we assume that the same process is used for naming objects and reading words. We can conclude that the visual memory hypothesis does not provide us with a useful understanding of reading.

Reading Among Those Who Are Deaf

If word reading is not based on visual memory, how do students who are deaf read? The evidence indicates that individuals who are deaf do not have an alternative visual route to skilled word reading. In fact, reading presents a major challenge to those who are deaf (Hanson, 1991; Lederberg, Schick, & Spencer, 2013; Leybaert, 2000). Most individuals who are deaf graduate high school with a third- or fourth-grade reading level (Lederberg et al., 2013; Leybaert, 2000). Over 95% of those who are deaf wear hearing aids. This means they have at least some residual sound input when using hearing aids, however limited. As a result, some individuals who are deaf are able to develop a sense of the segmental nature of the spoken language and develop some degree of phonological awareness, even if limited. The correlation between phonological awareness and reading is similar in both the deaf and hearing populations (Hanson, 1991). It will become clear in Chapter 4 why phoneme-level awareness is so essential for proficient reading.

If reading were based upon visual memory, we would expect that individuals who are deaf would not have such difficulties learning to read. However, this is not the case. The letters of printed words are designed to represent individual phonemes within spoken language. Those who do not have sufficient access to the spoken language cannot easily connect the letter sequences in written words to the sounds in the spoken language.

The Role of Visual Memory in Reading

While visual memory is not the mechanism we use to establish memories of printed words, we must not overlook the fact that visual memory *is* involved in learning letter names and letter sounds. Correctly saying a name or sound that goes with a particular letter involves pairing a visual memory with a phonological memory. This is parallel to object naming (e.g., a tree or a chair). When children struggle to learn letter sounds, however, there is little evidence those struggles result from poor visual memory. Studies suggest that when students have difficulties with visual–phonological paired-associate learning, it is the phonological aspect that is problematic, not the visual (Litt, de Jong, van Bergen, & Nation, 2013; Litt & Nation, 2014).

Based upon the evidence previously presented, it seems reasonable to conclude that while we *input* written words visually, we do not *store* them visually.

This should not be surprising because cognitively, input and storage represent different concepts. Written words are stored on multiple levels simultaneously: orthographically (the word's spelling), phonologically (the word's pronunciation), and semantically (the word's meaning). How this occurs is the topic of Chapter 4.

Why the Whole-Word Approach Does Not Help Weak Readers

The whole-word approach does not provide any concrete mechanism for storing words so that they become familiar, instantly accessible sight words. It is clear that the visual memory hypothesis, which is the foundation of the whole-word approach, does not represent how we remember words. Even though the whole-word approach does not provide an adequate understanding of how words are stored, does it nonetheless provide some helpful teaching strategies?

A primary teaching strategy within the classical whole-word approach is the use of multiple exposures to words so that those words become memorized. Children with reading difficulties do, in fact, develop a sight vocabulary (see Chapter 8). However, it is very limited compared to their peers. So, even students with reading problems are remembering *some* words. What words are they storing? Typically they store common words they have seen dozens, or even hundreds, of times before. Thus, even though they are not remembering words via visual memory, they are storing words somehow as a result of the multiple repetitions.

The problem with this conventional teaching strategy of multiple repetitions of words is that it works very inefficiently and does not close the gap between weak readers and their peers. For example, one study showed that fourth graders with reading disabilities required more than twice as many learning trials to remember new words as typically developing first graders (Ehri & Saltmarsh, 1995). Providing extensive practice does not adequately solve the problem.

The Rapid Development of Sight Words

From second grade on, typically developing readers are able to store a new word permanently in only one to four exposures (Bowey & Miller, 2007; Bowey, & Muller, 2005; Castles & Nation, 2006; Cunningham, 2006; Cunningham, Perry, Stanovich, & Share, 2002; de Jong & Share, 2007; Ehri & Saltmarsh, 1995; Nation, Angell, & Castles, 2007; Reitsma, 1983; Share, 1999, 2004a). While this seems surprising, a moment's reflection on typical reading growth reveals why this should *not* be surprising. Consider that typically developing readers enter first grade able to read between 100 and 500 familiar words. Two years later, those children enter third grade with a sight vocabulary that is between 3,000 and

8,000 words. Doing the math, it becomes clear that to make that kind of growth, children do not have the opportunity to see each of those 3,000 to 8,000 words 15, 20, or 30 times before they remember them. Indeed, the speed with which children turn unfamiliar words into familiar sight words in first and second grade is a key predictor of who will struggle in reading later on. A central component of word-level reading difficulties is the inability to quickly add words to one's sight vocabulary (van den Broeck & Geudens, 2012; van den Broeck, Geudens, & van den Bos, 2010).

In sum, the whole-word approach was developed long before researchers understood how words are remembered for instant retrieval. Whole-word teaching strategies were derived from that faulty hypothesis. For at-risk or struggling readers, approaches are needed that allow words to be added to their sight vocabularies quickly and reliably.

THE THREE CUEING SYSTEMS MODEL OF READING

The three cueing systems model, sometimes called the *meaning, structure, visual approach,* is based on the psycholinguistic guessing game theory of reading (Goodman, 1976, 2005; Smith & Goodman, 1971). The three cueing systems approach has been ubiquitous in literacy education for the past 25 to 35 years (Goodman, 2005). It is the theory of reading behind whole language, also known as the *literacy-based approach* to reading. The three cueing model is also a major component of balanced instruction (Goodman, 2005) and it forms the basis of Reading Recovery and the Leveled Literacy Intervention (LLI; see Chapter 11). This model proposes that skilled readers identify words using three interactive cueing systems: contextual, linguistic, and grapho–phonic (Goodman, 1996, 2005).

The three cueing systems theory has been impervious to the large body of empirical reading research that has accumulated since it was first proposed in the 1960s. This is likely due to the fact that the findings from this body of research have been inconsistent with the basic assumptions of the three cueing systems model. As mentioned in Chapter 1, its primary advocates have discouraged educators from considering the scientific findings on reading, preferring to appeal to teachers' intuitions and experiences (Goodman, 1989, 1996, 2005; Smith, 1999). The three cueing approach has been the subject of many studies that directly compared it with the phonics approach, also called the *code-emphasis approach.* The code-emphasis approach explicitly and systematically teaches students letters and sounds starting in kindergarten. The code-emphasis approach consistently yields better results in word reading and better reading comprehension than the three cueing systems approach, particularly for weaker readers

(Brady, 2011; Bryant, Nunes, & Barros, 2014; Christensen & Bowey, 2005; Ehri, Nunes, Stahl, & Willows, 2001; Foorman, Francis, Fletcher, Schatschneider, & Mehta, 1998; NICHD, 2000; Stahl & Miller, 1989). Despite research to the contrary, three cueing systems advocates claim that systematic instruction in phonics is unnecessary and hinders comprehension (Goodman, 1996, 2005; Smith, 1999), yet they provide no research to support those contentions.

The three cueing systems approach says readers only sample from the words and letters in the texts they read and that they rely primarily on semantic context to construct meaning from print (Goodman, 1976, 1996, 2005; Smith, 1999).

> We don't have to identify individual words before we can work out what they are . . . . We have no more need to identify and classify individual letters in order to understand written words than we need to identify and classify individual eyes, noses, and mouths before we can recognize faces. (Smith, 1999, p. 151)

The claim is that readers only sample from the words on the page and use "just as little of the cues from text as necessary to construct meaning" (Goodman, 1981, p. 477; see also Goodman, 1996). After providing a passage with typographical errors, Goodman (1996) says "if you didn't notice anything wrong . . . you may turn out to be among the more proficient readers" (p. 39). Goodman (1996) provides many illustrations of reading phenomena that he believes support his model, such as not noticing certain typographical errors or missing a doubling of the word *the* when one instance ends a line and the other begins a line. Yet every phenomenon used to illustrate this view has been the subject of multiple, scientifically oriented studies, and the results are inconsistent with Goodman's explanation of these phenomena (e.g., Adams, 1990; Adelman, 2012a, 2012b; Crowder & Wagner, 1992; Lupker, 2005; Rayner, Pollatsek, Ashby, & Clifton, 2011; van Orden & Kloos, 2005). While advocates of the three cueing systems model build their theory upon intuitive inferences from peculiar reading phenomena, scientists examine these phenomena more rigorously using a wide variety of methods to develop defensible explanations of how reading works (see Rapid Reference 1.3 in Chapter 1).

The problems with the three cueing systems model are quite extensive and have been addressed by numerous researchers (Ehri, 1998b; Foorman, 1995; Hempenstall, 2002; Liberman & Liberman, 1990; Stahl, 1999; Stahl & Kuhn, 1995; Stahl & Miller, 1989; Stanovich, 1980, 1993). A meta-analysis of whole language instruction with low SES students (typically at risk for reading difficulties) indicated that it displays weaker results than traditional basal reading series, which tend to be based on the whole-word approach with small doses of phonics, and eclectic approaches (Jaynes & Littell, 2000). This is interesting given that even these latter approaches have been shown to be less effective than explicit phonics instruction.

What follows are the most critical difficulties with the three cueing systems model. The focus is on the assumptions that are likely to have the largest impact on reading instruction and reading difficulties.

- *Skilled word recognition does not require context.* The three cueing systems model claims that semantic context is the most prominent of the three interactive cueing systems (Goodman, 1996, 2005; Smith, 1999). However, literally hundreds of studies have demonstrated that skilled readers instantly and effortlessly recognize any one of the thousands of written words they know when those words are presented in isolation (for reviews of this research see Adelman, 2012a, 2012b; Crowder & Wagner, 1992; Frost, 1998, 2005; Grigorenko & Naples, 2008; Halderman, Ashby, & Perfetti, 2012; Pugh & McCardle, 2009; Rayner & Pollatsek, 1989; Rayner et al., 2011; van Orden & Kloos, 2005). One only needs to hand a list of words to a skilled reader. Without the benefit of context, that individual will rapidly and effortlessly identify the words from the list. For skilled readers, context is therefore *not* a primary factor in recognizing words, nor is it even required.

  Context is helpful in identifying *unknown* words and is also required to grasp the *meaning* of words with multiple meanings (e.g., what does *ring* mean?). However, context is not required to recognize familiar words (except for homographs with differing pronunciations, such as *dove/dove, read/read,* and *wind/wind*). If a reader requires context to identify a word, it means the word is not familiar. But for familiar words, no guessing from context is involved.

  Decades ago, research indicated that with good readers from third grade on, word reading was so quick that recognition occurred before the benefits of context could take place (Stanovich, Nathan, West, & Vala-Rossi, 1985). This finding has received additional support in recent years using a variety of techniques, including high-tech neuroimaging and brain electrophysiological studies (Forster, 2012; Maurer & McCandliss, 2008; Perfetti, 2011). This research indicates that when we see a word, the areas of the brain responsible for orthography (familiar spellings) and phonology (pronunciation) activate sooner than the areas responsible for the semantic system (meaning). The evidence seems to suggest that readers recognize a word's spelling and its pronunciation before recognizing its meaning.

Of course, the speech-motor production capabilities are not able to produce the word's pronunciation that quickly. Yet a word's phonology and even its morphology (Cunnings & Clahsen, 2007) appear to be available before its meaning. Contrary to the three cueing systems assumption that skilled readers require semantic information to determine a word's identity, it seems that the word's identity is available a fraction of a second before its meaning. In sum, there is overwhelming evidence that a central element of the three cueing systems model, which is that context is a critical element of skilled word recognition, is incorrect.

- *Guessing words from context is not as efficient as phonic decoding.* The three cueing systems model strongly advocates guessing words as a primary way to read. Indeed, the original name for this model was the *psycholinguistic guessing game* (Goodman, 1976). While contextual guessing facilitates the identification of *unfamiliar* words (Cunningham, 2006; Landi, Perfetti, Bolger, Dunlap, & Foorman, 2006), in most cases it is less efficient than sounding out unknown words. Also, phonic decoding combined with contextual guessing is more accurate than either strategy alone (Share, 1995).

  Skilled readers can identify unfamiliar words with a high degree of accuracy by sounding them out, even irregular words (Frost, 1998; Share, 1995). By contrast, researchers have found that even proficient readers are not skilled at correctly guessing words from context. The accuracy rate is only about 25% (Hempenstall, 2002; Tunmer & Chapman, 1998). One advocate of the three cueing systems approach complained that research showing skilled readers correctly guess from context only 25% of the time was an underestimate. However, at 36%, his results were not much higher (Kucer, 2011), and far below the 80% to 90% accuracy rate of skilled readers sounding out unfamiliar words (Frost, 1998; Share, 1995). Also, the speed of skilled readers in sounding out decodable, unfamiliar, or nonsense words is extremely fast, with reaction times closely approaching the speed of pronouncing known words (for a review, see Frost, 1998). This is true even among skilled 9- to 12-year-olds (Simos et al., 2013).

- *Poor readers, not skilled readers, rely heavily on context.* In contrast to skilled readers, weak readers rely heavily on context for word reading (e.g., Aaron, 1989; Corkett & Parrila, 2008; Nation & Snowling, 1998; Stanovich, 1980). This is likely due to their limited pool of familiar words as well as their poor phonic decoding skills (Rack, Snowling, & Olsen, 1992; van den Broeck, Geudens, & van den Bos, 2010; van den Broeck & Geudens, 2012). If readers have a limited sight vocabulary and thus routinely encounter many unfamiliar words, and also if they lack sufficient phonic decoding skills to figure out the words, their only recourse is to rely on the context to figure out many of the words they read.

Thus, it appears that the strategies promoted by the three cueing systems model parallel how poor readers approach text rather than how skilled readers approach text (Hempenstall, 2002; Liberman & Liberman, 1990). The implication is that this model advocates teaching all children reading strategies that are typically used by weak readers rather than teaching students to approach reading the way skilled readers do. Fortunately, most readers survive this type of approach. Liberman and Liberman (1990) estimate that about 75% of students will learn to read "no matter how unhelpful the instruction" (p. 54). But if weak readers are encouraged to use weak-reader-style strategies (contextual guessing and not focusing on the precise spelling patterns within words), then how can they rise above that weak reading style and become proficient readers? We have no evidence that the three cueing systems model provides poor readers with any kind of path out of their reading difficulties.

- *Contextual guessing does not promote sight-word learning in poor readers.* Research suggests that with weak readers, contextual guessing facilitates word *identification* but does not promote written word *memory* (Archer & Bryant, 2001). Some research suggests contextual guessing actually hinders word learning (Landi et al., 2006). If weak readers can correctly guess a word from context, they do not have to carefully notice the letter sequence of that word to assist them in making it a familiar sequence for later recognition. If students are not required to notice the spelling pattern when identifying a word, then how does that word ever become familiar? For weak readers, contextual guessing allows them to bypass the orthographic mapping process (described in Chapter 4), which secures a particular written word in memory for later, instant recall.

- *Semantic errors are not a sign of better reading development than phonetic errors.* The three cueing systems approach relies heavily on "miscue analysis," which examines the kinds of reading errors children make (though three cueing advocates do not consider these to be "errors"). The model proposes that when a child misreads a word by substituting another word that is similar in meaning (saying "hand" for "wrist"), this demonstrates a better use of context and signifies superior reading development than making a phonetic reading error (saying "writ" for "wrist"). Yet studies have consistently shown the opposite. Poor readers are more likely to make semantic errors (Krieger, 1981; McGuinness, 1997) in which they substitute a word that fits the context but is not spelled like the word they are attempting to read. Countless studies have shown that as readers develop, their phonic decoding skills advance compared to younger readers and weaker readers (McGuinness, 1997; Share, 1995, 2011). As reading skills improve, their reading errors become more phonetically oriented and less semantically oriented. This is precisely the opposite of what the three cueing systems approach proposes.

- *One of the three cues in the three cueing model is not related to word reading.* According to the three cueing systems model, one of the three cues used to identify words is syntactic information (or "structure" in the meaning-structure-visual terminology). Yet research has shown that syntactic skills do not distinguish good word-level readers from poor word-level readers (Shankweiler et al., 1995; Vellutino et al., 1996). In other words, there is no correlation between syntactical skills and word-level reading. While syntax is absolutely essential for comprehension, it is not critical for word-reading development.

Summary of the Three Cueing Systems Model

The above discussion indicates that the three cueing systems model is inconsistent with research on the nature of reading. One of the three systems is unrelated to word-reading development altogether (syntactic). Another cueing system is highly inefficient for word-level reading and is used as a compensating strategy by weak readers (semantic/contextual), and the third has great potential but is discouraged from being taught or used in any kind of explicit or systematic way (grapho–phonic) (Goodman, 1996; Smith, 1999). Despite all of the research that is inconsistent with the three cueing systems model, it continues to be a very popular approach for teaching children to read via balanced instruction, whole language, and the literacy-based approach, but also with children who have reading difficulties (via Reading Recovery and Leveled Literacy Intervention, see Chapter 11).

It seems most students will learn to read regardless of the teaching method (Liberman & Liberman, 1990). Students who enter first grade with good literacy readiness skills do well with any approach, whereas weak readers do not (Foorman et al., 2001; Foorman & Torgesen, 2001; Juel & Minden-Cupp, 2000; Tunmer, Chapman, & Prochnow, 2002). The evidence suggests the three cueing systems approach is not effective with weak and at-risk readers, and it may actually be counterproductive with such students (Tunmer et al., 2002).

What practitioners can take away from this is that *reading is not a matter of skilled guessing*. Poor readers need to become proficient in the code of printed English, as has been established in countless studies (for reviews, see Brady, 2011; NELP, 2008; NICHD, 2000; Share, 1995). They also need to build a large sight vocabulary (Ehri, 2005a). No amount of guessing ability will close the gap between poor readers and their typi-

> ## DON'T FORGET
> ....
> Skilled reading is not a matter of skilled guessing. Poor readers need to become proficient in the code of printed English and to build a large sight vocabulary. No amount of guessing ability will close the gap between poor readers and their typically developing peers.

cally developing peers, despite the strong and persuasive claims used to promote the three cueing approach (Ehri, 1998b; Goodman, 1996, 2005; Hempenstall, 2002; Smith, 1999; Stanovich, 1993).

Why the Three Cueing Systems Approach Does Not Help Weak Readers

It should be clear from the information previously presented why the three cueing systems model does not address the needs of struggling readers. It appears that the three cueing systems model simply reinforces the kinds of habits that naturally occur among children who struggle in reading. It provides no avenue for weak readers to close the gap with their same-age peers.

THE PHONICS APPROACH TO READING

As mentioned, the phonics approach to beginning reading instruction has consistently demonstrated superior outcomes in word-level reading and reading comprehension compared to the whole-word and whole language approaches. This should not be misinterpreted to mean that if all children were taught via phonics, most or all reading difficulties would be resolved. There are problems with traditional phonics instruction that need to be recognized and addressed.

First, in weak readers, phonics helps with identifying unfamiliar words, but does not necessarily promote instant word recognition. This is a significant problem because skilled readers primarily read by instant recognition based on a large sight vocabulary.

Second, phonics instruction does not close the gap between weak readers and their peers in a sizable proportion of cases. Various studies using explicit, systematic phonics intervention with weak readers who displayed phonic decoding difficulties have yielded a broad range of results, from outstanding (12–20 standard score point improvement; Simos et al., 2002; Torgesen et al., 2001), to very limited results (3–8 standard score points; Lovett et al., 1994), to discouraging results (0 standard score point improvement; Vaughn et al., 2012). These studies indicate that by itself, phonics will not adequately address word-level reading difficulties. However, Chapter 4 will make it clear why it is an essential part of addressing the needs of poor word-level readers.

Additional evidence that phonics instruction does not normalize the reading performance of many weak readers comes from studies of programs that are deemed by many as the "gold standards" of phonics intervention: the Orton-Gillingham method, the Wilson method, and DISTAR/Reading Mastery. These programs display mixed results in the research (Ritchey & Goeke, 2006). One of the overall findings regarding these intensive phonics interventions is that students display improved phonics skills as a result of these programs, but often show limited improvements in overall word reading (Compton, Miller, Elleman, & Steacy, 2014; Kuder, 1990; Ritchey & Goeke, 2006; Stebbins, Stormont, Lembke, Wilson, & Clippard, 2012). Chapter 4 will make clear why these programs display such results.

SUMMARY

It is fair to assume that all reading methods were developed based on one factor: the desire to do what works best for children. But to address the needs of weak readers, good intentions are not sufficient. Taking a cue from the Wright brothers, we need to recognize that a large body of "wind tunnel" research exists that identifies the most effective elements for teaching children to read. It also helps us understand why some children struggle in reading. This research has shown that nearly all of the major assumptions underlying the three classical approaches to reading instruction do not accurately represent how reading works. Only the phonics approach to encountering unfamiliar words has research support. But even the phonics approach does not address the needs of a large proportion of struggling word-level readers. To address their needs, we must consider the findings from the scientific study of reading, reviewed in the next two chapters. No matter how they are rearranged, repackaged, or persuasively marketed, none of the classic approaches can compete with the effectiveness displayed in the best studies generated by scientific inquiry into reading over the past 25 years.

🕮 TEST YOURSELF 🕮

....

1. **All three of the major approaches used to teach reading (whole word, phonics, whole language) have been well established in public education since the**
   (a) 1970s.
   (b) 1960s.
   (c) 1940s.
   (d) late 1800s.

2. **Why were the Wright brothers successful while other attempts at flight failed?**
   (a) While other attempts at flight were based on intuitions about what *should* work, the Wright brothers tested designs in a wind tunnel to find out what *did* work.
   (b) They had engineering degrees and their "competitors" did not.
   (c) Their experience in making bicycles gave them the edge over the others.
   (d) They were the lucky ones whose hit-or-miss attempts just happened to work.

3. **Multiple reviews of reading research published between the 1960s and the 2000s:**
   (a) Display such wildly inconsistent results that it is unclear how educators should teach reading.
   (b) Indicate that systematically teaching students letter-sound relationships has advantages over not directly teaching the code of written English.
   (c) Concluded that while teaching phonics helps some kids, the majority of students learn best with meaning-based reading instruction that does not use phonics.
   (d) Concluded that all of the classic teaching approaches yield similar results.

4. **What did this chapter say about the term *research based*?**
   (a) It is a legally protected term, much like professional titles are protected by licensure (e.g., *physician* or *psychologist*).
   (b) While it is not a legally protected term, it has been carefully defined by various professional organizations.
   (c) It is an unprotected term so any company can call a program research based even if it is not.
   (d) It is restricted to programs that have been shown to be effective in the empirical research literature, but does not apply to programs that simply incorporate some research-based techniques.

5. **All of the following statements are true about the terms *word recognition* and *word identification* except:**
   (a) These words are often used interchangeably in research and in education.

(b) This chapter reserves the term *word recognition* for the reading of familiar words.

(c) Most of our reading tests maintain a clear distinction between word recognition and word identification.

(d) The term *word identification* can include "identifying" words via guessing, phonic decoding, or the instant recognition of a familiar word.

6. **Reading researchers have rejected the idea that we remember words based upon some sort of visual memory process. Which of the following indicates why?**

(a) Findings from MiXeD-cAsE studies are inconsistent with the visual memory hypothesis.

(b) Students with poor memory for words often have average visual memory skills.

(c) The correlation between word reading and phonological awareness is strong, while the correlation between visual memory and word reading is weak to non-existent.

(d) The areas of the brain involved in visual memory are different from the areas of the brain involved in instant recognition of written words.

(e) All of the above are reasons why researchers reject the visual memory hypothesis.

7. **All of the following are true about reading among those who are deaf except which one?**

(a) Those who are deaf learn to read efficiently through visual memory processes because they do not have access to the phonology of the language.

(b) The correlation between phonological awareness and reading is the same in the deaf population as it is in the hearing population.

(c) The average student who is deaf graduates high school at about a third- or fourth-grade reading level.

(d) Most individuals who are deaf have some residual hearing that is boosted with hearing aids, which allows them some extremely limited access to the phonology of the language, and this likely affects reading skill development.

8. **For typically developing students, how many times do they need to see a new word before it is committed to memory and instantly recognized thereafter?**

(a) 1–4

(b) 5–10

(c) 10–15

(d) 20+

9. **From the perspective of the scientific investigation of reading, which of the following is a major concern about the three cueing systems approach to reading?**

(a) It proposes that among skilled readers, context plays a major role in word reading, yet skilled readers instantly identify words without context, and it is weak readers who rely heavily on context.

(b) One of the three cues does not even correlate with word-level reading (i.e., syntactic cues).

(c) Guessing from context is not as efficient as phonic decoding, yet the former is considered primary and the latter is considered only useful as a backup.

(d) All of the above represent concerns about the three cueing systems approach.

10. **Which of the following approaches to teaching literacy are strongly influenced by the three cueing systems approach?**

(a) Whole language

(b) The literacy-based approach

(c) Balanced instruction

(d) All of the above

Answers: 1. d; 2. a; 3. b; 4. c; 5. c; 6. e; 7. a; 8. a; 9. d; 10. d

Three

A PRACTICAL FRAMEWORK FOR UNDERSTANDING AND ASSESSING READING SKILLS

THE SIMPLE VIEW OF READING

The *simple view of reading* is a practical framework researchers use either explicitly or implicitly to organize the most useful findings from a vast amount of reading research (e.g., Aaron, Joshi, Gooden, & Bentum, 2008; Catts, Adlof, & Weismer, 2006; Nation, 2005; Vellutino, Fletcher, Snowling, & Scanlon, 2004). Yet the *simple view of reading* is not just for researchers. School psychologists, teachers, and curriculum coordinators will also find it to be a practical and insightful framework for understanding the reading process, pinpointing the sources of reading difficulties, and guiding lesson planning. In fact, in recent years, the British government has incorporated the simple view of reading into its national reading strategy (Department for Education and Skills, 2006; Stuart, Stainthorp, & Snowling, 2008), suggesting it may be worth considering when developing instructional programs.

Philip Gough and colleagues first presented the simple view of reading in 1986 (Gough & Tunmer, 1986; Hoover & Gough, 1990; Juel, Griffith, & Gough, 1986). It begins with the axiom that the purpose of reading is to understand what one reads. The simple view of reading proposes a logical distinction between two broad skills that are required for reading comprehension: *decoding* and *linguistic comprehension*, that is, the ability to transform print into spoken language (orally or silently) and the ability to understand the spoken language. The simple view says that if a student can quickly and effortlessly read the words in a given passage, *and* if that student can understand that same passage when it is read to her, it follows that the student should be able to comprehend that passage when she reads it herself. While this may seem rather obvious, it runs counter to the most common way that literacy has been taught for the past two or three decades in the United States.

In large measure, the simple view of reading originated as a response to the psycholinguistic guessing game or three cueing systems approach to reading discussed in Chapter 2. It was also intended to make sense of the existing research at the time it was first presented (Gough & Tunmer, 1986; Juel et al., 1986). The research basis for the simple view of reading has been quite impressive since its inception because each element in the model had already been the subject of many studies. In addition, since the model was formalized, it has been directly tested in over 100 studies with children, adults, typical learners, and learners with various disabilities in English and in other languages (Aaron, Joshi, Palmer, Smith, & Kirby, 2002; Aaron et al., 2008; Catts, Hogan, & Fey, 2003; Catts et al., 2006; Goff, Pratt, & Ong, 2005; Harlaar et al., 2010; Hoover & Gough, 1990; Joshi & Aaron, 2000; Kendeou, Savage, & van den Broek, 2009; Munger & Blachman, 2013; Ricketts, 2011; Ricketts, Jones, Happé, & Charman, 2013; Ripoll Salceda, Alonso, & Castilla-Earls, 2014; Sabatini, Sawaki, Shore, & Scarborough, 2010; Tiu, Thompson, & Lewis, 2003; Verhoeven & van Leeuwe, 2008).

The Most Basic Form of the Simple View of Reading

The simple view of reading can be understood on multiple levels. This section of the chapter covers its most basic level. The next section will describe the expansions Gough and colleagues made to this basic level, along with additional elements that have emerged from the research since the simple view was originally presented. This latter, more expanded

> **DON'T FORGET**
>
> The expanded form of the simple view of reading presented in this chapter can be a powerful organizing framework for understanding and assessing reading, as well as for preventing and correcting reading difficulties.

form can be a powerful organizing framework for understanding and assessing reading, as well as for preventing and correcting reading difficulties.

Gough and colleagues present the simple view of reading in mathematical form:

$$R = D \times LC$$

Reading comprehension = Decoding × Linguistic comprehension

Decoding simply refers here to word-level reading, and *linguistic comprehension* refers to the ability to understand the spoken language in which the words are written. Later in the chapter, decoding and linguistic comprehension will be broken down into their constituent parts. For now, we will explore the simple view at its most basic level of $R = D \times LC$ to see how it helps us understand reading.

Illustrating the Simple View of Reading

Read the two lines of English shown in Figure 3.1.

Any difficulty? These are English words that you are very familiar with—at least orally. These English words have been transliterated into Greek and Russian letters. Chances are that most readers cannot decode these because they are not familiar with the alphabetic codes of Greek or Russian. This illustrates the critical importance of word-level reading. If one cannot determine the words, the meaning cannot be ascertained (each line in Figure 3.1 says the same thing: school psychology).

Now read the following paragraph and answer the comprehension questions:

The snables tramped the mengs to the dwip. The dwip fropped. The mengs clambed a sib boogle. The snables gicked and gicked.

Question 1: What did the snables do to the mengs?

Question 2: What happened to the dwip?

Question 3: What kind of boogle did the mengs clamb?

Question 4: What did the snables eventually do?

Chances are that with very little effort you correctly answered the comprehension questions without really understanding what you read. This is because you understand basic grammar and could detect nouns, verbs, and adjectives. This basic grammatical knowledge is all that is needed to correctly answer the simple informational questions. The reason you did not comprehend what you read is that you would have been unable to understand it even if it were *read to you*. In other words, because you lacked the necessary oral vocabulary and background knowledge for this passage, you had no understanding of it. Your lack of comprehension was due to a problem with oral language comprehension, not decoding.

These examples illustrate the necessity of being able to identify the written words and to understand the language used by the author. Difficulties with either will hinder reading comprehension.

Σχοολ ψυχολογυ

схоол психологи

Figure 3.1 English Words in Non-English Scripts

Case Illustrations of the Simple View of Reading

The following are four examples of the simple view of reading in the context of psychoeducational evaluations I conducted. Students' real names have been replaced.

Devin, grade 6
    Designation: specific learning disability (SLD)
    Verbal IQ: 106
    Word-reading skills at the early-second-grade level
Keith, grade 7
    Designation: traumatic brain injury (TBI)
    Verbal IQ: 99
    Word-reading skills at the late-first-grade level

Gough says a score of 1 represents perfectly good skill and 0 represents negligible skill. Various decimals represent the degree of the student's ability. Because the verbal IQ of these boys was average, we assume they would be capable of understanding a sixth- or seventh-grade level passage if it were *read to them*. Thus, they will be assigned a score of 1 for language comprehension. Yet they will be assigned a 0 for word reading because at their respective grade levels, their word reading skills were non-functional. If we do the math, we see that $1 \times 0 = 0$. According to the simple view, these boys are not readers. This conclusion may not seem particularly insightful, because everyone knew they were not readers before the evaluation was conducted! But the value of the simple view is that it makes *explicit* the relative contributions of both word-level reading and oral language to reading comprehension. In these "textbook" cases, the simple view indicates that the lone reason for the reading comprehension difficulties was poor word-reading skills. Just as the simple view would predict, both boys had extremely weak reading comprehension, comparable to average second graders. This is a nonfunctional level of reading comprehension when encountering sixth- or seventh-grade reading material.

As a contrast to Devin and Keith, consider the following cases:

Emily, grade 6
    Designation: speech or language impaired (SLI)
    Verbal IQ: 71
    Word-reading skills at the sixth-grade level
Molly, grade 5
    Designation: intellectual disability (ID) (Down syndrome)
    Verbal IQ: 72
    Word-reading skills at the fifth-grade level

Because the verbal IQ scores of these girls were so low, they could be assigned a 0 for language comprehension, meaning they were incapable of answering oral comprehension questions at the fifth- or sixth-grade level. We will assign them a full score of 1 for word-level reading. They could read any words up to their grade level. Because $0 \times 1 = 0$, the simple view says they are not readers. Once again, the simple view is stipulating *why* they are not readers: They lack the language skills to understand what they read. Their word identification was more than adequate and therefore was not a contributing factor to their reading comprehension difficulties. The simple view predicts both girls would have poor reading comprehension, which was indeed the case. Emily's reading comprehension was at the first-grade level and Molly's was at the kindergarten level.

At its most basic level, the simple view concretely specifies why a student has poor reading comprehension. As mentioned, these are textbook cases. They are included to highlight how both word-level reading and language comprehension can affect reading comprehension. However, most cases are not this clear. Often there is a combination of word-level reading and language issues contributing to poor reading comprehension. Even then, the most basic level of the simple view can suggest the relative contribution of these factors to weak reading comprehension.

Conclusions from the Case Illustrations

These cases illustrate the necessity of having good language comprehension *and* good word-level readings skills to be a good reader. Often, the source of a student's poor reading comprehension may not be clear to teachers or parents when the relative contributions of word reading and oral language comprehension have not been directly measured. The three cueing systems model of reading very deliberately does *not* disengage word reading from oral language comprehension. At its very core, that approach represents a merging of these two broad skills. Also, many reading tests, including high-stakes tests, give students a single score, masking the contributions of word reading and language comprehension to that score.

These cases also illustrate that the simple view of reading is not limited to students with learning disabilities. All four students had different special education designations. The simple view applies to any weak reader, including weak readers who do not qualify for special educational services. It even helps understand the relative contribution of word reading and language skills to the reading comprehension skills of average readers and superior readers (i.e., superior readers *are* superior readers because they have strong word-reading skills and strong language comprehension skills).

In addition, the cases illustrate that word reading and oral language comprehension are relatively independent abilities, each comprised of different sets of skills (Fletcher et al., 2007; Hulme & Snowling, 2009; Nation, 2005). Students do not need a high verbal IQ to become skilled word readers, as illustrated by Emily and Molly. At the same time, students with high verbal IQ scores can be poor word-level readers, despite good effort and instruction. The classic dyslexic individual has well-developed language comprehension but struggles when reading words.

Implications for Students with Low Verbal Skills

The fact that word-level reading and oral language comprehension involve minimally overlapping skill sets has important implications for students with poor language skills and students with generally low IQ scores. It would be easy to assume that word-level reading problems displayed by those with low IQ scores, low language skills, or even emotional/behavioral problems, are side effects of those cognitive, linguistic, or behavioral issues.

> **DON'T FORGET**
>
> Given the mechanics of how word-level reading works (see Chapter 4), it is clear that most students with ID, SLI, or *emotional disturbance/behavior disorders* (ED/BD) can achieve word-level reading skills at much higher levels than previously assumed (see Chapters 10 and 11).

However, that is a questionable assumption. Although factors like general intelligence, language skills, and emotions/behavior certainly affect reading comprehension, they are not central factors in word-level reading. There is plenty of research to suggest that students with poor language skills and low verbal intelligence scores can be good word-level readers when given opportunities for the proper preventive instruction and/or intervention (Allor, Mathes, Roberts, Cheatham, & Champlin, 2010; Catts et al., 2006; Hulme & Snowling, 2009; Nation, Snowling, & Clarke, 2007). Research has also shown quite clearly that the factors that prevent poor readers with high IQ scores from developing skilled word recognition are the very same factors that are responsible for poor word-level reading among those with low IQ scores. This well-established research finding is one of several reasons for the demise of the IQ/achievement discrepancy definition of a reading disability. Discrepancies between IQ and achievement do not cause word-reading problems. Rather, deficits in the skills that underlie word-level reading cause those problems. The component skills of word reading can be strong or weak, independently of IQ test performance. Consider Emily and Molly mentioned earlier. They had low IQ scores, yet were strong in all of the skills that are required for word-level reading. They were not miracle kids with some sort of word-reading savant skill. Rather, their phonemic awareness, phonic decoding, rapid automatized naming, and working memory were all tested in their triennial evaluations, and all of those skills were at or above the 50th percentile. As a result, we would *expect* that they would be skilled in word-level reading.

It is encouraging to see that over the last two decades, some of the standardized achievement batteries have added subtests that include aspects of oral language comprehension, typically listening comprehension (e.g., K-TEA-3; WRMT-III; WIAT-III; WJ-IV). While these oral language subtests were not added to assist practitioners in using the simple view of reading framework, we can nonetheless use those subtests for that very purpose (see Chapter 9).

The First Diagnostic Question

The most basic level of the simple view leads us to ask a helpful diagnostic screening question. When a teacher says a student struggles with reading comprehension, the first question to ask is: What if you read the passage to him, would he understand it? The answer to this question will help with designing a reading evaluation.

If the teacher confidently affirms that the student can easily understand things read to him, this suggests that his reading comprehension problem is likely due to a weakness in word-level reading. However, if the teacher says that the student probably would not understand very well even if it were read to him, there are two possibilities. One possibility is that the student has difficulties with language comprehension. This is not always obvious. There can be subtle language problems that may not show up in ordinary verbal and social interactions yet they may have an impact on a student's reading comprehension (Hulme & Snowling, 2011). The other possibility is that the child may have difficulties with listening comprehension due to inattentiveness, not language comprehension problems (Aaron et al., 2002; Cain & Bignell, 2014). In either case, a student may also have a word-reading problem. So, the follow-up question would be: What is the student's oral reading like? Is it fast and accurate or is it effortful? This will help to narrow down the source or sources of the reading difficulty.

If a teacher indicates that a child would struggle with understanding a passage even if it were read to him or her, it seems judicious to bring the case to the attention of a speech–language pathologist. The language batteries used by speech–language pathologists can provide helpful details about a student's language skills, including detecting subtle language difficulties that can affect comprehension but are not easily noticed from routine teacher–student interactions.

Figure 3.2 provides an overview of how these two simple view–based questions may clarify the type of reading difficulty a student is experiencing. It includes references to the types of reading difficulties described in the next section. Please note that these types of reading difficulties (in Figure 3.2 and in the next section) are descriptors of empirically established patterns of reading difficulties and do not assume that a student has an educational disability under the *Individual's with Disabilities Education Improvement Act* (IDEA). These common types of reading problems occur across various disability categories (as we saw with the case studies described earlier) as well as with nondesignated weak readers. The value of these descriptors is that they result in a different intervention protocol and often a different assessment protocol.

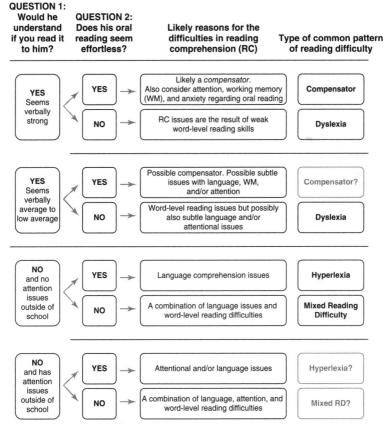

Figure 3.2 Two Questions to Consider When Students Display Reading Comprehension Difficulties

TYPES OF READING DIFFICULTIES/DISABILITIES

Gough and Tunmer (1986) organized three different types of reading difficulties under the simple view of reading framework. These three types have withstood the test of time in terms of research validation (Compton, Miller, Elleman, & Steacy, 2014; Nation, 2005). They are dyslexia, hyperlexia, and mixed subtype (Gough & Tunmer, 1986). A fourth, the compensator type, has been added and will also be described in this section. Figure 3.3 displays the relationship between these types of reading difficulties. Both word reading and language comprehension lie along a continuum, so there are many ways that these types of reading difficulties may play out in a given case, depending on where a student lies along each continuum.

Dyslexia

Dyslexia has developed a mystique in our popular culture. Many people presume it has something to do with visual–perceptual deficits. This is despite the fact that by the late 1970s, research had accumulated indicating this is not the case (Vellutino, 1979). Simply defined, *dyslexia* refers to a difficulty in developing word-level reading skills despite adequate instructional opportunities (Fletcher et al., 2007; Hulme & Snowling, 2009; Vellutino et al., 2004). That is much less intriguing than the popular discourse about dyslexia, which often focuses on the reversals and transpositions of letters. However, these are not defining characteristics, nor do they have anything to do with visual processing (Ahmed, Wagner, & Kantor, 2012; see Chapter 4). In the simple view, the dyslexic has adequate language comprehension but poor word-level reading skills. Devin and Keith, presented above, represent examples of dyslexia, despite their differing IDEA designations.

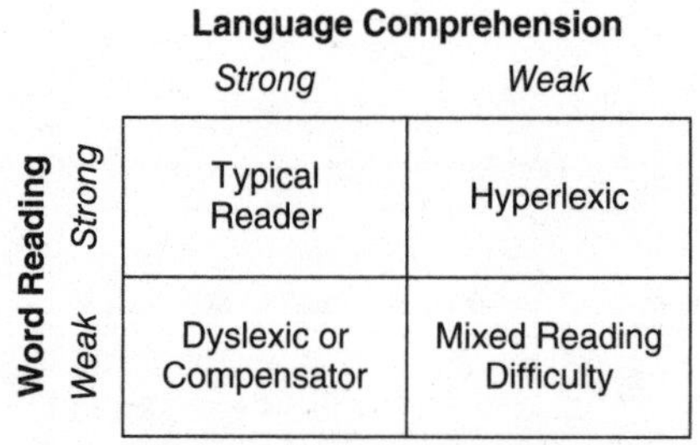

	Strong	Weak
Strong	Typical Reader	Hyperlexic
Weak	Dyslexic or Compensator	Mixed Reading Difficulty

Language Comprehension

Word Reading

Figure 3.3 Types of Reading Difficulties Organized Under the Simple View of Reading

Hyperlexia

Hyperlexics can read words at a level above what they can understand. The prefix *hyper-* is from a Greek word meaning "above" or "over." Hyperlexics typically have language-related deficits that keep them from comprehending what they read. Hyperlexia is far less common than dyslexia and the mixed type of reading difficulty (Nation, 2005; Shankweiler et al., 1995). In the earlier case illustrations, Emily and Molly both display hyperlexia, despite having different IDEA classifications.

Teachers sometimes refer to hyperlexics as "word callers." A popular notion among some educators is that phonics instruction promotes word calling and compromises reading comprehension. Research has shown the opposite. Numerous studies have indicated that students who receive early systematic phonics instruction have better reading comprehension at the end of the second and third grades (Foorman, Francis, Fletcher, Schatschneider, & Mehta, 1998; NICHD, 2000). This is because they can more accurately read the words, and being able to read the words provides the oral language system with the input needed for comprehension. Poor word reading means that the oral language system often receives inadequate input for comprehension. There is no evidence to suggest that any particular form of reading instruction is the source of hyperlexia. Rather, the evidence suggests that hyperlexia is based on difficulties with general language comprehension (Catts et al., 2006; Hulme & Snowling, 2009, 2011; Nation, 2005).

Mixed Type

Those with the mixed type of reading difficulty display weaknesses both in language comprehension and in word-level reading. Most individuals with intellectual disabilities and a substantial portion of individuals designated as speech or language impaired have this mixed type of reading disability (Catts et al., 2003; 2006; Nation, Clarke, Marshall, & Durand, 2004). However, we are all familiar with other students who have milder language difficulties along with mild to moderate decoding difficulties that combine to produce weak reading comprehension.

Compensator Type

This type of weak reader was not presented in the original simple view and has received very limited direct treatment in the research literature (Berninger & Abbott, 2013; Kilpatrick, 2014b, 2015a, 2015b). One must look for this type of reading problem among the subtypes found in studies of late-emerging poor readers (e.g., Catts, Tomblin, Compton, & Sittner Bridges, 2012; Leach, Scarborough, & Rescorla, 2003; Lipka, Lesaux, & Siegel, 2006).

Compensators typically have strong language skills. Their reading comprehension is substantially below their language skills but still average. Also, their word-reading skills are lower than their reading comprehension but are average or low average. Because their overall reading skills are in the average range, they typically do not arouse much attention from their teachers. These children are often referred by parents who complain about the effort it takes to get through reading all of the homework. Sometimes, these students express dissatisfaction with reading. While compensators have not received much research attention, it is suspected that most school psychologists have had experience with this type of student. Parents and teachers have a hard time putting their finger on the problem, yet they know something is not quite right.

Kilpatrick (2014b, 2015b) used a multiple case study approach with individuals drawn from 525 psychoeducational evaluations generated by the author between 2001 and 2011 and who met three criteria: (1) a Verbal IQ ≥ 105, (2) reading comprehension scores above the bottom 30% (i.e., ≥92), and (3) a below-average score (≤85) in one of the following skill areas: phonemic awareness, working memory, or rapid automatized naming. Twenty-two students from grades 2 to 7 met all three criteria.

There was a consistent pattern among these compensators (see Figure 3.4). Their average verbal IQ score was 113 and their average reading comprehension score was 98, a full standard deviation below their verbal skills. Their average timed and untimed word reading and spelling were each 92, and untimed nonsense word reading was 94 and untimed phonemic awareness was 93. However, their timed nonsense word reading, which is presumably a more valid index of their proficiency at phonic decoding (see Chapter 7), averaged 84 and

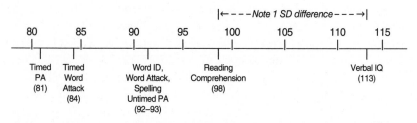

Note: PA = phonemic awareness; SD = standard deviation; Word Attack & Word ID = nonsense word-reading and real word-reading subtests from WRMT-R

Figure 3.4 Common Skill Pattern of Compensating Readers (Mean Performances)

their timed phonemic awareness, also likely to be a more valid index of their phonemic proficiency (see Chapter 6), was 81. In all, 94% had poor automatic (i.e., advanced) phonemic awareness and 90% had poor timed/automatic phonics skills. It appears from these multiple case studies that one or more of these lower-level linguistic skills were compromising word-level reading development. Because the students had strong language skills, however, they were able to create the impression that their reading was at least average. Tunmer and Chapman (2012) have demonstrated that students with strong vocabulary skills are more adept at determining unfamiliar words even when they are not correctly sounded out phonically (a skill called *set for variability*, described in Chapter 4). This suggests that given their strong verbal skills, compensators can correctly identify more words than those with average or lower language skills, thus creating the impression that they have sufficient word identification skills. However, word-level reading is effortful for them, and this effort presumably draws away valuable working memory resources from the task of comprehension, which can explain why their reading comprehension was a standard deviation below their language comprehension. Most compensators do not receive remedial instruction because their overall reading scores tend to be in the average range. Anecdotal comments from the reports from which Kilpatrick (2014b) drew suggest these students often disliked and avoided reading. The implication is that children who could be among our highest achieving students dislike reading because of some underlying lower-level skills (i.e., phonemic awareness and letter-sound proficiency) that are quite correctable (see Chapter 11).

The timed nonsense word subtests from the universal screeners (e.g., DIBELS, Aimsweb, easyCBM) are a great resource for detecting many of the students with the compensating pattern. However, it is suspected that teachers are not likely to pay much attention to a low nonsense word reading score when a student's word reading and comprehension are average. The universal screeners discontinue timed phonemic awareness at the end of first grade, before compensators' problems typically surface (Leach et al., 2003). Also, the phonological awareness task in the universal screeners is segmentation, which is less sensitive to reading difficulties than other phonological awareness tasks (Kilpatrick, 2012a, 2012b; Swank & Catts, 1994). This is discussed in detail in Chapters 4 and 6.

The compensator type of reading difficulty would not qualify a student as an individual with a learning disability under IDEA, nor should it. Nonetheless, it is a genuine problem for these students because they underperform in reading. Given that reading is critical for all school subjects, the compensator's struggles can have a broad educational impact. While technically not a disability, the compensator pattern is nonetheless disabling in that it keeps the reading comprehension of these students substantially below their language comprehension. Such students could receive Tier 2 remediation to directly address their difficulties.

Implications of the Four Types of Reading Problems

There are important assessment and intervention implications of the four types of reading problems. For assessment, the battery of tests used for each type will differ substantially. The dyslexic and the compensator require more tests of word-level reading, along with an assessment of the skills upon which word-level reading are based. By contrast, only cursory word-level reading tests would be administered to the hyperlexic, who instead would receive more language-oriented tests, including a language evaluation by a speech–language pathologist. The mixed reading disability will require both types of assessment.

For intervention, the student with dyslexia and the student with hyperlexia do not make good small group partners because their needs are so different. Even students with a mixed reading disability are not good candidates as small group partners with either hyperlexic or dyslexic students.

THE COMPONENTS OF READING

Throughout the remainder of the chapter, the components of word-level reading and language comprehension will be presented. Many of these will be described in more detail later in this volume. For now, it will be helpful to see how each of the parts of the reading puzzle can be usefully organized under the simple view of reading. The simple view provides a blueprint for our assessments of students who struggle in reading. Such assessments can identify the likely reason(s) a student struggles. These assessment results will form the basis of intervention efforts because they will allow teachers to know which aspects of the reading process require attention.

Gough and colleagues subdivided word-level reading and language comprehension into various subskills (Juel et al., 1986). Word reading is based upon two components: cipher knowledge and word-specific knowledge. *Cipher knowledge* is based on phonological awareness and exposure to print. Juel et al. (1986) did not develop the linguistic comprehension side of the simple view equation other than to say that verbal intelligence represents an important foundation for linguistic comprehension. Figure 3.5 displays Gough and colleagues' breakdown of the simple view of reading. This provides more clarity regarding the skills underlying reading beyond the basic $R = D \times LC$. Since the simple view was formulated,

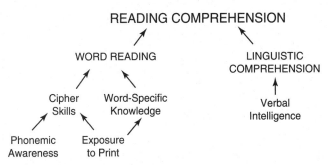

Figure 3.5 Reading and Its Components Based on the Original Formulation of the Simple View of Reading
Source: Juel et al. (1986).

there has been extensive research that allows for more detailed specification of the various components of the reading process. In what follows, the original breakdown of skills by Gough and colleagues and the additional skills subsequently identified by that research will be presented in an integrated fashion.

Intervention-Oriented Assessment Based on the Expanded Simple View of Reading

Before presenting the components of the expanded simple view of reading, it may be helpful to consider some of the potential benefits of using the simple view to organize and plan assessment and intervention.

Assessment Implications

With a few exceptions, the various component skills needed for reading can be directly evaluated by a school psychologist, speech pathologist, and/or literacy specialist via commonly used tests or test batteries. Chapters 6 through 9 will discuss this in detail. The goal is to improve our understanding of the student's needs in order to develop an intervention plan that is likely to normalize the student's reading skills or, at minimum, improve reading substantially more than conventional remediation efforts.

Intervention Implications

An assessment informed by the simple view of reading should help evaluators develop a reasonable hypothesis regarding why a student is struggling in reading. That information then forms the basis of an intervention plan. Several of the specific skill areas can be directly corrected, such as phonological awareness and vocabulary. Others cannot be directly corrected, such as rapid automatized naming and working memory. However, using various instructional techniques, we can minimize the impact of these "noncorrectable" weak skills on reading. Such instructional techniques are unnecessary for students who do not have those specific deficiencies. This is why the assessment of these components is important.

THE COMPONENTS OF WORD-LEVEL READING

First, the components of skilled word reading will be described, followed by the factors that affect language comprehension. To best understand the following presentation of the components of word-level reading, it may be helpful to review some terminology introduced in earlier chapters. Rapid Reference 3.1 provides such a review.

≋ *Rapid Reference 3.1 Terms Related to Word-Level Reading*

Due to the inconsistency in how the terms *decoding* and *word identification* are used within the research field and within education, the following are the operational definitions used throughout this book.

Word-level reading and *word reading* will be used interchangeably. These terms refer to an individual's ability to accurately pronounce written words, with no presumption about prior familiarity. These terms apply to the whole enterprise of correctly reading words regardless of whether they are recalled from memory, sounded out, or correctly guessed from context, and regardless of whether they are phonically regular or irregular. In essence, these terms refer to the correct pronunciation of written words.

Word recognition will be used for instant and effortless recall of familiar words. It is a subcategory of word-level reading.

A *sight word* is a word that is instantly recognized from memory, regardless of whether the word is phonically regular or irregular. This term overlaps with word recognition because sight words are the type of words that are instantly recognized.

Sight-word vocabulary, sight vocabulary, and *orthographic lexicon* are used interchangeably to refer to all the words that are familiar and instantly recognizable to a given student.

Phonic decoding refers to the process of sounding out a word using letter-sound knowledge and blending those sounds together to pronounce the word. In the research literature, this process is referred to as *phonological recoding* or simply *recoding* (Scarborough & Brady, 2002; Share, 1995). However, in this volume, the term *phonic decoding* will be used.

Guessing refers to when a student uses semantic, contextual, linguistic, or picture cues to identify an unfamiliar word. This often occurs in combination with phonic decoding.

Because of its variable use in research and education, *decoding* will not be used in this book other than in the phrase *phonic decoding* or occasionally when referring to the original simple view of reading formulation (i.e., "decoding and linguistic comprehension").

The Two Components of Word-Level Reading in the Simple View

The simple view postulates two skills that comprise one's ability to read words: cipher knowledge and word-specific knowledge. *Cipher knowledge* refers to the ability to use the code of written English to pronounce words. *Word-specific knowledge* refers to familiarity with a given word or word part, based on past experience with that word.

Cipher Knowledge

A *cipher* is a code. Not all codes are alike (Gough & Walsh, 1991). For example, consider the following code: 007. Most readers will recognize this code as referring to James Bond. There is, however, a problem with this type of code. Who is 008? How about 004 or 013? We simply do not know. The fact that we know that 007 refers to James Bond provides us with no help in figuring out to whom the other codes refer.

In some respects, Chinese written language works this way. For example, China has two main spoken languages, referred to in the West as Mandarin and Cantonese. Mandarin and Cantonese speakers do not understand each other in terms of oral language. However, speakers of those two languages can read the exact same book or newspaper written with the same Chinese characters. This is because the written form is not tied to the oral pronunciations. Roughly speaking, each character in the Chinese written language stands for a different word, and one must learn each character and word in its own right, just like one must learn the numbers associated with the secret agents in Her Majesty's Secret Service (e.g., 007).

A cipher type of code works very differently. Consider the following:

Kbnft Cpoe

This is a cipher because once you know what the cipher is, you can decode other words written using this cipher (Gough & Walsh, 1991). If you are not able to figure it out, this is a cipher-based code for James Bond. The cipher is, on one level, the secret to unlock the code. The key to this cipher is that each letter in James Bond's name has been shifted forward by one letter of the alphabet. Once you know this cipher/key, you can decode anything written using this cipher (hence our English word *decipher*). Unlike Chinese, alphabet-based writing systems use a cipher, not an arbitrary code, such as 007.

The cipher of English exists on two levels. The most basic level of the cipher is recognition that letters in written words represent sounds, or *phonemes,* in spoken language. On the second level, the cipher refers to the more detailed knowledge about those specific letters and sounds (e.g., that the letter *t* represents the phoneme /t/, *m* stands for the phoneme /m/, and *r* stands for /r/). According to the simple view, without this knowledge of the cipher one cannot efficiently read words. Note how earlier in the chapter you probably could not read the words "school psychology" printed in the ciphers of the Greek and Russian alphabets. Because you were not familiar with the specific letter-sound relationships in those ciphers, the words could not be deciphered.

Word-Specific Knowledge

Whereas the cipher is concerned with the correspondences between letters and sounds, word-specific knowledge refers to how these correspondences apply to particular words and to letter patterns within words. To have word-specific knowledge, the reader must have had one or more previous encounters with a given word. The concept of word-specific knowledge is roughly synonymous with the concept of known, familiar sight words. Yet, word-specific knowledge is not independent of letter-sound knowledge. Rather, to a very large degree, word-specific knowledge is based on one's cipher knowledge (Cardoso-Martins, Mamede Resende, & Assunção Rodrigues, 2002; Dixon, Stuart, & Masterson, 2002; Ehri, 1998a, 2005a, 2005b, 2014; Ehri & Saltmarsh, 1995; Ehri & Wilce, 1985, 1987; Frost, 1998; Gough & Walsh, 1991; Rack, Hulme, Snowling, & Wightman, 1994; Share, 1995, 1999, 2011). One thing that should be clear from Chapter 2 is the fact that sight-word knowledge is *not* based on visual memory. Sight-word knowledge is built up from basic letter-sound knowledge and experience with specific words (Cunningham, 2006; Laing & Hulme, 1999; Nation, Angell, et al., 2007; Rack et al., 1994; see Chapter 4).

Consider the words *sent, cent,* and *scent.* The only way to tell them apart is through word-specific knowledge. All of these words are pronounced in the same way. In fact, all homophones require word-specific knowledge to properly determine their meaning. But word-specific knowledge is not restricted to homophones. It applies to *all* known words, regular or irregular, homophonic and nonhomophonic. For example, the pronunciation of the word *been* in the United States represents a very rare example of an irregular use of the *ee* vowel digraph (in Great Britain and Australia, *been* rhymes with *seen* and *teen*). A student must learn not to pronounce *been* to rhyme with *seen* and *teen*. Only prior experience with the word *been* will allow the student to develop that word-specific information. In contrast, a phonically regular word like *teen* can be sounded out even if a beginning reader has never seen it before. In order for it to become a familiar and instantly recognizable word, the student must have had past experience with the word *teen* and know that it is pronounced to rhyme with *green* or *seen* and not with *been*. Thus, word-specific knowledge refers to all known words, regular or irregular.

The concept of word-specific knowledge also applies to parts of words (Bowey & Hansen, 1994; Bowey & Underwood, 1996), although we do not have a separate term for that, other than *orthographic knowledge*. For example, children learn that -*ight* is pronounced /ite/ in the words *night, right, sight,* and *bright*. If a child knows the word *night* and as a result correctly sounds out the word *bright*, the entire word *bright* will eventually become a sight word, and thus part of that student's word-specific knowledge. But before that can happen, the correct pronunciation of the -*ight* pattern must be familiar to that reader, even though -*ight* is not a word. This *pattern-specific orthographic knowledge,* as it could be called, allowed the student to correctly sound out *bright* in the first place. Average fourth-grade readers pronounce the nonsense word *nalk* to rhyme with *talk* and *walk,* even though that is not consistent with a standard letter-sound conversion process. By contrast, many second graders pronounce *nalk* to rhyme with *talc,* adhering more rigidly to the phonic regularities (Bowey & Underwood, 1996). Thus, by fourth grade, typical readers have developed pattern-specific knowledge of -*alk* and similar letter sequences, even though these subword patterns are not themselves words (Bowey & Underwood, 1996; Frost, 1998; Kilpatrick & Cole, 2015).

As mentioned, word-specific knowledge is based largely on cipher knowledge. Without letter-sound knowledge, one cannot effectively develop word-specific knowledge (Frost, 1998; Share, 1995, 2011). For example, what if the spoken words *cat, hat,* and *sat* were represented by the written sequences *rbq, msw,* and *plz*? It would likely take a long time and much rote memorization to develop word-specific knowledge and instantaneous recognition of those random letter sequences because there is no connection between the letters and the sounds in those words. It is also likely that many previously learned words would be forgotten (i.e., which one is *rbq* again?). There is no evidence that a sight-word vocabulary can be efficiently built upon visual memorization of sequences independently of their letter-sound knowledge (see Chapter 4). By contrast there *is* extensive evidence that students use those letter-sound/cipher skills to build instantly recognizable sight words (Cardoso-Martins et al., 2002; Cunningham, 2006; Cunningham et al., 2002; de Abreu & Cardoso-Martins, 1998; Dixon et al., 2002; Ehri, 1998a, 2005a, 2014; Ehri & Saltmarsh, 1995; Ehri & Wilce, 1985; Laing & Hulme, 1999; McKague, Davis, Pratt, & Johnston, 2008; Nation et al., 2007; Rack et al., 1994; Scott & Ehri, 1990; Share, 1995, 1999, 2011; see Chapter 4).

The Basis of Cipher Knowledge

The original formulation of the simple view proposed that cipher knowledge is based on phonemic awareness and exposure to print (Juel et al., 1986). The following lists the most well-established factors related to the development of cipher knowledge, incorporating updated research since the simple view of reading was first proposed:

- Letter-sound/orthographic knowledge
- Phonological awareness
- Phonological blending
- Working memory
- Morphological knowledge/awareness
- Vocabulary/phonological long-term memory
- Rapid automatized naming
- Visual/phonological paired-associate learning

Each of these will be presented below but will also receive further treatment in later chapters. They are introduced to illustrate how the various parts of the reading process are organized under the simple view framework to assist assessment and instruction.

Letter-Sound Knowledge

There is no question that letter-sound knowledge is an element that is necessary for skilled word-level reading in an alphabet-based writing system. The amount of supporting literature on this is extensive (for reviews, see Adams, 1990; Brady, 2011; Frost, 1998; NICHD, 2000; Share, 1995; Treiman, 2006). Letter-sound knowledge is essential for both phonic decoding and for storing words in one's sight vocabulary (see Chapter 4). To develop word-level skills, students need to know the correspondences between graphemes (letters) and phonemes (sounds). A *grapheme* is one or more letters that represent a single sound (e.g., *r, m, ee, th*). Recall that a *phoneme* is the smallest distinguishable unit within the speech stream (e.g., *cat* has three phonemes and *shoe* has two).

Orthographic Knowledge

Orthographic knowledge involves two related concepts. The first includes general knowledge about what is permissible and impermissible in English spelling. For example, every word has a vowel, so *tbl* is impermissible (researchers call impermissible patterns *orthographically illegal*). Another example is that although there are words with doubled letters in English (*happy, knitting*), there are none with tripled letters (e.g., *feeet, talll*). Other examples could be given. This represents the first level of orthographic knowledge, and it goes by multiple names in the research literature (e.g., *orthographic sensitivity, orthotactic awareness, graphotactic awareness*). Second, orthographic knowledge relates to the learning of common patterns in words (e.g., *ight, alk, ing, ence, ance, ent, tion*). This was discussed previously. Both of these aspects of orthographic knowledge (orthotactic awareness and familiarity with specific patterns) could be considered an advanced form of phonic knowledge (Vellutino, Scanlon, & Tanzman, 1994). This will be further addressed in Chapter 7.

Phonological Awareness

As mentioned, *phonological awareness* is the ability to notice the sound structure of spoken words. Chapter 4 will detail the importance of phonological skills, ranging from the earliest stages of reading development (learning letter names and sounds) to the most advanced orthographic mapping skills in which new words are quickly and reliably added to the sight vocabulary. Every point in a child's development of word-level reading is affected by phonological awareness skills. It should therefore come as no surprise that children with difficulties in phonological awareness struggle in reading. To reinforce the importance of phonological awareness, several highlights drawn from the extensive phonological awareness research literature are listed below. These are listed here because this information is not as widely known. Most of these will be further discussed in Chapters 4 and 6.

- Phonological awareness difficulties represent the most common source of word-level reading difficulties (Hulme, Bowyer-Crane, Carroll, Duff, & Snowling, 2012; Melby-Lervåg, Hulme, & Halaas Lyster, 2012; Vellutino et al., 2004).
- Phonological awareness is essential for skilled reading. Most children develop this skill naturally, but weak readers will have limited progress in reading unless they receive phonological awareness training (Burt, 2006; Liberman & Liberman, 1990).
- Phonemic awareness is needed for efficient sight-word learning (Dixon et al., 2002; Ehri, 2005a; Laing & Hulme, 1999).

- The most common phonemic awareness task, phoneme segmentation (DIBELS, Aimsweb, easyCBM, etc.), is one of the least sensitive phonological awareness tasks. Beyond first grade, it is not a good indicator of the degree of phonemic proficiency needed for skilled reading (Kilpatrick, 2012a, 2012b; Swank & Catts, 1994).
- Phonological awareness continues to develop in typical readers beyond first grade (Kilpatrick, 2012a; Lipka et al., 2006; Wagner, Torgesen, Rashotte, & Pearson, 2013), even though most programs and assessments discontinue training and assessing phonological awareness at the end of first grade (e.g., DIBELS, Aimsweb, easyCBM). This later-developing phoneme proficiency significantly impacts reading development (Ashby, Dix, Bontrager, Dey, & Archer, 2013; Booth, Mehdiratta, Burman, & Bitan, 2008; Caravolas, Volín, & Hulme, 2005; see Chapter 4).

DON'T FORGET

....

Every point in a child's development of word-level reading is substantially affected by phonological awareness skills, from learning letter names all the way up to efficiently adding new, multisyllabic words to the sight vocabulary.

In later chapters, we will examine how to leverage the emerging research on the role of phonological awareness in orthographic learning. Indeed, those highly successful intervention results described in Chapter 1 involved eliminating the phonological awareness difficulties in those weak readers. Other intervention studies that did not eliminate phonological awareness deficits had less impressive outcomes.

Phonological Blending

Phonological blending refers to the ability to identify a word (or nonsense word) after hearing that word one part at a time (NICHD, 2000). It could involve blending syllables, onsets and rimes, or phonemes. Phonological blending plays an important role in the phonic decoding of unfamiliar words. Once all of the sounds associated with the letters in the words are identified, the student must blend those sounds to activate the word.

Most resource teachers and first-grade teachers have experienced the following: A child sees a word like *cat* for the first time. The child begins by pronouncing a /k/. The teacher gets excited because the child used the hard *c* sound. The child pronounces the /ă/ sound, which further excites the teacher because the child used the short *a* sound. After the child correctly pronounces the /t/, the teacher is beaming and expects to hear the child pronounce the word. Instead, the child looks at the teacher saying, "So what's the word?" The teacher responds,

"What do you mean? You just sounded it out!" This child has a problem with phonological blending. Hearing parts of words in isolation, the student cannot blend them into a word. Phonological blending difficulties undermine phonic decoding because phonic decoding is made up of two skills, letter-sound knowledge and phonological blending (NICHD, 2000; see Chapter 4).

Rapid Automatized Naming

Rapid automatized naming (RAN), or simply *rapid naming*, was first identified as a factor affecting reading by Denkla and Rudel (1976). It has been incorporated into hundreds of studies on reading acquisition and reading difficulties (de Jong, 2011; Georgiou, Parrila, Manolitsis, & Kirby, 2011; Lervåg & Hulme, 2009; Wagner & Torgesen, 1987). RAN problems do not have as big of an impact on reading as phonological awareness (Georgiou et al., 2011; Pennington, Cardoso-Martins, Green, & Lefly, 2001). Students who display RAN deficits but no phonological awareness deficits have reading difficulties that are typically milder than students with poor phonological awareness (Powell, Stainthorp, Stuart, Garwood, & Quinlan, 2007). This is fortunate because there is currently no known way to directly improve RAN (de Jong & Vrielink, 2004). There is, however, evidence that improvements in RAN task performance may occur following substantial improvements in reading (Kerins, 2006; Krafnick, Flowers, Napoliello, & Eden, 2011; Torgesen et al., 2010; Vaughn, Linan-Thompson, & Hickman, 2003; Vukovic & Siegel, 2006; Wolff, 2014).

The *double-deficit phenomenon* is a term used to refer to a student who has a difficulty in both phonological awareness and RAN. The reading problems experienced by students with the double deficit tend to be more severe (Pennington et al., 2001; Steacy, Kirby, Parrila, & Compton, 2014; Wolf & Bowers, 1999), though that is not always the case (Vukovic & Siegel, 2006).

RAN involves rapidly naming digits, letters, objects, or colors from an array (see Figure 3.6). Children who name such items more slowly than average tend to struggle in reading (Lervåg, Bråten, & Hulme 2009; Moll et al., 2014; Vellutino et al., 1996; Wagner & Torgesen, 1987). The precise reason for this is unclear, despite more than 30 years of research. More will be said about this in Chapter 6.

4	1	6	3	9	2	6	1	8
2	8	6	9	3	5	1	6	4
6	9	5	4	9	2	4	1	3
9	5	8	2	4	1	6	4	9

Figure 3.6 A Sample of a Rapid Naming Task With Digits

Working Memory

There is an extensive research base establishing a relationship between working memory difficulties with word-reading problems (Swanson, Zheng, & Jerman 2009; Wagner & Torgesen, 1987), ranging from beginning readers (Vellutino et al., 1996) to adults (Macaruso & Shankweiler, 2010). Working memory can be distinguished from short-term memory (Swanson et al., 2009), with the former involving a more active, central executive component and the latter being more passive and phonological in nature. Short-term memory is slightly more affiliated with word reading, and working memory is slightly more affiliated with reading comprehension (Swanson et al., 2009). However, this distinction is based on large factor analyses. The overlap is so great that a distinction cannot be reliably made in the context of individual evaluations. As a result, *working memory* and *short-term memory* will be used interchangeably in this volume. Poor working memory is common among children with learning difficulties, regardless of disability category. It is not common among typically achieving students (Alloway, Gathercole, Adams, & Willis, 2005; Vellutino et al., 1996). Working memory is associated with both sides of the simple view equation: word-level reading and linguistic comprehension. Despite hundreds of studies, the precise relationship between working memory and word reading is not yet clear (for a few possibilities, see Chapter 6).

Vocabulary/Phonological Long-Term Memory

There is a moderate correlation between vocabulary and word-level reading skills (Catts, Fey, Zhang, & Tomblin, 1999). Vocabulary is essential for language comprehension. Also, there is extensive research showing that semantic characteristics of words affect the speed of retrieval of *familiar* words (e.g., Adelman, 2012a, 2012b; Lupker, 2005; van Orden & Kloos, 2005). Yet the phenomenon of hyperlexia demonstrates that vocabulary knowledge is not a requirement for turning unfamiliar words into instantly pronounceable sight words. How, then, does vocabulary fit in?

It appears that a word's semantic properties play a role in how quickly an unfamiliar word becomes a sight word (Duff & Hulme, 2012). For example, concrete written words are learned in fewer learning trials than abstract words (Laing & Hulme, 1999). However, it appears that the semantic properties only facilitate the speed with which new words are learned because students quite capably learn abstract words, even if more slowly than concrete words. But knowing the meanings of words is not required for words to become sight words. Hyperlexics can instantly recognize words for which they do not know the meaning (Bishop, Hayiou-Thomas, McDonald, & Bird, 2009). Fernandes, Kolinsky, and Ventura (2009) taught adults nonsense words, and those meaningless words became "lexicalized," that is, they became instantly recognizable sight words, in spite of remaining meaningless. So, while meaning facilitates word learning and speeds recognition (in milliseconds), it is not required in order to develop a sight-word vocabulary.

To understand how hyperlexics develop sight words, it is important to distinguish between the semantic lexicon and the phonological lexicon. Researchers use the term *lexicon* to refer to the pool of words mentally available to a student. The *semantic lexicon* refers to the pool of words for which an individual has partial or full knowledge of the words' meanings. The *phonological lexicon* is broader and encompasses the entire semantic lexicon plus all of the words that are immediately recognized as familiar sounding, even if the meaning is not known. The phonological lexicon also includes word parts (Adelman & Brown, 2007; Andrews, 1992; Bowey & Hansen, 1994; Bowey & Underwood, 1996; Nation & Cocksey, 2009b; Peereman & Content, 1997). For example, /ip/ is not a word, but it is phonologically familiar because it is found in over 20 single-syllable words in English (e.g., *chip, dip, flip, lip, sip*). Likewise, /ing/ is not a word, but it is in the phonological lexicon of English speakers because it is found in so many English words.

If a word sounds familiar, that means it is already stored in long-term memory as a familiar spoken word, whether or not the meaning is known. Phonological long-term memory provides the anchoring points for connecting letter strings (i.e., printed words) with phoneme strings (i.e., the sounds in the stored spoken words). Hyperlexics apparently use these familiar-sounding words to connect the printed letter strings used to spell those words. The role of the phonological lexicon in word reading will be covered in Chapter 4.

Morphological Awareness

Morphological awareness refers to the ability to recognize the meaning of parts of words such as roots, affixes (i.e., prefixes and suffixes), and grammatical endings such as -*s*, -*ed*, *ly*, and -*ing*. Students with reading difficulties perform more poorly on morphological awareness tasks than their peers (Casalis, Cole, & Sopo, 2004; Deacon, Parrila, & Kirby, 2006). A review of research on morphologically oriented interventions found a modest improvement in reading comprehension, phonological awareness, nonsense word reading, and vocabulary, but there was no direct impact on real-word reading (Goodwin & Ahn, 2010; see also Deacon & Kirby, 2004). Studies show that morphological awareness contributes independent variance to reading beyond phonological awareness, though it is difficult to separate the two, because both involve pulling words apart (Casalis et al., 2004).

In fact, one study showed that a phonological awareness intervention increased morphological awareness (Kirk & Gillon, 2007), and as just mentioned, morphological training can improve phonological awareness. The precise role of morphological awareness in word-level reading development is not yet clear but it has been receiving an increasing amount of research attention in the last 15 years.

Visual–Phonological Paired-Associate Learning

There is a correlation between visual–phonological paired-associate learning and word-level reading (Hulme, Goetz, Gooch, Adams, & Snowling, 2007; Messbauer & de Jong, 2003; Treiman, Sotak, & Bowman, 2001; Vellutino et al., 1996). The intuitive idea would be that when a student sees a written word (visual) and says it (phonological), paired-associate learning has been demonstrated. However, as was shown in Chapter 2, memory for written words is *not* based upon a process of visual–phonological paired-association learning.

> **CAUTION**
> ....
> Contrary to a long-held assumption, reading problems do not appear to be the result of some sort of "cross-modal" learning problem. The difficulties appear to be on the phonological end of any visual–phonological learning.

What, then, might be the connection? It appears that only paired-associate learning tasks requiring verbal output (i.e., visual–verbal and verbal–verbal, but not visual–visual or verbal–visual) correlate with reading in typically developing readers (Litt et al., 2013) and in students with reading disabilities (Litt & Nation, 2014). It was discovered that the verbal output fully accounted for the relationship between paired-associate learning and reading (Litt & Nation, 2014; Litt et al., 2013). This narrows the possible explanations. Contrary to a common assumption, the issue with poor readers is not some sort of "cross-modal" learning problem, nor is it a general paired-associate learning difficulty. Litt and Nation (2014) discovered that dyslexic students could represent a newly learned "phonological form" (in this case a nonsense word) immediately in memory, but were more likely than their nondisabled peers to forget it moments later. Transferring newly learned phonological representations into a well-established long-term memory seems to be an issue for students with dyslexia. This is consistent with the suggestion by Hulme et al. (2007) that perhaps poor visual–verbal paired-associate learning slows the learning of letter names and letter sounds. This would make sense given that learning both letter names and letter sounds involves paired-associate learning of visual–phonological stimuli. Since letter-sound knowledge is foundational to every aspect of word reading, a disruption or lag in letter learning would be an important contributing factor to word-level reading development. This notion gains support from neurophysiological research indicating that there is a longer time frame for fully automatizing letter-sound connections than previously thought (Froyen, Bonte, van Atteveldt, & Blomert, 2009), and subtle lags may not be noticeable in ordinary responding but still affect early reading skills.

Another view suggests there is no causal connection between poor visual–phonological paired-associate learning and poor reading. Rather, both are a reflection of a third factor: poor phonological processing. Indeed, de Jong, Seveke, and van Veen (2000) found that phonological awareness skill predicted how well children would learn new words via paired-association learning, and training students weak in phonological awareness improved their ability to do visual–verbal paired-associate learning. While research has been able to narrow the possibilities, there continues to be some uncertainty regarding the relationship between visual–phonological paired-associate learning and reading.

The Basis of Word-Specific Knowledge

Beyond exposure to print, Gough and colleagues (Gough & Tunmer, 1986; Hoover & Gough, 1990; Juel et al., 1986) did not break down word-specific knowledge into component parts. Since the simple view was proposed, much research has accrued allowing us to better understand the prerequisite skills for word-specific knowledge (i.e., sight vocabulary development). These skills overlap substantially with those needed for cipher knowledge (Ehri, 2005a; Share, 1995, 2011), which should not be surprising because cipher skills are essential for word-specific knowledge. The following list identifies the key components of word-specific knowledge (items with a question mark play an uncertain role):

- Cipher skills/phonic decoding
- Phonemic awareness
- Vocabulary/phonological long-term memory
- Working memory (?)
- Rapid automatized naming (?)
- Morphological knowledge/awareness (?)

Phonological blending is not listed here because its contribution appears to be limited to the domain of cipher skills. David Share's empirically supported self-teaching hypothesis (1995, 1999) indicates that for typical readers, the process of sounding out new words and interacting with the letters and sounds helps to build word-specific knowledge. In Chapter 4, orthographic mapping will be discussed. Orthographic mapping goes beyond the self-teaching hypothesis model to specify precisely how word-specific knowledge is established. The orthographic mapping model indicates that phoneme-level awareness skills are required to make connections between word-specific letter sequences and the phoneme sequences of oral words stored in phonological long-term memory. For this reason, the phonological awareness item from the list of components of cipher skills has been changed to *phonemic* awareness (phonemic awareness is a subcategory of phonological awareness that deals specifically with phonemes). Rapid automatized naming, short-term memory, and morphological awareness each have a question mark next to them because, although there is reason to believe they are involved in developing word-specific knowledge, the research is not entirely clear on this.

Because they were already described, there is no reason to discuss these components (or presumed components) of word-specific knowledge here. However, they play a somewhat different role in word-specific knowledge compared to their role in cipher skills, and these differences will be explained in Chapter 4.

Figure 3.7 provides an illustration of the various components of the word-reading aspect of the simple view of reading. It allows evaluators and teachers a "bird's-eye view" of the various skills required to read words proficiently.

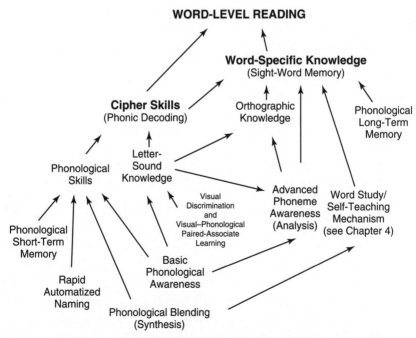

Figure 3.7 Word-Level Reading in an Expanded Simple View of Reading

For evaluators, it provides a framework for considering skills that may need to be examined in order to have a clearer understanding of the possible source(s) of word-reading difficulties. Chapters 6 through 8 will discuss the assessment of these skills.

THE COMPONENTS OF LINGUISTIC COMPREHENSION

Far less research has been done on the components of linguistic comprehension that affect reading comprehension compared to the components of word-level reading (Fletcher et al., 2007). However, the current body of knowledge allows a working understanding of the skills that affect reading comprehension.

Generally speaking, the language comprehension skills of K–12 students represent the outer limit of their potential for reading comprehension. "Children cannot understand written language any better than they can understand oral language" (Fletcher et al., 2007, p. 188). Numerous studies have shown that if word-level reading skills are strong, then a student's reading comprehension very closely parallels his or her language comprehension (Carver, 2003; Diakidoy, Stylianou, Karefillidou, & Papageorgiou, 2005; Fletcher et al., 2007; Hulme & Snowling 2009; Nation, 2005). When word-level reading is not an issue, reading comprehension and listening comprehension appear to be two sides of the same coin, and concurrent measures of these two skills have very high intercorrelations (Fletcher et al., 2007). For example, Hedrick and Cunningham (2002) found that between grades 3 and 5, students who did a large amount of reading improved their listening comprehension skills more than students who did less reading, all other things being equal. Research on poor comprehenders with good word-level reading skills indicates that their poor comprehension is not confined to reading, but also includes oral language comprehension difficulties (Catts et al., 2006; Fletcher et al., 2007; Hulme & Snowling, 2009, 2011; Nation, 2005).

The following is a list of the components of linguistic comprehension that appear to influence reading comprehension, most of which will be discussed in more detail in Chapter 5:

- Vocabulary–semantic knowledge
- Syntactic–grammatical knowledge
- Background knowledge
- Working memory
- Attention
- Inferencing
- Comprehension monitoring
- Nonverbal visual-spatial skills

In what follows, studies that focused on language comprehension are described alongside studies of reading comprehension. This reflects the current state of the research. Nearly all of the studies cited in the following sections that examined reading comprehension involved students who were skilled word-level readers but poor comprehenders. This eliminates the potential word-reading confound. When word reading is skillful (the typical reader and the hyperlexic), the differences between language comprehension and reading comprehension are negligible (Catts, 2009; Fletcher et al., 2007; Hulme & Snowling, 2009; Kamhi, 2009; Nation, 2005).

Vocabulary–Semantic Knowledge

There is little question that vocabulary influences language comprehension. While the correlation between word-level reading and general intelligence scores is not particularly high, the correlation between verbal intelligence scores and reading comprehension is quite strong (Fletcher et al., 2007; Gresham & Vellutino, 2010; Hulme & Snowling, 2009). In an article designed to demonstrate that IQ/achievement discrepancies are not relevant for determining a reading disability, Gresham and Vellutino (2010) state: "Indeed, knowledge and skills assessed by most tests of intelligence are important for language and reading comprehension (e.g., vocabulary knowledge, use of inference, reasoning, etc.), and will undoubtedly contribute to individual differences on tests of these abilities" (p. 199).

Students who are good decoders and poor comprehenders typically perform poorly on tests of vocabulary knowledge (Catts et al., 2006; Nation, 2005). Cain, Oakhill, and Lemmon (2004) found that 9- and 10-year-old poor comprehenders took more practice trials to learn novel vocabulary than their average-comprehending peers. While many of these poor comprehenders do not have language difficulties low enough to be considered speech or language impaired (Nation, 2005), approximately a quarter of them do (Catts et al., 2006).

Syntactical–Grammatical Knowledge

Syntax deals with the order of words in sentences. *Grammar* refers to a variety of linguistic concepts that include singular/plural, verb tense, and parts of speech. A combination of grammatical and syntactical knowledge allowed you to success-fully answer the comprehension questions earlier in the chapter about the snables. The snables paragraph shows that we can distinguish grammatical–syntactical knowledge from vocabulary–semantic knowledge.

Generally speaking, grammar and syntax do not usually represent a unique source of difficulty for poor comprehenders, independent of vocabulary–semantic knowledge. Typically, children who demonstrate weak grammar also have difficul-ties with semantics; their language difficulties are more global. However, it appears some students have weak semantic knowledge but fairly intact grammatical and syntactic knowledge. Traditional cognitive and reading assessments do not evaluate grammar and syntax. However, difficulties in these areas can be assessed via a speech-language evaluation.

Background Knowledge

There are multiple types of background knowledge that affect language comprehension as well as reading comprehension, including general world knowledge, specific topical knowledge, knowledge that allows one to build a situation model, and knowledge of the genre of what one is listening to or reading (Catts, 2009; Fletcher et al., 2007; Kamhi, 2009; Nation, 2005). In fact, some have argued that background knowledge is the key to language comprehension and that even those with low-average to below-average language skills can have good comprehension when listening to or reading material about which they have good prior knowledge (Catts, 2009; Kamhi, 2009).

Working Memory

While not as strong of a factor as language (Goff et al., 2005), working memory is considered a "core process" (Fletcher et al., 2007) in language and reading comprehension. One needs to temporarily capture and maintain the specific words and grammatical constructions in any given sentence or group of sentences in order to comprehend that information (Gathercole & Galloway, 2008). In a longitudinal study, Cain, Oakhill, and Lemmon (2004) found that working memory accounted for unique variance in reading comprehension at ages 8, 9, and 10, after vocabulary/general language skills had been accounted for.

Attention

Attention appears to play a role in language/listening comprehension and reading comprehension (Cain & Bignell, 2014; Kendeou, van den Broek, Helder, & Karlsson, 2014; Kieffer, Vukovic, & Berry, 2013; Miller et al., 2013). This is not surprising, because if a student is not focused on what she is listening to or reading, we would expect comprehension to be negatively affected.

Inferencing

Poor comprehenders typically can understand and extract literal information from text, but they struggle with inferring what was not explicitly stated (Fletcher et al., 2007; Kendeou et al., 2014). Inferencing often requires the application of the background knowledge a student brings to the text. Yet it is more than this, because poor comprehenders demonstrate difficulties on inferencing tasks even when oral language skills, working memory, and background knowledge are controlled for (Fletcher et al., 2007).

Comprehension Monitoring

While tired or distracted or when reading difficult material, we have all had the experience of noticing we did not understand the last few sentences or even paragraphs. In such cases we go back and reread. The fact that we noticed this means we were using comprehension monitoring. Poor comprehenders are less likely to notice when they did not comprehend something and often continue reading without going back to clarify (Fletcher et al., 2007; Hulme & Snowling, 2009; Nation, 2005). It is not clear whether comprehension monitoring is a cause of reading comprehension problems or simply a byproduct. If a student routinely does not understand what he reads, that student may be less inclined to go back and reread.

Nonverbal, Visual–Spatial Skills

Listening and reading comprehension have been shown to correlate with visual–spatial–perceptual (VSP) skills (Adlof, Catts, & Lee, 2010; Joffe, Cain, & Marić, 2007; McCallum & Moore, 1999; Stothers & Klein, 2010; Stroud, Blommers, & Lauber, 1957). For example, Adlof et al. (2010) found that nonverbal IQ measures taken in kindergarten were key predictors of eighth-grade reading comprehension, but not of eighth-grade word-level reading. In addition, certain types of visual imagery training have been demonstrated to provide

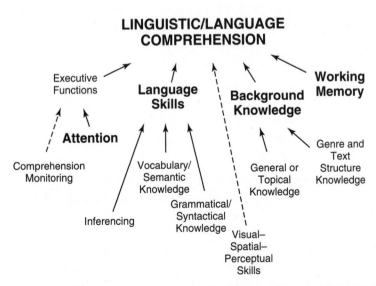

Figure 3.8 The Components of Linguistic Comprehension in an Expanded Simple View of Reading

benefits for both listening comprehension and reading comprehension (Center, Freeman, Robertson, & Outhred, 1999; Johnson-Glenberg, 2000; Oakhill & Patel, 1991). Hulme and Snowling (2009) describe VSP skills as a factor in reading comprehension that deserves more attention.

Figure 3.8 illustrates the relationship among the various components of linguistic comprehension within the expanded form of the simple view of reading. Students referred for reading comprehension difficulties that cannot be accounted for by word-reading deficits will likely display weak performance on assessments of one or more of the components depicted in Figure 3.8. This allows an evaluator to pinpoint the likely reasons for the student's struggle. Chapter 9 will discuss the assessment of these various comprehension-related components. Once these weak areas are identified, they will provide the blueprint for intervention.

SUMMARY

The simple view of reading is a way of organizing the empirical findings about the components needed for skilled reading. It begins by dividing reading comprehension into two broad skills: word-level reading and language comprehension. Each of these broad skills can be further subdivided based upon research into the various components influencing those broad skills. The simple view of reading has the potential of driving our Tier 1 instruction. Doing so would ensure that each of the key components involved in learning to read would receive proper instructional attention. It should also drive our assessments of children with reading difficulties. This would allow us to pinpoint the reasons why a student struggles. Tier 2 and 3 instruction/intervention can focus on addressing the specific components that are compromising the student's reading development.

The simple view of reading applies to poor readers with IDEA disabilities (SLD, SLI, ID, ED/BD, TBI) and poor readers not considered disabled. Thus, when asked the question, "Why is this child struggling in reading?" we would no longer answer, "because the child has an intellectual disability (or SLI or ED/BD or whatever)." Those disability categories do not cause reading difficulties—specific reading-related skill deficits cause reading difficulties. The answer to the question about why a student with an intellectual disability struggles in reading would be something like, "because the child has poor phonemic awareness along with difficulties with vocabulary and background knowledge." Now a teacher knows where to focus instructional efforts.

Although unresolved issues regarding reading problems remain, researchers now have a well-grounded understanding of the nature and causes of most reading disabilities (Fletcher et al., 2007; Hulme & Snowling, 2009; Vellutino et al.,

2004). Informed by the expanded simple view of reading, teachers and educational evaluators can approach reading difficulties with confidence that they can pinpoint and address the sources of almost any reading problem. Chapters 6 through 9 show how to assess each component of the expanded simple view of reading. Chapters 10 and 11 demonstrate how to prevent and/or correct most reading difficulties.

🖎 TEST YOURSELF 🖎

1. **The simple view of reading proposes that reading is**
   (a) The product of decoding and linguistic comprehension.
   (b) Simple to learn but made more complex by the teaching methods we use.
   (c) Simple when taught early, but only more complex if the window of opportunity has passed.
   (d) All of the above are proposed by the simple view of reading.

2. **The current status of the simple view of reading is that it**
   (a) Is a great idea awaiting experimental evaluation.
   (b) Is a theoretical framework with extensive research validation.
   (c) Is valid for most students, but not for English language learners.
   (d) Is valid for most students, but not for those with IDEA disabilities.

3. **Hyperlexia refers to a case in which**
   (a) Word-level reading is far below one's reading comprehension.
   (b) Word-level reading is far above one's reading comprehension.
   (c) Word-level reading and reading comprehension are both above average.
   (d) Word-level reading and reading comprehension are both below average.

4. **According to the simple view of reading framework, what can be said about those with low IQs?**
   (a) They should at least be hyperlexic and not poor at both word reading and language comprehension.
   (b) They should at least be dyslexic and not poor at both word reading and language comprehension.
   (c) Given their low IQs, we cannot expect reading improvement.
   (d) They should be expected to reach a normal reading level if they are given enough time.

5. **All of the following are suggested in the chapter about compensating readers except:**
   (a) They tend to have strong verbal skills.
   (b) Because their reading scores are average, they are not a concern.

   (c) Lower-level skills such as phonological awareness limit their word-level reading, which thus prevents their reading comprehension from being as high as their language comprehension.

   (d) They are often difficult to detect, especially early in their reading careers.

6. What appears to be the benefit of using the simple view of reading framework to guide reading assessments?

   (a) It will make such assessments much briefer.

   (b) It will allow evaluators to better understand reading skills without formal assessment.

   (c) It will allow evaluators to assess skills that underlie reading that may be contributing to the reading difficulty.

   (d) Many achievement batteries are based on the simple view of reading.

7. What appears to be the benefit of using the simple view of reading framework to guide reading instruction and intervention?

   (a) It will make lesson planning easier.

   (b) It will allow one to better understand reading skills without formal assessment.

   (c) It will allow teachers to address the skills that are the likely source of a student's reading difficulty.

   (d) Most reading series are already based on the simple view of reading.

8. All of the following are related to cipher knowledge except

   (a) Letter-sound knowledge.

   (b) Inferencing skills.

   (c) Phonic decoding.

   (d) Phonological awareness.

9. Word-specific knowledge

   (a) Is based on an overlapping set of skills with cipher knowledge.

   (b) Requires past experience with specific words.

   (c) Overlaps with the concept of a sight word.

   (d) All of the above.

10. The linguistic comprehension aspect of the simple view of reading is based on all of the following *except*

   (a) Word-reading skills.

   (b) Vocabulary knowledge.

   (c) Background knowledge.

   (d) Working memory.

Answers: 1. a; 2. b; 3. b; 4. a; 5. b; 6. c; 7. c; 8. b; 9. d; 10. a

Four

UNDERSTANDING WORD RECOGNITION DIFFICULTIES

When reading is flowing at its best, for example in reading a mystery novel in which the vocabulary is very familiar, we can go along for many minutes imagining ourselves with the detective walking the streets of London, and apparently we have not given a bit of attention to any of the decoding processes that have been transforming marks on the page into the deeper systems of comprehension.

—LaBerge and Samuels (1974, p. 314)

Skilled readers are familiar with all, or almost all, of the words they read. For them, the word-reading process is automatic and performed without effort or conscious awareness. When they encounter an unfamiliar word, they quickly and efficiently sound out the word, often with help from context (Frost, 1998; Share, 1995; Tunmer & Chapman, 1998, 2012).

By contrast, individuals with reading difficulties display inefficient word-level reading skills. Many of the words they encounter are unfamiliar. They must use phonic decoding and contextual guessing to identify these words. Because their phonic decoding is weak, their word reading requires much conscious effort. A common result is a compromise of their reading comprehension (Fletcher, Lyon, Fuchs, & Barnes, 2007; Hulme & Snowling, 2009; Nation, 2005).

THE IMPORTANCE OF THIS CHAPTER

The present chapter forms the heart of this volume. Much of the material on assessment (Chapters 6–8) and prevention/intervention (Chapters 10, 11) are based upon the understanding of the reading process described in this chapter. It will provide information that can help answer the following questions:

- Why do some students have word-level reading difficulties or disabilities?
- Why do some students struggle with learning phonics?
- Why do some students with reading problems reverse or transpose letters?
- Why do students with reading problems have limited sight vocabularies?
- Why do students with reading problems struggle with reading fluency?
- Why do students struggle with reading comprehension?
- How does this affect students whose native language is not English?
- Why do most intervention studies with weak readers show minimal to modest gains but others demonstrate very large improvements?

This is an ambitious set of questions. Nevertheless, these questions can be answered by drawing from the scientific research on reading over the past 30 years. Before we can apply these findings to struggling readers, we must first acquire an in-depth understanding of the very nature of how written words are read and remembered. This will form the foundation for the assessments and interventions that will be described throughout the remainder of the book.

INTRODUCING ORTHOGRAPHIC MAPPING

An important key to answering this ambitious set of questions is to understand a process called *orthographic mapping*. It will be described in detail later in the chapter. It is briefly introduced here because of its overarching significance for almost everything that follows in this chapter. First, a definition:

Orthographic mapping is the process readers use to store written words for immediate, effortless retrieval. It is the means by which readers turn unfamiliar written words into familiar, instantaneously accessible sight words.

Orthographic mapping is the encoding process responsible for word recognition and explains how readers build a sight vocabulary. Orthographic mapping establishes a stable memory of spelling patterns. Skilled readers develop orthographic mapping skills naturally, simply by interacting with letters and words. By contrast, students with word-level

DON'T FORGET

Orthographic mapping is the process that readers use to store written words for instant and effortless retrieval. It is the means by which readers turn unfamiliar written words into familiar and instantly recognizable sight words.

reading difficulties do not naturally develop orthographic mapping. As a result, they experience great difficulty developing a sight-word vocabulary (Ahmed, Wagner, & Kantor, 2012; Dixon et al., 2002; Ehri, 2005a; Kilpatrick, 2014a; Van den Broeck & Geudens, 2012; Van den Broeck, Geudens, & van den Bos, 2010).

The Multiple Meanings of the Term *Orthography*

To understand orthographic mapping, it may be useful to define the term *orthography*. Orthography comes from two classic Greek words: *orthos,* meaning straight, right, correct (an *ortho*dontist straightens or corrects teeth); and *graphē*, which means a writing or an inscription. Thus, orthography literally means "correct writing." In reading research, *orthography* is used to refer to the correct spelling of words. For example, *brain* is correct orthography while *brane* is not. *Cent* is the correct orthography for a U.S. penny, but *scent* is the correct orthography when that same spoken pronunciation refers to an aroma. Like other terms used in research, orthography has multiple meanings. These are highlighted in Rapid Reference 4.1.

≡ *Rapid Reference 4.1 Multiple Uses of the Term Orthography*

The terms *orthography* and *orthographic* are used in multiple ways:

- Orthography can refer to the correct manner in which specific written words are spelled (e.g., *Italy* is a country but *Italee* is not).
- Orthography can refer to the writing system associated with a particular spoken language (English orthography vs. French orthography vs. Chinese orthography).
- Orthography can refer to the conventions of spelling, that is, what patterns are permitted and/or what patterns are common (e.g., -*ck* usually ends a word rather than -*k* or -*c* alone).
- Orthography can refer to an awareness of common patterns in words that are consistent across words but are inconsistent when using a letter-by-letter phonic conversion process, such as -*ight*, -*alk*, or -*ing*).

What ties these usages together is the idea that orthography refers to the patterns and principles by which spoken language is correctly represented in writing.

Orthography in Reading and Spelling

The memory students develop for the specific spellings of words appears to function on two broad levels: recall and recognition. Orthographic *recognition* is the essence of word recognition—a particular orthographic sequence is instantly recognized as a familiar word. Yet to correctly spell words, orthographic *recall* is necessary (i.e., it is *boat* not *bote*). Orthographic recall appears to require a more detailed, well-encoded memory of orthographic sequences. Word recognition in reading requires sufficient detail to distinguish between the many look-alike words in English (*black, block, blink, brink*, etc.). However, many words can be easily recognized that cannot be easily spelled, such as *tongue, bouquet, colonel, rendezvous,* or *licorice.*

> **DON'T FORGET**
> ....
> Recall that a *sight word* is a word that is instantly and effortlessly recalled from memory, regardless of whether it is phonically regular or irregular. A *sight-word vocabulary* (or simply *sight vocabulary*) refers to the pool of words a student can effortlessly recognize. Sight words and the sight vocabulary represent the *content* of word recognition. Word recognition involves accessing familiar sight words.

> **DON'T FORGET**
> ....
> Individuals with reading problems commonly display difficulties in *both* phonic decoding *and* instant word retrieval. Phonic decoding and orthographic mapping are so central to the development of proficient reading that research on both of these word-level reading processes should drive our assessments, instructional practices, and intervention efforts.

HOW SKILLED WORD READING DEVELOPS

For the majority of children, reading development occurs quite naturally, as long as they are taught to read. By contrast, those with word-reading difficulties struggle to identify words via phonic decoding (Rack, Snowling, & Olson, 1992) *and* they have limited sight vocabularies (Ahmed et al., 2012; van den Broeck et al., 2010; van den Broeck & Geudens, 2012). Their typically developing peers acquire phonic decoding skills whether or not they are directly taught them (Bitana & Karni, 2003; Carroll, 1956; Dixon, 2011; Liberman & Liberman, 1990), and with an appropriate amount of exposure to text, they build a large sight vocabulary. How do they do this?

Understanding the Pieces of the Word-Reading Puzzle

A comprehensive understanding of the complex process of learning to read words requires knowledge of the specific components needed for both phonic decoding and for orthographic mapping (i.e., sight-word learning). A compromise in any of the components usually results in difficulties with reading acquisition. These components include: (a) proficient letter-sound knowledge, (b) proficient phonological awareness (basic and advanced), (c) phonological blending, and (d) vocabulary/phonological long-term memory.

Letter-Sound Knowledge

To read an alphabet-based writing system, children must learn the sounds associated with the letters. Some languages like Turkish and Swahili have a one-to-one correspondence between the sounds in the spoken language and the letters in the written language. English is the most inconsistent alphabetic orthography (Seymour, Aro, & Erskine, 2003). Yet, regardless of whether the orthography is the most consistent (Turkish) or the least (English), letter-sound knowledge is essential for reading (Ziegler & Goswami, 2005). It will be demonstrated below that letter-sound knowledge is central to both phonic decoding and sight-word learning.

> **CAUTION**
>
> ....
>
> Contrary to any intuitions we may have about sight-word learning, a substantial amount of research shows that letter-sound knowledge is central to both phonic decoding *and* sight-word learning.

Phonological Awareness—Basic and Advanced

Phonological awareness involves noticing and/or manipulating the sound structure of spoken language (Brady & Shankweiler, 1991; Scarborough & Brady, 2002; Wagner & Torgesen, 1987). When attempting to interface phonological awareness with reading development, we can broadly define three levels of phonological awareness development: early, basic, and advanced. This general scenario parallels what has been known about phonological awareness development for decades (Adams, 1990; Cassady, Smith, & Putman, 2008). Reviewing the phonological awareness research from the 1970s and 1980s, Adams (1990) outlined five levels of difficulty in phonological tasks, and subsequent research has generally supported her hierarchy (e.g., Cassady et al., 2008). However, in what follows, a more streamlined, three-level approach is presented as we have come to know more about the relationship between phonological development and reading.

Early phonological awareness skills (roughly corresponding to the first two levels of the skill hierarchy outlined in Adams, 1990) typically develop in preschoolers and include rhyming (e.g., *cat, hat, sat, mat*), alliteration (e.g., *the big brown bear*), being able to segment words into syllables (e.g., /car/ /pen/ /ter/), and being able to identify the first sounds in words (a skill that overlaps with alliteration). There is evidence that these early phonological awareness skills facilitate the development of letter-sound knowledge (Cardoso-Martins, Mesquita, & Ehri, 2011; Juel, Griffith, & Gough, 1986; Kim, Petscher, Foorman, & Zhou, 2010).

Basic phonological awareness develops throughout kindergarten and first grade. Basic phonological awareness skills include phoneme blending and phoneme segmentation (corresponding to the third and fourth levels of Adams' hierarchy) and are generally mastered by most students by the end of first grade (Kilpatrick, 2012a; Swank & Catts, 1994; Wagner, Torgesen, & Rashotte, 1997). This is why the segmentation subtests from the universal screening batteries (DIBELS, Aimsweb, easyCBM) are discontinued after first grade. These basic phonological skills are instrumental in phonic decoding and early spelling.

Advanced phonological awareness (Adams' fifth and highest level) continues to develop until about third or fourth grade. Tests that involve manipulating phonemes, such as deleting, substituting, or reversing phonemes within words, appear to tap into this advanced level of phonological awareness/proficiency. Advanced phonemic awareness appears to be needed for efficient sight vocabulary development (Caravolas, Volín, & Hulme, 2005; Vaessen & Blomert, 2010).

Phonological Blending

Phonological blending is technically a type of phonological awareness. Most phonological awareness tasks (e.g., segmentation, isolation, and manipulation) involve taking apart spoken words. By contrast, blending involves putting sounds together to make a word (or nonsense word); this is sometimes referred to as *phonological synthesis* (i.e., putting sounds together). Other tasks involve *phonological analysis* (i.e., taking words apart) (NICHD, 2000; Scarborough & Brady, 2002). Despite the fact that phonological awareness/analysis and phonological blending/synthesis are highly inter-correlated and load on a single factor in factor analytic studies (Schatschneider, Fletcher, Francis, Carlson, & Foorman, 2004; Schatschneider, Francis, Foorman, Fletcher, & Mehta, 1999), they will be discussed separately in this volume for two reasons.

First, while phonological analysis and synthesis are closely interrelated, they appear to contribute to reading in different ways (see Figures 4.2 and 4.3 later in the chapter). Second, many struggling readers beyond first grade display average blending skills but poor phonological awareness/analysis tasks, yet rarely do students show the opposite pattern (Kilpatrick, 2012a; see Chapter 6). There is evidence that blending skills develop sooner than analysis skills, and that students can have good blending skills and inadequate reading development (Fox & Routh, 1976, 1983; Kilpatrick, 2012a). Only when both blending and analysis skills are mastered do we see benefits for reading development (Fox & Routh, 1976, 1983; see Chapter 11). For these reasons, blending (synthesis) will be discussed separately from phonological awareness (analysis) skills.

Blending and Phonic Decoding   Phonic decoding involves two elements: letter-sound knowledge and blending. A reader identifies the most common sounds that go with the letters and then *blends* those sounds together to pronounce a word. The National Reading Panel report stated: "The process of decoding words never read before involves transforming graphemes[1] into phonemes and then blending the phonemes to form words with recognizable meanings. The PA [phonological awareness] skill centrally involved in [phonic] decoding is blending" (NICHD, 2000, pp. 2–11).

The Set for Variability and Phonological Blending   Readers do not need to pronounce words completely or correctly to accurately identify them, as long as they are close enough phonetically (Share, 1995). This is due to a skill called the *set for variability,* which refers to "the ability to determine the correct pronunciation of approximations to spoken English words" (Tunmer, 2011, p. xii). Tunmer and Chapman (2012) found that those with better oral vocabulary were better at determining words based upon the set for variability. This has important significance for some students with word-reading difficulties, particularly older students. As children grow older, their vocabularies increase and they are presumably better able to correctly determine words based upon partial phonic decoding or even inaccurate phonic decoding. We have a natural linguistic tendency to try to determine a word based upon partial information. Research has shown that adults and even infants between 18 and 21 months old can quickly determine some words based upon their initial sound (Fernald, Swingley, & Pinto, 2001).

Tunmer and Chapman (1998, 2012) used a test in which irregular words were pronounced by the examiner according to phonic regularity (e.g., the word *prove* was pronounced to rhyme with *drove*). Children heard these words in isolation, but in a later session heard them in a sentence context (e.g., "The dog had to have a *wash*"; *wash* was pronounced like *cash*). Tunmer and Chapman (2012) found that students at the end of first grade who more accurately identified the mispronounced words (i.e., better set for variability skills) were

---

[1]A *grapheme* refers to the letter or letters used to represent a single phoneme. Most graphemes are single letters (e.g., *m* for /m/), but some are multi-letter (e.g., *ch, sh, th, ee, oa,* or *igh* as in *light* each represent single phonemes).

more accurate at determining words via phonic decoding. Set for variability thus boosts the likelihood of correctly determining an unfamiliar irregular word or an unfamiliar regular word that has been sounded-out incorrectly. Also, it may allow students with stronger vocabularies to correctly determine words on word-reading tasks, particularly untimed tasks. This means untimed word identification tests may overestimate the reading proficiency of some students (see Chapter 8). The set for variability phenomenon also helps us understand why the compensating-type of readers described in Chapter 3 appear to have fairly typical word-reading performance. A student's skill in phonological blending, along with the set for variability, can be combined with contextual cues to determine many of the unfamiliar words the student will encounter.

Vocabulary and/or Phonological Long-Term Memory

We can distinguish between the semantic lexicon and the phonological lexicon. The *semantic lexicon* refers to the pool of words for which an individual has partial or full knowledge of each word's meaning. The *phonological lexicon* is broader and includes: (a) the entire semantic lexicon, (b) words that are orally familiar but whose meanings are unknown (Nation & Cocksey, 2009a), and (c) familiar parts of words (e.g., *-ing, -ence, -ip,*) (Adelman & Brown, 2007; Andrews, 1992; Bowey & Hansen, 1994; Bowey & Underwood, 1996; Nation & Cocksey, 2009b; Peereman & Content, 1997). In long-term memory, entries in the phonological lexicon include all familiar-sounding words and word parts.

Having familiar words and word parts in phonological long-term memory helps both phonic decoding and sight-word learning (Duff & Hulme, 2012; McKague, Pratt, and Johnston, 2001; Nation & Cocksey, 2009a). In phonic decoding, the phonological lexicon will help the student activate a familiar-sounding pronunciation after sounding out an unfamiliar printed word. Also, the phonemes that make up the sounds of words in the phonological lexicon will act as anchoring points for remembering the spelling sequence in written words. This is central to orthographic mapping/sight-word learning, which is described in detail later in the chapter.

McKague and colleagues (2001) taught 20 nonsense words to 44 first graders. The researchers assigned meanings to 10 of those nonsense words using stories that included those new vocabulary words seven times. They also taught 10 nonsense words with no meanings. Students became orally familiar with all 20 nonsense words. Two or three days later, the students were tested on the previously learned nonsense words plus some new nonsense words. Students were faster and more accurate in their reading of the nonsense words they had previously learned than on the newly encountered nonsense words. But the semantic element made no difference. They did equally well on both types of previously learned nonsense words: those with meanings attached and those without. The key seems to be that they were orally/phonologically familiar—that is, they were in the phonological lexicon.

Nation and Cocksey (2009a) evaluated 7-year-old children's phonological long-term memory with a lexical decision task. The children had to indicate whether a word spoken by the examiner was a real word or a nonsense word. Then, their word reading was evaluated a week later, including the real words from the previous week. During the third week, they were asked to give definitions of the target words, with ratings of 0, 1, or 2, similar to the scoring of the Wechsler Vocabulary subtest. They found that knowing the word's definition provided no additional help in quickly and accurately reading the words than simply being orally familiar with the words. Studying 5- and 6-year-olds, Duff and Hulme (2012) similarly found that nonsense words that were given meanings were learned to mastery with the same speed as nonsense words that were orally familiar but had no meaning. They provided children with 88 exposures to the nonsense words with and without meaning, and nonsense words with meanings were taught in isolation, in sentences, and in stories. With that many exposures to the words and their meanings, it seems that any potential benefit that a word's meaning would have for word learning would have surfaced.

Many studies over the past 40 years have demonstrated a strong correlation between vocabulary knowledge and word-reading development. However, the emerging research suggests that it is the phonological lexicon (in which the semantic lexicon is fully embedded) that may have the lion's share of responsibility for sight-word reading development. In other words, vocabulary may be correlated with word-reading development primarily because it is a component of a child's phonological lexicon. These recent studies are suggesting that the semantic element plays a smaller role in word learning than previously thought. For example, in their regression analysis, Nation and Cocksey (2009a) found that vocabulary knowledge contributed nothing to word reading beyond their lexical decision task (a direct test of phonological long-term memory), yet performance on the lexical decision task accounted for an additional 18% of the variance above and beyond performance on the vocabulary task. These findings seem to echo an earlier comment by Torgesen et al. (1999), "The type of verbal ability required in the growth of word-level reading skills is primarily phonological in nature" (p. 589).

This finding helps our understanding of multiple phenomena found in the reading research literature, including hyperlexia, poor word reading among students of low SES, and the reading patterns of many ELL students. It also clarifies one aspect of dyslexia. Each of these will be examined in turn.

Hyperlexia   The findings regarding the role of the phonological lexicon in word learning help make sense of the phenomenon of hyperlexia. It seems that hyper-lexics can read many words for which they have no semantic knowledge, as long as the word is orally familiar to them. If they have heard the word, it is in their phonological lexicon, so they can still learn to read it even if it is not in their semantic lexicon.

Low SES Readers   There is a large vocabulary gap between students of high SES and those of low SES. Some studies have indicated that infants and toddlers in high SES homes may hear as many as 10 times more words spoken in a given day than infants and toddlers in low SES homes (Hart & Risley, 2003). While this finding helps account for the vocabulary gap, it may also point to a phonological lexicon gap. It seems that students from low SES backgrounds are more likely to arrive at school having heard far fewer words, and therefore having fewer words in their phonological lexicon. This likely puts them at a disadvantage in learning to read. Couple this with the fact that exposure to words in the preschool years also promotes phonological awareness (Burgess, Hecht, & Lonigan, 2002; Metsala, 2011), assuming no genetically based phonological-core deficit, and the reasons for the reading gap between low SES and high SES students come into sharper focus. Students from high SES backgrounds likely have larger phonological lexi-cons, which facilitates orthographic mapping.

ELL Students   Many students whose native language is not English display a pat-tern in which their word-level reading skills progress more quickly than their comprehension (Farnia & Geva, 2013; Sparks, Patton, Ganschow, & Humbach, 2012). The findings about the role of the phonological lexicon described above help us understand why. These students are living in an English-speaking environ-ment (school and the broader culture), so they are orally exposed to many words that are not yet in their semantic lexicons. This puts them in a ready position to learn to read those words, so long as they have adequate phonological aware-ness skills and letter-sound knowledge. Yet with a limited semantic lexicon, their reading comprehension is substantially weaker.

Dyslexia   Many individuals with the dyslexic reading pattern have average or better vocabulary skills. This means their phonological lexicons are more than adequate for reading. However, the phonological-core deficit prevents them from having ready access to the phonemic properties of the words in their phonological lexicons. That is, phonemic awareness difficulties prevent them from connecting the phonological lexicon with the printed form of the language. Thus, of the components needed for word-level reading—letter-sound knowledge, phonological blending, phonemic awareness, and phonological long-term memory—the difficulties experienced by those with the dyslexic pattern can be narrowed down to some combination of the first three.

Vocabulary is obviously essential for comprehension. In the context of the simple view of reading, it appears that vocabulary belongs primarily on the language comprehension side of the simple view equation, not necessarily on the word-reading side. The distinction between the semantic and phonological lexicons is fairly recent, long after the simple view was developed. Yet it testifies to the power of the simple view due to the dissociation between the skills involved in word reading and the skills that contribute to language comprehension.

This, however, is not the whole story. Some studies show that words with the semantic property of being more concrete (e.g., *red, Mom, truck, light*) are learned more quickly than words that are more abstract (e.g., *then, by, might, yet*) (Duff & Hulme, 2012; Laing & Hulme, 1999). This finding seems inconsistent with the finding that vocabulary plays little or no discernible role in sight-word development. Duff and Hulme (2012) did two experiments; the first demonstrated that meaning did not influence word learning (described above), whereas the second indicated that concrete words were easier to learn to read than abstract words. These authors could not adequately explain these contrasting findings and acknowledged this question requires further inquiry. Regardless, there is enough research to suggest that on some level, semantic knowledge has some degree of impact on word learning, even if it is not substantial enough to show up in all types of experimental paradigms. Nonetheless, studies of the relationship between word learning and the phonological versus semantic lexicons using multiple research designs indicate that oral familiarity with a word plays the primary role in sight-word development, and any benefits of the semantic properties appear to be secondary.

Summary of the Puzzle Pieces

The four puzzle pieces that together explain both phonic decoding and sight-word acquisition are: (1) letter-sound knowledge, (2) phonological awareness/analysis (basic and advanced), (3) phonological blending, and (4) vocabulary/

phonological long-term memory. Each will be examined in more detail in the context of how they contribute to word-level reading skills.

THE EARLY STAGES OF THE READING PROCESS

Children in preschool and even early kindergarten who do not yet know letters and sounds try to make sense of print by using visual features of words. Mason-heimer, Drum, and Ehri (1984) conducted a seminal study demonstrating that 2- to 5-year-old preschoolers could not identify common words in environmental print without their corresponding contexts or logos. For example, *PEPSI* was quickly read when it was embedded in the product's logo but not when presented apart from the logo. Also, children said "Pepsi" when the spelling inside the logo was changed to *PEWSI* or *PEPSO* or *XEPSI*. The preschoolers were asked to look carefully to see if there was anything wrong, yet they were not able to detect these misspellings. Children may also focus on visual features within words, such as noticing the tail at the end of the word dog or the two "eyes" in the center of the word *look*. These types of cues are limited in number (Ehri, 2005a). It is not until children learn the alphabet that a reliable system of remembering words becomes established.

Three Levels of Reading Development

Theorists have divided reading development into various stages or phases. There is no intention to review those here. What is provided is a useful set of three developmental levels that helps organize and integrate research related to phonological awareness development, reading acquisition, and reading difficulties:

Level 1: *Letters and sounds.* Children learn letter names and letter sounds.
Level 2: *Phonic decoding.* Children combine letter-sound knowledge with phonological blending to sound out unfamiliar words.
Level 3: *Orthographic mapping.* Children efficiently expand their sight vocabularies.

These three levels overlap in the sense that some rudimentary orthographic mapping can occur before phonic decoding skills emerge (Ehri & Wilce, 1985; Kilpatrick, 2015c; Rack, Hulme, Snowling, & Wightman, 1994). However, *efficient* orthographic mapping presumes workable phonic decoding skills, which is why it is represented as a level beyond phonic decoding. Also, these developmental reading levels align closely with the three levels of phonological awareness development described earlier in the chapter (see Rapid Reference 4.2).

≋ Rapid Reference 4.2 Developmental Levels of Phonological Awareness and Reading

Phonological Skill Development	Word-Reading Development

1. Early phonological awareness
    Rhyming, alliteration, first
    sounds
	1. Letters and sounds
	    Requires simple phonology to learn
	    sounds

2. Basic phonemic awareness
    Blending and segmentation
	2. Phonic decoding
	    Requires letter sounds and blending

3. Advanced phonemic awareness
    Phonemic proficiency
	3. Orthographic mapping
	    Requires letter-sound skills and advanced
	    phonological awareness

Looking ahead, it will become clear that students with word-level reading difficulties often get "stuck" in the second level and never develop proficiency at the third. Others, typically as a result of remedial phonics instruction, master the second level but do not have adequate phonemic awareness to become skilled at the third.

Level 1: Learning Letter Sounds

Research has demonstrated that basic phonological awareness skills and letter-name knowledge are important contributors to learning letter-sound relationships (Cardoso-Martins et al., 2011; Share, 2004b). Studies also show that not all letter-sound relationships are of equal difficulty to learn. Some letters have their sound at the beginning of the letter's name (e.g., *b, d, c; bee, cee, dee*), whereas others have the letter's sound embedded in the letter's name (e.g., *f, l, m; ef, el, em*), and still other letters have sounds not contained in the letter's name (e.g., *h, w, y*). Letters that contain their sound in the initial position in their names are more easily learned than those whose sounds are second in the letter name or not in the name at all (Cardoso-Martins et al., 2011; Share, 2004b; Treiman, Tincoff, & Richmond-Welty, 1996; Treiman, Weatherston, & Berch, 1994). This indicates that among preschoolers and kindergarteners, there is a strong phonological component to learning letter sounds. Also, studies that involved training phonological awareness skills improved the speed with which preschoolers and early kindergarteners learned letter sounds (Cardoso-Martins et al., 2011; Williams, 1980).

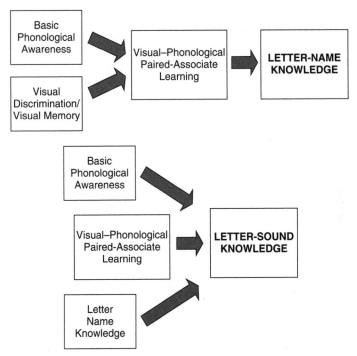

Figure 4.1 Skills Involved in Letter-Name and Letter-Sound Knowledge

Figure 4.1 displays the component skills in learning letter names and letter sounds. Note that phonology is critical for both.

Level 2: Phonic Decoding

It appears that phonic decoding and sight-word learning develop in tandem during normal reading acquisition, though they do not develop in the same way or at the same rate. Both are based upon the alphabetic principle.

The Alphabetic Principle

The alphabetic principle is neither a skill nor a strategy; it is an insight. The *alphabetic principle* is the insight that there is a direct connection between the sounds of spoken language and the letters in the written words. This is obvious to skilled readers but not prereaders or many students with the phonological-core deficit. The alphabetic principle is central to both phonic decoding and sight-word learning. Yet even when weak readers develop the alphabetic principle insight (typically via remedial instruction), they are limited in how efficiently they apply it.

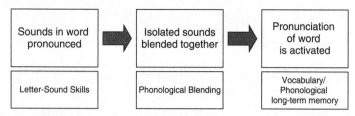

Figure 4.2 Phonic Decoding. The contribution of letter-sound knowledge and phonological blending to activate the spoken form of words

Development of Phonic Decoding Skills

Figure 4.2 provides a basic display of the skills involved in phonic decoding. If a student can sound out the letters in a word, and can blend those sounds together, it is likely that she will determine the spoken form of the word. The resulting pronunciation should activate a word in phonological long-term memory. Phonic decoding is essential for skilled reading development. Regardless of the teaching method used, all skilled readers develop basic phonic decoding skills (see Chapter 10). Phonic decoding allows readers to independently determine many of the new words they encounter (Share, 1995).

Phonic decoding works well for phonically regular words. What about irregular words, often called *exception words*?

> When beginning readers apply their developing knowledge of letter-sound relationships to unknown exception words, the resulting partial decoding will often be close enough to the correct phonological form that they will be able to arrive at a correct identification, but only if the word is in their listening vocabulary [i.e., phonological long-term memory]. (Tunmer & Chapman, 2012, p. 124)

DON'T FORGET

The terms *irregular words* and *exception words* are used interchangeably in this volume. These terms refer to words that do not display the regular or consistent phonic patterns and would not be pronounced correctly using a traditional letter-sound conversion process (e.g., *both, some, what, put*).

McGeown, Medford, and Moxon (2013) found that students with good phonic decoding skills took a more phonetic approach to sounding out irregular words than those with weaker phonics skills who relied more on the overall look of the word. Those approaching irregular words phonically were more successful at reading them correctly than those who used the more "visual" approach. Phonic decoding, with help from the set for variability and sentence context, can allow students to identify most of the unfamiliar words they encounter.

Phonic Decoding and the Self-Teaching Hypothesis

A growing amount of research suggests that for typically developing readers, phonic decoding may be the gateway to sight-word learning. By itself, phonic decoding is not capable of producing a sight-word memory, yet it appears to provide the opportunity for such learning. This research stems from investigations of David Share's self-teaching hypothesis (Bowey & Miller, 2007; Bowey & Muller, 2005; Cunningham, 2006; Cunningham et al., 2002; de Jong & Share, 2007; Frost, 1998; Nation, Angell, & Castles, 2007; Share, 1995, 1999, 2004a, 2011).

The self-teaching hypothesis proposes that once children become somewhat proficient at phonic decoding, they can teach themselves to read. For each encounter with a new word, they attend to the internal structure of that written word in order to sound it out. Such encounters help them establish an orthographic representation of that word in long-term memory.

An example of an experimental test of Share's self-teaching hypothesis is to expose students to new words a certain number of times during silent reading. At a later date, the students are tested to see if they learned the precise spellings of those words. Different studies exposed students to words a different number of times, ranging from one to eight. Depending on the study, an opportunity was provided to display learning the following day, the following week, or the following month. Various grade levels have been studied from second grade on.

An example of a new word would be the nonsense word *Yait*. Children silently read a story about *Yait*, the coldest city in the world. As they read about this fictitious city, some students received multiple exposures to the word, while others only saw it once in the opening line. A homophone task is given to determine if the new word was learned. The students are queried about the paragraph they read previously and asked whether the city was *Yate, Yait, Yaet,* or *Yat*. Students select the correct spelling with a high degree of accuracy. In studies in which they were asked to spell the new word they had learned (all words could be phonically spelled in more than one way), they also displayed a high degree of accuracy. Also, reaction times were faster to the previously seen version of the word (e.g., *Yait*) than its homophonic alternative (*Yate*). The finding from these studies has been that children add new words to their sight vocabulary by sounding them out independently, either silently or orally, with no help from the experimenter, and the precise spelling is recognized later. This supports the self-teaching hypothesis.

The self-teaching hypothesis reinforces earlier research showing that in typically developing readers, the learning of new sight words occurs after one to four exposures (Reitsma, 1983). This is an important factor in understanding skilled reading among young readers from second grade on. When students require many exposures before they learn a given word, that suggests that their sight vocabularies will grow very slowly. Also, the self-teaching hypothesis helps us understand how children develop such a large sight vocabulary on their own, without having to seek help from others every time they encounter new words.

Despite the important contributions of the self-teaching hypothesis, it stops short of explaining precisely *how* words are stored in long-term memory. It provides the context surrounding orthographic learning. However, orthographic mapping, which was introduced earlier, picks up where Share's theory leaves off. While the self-teaching hypothesis provides the context for sight vocabulary learning, orthographic mapping explains *how* words are remembered.

Level 3: Sight Word Learning via Orthographic Mapping

Orthographic mapping is the process we use to store printed words in long-term memory. Orthographic mapping was originally described by Linnea Ehri back in the late 1970s (Ehri, 1998b). She began providing empirical data for orthographic mapping in the mid-1980s (e.g., Ehri & Wilce, 1985), but it was not until an independent team of British researchers designed a rather "airtight" set of tests of Ehri's theory (Rack et al., 1994) that it became widely recognized in the research literature. Numerous studies by Ehri and by independent researchers began to follow (Cardoso-Martins, Mamede Resende, & Assunção Rodrigues, 2002; de Abreu & Cardoso-Martins, 1998; Dixon et al., 2002; Ehri & Saltmarsh, 1995; Laing & Hulme, 1999; McKague et al., 2001, 2008; Roberts, 2003). It is now considered "the most complete current theory of how children form sight word representations" (Torgesen, 2004b, p. 36).

How Sight Words Are Stored

Orthographic mapping requires: (a) advanced phoneme awareness, (b) letter-sound knowledge, and (c) phonological long-term memory. These three interact with one another in such a way as to produce a long-term orthographic memory of all of the words that we learn. There is nothing intuitive about the process of orthographic mapping, which is likely why it eluded researchers for nearly 100 years. The orthographic mapping principle helps us organize and make sense of most of the research on word-level reading skills in typically developing students and in struggling readers.

Phonological Lexicon as Anchor Phonological long-term memory represents familiar sounding words and word parts, regardless of whether the meanings

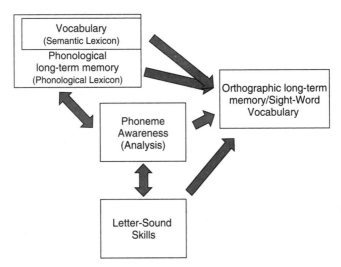

Figure 4.3 The Orthographic Mapping/Sight Word Learning Process. Sounds in the phonological lexicon map onto letters via phoneme awareness/analysis to produce an orthographic memory of written words

of the words are known. Orthographic mapping proposes that we use the pronunciations of words that are already stored in long-term memory as the anchoring points for the orthographic sequences (letters) used to represent those pronunciations. Efficient orthographic mapping requires good letter-sound proficiency as well as advanced phonemic proficiency (see Figure 4.3).

Consider a first grader's first encounter with the word *sit*. She already has the oral word *sit* well anchored in the phonological lexicon. How is she going to turn this unfamiliar written word into a familiar sight word? The self-teaching hypothesis describes the first step. To sound out the word *sit*, she will need to attend to the individual letters and sounds in that word. By itself, this is not enough to remember that printed word. In order to establish the precise orthographic representation of the word *sit* in long-term memory, this first grader will need to anchor that sequence to something in memory. Her letter-sound skills and her phonemic analysis skills will be the keys.

The fact that she successfully sounded-out the word *sit* indicates that she has good letter-sound skills. Phonic decoding also requires phonological blending, but not phonemic awareness/analysis skills. To anchor or bond the printed word *sit* to the spoken word *sit*, she will need to be able to pull apart the spoken word *sit* into its individual phonemes. She will then align those phonemes to the printed letter sequence used to represent the oral word *sit*.

If she can determine that *sit* is made up of the sounds /s/, / ĭ /, and /t/ (see Rapid Reference 4.3 for how sounds are represented in print), she is in a position to align those corresponding sounds—already well established in memory—onto the sequence of letters *s-i-t*. If she can notice the /ĭ/ sound in the middle of *sit*, the /t/ sound at the end of *sit*, and the /s/ sound at the beginning of *sit*, she can easily align those sounds/phonemes onto the corresponding letters in the printed word *sit*. This connection-forming process allows her to map the pronunciation of that spoken word onto its printed spelling. Figure 4.4 on p.107 illustrates this process.

≡ Rapid Reference 4.3 Representing Sounds in Print

In the reading research, the most common way sounds are represented is to place slash marks on either side of the letter that is typically associated with that sound. The International Phonetic Alphabet is often used in research reports, but in this volume, traditional phonics conventions will be used.

Consonants
> *Examples:* /m/ /r/ and /t/ represent the sounds associated with the letters *m, r,* and *t.* The letter *c* can be represented by /k/ or /s/, depending on the word (e.g., *cat* vs. *cent*).

Vowels
- The "short" vowels are represented with the curved symbol above the letter.
  > *Examples:* The vowel sounds in *top* and *set* would be represented by /ŏ/ and /ĕ/.
- The "long" vowels are represented by a straight bar above the letter.
  > *Examples:* The vowel sounds in *cake* and *tried* would be represented by /ā/ and /ī/.

Whole words and word parts
- Whole-word pronunciations or word parts are marked by slash marks on either side and with letters represented phonically.
  > *Examples:* The full pronunciation of the words *red* and *side* and the word parts *un* and *op* would be represented as /rĕd/, /sīd/, /ŭn/, and /ŏp/.

On one level, orthographic mapping goes in the opposite direction of phonic decoding. Phonic decoding starts with the letters and uses letter-sound knowledge and blending to activate a spoken word. There is no need to pull apart the sounds of the words. In phonic decoding, the sounds are already pulled apart.

The task is to blend those parts. By contrast, orthographic mapping requires one to analyze the pronunciation of words in the phonological lexicon. These now-separated phonemes will be used as the anchoring points for the individual letters in the written word. Roughly speaking, think of phonic decoding as going from text to brain and orthographic mapping as going from brain to text. This is, however, an oversimplification because orthographic mapping involves an interactive back and forth between the letters and sounds. However, it is important that we do not confuse orthographic mapping with phonic decoding. They use some of the same raw materials (i.e., letter-sound knowledge and phonological long-term memory), but they use different aspects of phonological awareness, and the actual process is different. Phonic decoding uses phonological blending, which goes from "part to whole" (i.e., phonemes to words) while orthographic mapping requires the efficient use of phonological awareness/analysis, which goes from "whole to part" (i.e., oral words to their constituent phonemes). Rapid Reference 4.4 provides some similarities and differences between phonic decoding and orthographic mapping.

≡ Rapid Reference 4.4 Similarities and Differences Between Phonic Decoding and Orthographic Mapping (Sight-Word Learning)

Similarities

Both are components of skilled reading
Both require letter-sound proficiency
Both have to do with sounds/phonemes

Differences

Phonic Decoding	Orthographic Mapping
An old teaching method	A comparatively recent discovery
A strategy for identifying unfamiliar words	A process for storing unfamiliar words
Goes from print to sound	Interactively goes between sound and print
Requires phonological blending	Requires phonemic awareness/analysis

The order of the phonemes in spoken words represents the anchoring element for remembering the order of the letters in written words. Aligning stored phoneme sequences to printed letter sequences (from brain to text) will allow that printed word to become familiar (see Figure 4.4 on p.107). It will no longer require sounding out or guessing. Efficient orthographic mapping will only occur if the student has adequate phonemic awareness/analysis. If he cannot pull apart the sounds in words, he cannot align those sounds to the order of the letters. This answers the question of why teachers should be doing "auditory training" (i.e., phonological awareness instruction) when word reading is "visual." We saw in Chapter 2 that word-level reading is not based on visual memory. Once the printed letters are visually entered into the language system, orthographic memory takes over.

Abstract Letter Representations   Recall from Chapter 2 that if a word is flashed on the screen for 1/20th of a second, skilled readers reliably identify the word but may not necessarily be aware of whether the word was printed in uppercase, lowercase, or mixed case. Also recall that memory for a written word is independent of a particular font. The reason for these phenomena is that in our orthographic memory system, we do not store words according to their visual properties. Rather, we store words based on an alignment between the letter sequence and the phoneme sequence in the word's pronunciation. Phonemic information regarding the pronunciation of words is already stored in long-term memory and ready to be used as a strong mnemonic for "attaching" or "bonding" printed letter sequences (i.e., written words) to these stored pronunciations.

Research has suggested for many years that we have an abstract representation of all of the letters in the alphabet (Adams, 1979; Bowers, 2000; Frost, 1998; van den Broeck & Geudens, 2012). Whether the letter in the word is A, a, or **a**, the perceptual information instantly translates to the abstract representation of the letter *a*. From there, the orthographic, letter-order information stored in long-term memory takes over, regardless of the actual physical features of the letters at the time the word was learned. So if a child learned the word *bear* in all lowercase, he will instantly recognize BEAR when he sees it, even though none of the uppercase letters in that word look like their lowercase counterparts (e.g., b/B, e/E). Word learning involves translating the physical properties of the letters to their abstract representation in our memory system. This phenomenon, well documented in the research (for reviews, see Adams, 1979; Bowers, 2000; Frost, 1998; van den Broeck & Geudens, 2012), helps us understand the findings from the mixed-case studies described in Chapter 2. When words were presented very quickly, individuals could input the letter string into long-term memory but did not have time to notice any details about the physical properties of those letters.

Thus, orthographic memory involves a connection-forming process in which the oral phonemes in spoken words are "bonded" (Ehri, 2005a) to the letters used to represent those phonemes.

> **DON'T FORGET**
> ....
> Phoneme awareness is essential for storing words in one's sight vocabulary.

The phoneme sequence of the word that is already established in long-term memory acts as the anchor for the written sequence of letters used to represent that phoneme sequence. The perceptual properties of the letters are not important, as long as they are legible to the reader. The only way a reader can access the phoneme sequence in order to anchor it to the spoken pronunciation is by phonemic awareness/analysis skills. Thus, phoneme awareness/analysis is essential for storing words in one's sight vocabulary (Ehri, 2005a, 2005b, 2014; Torgesen, 2004a, 2004b). Then, after one to four exposures to that new letter sequence, all connections are made and secured. The sequence becomes instantly familiar and is not confused with similar-looking words with different sequences (e.g., *trail/trial, silver/sliver*). From that point on, the entire familiar sequence activates the entire spoken pronunciation *as a unit* because our eyes can simultaneously perceive all the letters in a given word (Rayner et al., 2011), so that whole sequence of letters is recognized as a stored, familiar sequence. This is why it *feels* like whole-word recognition because of the speed and reliability of the recognition process when one encounters familiar letter strings.

Insights from Neuroimaging

Neuroimaging research has provided important clues to how this mapping process takes place (Dehaene & Cohen, 2011; Frost et al., 2009; Halderman, Ashby, & Perfetti, 2012; Glezer, Kim, Rule, Jiang, & Riesenhuber, 2015; Simos et al., 2013). There is an area called the *fusiform gyrus* that overlaps the temporal and occipital lobes in the lower part of our cortex in both the left and right hemispheres. The right fusiform gyrus appears to mediate memory for faces, and the left fusiform gyrus appears to store and activate unitized letter sequences in printed words.

Research related to the left fusiform gyrus suggests that our brains have the ability to perceive and store very subtle and fine-grained sequential associations between specific letter sequences and spoken pronunciations. This allows for the *unitization* of previously encountered sequences to instantly activate their spoken form. For this to happen, it appears that both phonological and letter processing must take place first, which are primarily mediated by left temporal and temporal-occipital areas (letter-sound processing) higher in the left hemisphere than the fusiform gyrus. The back portion of the left frontal lobe, which is heavily involved in processing spoken words, also appears to be involved in this process. It seems that without the connections made between the spoken pronunciations and the letter sequences, the fusiform gyrus is not much involved. But once these connections are made, the fusiform gyrus appears to mediate the storage and retrieval of the precise unitized letter sequences that are attached to their corresponding pronunciations (Dehaene & Cohen, 2011).

Translated back into educational terms, the neurophysiological findings are consistent with the integration of Share's self-teaching hypothesis and Ehri's orthographic mapping. The self-teaching hypothesis suggests that the letter-sound processing involved in phonic decoding promotes orthographic memory.

Simos et al. (2002) found that the left fusiform gyrus was not very active when dyslexics read text. However, following the correction of the dyslexics' phonemic awareness problems and the normalization of their reading skills, Simos et al. (2002) found normal left fusiform gyrus activity in these students.

CAUTION

Contrary to the claims of a popular viral e-mail, multiple experimental studies have demonstrated that skilled readers perceive every letter in the words they read (Crowder & Wagner, 1992; Rayner et al., 2011), unless they are skimming. We can accurately recognize words flashed on a screen for 1/20th of a second with no context. This is true even if the word looks like other words. We can instantly and flawlessly recognize words like *black, block, blink, blind, bland, brick, brink, blank*, etc., when they are presented in isolation for 1/20th of a second. Unless we perceive each of the letters, there is no explanation for how we could accomplish this.

The e-mail in question contains words with medial letters jumbled around, and it claims that we don't attend to every letter in every word we read. It also claims this was confirmed by a study conducted at Cambridge University. First, no such study came out of Cambridge University with that conclusion (Davis, 2012). Second, the suggestion that we do not perceive every letter of the words we read is also not accurate.

How, then, can we read the e-mail with semi-jumbled words? The same way we read items with typos or with poor handwriting. We use contextual facilitation. Context helps us resolve uncertainties in words when the "signal" is compromised. This jumbled word paradigm has been used for years to study various reading phenomena, but researchers do not draw the conclusion that the e-mail draws. Davis (2012) and Grainger and Whitney (2004) provide some technical interpretations of this phenomenon that go beyond contextual facilitation. It can be concluded that although the e-mail is entertaining, it is inconsistent with the empirical reading research.

Establishing Letter Sequences in Memory

Consider a beginning reader who encounters a two-letter word, such as *at, if,* or *up,* and she correctly sounds it out. She can then notice the relation between the two phonemes in the spoken word and that letter sequence. Connecting the pronunciation to that letter sequence helps to make that letter sequence familiar. Once those connections are made in memory, those two letters *as a familiar unit* activate the full pronunciation of the word. For example, when a child sees the word *at,* she no longer has to break that word apart. Rather, those two letters together are a familiar sequence and are now connected as a unit. With apparent thanks to the sequential precision offered by the left fusiform gyrus, the student now can provide an instant pronunciation of /ăt/. The raw materials she needed for this unitization process were (a) letter-sound knowledge, (b) a previously stored entry in the phonological lexicon (i.e., /ăt/), and (c) phoneme awareness (in order to pull apart phonemes in the spoken word *at*).

The student is now able to instantly recognize simple letter sequences due to this rudimentary orthographic mapping process. This builds up to sequences that are longer, such as three or more letters. The process is not restricted to sequences of letters that are spoken words. It also includes sequences of letters that represent parts of words. For example, when a student sees *op* in *top* or *hop,* she will have an association between the *o* and the *p* so that *op* becomes its own, unified sequence, even though it is not a word (Bowey & Hansen, 1994; Bowey & Underwood, 1996; Ehri, 2005a, Nation & Cocksey, 2009b; Kilpatrick & Cole, 2015). As a result of this connection-forming process, children begin to build up familiar orthographic sequences, whether words or word parts. This is the essence of sight-word acquisition.

Retrieving Familiar Sequences (Word Recognition)

The speed with which readers can recognize written words is quite impressive. To understand how retrieval of known words can be so rapid, consider how your Internet browser anticipates the web address that you are typing. If I type www.a, my browser immediately pops up www.apple.com (I have a Macintosh computer) along with other alternatives listed below whose addresses begin with www.a. My browser's "guess" will narrow when I add a second letter, let's say www.ad. It will continue to narrow down the possibilities until there are not many choices left given the number of letters already typed, until www.adobe.com, for example, is the only remaining candidate. In a sense, our brains function in a similar way, except far more efficiently. Our brains have a major advantage over our Internet browsers when it comes to such "guessing." The browser has to guess based upon one letter at a time presented in serial order, narrowing the possibilities as each new letter is added. By contrast, our eyes take in *all* of the letters of the word simultaneously (Crowder & Wagner, 1992; Rayner et al., 2011), so no guessing is needed. There is no waiting to find out what the next letter is; the reader has access to all the letters simultaneously. To continue with our Internet analogy, it would be like copying www.adobe.com and pasting it into the browser's search line. If that happened, the browser would provide no alternative guesses and would instantly access the exact site. There is simply no need for narrowing down or guessing when all of the needed information to access the site is already present.

In a similar way, written words represent specific entries in the orthographic lexicon, which is directly connected to the phonological lexicon (pronunciation) and normally the semantic lexicon (meaning). Because all of the letters of a word can be perceived in a single glance, the recognition of the entry in orthographic memory is instantaneous. To further the analogy, each written word is like a specific "web address" to a specific "site" in our orthographic, semantic, and phonological lexicons. Access is instant because all of the addressing information is provided to the system simultaneously.

Some lexical "addresses" such as *pair, pare,* and *pear* have a single entry in the phonological lexicon because they share the same pronunciation. Yet, they have different entries in the orthographic and semantic lexicons because their spellings and meanings are different. Other words such as *ring* have a single entry in both the phonological and orthographic lexicons, but multiple entries in the semantic lexicon. Finally, there are words such as *dove, wind,* and *lead.* Each of these words has a single entry in the orthographic lexicon. But because they each can be pronounced two different ways, resulting in different meanings, they have different entries in the phonological and semantic lexicons. Such is the English writing system! This raises the question of how orthographic mapping deals with English words with phonically irregular spelling patterns.

LEARNING TO READ IRREGULAR WORDS

The orthographic mapping process does not presume that letters and sounds are consistently related to one another, as in written languages such as Italian or Spanish. Indeed, most readers of English develop word-level reading skills quite successfully, even though English is the least consistent alphabet-based written language (Seymour et al., 2003). This is because orthographic mapping does *not* require perfect regularity to letter-sound relationships. Linnea Ehri, who developed the orthographic mapping theory, says:

> Exception words are only exceptional when someone tries to read them by applying a decoding strategy. When they are learned as sight words, they are secured in memory by the same connections as regularly spelled words, with only the exceptional letters unsecured. (Ehri, 2005a, pp. 171–172)

To understand how orthographic mapping handles irregular words, we must first define more precisely what constitutes an "irregular" or "exception" word in English.

The Nature of Letter-Sound Irregularities

Regular words display a meaningful and consistent relationship between their sounds and the letters. The word *top* is a regular word that has meaningful connections between the letters and its phonemes (/t/ /ŏ/ /p/). By contrast, the written word *one* is an irregular word with minimal connection to the spoken sequence /w/ /ŭ/ /n/. The only regular element in *one* is the connection between the letter *n* and the sound /n/. The /w/ sound at the beginning has no letter to represent it such as in the homophone *won*. Also, the letter *o* in *one* does not represent that letter's typical sound. Finally, the silent *e* does not influence the previous vowel in the way that the silent *e* typically does.

Fortunately, the words *one* and *once* are extremely rare cases in which an English written word is so poorly related to the spoken sequence. *One* and *once* are unique in that there is a sound in the spoken word that is not represented in the written word (i.e., /w/). Nearly all other irregular words

> **DON'T FORGET**
>
> The vast majority of exception words have only a single irregular letter-sound relationship.

in English represent every sound in the spoken word, even if they represent some sounds irregularly. What is also surprisingly uncommon is for an irregular word to have more than one irregular grapheme-sound connection. The vast majority of irregular words have only a single irregular letter-sound relationship. For example, the word *island* has one unusual silent letter. In the words *been, from, both,* and *put,* the only letter-sound irregularity is how they represent a single sound—the

Table 4.1 The Most Common English Words That Contain More Than One Irregular Letter-to-Sound Correspondence

of	one	once	iron	tomb
sugar	ocean	tongue	rhythm	stomach
bouquet	suede	chauffeur	ukulele	colonel

vowel. Some of the most common words that contain more than one irregularity are found in Table 4.1. Only a few of these (e.g., *of, one, once,* and the suffix -*tion*) would be encountered by beginning readers.

Routine, singular violations in irregular words present very little difficulty for orthographic mapping. First, there is evidence that when readers encounter new, irregular words, they create a "phonological framework" based on the regular letter–phoneme correspondences. They then make a mental note of the irregular element (Ehri, 2005a; Frost, 1998; Katz & Frost, 2001; Share, 1995; Van Orden & Kloos 2005). For example, when a first grader sees the word *island* for the first time, the child might say *iz-land*. But the child can quickly notice that the *s* is silent and that the five other letters do their "normal job." The regular letter-sound correspondences function as the phonological framework for building the orthographic sequence in long-term memory (Katz & Frost, 2001). The single deviation is noted for future reference. The child instantly recognizes *island* from that time on as a familiar word (Frost, 1998; Katz & Frost, 2001; Share, 1995; Van Orden & Kloos 2005).

Another example is the word *been.* For a child who is skilled in phonemic awareness and letter-sound knowledge, it would be rather easy, after first becoming aware of the irregularities in the written word *been,* to say, "Oh, *that's* how we spell it." The child already perceives the sounds in that word due to his phonemic awareness. While he expects it to be spelled *b-e-n,* he makes a mental note that it is spelled *b-e-e-n* and identifies it correctly thereafter. The *ee* in the word *been* gets mapped onto the /ĕ/ in his phonological long-term memory for that specific word (hence the component of word-specific knowledge in the simple view of reading). With much ease he would associate the /b/ with *b* and the /n/ with *n*; the only adjustment is the way the vowel sound is represented. Words that have more than one violation of regularity may require additional attention and perhaps additional exposures before securing the written word in permanent memory.

Adjusted Mappings for Regular Words

Mapping irregular words is similar to mapping some types of regular words (see Figure 4.4). From an orthographic mapping perspective, there are two kinds of

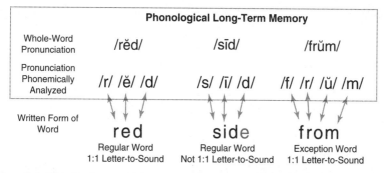

Figure 4.4 The Orthographic Mapping Process. Whole-word pronunciations are phonemically analyzed and then connected with printed letter strings

phonically regular words. One type of regular word has a one-to-one correspondence between letters and sounds, such as *red, hat,* and *stop.* Researchers call these *transparent words* (Laing & Hulme, 1999; Rack et al., 1994). However, many phonically regular words have more letters than sounds, including (a) silent *e* words (e.g., *make, ride*), (b) vowel digraph words (e.g., *seen, coat*), and

> **DON'T FORGET**
> Mapping irregular words is not a significant problem for orthographic mapping. The process is similar to mapping the many regular words for which an adjustment must be made as the child aligns letters to the phonemes in memory.

(c) words with consonant digraphs (e.g., *ca__sh, th__at*). In these cases, there is not a one-to-one correspondence between letters and sounds. Therefore, even with many regular words, an adjustment must be made as the child maps these regular words to the stored phonemes in the phonological lexicon.

In addition, there is the case of mapping phonically regular multisyllabic words. It is common for multisyllabic words to have a reduced vowel sound in the nonstressed syllable. For example, the vowels *i, a,* and *o* in the nonstressed syllables of *an__imal, ba__lloon,* and *dino__saur* do not use their typical short or long vowel sounds. Each of these reduce to a schwa sound, which is like a very quick, short *u* sound (/ŭ/) and is represented in print as an upside down letter *e* (i.e., /ə/ or /ə/). Some vowels in multisyllabic words get reduced to a short *i* sound (/ĭ/), such as the reduced vowels in *market* and *magnet* (for which dictionary.com gives the phonetic spellings as *mahr-kit* and *mag-nit*). This common phenomenon parallels the kind of mapping "adjustment" that needs to be made in irregular words when a vowel is irregular (e.g., *many, off*).

Children with typical reading development appear to have little difficulty mapping these sequences to long-term memory. Note also that many irregular words are transparent due to their one-to-one letter-to-sound pattern (e.g., *from, most, put*), even if one of those correspondences is not phonically regular.

Phonically regular words with more letters than sounds and phonically regular multisyllabic words with a vowel reduction are routinely encountered as children map words to their sight vocabulary. These phenomena require adjustments similar to those required for irregular words. This means that the kinds of adjustments needed for most irregular words are quite routine, which helps us understand why typically developing readers have little difficulty mapping irregular words. However, for weak readers, irregular words present difficulties because they are not good at mapping in the first place. The irregularities present an additional challenge. With many weak readers, a good grasp of phonic regularity cannot be assumed.

> # DON'T FORGET
> ....
> Despite their irregularities, exception words are secured in long-term memory by the same orthographic mapping process as regular words. The extra adjustment needed to encode an irregular word into permanent memory through orthographic mapping is far more efficient and reliable than any known alternative.

All of this helps to illustrate Ehri's statement earlier that, despite their irregularities, exception words are secured in long-term memory by the same orthographic mapping process as regular words. There is no parallel "visual memory" alternative for efficiently storing exception words. The alignment of the letter sequences to phoneme sequences in memory appears to be the only effective way to build the orthographic lexicon. In Chapter 2, it was noted that visual memory provides no reliable or efficient way to remember written words. The minor adjustment needed to encode an irregular word into permanent memory through orthographic mapping is far more efficient than any other known alternative.

Implications of Orthographic Mapping and Exception Words

The fact that all words, including exception words, are stored via orthographic mapping has implications for reading instruction. This will be covered in more detail in Chapter 11. For now, it is noted that the very common instructional suggestion that weak readers should learn irregular words as unanalyzed wholes is based on intuition and tradition and is not supported by any empirical research. Indeed, presenting weak readers with words as unanalyzed wholes directs attention away from the phonological framework within exception words, and

attention to the phonological framework is the very basis for efficiently
storing those words. Typically developing students learn words presented
as wholes because they are good
orthographic mappers. They naturally
analyze any whole word phonemically
and establish an orthographic representation of that word. Weak readers,
however, do not naturally engage in
orthographic mapping because they

> **CAUTION**
>
> The irony of the teaching practice of
> presenting irregular words to be
> learned as unanalyzed wholes is that
> exception words require *more*
> letter-sound and phonemic analysis
> than regular words, not less.

lack the advanced phonemic awareness skills and often the letter-sound proficiency to reliably store words. The irony of the teaching practice of presenting
irregular words to be learned as unanalyzed wholes is that exception words require
more analysis and attention than regular words, not less.

THE RESEARCH ON ORTHOGRAPHIC MAPPING

One of the early empirical investigations of orthographic mapping was a study by
Ehri and Wilce (1985). Preschoolers and beginning kindergarteners were taught
two types of words. One type was a modified phonetic form of words (e.g., TRDL
for *turtle* and NE for *knee*). The other was a visually distinctive form of words
with no phonetic correspondence (e.g., Y^MP for *turtle* and Fo for *knee*). They
found that nonreaders with little or no letter-sound knowledge learned the visually distinctive words more easily than the phonetic forms. By contrast, the children with basic letter-sound knowledge found the phonetic spellings easier to
remember. It seems that as soon as children have letter-sound knowledge, they
use it to create connections between the written and spoken forms of words. Such
connections make those letter sequences memorable and familiar.

Rebecca Treiman and colleagues (Treiman et al., 1996; Treiman & Rodriguez,
1999; Treiman, Sotak, & Bowman, 2001; see also Roberts, 2003) found that
even before preschoolers could read any basic words or sound out any nonsense
words, they still used letter *name* knowledge to "map" sounds in spoken words
to printed sequences. For example, they would present the students with 15
two-letter sequences (e.g., KN, TM) as words to be learned. All letter sequences
had three different pronunciations counterbalanced across students (each student was exposed to only one pronunciation of each sequence). One involved a
word in which the first two phonemes of the word matched the first letter's name
(e.g., KN would be read as *cane;* the /k/ /ā/ matched the first letter's name, i.e.,

"kay"). The second type of word had the letter *sound* at the beginning, but not the letter's name (e.g., KN was to be read as *cone*). The third involved visually distinctive presentations of the words that had no letter-sound correspondence (e.g., ᴷN would be read as *goal*). With counterbalancing, each child was taught 15 different two-letter "words," five of each type. They received multiple learning sessions over a few weeks.

The results indicated that children were far more successful learning the "words" that contained the letter's *name* in the first position. Having only the letter *sound* in the initial position was no more helpful than the visually distinctive presentations with no letter-sound correspondences. These young children did not yet know all of their letter sounds, but they knew letter names, so they could map the spoken word to the first letter of the "words" only when it aligned with the letter's name. This suggests that preschoolers who cannot read or sound out words, but who know letter names, naturally attach what limited phonological properties they have available to the letter sequences they are taught. This early mapping approach was far more successful than the visual memory strategy.

Mapping Starts Early

One thing that we have learned from Ehri and Wilce (1985) and the studies by Rebecca Treiman and colleagues (see also Roberts, 2003) is that the mapping of words to sight vocabulary, even if only partial, begins extremely early in the reading process, even before phonic decoding develops (Kilpatrick, 2015c; Rack et al., 1994). That is why it was said above that the three "levels" of word-reading development (i.e., letter-sound, phonic decoding, and orthographic mapping) overlap somewhat.

In the studies just mentioned, children were not capable of phonic decoding, which suggests that sight vocabulary learning and the learning of phonic decoding develop in parallel. Kilpatrick (2015c) examined beginning kindergarteners who were unable to sound out any basic nonsense words, even with prompting and practice trials. Those kindergarteners who had successfully learned six sight-words taught to that point in kindergarten (when presented embedded with other distractor words) had far higher phonological awareness skills than those who learned fewer of the taught words. The early mapping of these preschoolers and beginning kindergarteners indicates that they use whatever limited phonological awareness they have available to help secure written words in memory. But given their developmental level, they have limited phonological awareness so their sight-word learning skills are also limited.

Rack et al. (1994) took the early work of Ehri and Wilce (1985) a step further, controlling for the "look" of the words. They taught 5-year-old nonreaders and beginning readers two types of modified words. One type had a stronger phonic element than the other. For example, the word *farmer* was represented as either *vmr* or *zmr*. The sequence *vmr* is phonologically closer to *farmer* than is *zmr*. The sounds /f/ and /v/ differ only in voicing (i.e., whether the vocal cords vibrate), whereas /f/ and /z/ are different in multiple ways. Like Ehri and Wilce (1985), they found that children with letter-sound knowledge made use of the more phonologically based letter sequences to remember the words compared to their visual foils, while those without letter-sound skills did not. For those with the good letter-sound skills, their correct readings of the taught (modified) words displayed genuine sight-word memory because these children were not capable of sounding out even the simplest nonsense words.

Phonological Awareness Is Key

Others have replicated this finding (de Abru et al., 1998; Cardoso-Martins et al., 2002; Dixon et al., 2002; Kilpatrick, 2015c; Laing & Hulme, 1999; Roberts, 2003). Of interest are the studies showing that students with better phonological awareness skills were more proficient at this mapping process than those with weaker phonological awareness skills (Dixon et al., 2002; Duff & Hulme, 2012; Kilpatrick, 2015c; Laing & Hulme, 1999; O'Connor, Jenkins, & Slocum, 1995). For example, Dixon et al. (2002) divided 5-year-olds into three groups based upon their level of phonological awareness skills: high, medium, and low. Their word learning results directly aligned with the students' phonological awareness skills: The children in the "high" group learned words far more quickly than the medium group, which learned somewhat more quickly than the low group.

Phonemic Proficiency and Mapping

Kilpatrick (2015c) studied 50 typically developing second graders and 57 typically developing fifth graders. Each student read a list of irregular words (from Adams & Huggins, 1985), along with the WRMT-R Word Identification and Word Attack subtests, and the Phonological Awareness Screening Test (PAST). The PAST includes a traditional correct/incorrect scoring, but also has a timing element. Responses occurring in 2 seconds or less are scored as "automatic." This is intended to assess the degree of proficiency of phonological awareness skills. In a regression analysis of the performance of the second graders, automatic phonemic awareness responses did not account for any unique variance in exception word reading beyond what could be accounted for by the tests of phonic decoding. However, with the fifth graders, automatic responding on the PAST accounted for a substantial and statistically significant amount of additional variance in untimed exception word reading after accounting for phonic decoding. Because correctly identifying exception words requires a more highly developed degree of orthographic skills, this study suggested that the more automatic and proficient the phonemic awareness, the more well developed were the students' sight vocabularies. Because the second graders had not yet achieved that same advanced level of phonemic awareness, this effect was not yet found. Caravolas and colleagues (2005) reviewed studies demonstrating the superiority of timed phonemic awareness in accounting for word learning (see also Vaessen & Blomert, 2010).

Indirect Evidence for Orthographic Mapping

Indirect support for orthographic mapping comes from many sources, including any research showing a close connection between sight-word learning and letter-sound knowledge, phonic decoding, and phonological awareness, even if such studies were not designed as direct tests of orthographic mapping (e.g., Ashby et al., 2013; Bowey & Miller, 2007; Bowey, & Muller, 2005; Burt, 2006; Caravolas et al., 2005; Cunningham, 2006; Cunningham et al., 2002; Dehaene & Cohen 2011; de Jong & Share, 2007; Frost, 1998; Halderman et al., 2012; Landi et al., 2006; Levy & Lysynchuk, 1997; Katz & Frost, 2001; McKague et al., 2008; Nation et al., 2007; Scott & Ehri, 1990; van den Broeck, & Geudens, 2012; van den Broeck et al., 2010; Vellutino et al., 1996). In addition, there are neurophysiological studies, described earlier, that are consistent with orthographic mapping (Dehaene & Cohen, 2011; Simos et al., 2002).

> ### DON'T FORGET
> ....
> The intervention studies of poor readers that have had the highest degree of success used approaches that are precisely what orthographic mapping indicates needs to be in place for a student to be an efficient reader.

The most exciting indirect evidence for orthographic mapping comes from a subset of intervention studies with weak readers. These studies produced improvements ranging from 12 to 25 standard score points on nationally normed word identification subtests (Alexander et al., 1991; Lennon, & Slesinski, 1999; Simos et al., 2002; Torgesen et al., 1999, 2001, 2003, 2010; Truch, 1994, 2003, 2004; Vellutino et al., 1996). Some included 1-, 2-, and even 4-year follow-ups and found the improvements were maintained over time. These studies were not intended as tests of orthographic mapping. What is important, however, is that these studies involved interventions that did *precisely* what the orthographic mapping theory would suggest needs to be done with weak readers. In each of these studies with highly effective outcomes, researchers provided intensive phonemic awareness training (to the advanced level), intensive phonic decoding training, and substantial opportunity for reading connected text. This combination of intervention elements presumably allowed these students to develop the *capacity* to quickly and reliably add words to their sight vocabularies. In essence, these interventions taught them to become effective orthographic mappers. See Chapter 11 for more details.

In addition, indirect support for orthographic mapping is provided by the numerous studies that have demonstrated that most reading difficulties can be prevented in at-risk beginning readers. The most successful prevention studies with kindergartners and first graders involved direct teaching of phonological awareness and letter-sound knowledge and provided opportunities to apply those skills with real words (NICHD, 2000; see Chapter 10). These are the central components of orthographic mapping.

Summary of Typical Reading Development

To this point, the presentation has focused on typical reading development. Preschoolers apply their basic phonological skills and visual memory skills to the paired-associate learning task of attaching names to letters. This letter-name knowledge, combined with early phonological awareness, helps to produce letter-sound knowledge (Cardoso-Martins et al., 2011). Readers then begin to use their developing letter-sound knowledge and phonological blending to sound out words via phonic decoding. As phonic decoding skills develop throughout first grade, it appears to directly promote more advanced phonemic awareness. Thus, for typically developing students, advanced phoneme awareness is not a *cause* of early reading skills. Rather, it is a *product* of beginning reading. When students interact with letters and sounds via letter-sound knowledge and then phonic decoding, such experiences refine their phonemic awareness skills. Then, as these more advanced phonemic awareness skills develop, there is a dramatic increase in the speed and efficiency with which students develop their sight vocabularies. The more words that are added to the sight vocabulary, the more fluent their reading becomes. Their reading fluency increases because their word-level reading is more effortless and "transparent," allowing for greater focus to be placed on reading comprehension.

All of this happens in typically developing readers quite naturally, regardless of instructional methodology, although early instruction in phonics and phonological awareness facilitates this developmental pattern even in typically developing students (NICHD, 2000). Children taught by the classic whole-word or whole language approaches will naturally develop the skills needed for orthographic mapping, in spite of the teaching approach. They will discover that they can quickly add words to their sight vocabulary via the connection-forming process inherent in orthographic mapping. They will find this process quite natural and effective, and far superior to trying to memorize words as unanalyzed wholes (whole-word approach) or trying to rely heavily on context to determine words (whole language approach).

The Central Nature of Phonology in Word-Level Reading

After reviewing the research on phonological processing skills, Ahmed et al. (2012) concluded that inadequacy in these skills are a "universal cause" of word-level reading difficulties (see also Vellutino et al., 2004). Based on the research described throughout this chapter, it should be clear that phonological processing skills heavily influence *every* aspect of word-level reading development:

- Phonological skills are an important contributor to the development of both letter-name and letter-sound knowledge.
- The phonological skill of blending is required for phonic decoding.
- Advanced phoneme awareness/analysis is central to sight-word development, being a key skill needed for orthographic mapping.

Given that phonological processing skills thoroughly permeate word-level reading development, it becomes clear why researchers have placed so much attention on these skills. It should also be clear why children with phonological processing difficulties struggle in reading: There is simply no aspect of word-level reading that is unaffected by phonological skills (Ahmed et al., 2012; Halderman et al., 2012). This is why the phonological-core deficit is far and away the most common reason why children struggle in word-level reading (Ahmed et al. 2012; Fletcher et al., 2007; Hulme & Snowling, 2009; Vellutino et al., 2004). We now turn to the relationship between word-reading development and the phonological-core deficit of reading disabilities.

HOW THE PHONOLOGICAL-CORE DEFICIT HINDERS READING DEVELOPMENT

Because every aspect of word-level reading development is heavily influenced by phonological abilities, students with difficulties in phonological skills struggle with some or all aspects of word-reading development. Each will be discussed in turn.

Letter-Name and Letter-Sound Knowledge

For decades, it has been known that letter-name and letter-sound knowledge predict later reading development. The most obvious and intuitive reason for this is that children need letter-sound knowledge to phonically decode words. This intuition is quite accurate and has strong empirical support (Brady, 2011; Ehri, 2005a; NICHD, 2000; Share, 1995, 2011). However, there is another likely reason why letter-name and letter-sound knowledge predict later reading skills. They may be early "markers" of the phonological-core deficit. This assumes children have had adequate opportunities at home and/or in preschool to learn letter names and sounds, which is not always the case.

Phonic Decoding Skills

When children with the phonological-core deficit are expected to phonically decode words in first grade, they may not have fully mastered their letter-sound skills. Yet they are expected to combine those weak letter-sound skills with another phonological processing skill—blending—to phonically decode words. This is why phonic decoding is weak for a very large proportion of phonological-core deficit children. They may lack full proficiency in letter-sound knowledge and they often have delays in phonological blending—the two skills needed for phonic decoding. Nonsense word reading, which is an index of phonic decoding skills, is usually weak in such children (Brady, 2011; Fletcher et al., 2007; Rack et al., 1992; Share, 1995).

While phonic decoding development promotes advanced phonemic awareness in typically developing readers, this is not the case for children with the phonological-core deficit. Even if they develop phonic decoding via intervention, this development of phonic decoding skills does not automatically prompt the development of the advanced phonemic awareness skills needed for efficient orthographic mapping. Those advanced skills will not develop unless they are directly trained.

Orthographic Mapping

Unlike typically developing readers, students with the phonological-core deficit do not naturally develop phonological awareness as a result of literacy instruction, at least not enough to promote reading development. O'Connor, Jenkins, and Slocum (1995), for example, intervened with at-risk kindergarteners. Two groups received different types of phonological awareness instruction with some

> **DON'T FORGET**
> ··
> In students with the phonological-core deficit, phonological awareness does not naturally develop via exposure to literacy activities, even explicit and systematic phonic instruction. Thus, phonological awareness must be directly trained in these students.

additional letter-sound instruction. A third group focused on letter-sound instruction. A fourth group was a control group of typically developing readers. All three at-risk groups made equivalent gains in speed of naming letters, though the two groups instructed in phonological awareness and the typically developing comparison group made large gains on multiple phonological awareness measures. By contrast, the group given letter-sound instruction made minimal gains on some phonological awareness measures and no gains on others. Importantly, the first two groups (those trained in phonological awareness) showed strong performance on a new word-learning task, with one of these phonologically trained at-risk groups performing comparable to the typically developing students. The third group (letter-sound training) performed far more poorly on the word-learning task than the other three groups. This basic finding can be multiplied across many studies (e.g., Ball & Blachman, 1988, 1991; Barker & Torgesen, 1995; Blachman, Ball, Black, & Tangel, 1994; Dixon et al., 2002; NICHD, 2000). In at-risk readers and poor readers, phonological awareness does not naturally develop via exposure to literacy activities, even explicit and systematic phonic instruction. Thus, phonological awareness must be directly addressed in students with the phonological-core deficit (see Chapters 10 and 11).

Because students with the phonological-core deficit almost never develop the advanced phoneme awareness skills on their own, sight-word development/orthographic mapping is a major struggle for them. Recent conceptualizations of the nature of word-level reading difficulties suggest that the inability to develop a large sight vocabulary is at the core of word-level reading disabilities (Staels & van den Broeck, 2014; van den Broeck & Geudens, 2012; van den Broeck et al., 2010). In languages that are phonically consistent, disabled readers have a high degree of reading accuracy, but struggle tremendously in fluency due to limited sight vocabularies (Seymour et al., 2003; Seymour, 2009; van den Broeck & Geudens, 2012; van den Broeck et al., 2010; Ziegler & Goswami, 2005). Most individuals with the phonological-core deficit can learn to accurately sound out words in highly consistent written languages. However, they are not storing those words for later instant access. This compromises fluency and comprehension.

As mentioned, advanced phonemic awareness skills must be directly taught if children with the phonological-core deficit are to develop them. There is ample evidence that with many individuals with a phonological-core deficit, their lack of advanced phonemic awareness

> **DON'T FORGET**
> ....
> If phonemic awareness is interfering with reading at any age, progress will be minimal unless the phonemic awareness difficulties are corrected.

skills continues into adulthood (Bruck, 1992; Downey, Snyder, & Hill, 2000; Thompkins & Binder, 2003) unless they are directly addressed (Truch, 1994). In Chapter 11, it will become clear that there is no "statute of limitations" on training phonemic awareness. If phonemic awareness is interfering with reading skills at any age, additional progress will be minimal unless the phonemic awareness difficulties are corrected (Bruck, 1992; Truch, 1994).

Understanding letter reversals and transpositions in poor readers

The mystique surrounding dyslexia (i.e., poor word reading despite prior instruction and adequate language skills) has been largely fueled by the phenomena of letter reversals and letter transpositions. Reversals involve writing a letter backward or reading a backward form of a letter. Far and away the most common is the b/d reversal. In three-dimensional space, they are the same. If you had a cut-out of the letter *b*, it could be a *b, d, p,* or *q* depending on how you hold it, so they are visually similar. Transpositions involve inaccurate letter order, such as reading *form* as *from,* or spelling *said* as *siad.*

Errors involving letter reversals and transpositions are common in typically developing beginning readers (Ahmed et al. 2012). However, because older poor readers often read at a level similar to beginning readers, they also make the kind of errors beginning readers make. The issue is developmental, not likely due to faulty visual-spatial-perceptual skills. In light of orthographic mapping, we now understand letter transpositions in weak readers more clearly. For students who are poor at mapping the correct letter order into long-term memory, the specific letter order of written words is not as helpful for them in either word reading or spelling.

An illustration may help. Let's say you did a memory study with two groups of adults, American sports fans and Australians who had no familiarity with American sports. You asked both groups to memorize the following "random" letter sequences: NFL, NASCAR, WNBA, PGA, NHL, MLB, NCAA, and NBA. Later you asked them to write down as many of the letter sequences they can recall. It is quite likely that some of the Australians may incorrectly write down NLF instead of NFL, but there is no chance that any of the American sports fans would make such a letter transposition. This is because these letter sequences are meaningful and well established in the memory of those fans, but there is nothing particularly meaningful or well established about those letter sequences to this particular group of Australians. In a similar way, good readers have the sequences of letters in written words well established in memory. By contrast, poor readers don't have a clear recognition of the logic of a given letter sequence because of their limited awareness of the phonemes in spoken words (i.e., poor phonemic awareness). They do not have a well-established memory for those letter sequences. As a result, they often read and spell words in which letters are not in the right order. It is not based upon a visual memory deficit (see Chapter 2). Rather, it is due to the fact that the written sequence of letters and the spoken sequence of phonemes have not been associated with one another in long-term memory to form an established, accurate memory of that letter sequence.

The Sensitivity of Phonemic Awareness Tasks

One of the difficulties in applying information from this chapter is that not all phonological awareness tasks are sensitive to the advanced phonological awareness skills needed for orthographic mapping. In typically developing readers, phoneme segmentation skills and phonological blending tend to reach ceiling by the end of first grade (Kilpatrick, 2012a, 2012b; Swank & Catts, 1994; Wagner et al., 1999), which is likely why the universal screeners (DIBELS, Aimsweb, easyCBM) discontinue their phonemic segmentation assessment at the end of first grade. But phonemic awareness skills continue to develop in typical readers until about third or fourth grade. This additional growth appears to affect reading development (Ashby et al., 2013; Caravolas et al., 2005; de Jong & van der Leij, 2002; Kilpatrick, 2012b, 2015c; Vaessen & Blomert, 2010; Wagner et al., 1999, 2013).

For example, using the Comprehensive Test of Phonological Processing (CTOPP) Elision, Blending Words, and Segmenting Words subtests, Kilpatrick (2012a) and Kilpatrick and McInnis (2015) found virtually no difference in raw scores in the Blending Words and Segmenting Words subtests between typically developing first and second graders. By contrast, there was a substantial raw score difference between first and second graders on the Elision subtest and the PAST. The Elision subtest and the PAST involve phonological manipulation, which taps into advanced phonological awareness skills (see Chapter 6). Kilpatrick and McInnis (2015) displayed growth in phonological manipulation raw scores beyond second grade and leveling off by fifth grade, among typically developing students, when automaticity of responding to phonological awareness prompts was taken into account. Vaessen and Blomert (2010) displayed nearly identical findings.

A casual look at the norm tables or the raw score-to-grade equivalent conversions on the CTOPP, the CTOPP-2, and the Woodcock-Johnson IV (WJ-IV) Phonological Awareness (WJ-III Sound Awareness) subtest protocol will bear this finding out. Raw scores on the phonological manipulation subtests continue to climb after first grade and do not level out until around third to fourth grade. Because all of the major universal screeners (DIBELS, Aimsweb, and easyCBM) only track basic phonological awareness, they are not sensitive to the advanced phonological awareness skills that are needed for orthographic mapping. This is important because many children with reading problems can develop the phonological awareness needed for letter-sound knowledge and can also develop the phonological blending needed for phonic decoding. However, their phonological awareness development stalls at that point due to a mild to moderate phonological-core deficit. Such students become slow, laborious readers (Fox & Routh, 1983). Students with more severe phonological-core deficits even struggle with letter-sound knowledge and basic phonic decoding.

Why Advanced Phonemic Awareness is Necessary for Efficient Sight-Word Learning

Theoretically speaking, the only phonemic awareness skill a student needs for orthographic mapping is segmentation. A student needs to be aware of each phoneme in the word to align those phonemes to the letters. This raises two questions. First, why then do phonemic manipulation tasks correlate better with reading than segmentation tasks? Second, why does one need to be able to manipulate phonemes to efficiently create orthographic memories?

To answer these questions, consider an analogy from basketball. The degree of shooting skill or proficiency a player needs to make baskets while playing in a game and being covered by a defender is substantially higher than the degree of shooting proficiency needed to make baskets when standing alone in the driveway taking shots at a basket. In a similar way, the degree of phonemic proficiency needed to instantly and effortlessly access phonemes after determining an unfamiliar word while reading connected text presumably represents a greater degree of phonemic proficiency than would be required to correctly respond on a conventional segmentation task. In this latter situation, all of one's working memory resources are devoted to the segmentation task. But while reading, one is focusing on multiple processes simultaneously. The student is identifying the letters and words and blending sounds, all while trying to comprehend what is being read by maintaining the accumulated meaning of the sentence in working memory. Because the individual's attention is split among multiple processes, very little is likely dedicated to accessing phonemes. Thus, phoneme manipulation tasks appear to be a proxy for the orthographic mapping process that occurs during the self-teaching situation, which involves reading connected text. Phoneme manipulation requires the proficient segmentation of letters while also doing other phoneme tasks, such as isolating the phoneme to be deleted or substituted, making the change, and blending the resulting sounds. In other words, phoneme manipulation tasks involve automatic and largely implicit access to phonemes while sharing working memory with other cognitive operations. Segmentation tasks do not do this. Thus, the answer to the second question is that it is not the actual task of manipulating sounds in words that is required for sight-word acquisition. Rather, orthographic mapping in the self-teaching context requires a particular level of phonemic proficiency, and manipulation tasks do a better job of reflecting the level of proficiency needed while segmentation tasks display a more basic level of phonemic proficiency.

The Causes of the Phonological-Core Deficit

Educators have to deal with the issues students present, regardless of the causes of those issues. For this reason, only a brief presentation of the causes of the phonological-core deficit will be provided.

Like many other human characteristics, the phonological-core deficit can be based on genetics and/or the environment. There is ample evidence for both (for reviews, see Metsala, 2011; Pennington & Olson, 2005; Vellutino et al., 2004). Children who have a biological parent with a history of reading difficulties are at a higher risk for reading problems. Extensive, multinational twin studies have been able to establish and narrow down some of the genetic components related to difficulties with reading acquisition. Lack of sufficient language stimulation in a child's early years can also be a significant contributor to phonological processing difficulties. The encouraging news, however, is the body of highly successful prevention and intervention research that was previously mentioned. The fact that there is a genetic, neurodevelopmental basis for most reading difficulties must not lead teachers or parents to despair. The intervention studies consistent with orthographic mapping resulted in substantial, often "normalizing" improvements that were maintained long after the intervention ended. While there may be a genetic/neurological basis for reading disabilities in a majority of cases, we should feel encouraged by the fact that there are ways to prevent and intervene to help children overcome those difficulties (see Chapters 10 and 11).

Rapid Automatized Naming and Working Memory

There are two other factors that appear to have a significant influence on the phonological-core deficit phenomenon: rapid automatized naming and working memory. Because there remains a large degree of uncertainty regarding the precise role they play in reading development, it was deemed more appropriate to treat these skills elsewhere. In addition to the description of these factors in the previous chapter, they will also be addressed in the chapters on assessment, prevention, and intervention (see Chapters 6, 10, and 11).

WORD-READING FLUENCY AND ORTHOGRAPHIC MAPPING

Understanding how children turn unfamiliar written words into highly familiar, instantly accessible sight words has broad implications for our perspectives on reading development and reading difficulties. One example is that it will affect our perspective on understanding and addressing reading fluency. *Fluency* refers to reading words quickly and accurately, but also with proper intonation or *prosody*. Prosody comes from two Greek words, *pros*, meaning "to" or "toward" and *odē*, meaning a song (hence the English word *ode*). Just as songs vary their pitch, so do readers vary their intonation as they read. Such prosody suggests that the reader comprehends the passage *as she reads it*, otherwise she would not likely know when to inflect her voice (Schwanenflugel & Ruston, 2008; Whalley & Hansen, 2006).

Efforts to address problems in reading fluency have received much attention in recent years, particularly since the release of the report of the National Reading Panel (NICHD, 2000). Fluency was one of the key areas of reading highlighted in that report. It appears that fluency deficits are often addressed by providing extra reading practice in general, or by using the specific intervention technique of repeated readings. The idea that additional practice is an efficient way to boost reading fluency in weak readers appears to be based on one or more implicit assumptions about the nature of reading fluency. However, these assumptions appear to be inconsistent with the scientific findings regarding how skilled reading develops.

One implicit assumption behind repeated readings (and similar practice-based approaches to fluency) seems to be that with sufficient exposure, children eventually generate some sort of "visual memory" of those oft-repeated words based on paired-associate learning. This assumption is a variation of the classic whole-word method described in Chapter 2. In that chapter, it was shown that the visual memory hypothesis does not reflect the scientific findings on how a sight vocabulary is built. It was also previously mentioned that typically developing readers, from second grade on, only need to be exposed to an unfamiliar word one to four times before it is permanently learned. By contrast, children with reading disabilities often do not "store" a word even after the maximum allotted 12 to 16 exposures in an experimental learning task (Ehri & Saltmarsh, 1995; Martens & de Jong, 2008). Any approach to fluency that relies primarily on extensive reading practice does not explain why some students require 10, 20, or more repetitions of new words while their typically developing peers require as few as one or two exposures.

> ### DON'T FORGET
>
> ···
>
> Familiar words are responded to very quickly. Variations in response times among familiar words are about 1/10th of a second. Thus, if a correctly read word is not instantly responded to, it is not likely a familiar word. It should not be assumed that students already know the words but simply need faster access to them.

Another implicit assumption seems to be that many or most of the words a student is expected to read are already stored in the student's sight vocabulary but require additional practice to become more quickly accessed. It is true that some familiar words are accessed more quickly than others based upon a variety of factors, such as the word's semantic, orthographic, or morphological properties; its frequency; and its phonic regularity, among other things (Adelman, 2012a, 2012b; Lupker, 2005; van Orden & Kloos, 2005). However, the reaction time difference between quickly accessed familiar words and less quickly accessed familiar words is only about 1/10th of a second! This would not be noticeable in real-world reading situations. Essentially, if a word is familiar, it is responded to instantly. By contrast, weak readers may require 1–3 seconds to phonically decode an unfamiliar word. It seems more reasonable to assume that poor fluency results from a limited sight vocabulary than to assume that the sight vocabulary is adequate but that these presumably familiar words are being accessed too slowly.

The scenario of word-level reading development described earlier in the chapter, particularly the aspect of orthographic mapping, provides an alternative explanation of the nature of word-reading fluency. Once students develop proficient orthographic mapping skills, they have the *capacity* to quickly and reliably add new words to their sight vocabulary, so long as they have ample reading opportunities. As they read, their large and continuously growing sight vocabularies allow them to instantly recognize all, or almost all, of the words in a given passage. The more words they instantly recognize, the more fluent their reading will be. Instant recognition typically means effortless recognition, and that leaves more working memory allotment available for comprehension, which loops back to better prosody, completing the whole fluency enterprise. The larger the sight vocabulary, the more quickly and easily one can move through text unhindered by having to phonically decode or guess at unfamiliar words. From this perspective, it appears that the best approach to addressing fluency is to be sure that a student has proficient orthographic mapping skills. Fluency is not seen as a separate reading subskill, but rather as a byproduct of having instant access to most or all of the words on the page (Ehri, 2005a, 2005b; Torgesen, 2004a, 2004b; Torgesen, Rashotte, Alexander, Alexander, & MacPhee, 2003).

> It is the necessity of slowing down to phonemically decode or guess at words that is the most critical factor in limiting the reading fluency of children with severe reading difficulties.... The most important key to fluent reading of any text is the ability to automatically recognize almost all of the words in the text. (Torgesen et al., 2003, p. 293)

However, this is not the whole picture. Research has shown that adult competent readers can instantly pronounce single-syllable nonsense words at speeds similar to real words (for a review, see Frost, 1998). If one has ever given a skilled reader in upper elementary school up to high school the TOWRE/TOWRE-2, which has a timed nonsense word reading subtest, it becomes clear how quickly competent readers can assemble single-syllable pseudowords. The instantaneous nature of this suggests minimal working memory involvement. This is likely true, to a lesser degree, with beginning readers as well. Harn, Stoolmiller, & Chard (2008) examined the manner in which first graders responded to the Nonsense Word Fluency subtest of the Dynamic Indicators of Basic Early Literacy Skills (DIBELS). Some pronounced the nonsense word as a whole unit (e.g., *wum*), others decoded then pronounced (/w/ /u/ /m/, *wum!*), others did partially unitized pronunciation (e.g., /w/ /um/), while still others only pronounced the sounds but never blended those sounds into a nonsense word (e.g., only /w/ u/ /m/). A large percentage of the students had a mix of these, but all had a dominant approach, and the largest percentage of students almost exclusively used the unitized "whole-word" pronunciation. These students displayed the best results on the Oral Reading

DON'T FORGET

It appears that the best approach to addressing fluency is to be sure that a student has proficient orthographic mapping skills. Fluency is not seen as a separate reading subskill, but rather as a byproduct of having instant access to most or all of the words on the page.

Fluency measure months later. To pronounce nonsense words as whole units presumably requires a higher level of proficiency than the other approaches because it involves letter-sound identification and phonological blending in a very quick and integrated fashion. Thus, phonic decoding proficiency was associated with subsequent reading fluency in first grade. This means that students with a large sight vocabulary and very proficient phonic decoding are going to be the ones who most fluently move through text. And given that both phonic decoding and orthographic mapping are based upon similar skills, the students with good orthographic mapping skills will also have good phonic decoding skills (though the reverse is not always true) and will be fluent readers.

Direct support for this view of fluency has come from multiple studies. One longitudinal study tracked students from first to third grade. Early phonic knowledge had a direct causal effect on word recognition development, and word recognition development had a direct causal effect on word-reading fluency (Eldredge, 2005). Jenkins, Fuchs, van den Broek, Espin, and Deno (2003) showed that typically developing fourth graders read words from lists or in context about three times faster than students with reading disabilities, and they read more accurately. In other words, the more words students could quickly recognize out of context (a fairly direct test of their sight vocabulary, given the timing element) was associated with how quickly they read words in context (fluency). Thus, the isolated word-reading proficiency was related to paragraph reading fluency. This supports the notion that fluency is a byproduct of the size of one's sight vocabulary and not its own distinct reading-related skill.

> **CAUTION**
> ....
> There is no compelling reason to consider fluency as an isolated skill. Rather, fluency appears to be a byproduct of having instant access to most or all of the words on the page.

A final note about fluency. When the National Reading Panel (NICHD, 2000) did their work from 1997 to 1999, the nature of reading fluency was not well understood. Indeed, they specifically indicated this in their report. But because fluency is so strongly related to reading comprehension, it has become its own, largely not-well-understood reading-related factor. Since the time of the reading panel, it seems educators have been trying to put their finger on this independent reading skill of fluency, when in fact research is now suggesting that it is best understood as a byproduct of the size of one's pool of sight words. It seems that we may do well to take our focus off fluency as a separate reading skill and focus our energies on building the orthographic lexicon (i.e., sight vocabulary).

Fluency and Comprehension

The process of figuring out unfamiliar words while reading requires a certain amount of working memory allocation. Any working memory effort devoted to reading unfamiliar words compromises the amount of working memory available for comprehension (Perfetti, 1985; Nation, 2005). In addition, poor readers with limited sight vocabularies are more likely to misread words using their weak phonic decoding skills and the unreliable strategy of contextual guessing. Word-reading errors provide faulty input to the comprehension system, and this can further hinder reading comprehension. By contrast, skilled readers devote all (or nearly all) of their working memory resources to comprehending what they read. This is because word recognition is generally accurate and effortless.

STUDENTS WHOSE NATIVE LANGUAGE IS NOT ENGLISH

Students who are not native speakers of English but who are learning to speak and read English during their pre-K–12 school years have been referred to by multiple terms over the last two decades: *English as a second language* (ESL) students (e.g., Adesope, Lavin, Thompson, & Ungerleider, 2011), *English as a foreign language* (EFL) students (e.g., Goldfus, 2012), *language minority learners* (LM) (e.g., Mancilla-Martinez, Kieffer, Biancarosa, Christodoulou, & Snow, 2011), *English language learners* (ELL) (e.g., Klingner & Artiles, 2006), or simply *English learners* (EL) (e.g., Calderón, Slavin, & Sánchez, 2011). Because ELL appears to be the most common acronym, it will be used in this volume.

ELL students make up a growing percentage of the K–12 school population in the United States, and they present interesting challenges in terms of literacy development. Over the last few decades, there has been an extensive number of studies conducted with ELL students related to almost every aspect of reading. Some of those studies are purely theoretical in that they help us better understand the nature of reading and language. Others have been more practical, addressing the challenges faced by ELL students and their teachers.

For our purposes in this chapter, it should be pointed out that the key skills involved in developing letter-name and letter-sound knowledge, phonic decoding, and orthographic mapping are the same across languages with any alphabetic-based orthography (Betts et al., 2008; Caravolas, 2005; Caravolas et al., 2005; Landerl et al., 2013; Sparks et al., 2012; Vaessen et al., 2010; Ziegler & Goswami, 2005). A common assumption is that word-level reading develops differently in a consistent orthography, such as Spanish, compared to a less-consistent orthography, such as English. This is not the case, at least not in terms of the three levels of reading development described earlier in the chapter. The *speed* with which word-level reading is mastered is strikingly different. Mastering the code of written English takes twice as long as languages with more consistent orthographies (Seymour, Aro, & Erskine, 2003). However, while it is easier to master word-level reading in a consistent orthography, the steps and processes involved in developing phonic decoding and a sight vocabulary are the same, regardless of the alphabetic orthography. Skilled reading in any alphabet-based orthography requires phonological awareness/analysis, phonological blending, letter-sound proficiency, and vocabulary/phonological long-term memory. Those with reading difficulties in other alphabetic orthographies struggle for the same reasons native English speakers struggle.

In English, poor reading speed and poor accuracy characterize those with reading disabilities. However, in consistent orthographies, reading problems are characterized by slower mastery of the written code. But after mastering the written code and phonic decoding, reading accuracy is good among those with reading disabilities due to the consistent orthography. However, individuals with reading difficulties in consistent orthographies display slow word-reading speed. This is the primary characteristic of individuals with reading disabilities in such languages. Their poor reading speed is due to a limited sight vocabulary, even if they can read all of the words via phonic decoding. In English, poor readers continue to demonstrate difficulties with reading accuracy because of the less consistent nature of English orthography (Caravolas, 2005; Landerl et al., 2013; Seymour et al., 2003; Ziegler & Goswami, 2005). If the word is not in one's sight vocabulary and it cannot be sounded out phonically, accuracy suffers. Thus, in both consistent and inconsistent orthographies, reading speed appears to be affected by the size of the reader's sight vocabulary. Difficulties with orthographic mapping are ultimately the source of reading problems beyond the early grades in alphabetic orthographies, regardless of the level of consistency (van den Broeck & Geudens, 2012; van den Broeck et al., 2010).

When learning to read English, many ELL students with limited English vocabulary function like hyperlexics. They develop word-level reading skills in the context of their limited English oral vocabulary. They hear many English words for which they have not yet acquired the meaning, and those words are in their phonological long-term memory. It is their phonological long-term memories that will function as the anchor for establishing printed letter sequences in their sight vocabularies. This assumes that students have sufficient phonological awareness to separate out the sounds in the spoken word. The evidence suggests that the best predictor of phonological awareness and word-reading development in a second language is a student's phonological awareness and word-reading development in the first language (Farnia & Geva, 2013; Sparks et al., 2012).

ANSWERS TO THE QUESTIONS POSED ABOUT READING DIFFICULTIES

At the start of the chapter, an ambitious set of questions was posed:

- Why do some students have word-level reading difficulties or disabilities?
- Why do some students struggle with learning phonics?
- Why do some students with reading problems reverse or transpose letters?
- Why do students with reading problems have limited sight vocabularies?
- Why do students with reading problems struggle with reading fluency?
- Why do students struggle with reading comprehension?
- How does all of this affect students whose native language is not English?
- Why do most intervention studies with weak readers show minimal or modest gains but others demonstrate very large improvements?

It is now time to respond to these questions.

Why do some students have word-level reading difficulties or disabilities? In the vast majority of cases, word-reading difficulties are the result of the phonological-core deficit. This can originate via genetics, the environment, or both.

Why do some students struggle with learning phonics? Poor phonological processing appears to interfere with phonic development on two levels. First, it delays the development of letter-sound knowledge. Second, phonological blending, if problematic, will decrease the efficiency of phonological decoding because it is one of the two skills required for phonic decoding.

Why do some students with reading problems reverse or transpose letters? Long assumed to be related to visual-perceptual skills, reversals and transpositions appear to be developmental. Poor readers who display reversals and transpositions function like beginning readers in most aspects of word-level reading, and beginning readers are prone to reversal and transposition errors. Transpositions, in particular, appear to be directly affected by the struggles these students have in anchoring the specific letter sequences in written words into long-term memory.

Why do students with reading problems have limited sight vocabularies? Advanced phonemic awareness, which typically develops from late first grade through third or fourth grade, is needed for proficient orthographic mapping. Orthographic mapping is the means by which we develop a sight vocabulary. Students with the phonological-core deficit typically do not develop these more advanced phonemic awareness skills and therefore have limited sight vocabularies. Also, poor letter-sound proficiency hinders sight vocabulary development.

Why do students with reading problems struggle with reading fluency? Students with reading difficulties who have the phonological-core deficit have limited sight vocabularies. Therefore, too many of the words in a passage require effort to identify, which inhibits fluency.

Why do students struggle with reading comprehension? Poor word-level reading is one of the most common reasons students struggle in reading comprehension. Beyond that, there are several additional issues, mostly language related, that affect the comprehension of both oral and written language (see Chapter 5). Students who are below average in oral language comprehension typically struggle in reading comprehension.

How does all of this affect students whose native language is not English? Phonic decoding and orthographic mapping work the same for ELL students as they do for native speakers of English. They require good letter-sound knowledge, phonological blending, and phonemic awareness. They also need to have English words stored in phonological long-term memory, even if they do not yet know the meaning of those English words. These four factors work together to produce a long-term memory of orthographic sequences (i.e., written words). Certainly ELL students face challenges for acquiring letter-sound knowledge if they already learned different sounds for the same letters in their own language, but most ELL students seem to adapt fairly well (Fitzgerald, 1995). Also, the oral language development of ELL students plays a large role in determining their progress in reading comprehension.

Why do most intervention studies with weak readers show minimal or modest gains but others demonstrate very large improvements? Studies that do not take into account all of the puzzle pieces that go into reading development do not display large gains in the reading performance of students with word-level reading problems. By contrast, studies that have demonstrated very large gains (12 to 25 standard score points) included three key features: (1) they aggressively "fixed" the phonological awareness problems and trained phonemic awareness to the advanced level, (2) they taught or reinforced phonic decoding skills, and (3) they gave students ample opportunities to read connected text. In sum, studies for which interventions are consistent with all three levels of word-reading develop-ment, particularly those consistent with orthographic mapping, have been highly successful. By contrast, studies that are not consistent with ortho-graphic mapping have not displayed the same degree of success. This will be presented in more detail in Chapter 11.

SUMMARY

In this chapter, findings regarding the process of both phonic decoding and word recognition were presented. As mentioned in Chapter 1, the findings related to how word recognition skills develop are not widely known. Yet, understand-ing word recognition development as described in this chapter, particularly the concept of orthographic mapping, represents the key to unlocking the mystery behind most reading difficulties.

When we combine the research on phonic decoding and orthographic mapping with the research into the phonological-core deficit of reading disabilities, we remove nearly all of the mystery behind the most com-mon word-level reading problems. While phonological awareness has received much attention in recent years, it is arguable that it has not received sufficient attention—its role in word-reading development appears to be *underestimated*. This is likely due to not understanding the differ-

> **DON'T FORGET**
>
> Although phonological awareness has received much attention in recent years, it is arguable that it has not received enough attention, or at least not the right kind of attention. Its role in word-reading development appears to be *underestimated*. Every step and every element of the word-reading process require a substantial amount of phonological abilities.

ences between early, basic, and advanced phonemic awareness, and the role each of these plays in word-reading development. Every step and every ele-ment of the word-reading process requires a substantial amount of phonological skills, whether phonological awareness/analysis (basic or advanced), phonologi-cal blending, or phonological long-term memory. Our phonological awareness tests are rough guides to the integrity of a child's phonological abilities. Unfor-tunately, we have been relying primarily on phonological segmentation tasks to assess phonological awareness, especially in our school-wide screenings. Yet phonological segmentation only covers phonological awareness development up to the end of first grade, and only to the second of the three levels of phonologi-cal skill development and word-reading development. It does not assess advanced phonemic awareness skills, which appears to be the level of phonemic proficiency needed for orthographic mapping (see Chapters 6 and 11).

From letter-name learning in a preschooler through the fast and effortless word-reading fluency of a skilled reader, the knowledge gained from the research on how word-reading develops can guide our evaluations of students with word-reading problems (see Chapters 6–8). The information in this chapter also provides us with a foundation for concrete recommendations about how to prevent reading difficulties in at-risk readers (Chapters 10) and how to correct most word-level reading difficulties (Chapter 11).

✍ TEST YOURSELF ✍

1. **What is *orthographic mapping*?**
   (a) Making sure all letter-sound relationships are systematically introduced in a developmentally appropriate fashion in kindergarten
   (b) A strategy for enhancing spelling instruction in younger students
   (c) A strategy for enhancing spelling instruction in older students
   (d) In reading, the mental process used to store words for later, instant retrieval

2. **Orthographic mapping requires**
   (a) Semantic knowledge of words.
   (b) Good visual memory and visual–auditory paired-associate learning.
   (c) Letter-sound proficiency and phonemic awareness proficiency.
   (d) All of the above are needed for orthographic mapping.

3. **Which of the following would most likely be the best demonstration of *advanced* phonological awareness?**
   (a) Quickly and accurately responding to a phonological blending task
   (b) Quickly and accurately responding to a rhyming, alliteration, or first-sound task
   (c) Quickly and accurately responding to a phonological manipulation task
   (d) Quickly and accurately responding to a phonological segmentation task

4. **Where does it appear that phonological blending fits into word-reading?**
   (a) When combined with letter-sound knowledge, it allows students to develop phonic decoding skills.
   (b) When combined with letter-sound knowledge, it allows students to develop orthographic mapping skills.
   (c) It seems to be a basic skill that leads to other phonological awareness skills like rhyming, alliteration, and first-sound identification.
   (d) It seems to have no direct impact on reading, only indirect given that it is a type of phonological skill.

5. **What is the significance of the phonological lexicon?**

   (a) It represents the "anchoring point" in long-term memory to store the letter sequences that represent written words.

   (b) It appears to assist in phonic decoding.

   (c) It appears to include the semantic lexicon (i.e., vocabulary knowledge) that helps us understand why vocabulary correlates with word reading.

   (d) All of the above are significant aspects of the phonological lexicon.

6. **At the earliest stages of reading development, what is the most effective way for children to remember words?**

   (a) By having words posted around their kindergarten classroom (e.g., having the word *chair* posted on a chair)

   (b) By anchoring letters in the word to whatever phonological aspects of the word they can notice/be aware of

   (c) By visual memorization techniques

   (d) All of the above are equally helpful for beginning kindergarteners.

7. **At which level of reading development are phonological skills important?**

   (a) Level 1: Letter-sound knowledge

   (b) Level 2: Phonic decoding

   (c) Level 3: Orthographic mapping

   (d) Phonological skills are important at all three levels.

8. **How are written words stored for later, instantaneous retrieval?**

   (a) Letter sequences in written words become aligned/attached to the phoneme sequences in spoken words.

   (b) The student becomes so proficient in phonic decoding that familiar words can be decoded in an instantaneous fashion.

   (c) Readers make use of good visual–spatial–perceptual memory to remember the order of the letters in a written word.

   (d) How we store written words is very uncertain.

9. **All of the following statements about learning irregular words are true *except* which one?**

   (a) Nearly the same process that is used to store phonically regular words is also used to store phonically irregular words.

   (b) Irregular words require a different storage process compared to regular words.

   (c) Very few words in the English language are irregular in more than one letter-sound connection.

   (d) The letter-sound connections that are regular within irregular words can be used to build a phonological framework for remembering them.

10. Which of the following ideas about reading fluency has the most research support?
   (a) Providing students with much reading practice is the key to fluency.
   (b) Reading fluency is a function of the size of a student's sight vocabulary.
   (c) Reading fluency is primarily based on students' processing speeds in terms of how quickly they can read the words they know.
   (d) Reading fluency represents an independent element in the bigger reading picture alongside phonemic awareness, phonics, and reading comprehension.

Answers: 1. d; 2. c; 3. c; 4. a; 5. d; 6. b; 7. d; 8. a; 9. b; 10. b

Five

UNDERSTANDING READING COMPREHENSION DIFFICULTIES

Comprehension is the obvious goal of reading, yet many students display a great deal of difficulty understanding what they read. Some of these students struggle due to poor word-level reading. They often can comprehend passages that are read *to* them, but their comprehension is weak when they read those same passages themselves. This is the dyslexic pattern within the simple view of reading framework. Other students may struggle because English is not their first language. Such students typically learn word-level reading skills more easily than they learn the vocabulary of spoken English. Still other students have no difficulties with word-level reading, yet they struggle to comprehend what they read. Typically, these students have language deficiencies that make it difficult to comprehend both written and oral language.

This chapter will examine factors that contribute to reading comprehension that are not primarily related to word-level reading. When word-level reading deficits have been ruled out as the lone source of weak reading comprehension, the next step is to examine language and other skills that affect reading comprehension. These deficits are found among students with the hyperlexic and mixed patterns of reading difficulties described in Chapter 3.

> **DON'T FORGET**
>
> The hyperlexic pattern involves reading comprehension difficulties despite skilled word-level reading. The mixed-difficulty pattern includes word-level reading difficulties in addition to below-average oral language comprehension. The presence of oral language difficulties is common to both patterns.

SPECIFIC READING COMPREHENSION IMPAIRMENT

A *specific reading comprehension impairment* (Hulme & Snowling, 2009; 2011) refers to a situation in which students "can read aloud accurately and fluently at a level appropriate for their age but fail to understand much of what they read" (Hulme & Snowling, 2011, p. 139). Recall that hyperlexics have word-level reading skills above their level of comprehension. For convenience, we will continue with the term *hyperlexic* as used in the context of the simple view of reading rather than the lengthier term *specific reading comprehension impairment*. Some students with this pattern have language skills low enough to qualify under IDEA as students with a speech or language impairment (SLI) (Catts, Adlof, & Weismer, 2006; Nation, 2005; Nation, Clarke, Marshall, & Durand, 2004) or a mild intellectual disability. Others have language skill deficits not severe enough to meet the criteria for SLI, but those deficits have a negative impact on their reading comprehension. Hulme and Snowling (2009, 2011) state that this pattern is more common than many realize and that milder cases of language difficulties often go unrecognized in the classroom.

CAUTION

Subtle language difficulties are not always easy to identify during routine day-to-day interactions with students. As a result, they typically do not prompt a referral for a language evaluation and often go unrecognized. However, their difficulties are substantive enough to make reading comprehension more difficult.

Hulme and Snowling (2009, 2011) provide a conservative estimate of the percentage of students who fit this pattern in the United Kingdom at about 3.3%. They base this upon a stratified sample of elementary school children from the normative sample of a test battery called the York Assessment for Reading and Comprehension. Of the 1,324 students in the sample, 10.3% displayed reading comprehension scores that were 1 standard deviation below their word-reading skills. However, because the 10.3% figure included students with average reading comprehension and superior word-reading, it was not an accurate estimate of the hyperlexic pattern. They next applied more stringent criteria that included only students (a) whose reading comprehension scores were at or below a standard score of 90; (b) whose word-reading standard score was 90 or above; and (c) whose word-reading was a full standard deviation above their reading comprehension. These criteria lead them to the estimate of 3.3% (Hulme & Snowling, 2011). This is a conservative estimate because it did not include students who, for example, had an 85 to 90 standard score in reading comprehension and a 95 to 100 standard score in word reading, even though such students would demonstrate similar problems in the classroom. Also, it only focused on the hyperlexic-type pattern. There are many students with subtle language difficulties who also have word-reading skill deficits, that is, the mixed type was not included in Hulme and Snowling's (2011) estimate (which is understandable since they were only investigating the hyperlexic pattern). Nonetheless, educators also need to recognize students whose subtle language difficulties result in both the hyperlexic and mixed patterns, the latter of which is more common (Fletcher, Lyon, Fuchs, & Barnes, 2007; Hulme & Snowling, 2009).

WHAT IS REQUIRED FOR SKILLED READING COMPREHENSION?

Various authors have reviewed the research investigating the skills that are needed for reading comprehension (Catts, 2009; Fletcher et al., 2007; Fuchs et al., 2012; Hulme & Snowling, 2009, 2011; Johnston, Barnes, & Desrochers, 2008; Kamhi, 2009; Nation, 2005; Perfetti, Landi, & Oakhill, 2005; Oakhill, Cain, & Elbro, 2015; Rapp et al., 2007). To comprehend text, readers must be able to represent what they are reading in memory (Rapp et al., 2007). Multiple operations must be performed simultaneously. Readers must be able to quickly and automatically identify the words. This fluent word recognition is necessary so that word reading does not draw attention or working memory resources from comprehension. Readers must be familiar with the vocabulary and the syntax of the language and have sufficient general and specific background knowledge related to what they are reading. They must be able to make adequate inferences, because much of what is conveyed in a text is not explicitly stated. Readers must be able to transfer information in and out of working memory. They must be able to attend to the important details while not letting the less important details detract from understanding of the text. Readers must be able to accumulate and then connect various references made to different characters, objects, and concepts as the passage develops and draw logical and causal connections between the various elements in the text. Strategies are applied based upon the genre of the text and the reader's purpose for reading. The use of various strategies, some conscious and some below conscious awareness, shifts throughout the reading of a given text. An important way for readers to create coherence is through the development of what has been termed a situation model (Perfetti et al., 2005; or sometimes a *mental model* (Oakhill et al., 2015). A *situation model* integrates vocabulary, syntax, background knowledge, and referential and logical connections found in the text. All of this has to occur within the limited attentional, metacognitive, and working memory resources available to the reader.

DON'T FORGET

....

Reading comprehension requires the activation and coordination of several skills and processes. A compromise in one or more of these skills and processes can result in difficulties in comprehending text.

This description illustrates that there are many points in the process where comprehension may break down. Word reading, vocabulary, syntax, background knowledge, inferencing, attention, metacognition, and working memory are all skills that are important for making sense of text. Each of these skills has its own continuum ranging from weak to strong, and if there is a weakness in any of them, it can negatively affect reading comprehension.

Kamhi (2012) and Rapp et al. (2007) have highlighted three general domains on which reading comprehension research has focused. These three broad domains of research are: (1) reader abilities, (2) text factors, and (3) task factors. These are each discussed in turn.

READER ABILITIES

A reader must possess several skills in order to comprehend text. The following is not intended to be an exhaustive list of these skills. The focus is on the major factors identified by researchers, with an emphasis on skills that can be assessed as part of a psychoeducational or language evaluation.

Vocabulary–Semantic Knowledge

Both children and adults have two semantic lexicons. One is comprised of words used in everyday conversations and is limited to a few thousand words. Programs that teach a second language, such as Pimsleur and Rosetta Stone, teach the most common 2,000 to 4,000 words an individual might need to function in that second language context. However, typical adults and even students from late elementary school on have a broader semantic lexicon of tens of thousands of words (Carroll, 2008). A student may be very proficient at using the more limited, day-to-day lexicon and thus arouse no suspicion of having semantic–vocabulary difficulties (Beck, McKeown, & Kucan, 2002). However, every school subject pushes beyond the day-to-day lexicon into larger semantic fields, including texts students are expected to comprehend. Some students who appear to have good verbal skills may have relatively limited semantic–vocabulary lexicons, which can significantly impact reading comprehension. Thus, an assessment of language skills should be a key element in an evaluation of students with reading comprehension difficulties.

Syntactical–Grammatical Knowledge

Syntax refers to the order of words in sentences. Despite its many complications, English has relatively simple and direct syntax, as anyone who has studied German, Greek, or Latin can attest. In active sentences, the subject typically goes before the verb (e.g., "Rob handed the book to Laura"). The subject of the sentence and the object of the preposition are easy to identify. The only major variation is a passive sentence (e.g., "The book was handed to Laura by Rob"). A minor syntactical difference between English and languages such as Spanish, Italian, French, and Portuguese is that, in English, adjectives precede nouns (big river) whereas they follow nouns in the others (e.g., Rio Grande). As a result, there are few syntactic complications for speakers of those languages when they learn English.

Grammar refers to a variety of linguistic concepts (e.g., singular/plural, verb tense, parts of speech). A combination of grammatical and syntactical knowledge allowed you to successfully answer the comprehension questions about the snables from Chapter 3. The snables paragraph demonstrates that we can distinguish grammatical–syntactical knowledge from vocabulary–semantic knowledge.

Grammar and syntax do not usually represent a *unique* source of difficulty for poor comprehenders, independently of vocabulary–semantic knowledge. Students with grammatical problems typically have semantic difficulties as well (Catts et al., 2006; Nation et al., 2004). By contrast, there are students with weak semantic knowledge but intact grammatical and syntactical knowledge.

> **DON'T FORGET**
> ....
> Skills in vocabulary, grammar, and syntax are essential for comprehending written and oral language. Most students with grammatical–syntactical skill deficits also have vocabulary deficits. However, many students with vocabulary deficits have average grammatical–syntactical skills.

Background Knowledge

There are multiple types of background knowledge that affect the comprehension of both oral and written language, including general world knowledge, specific topical knowledge, knowledge that helps to build a situation model, and knowledge of the genre of the text one is reading (Catts, 2009; Fletcher et al., 2007; Kamhi, 2009, 2012; Nation, 2005; Oakhill et al., 2015). Some have argued that background knowledge is the key to comprehension (Catts, 2009; Kamhi, 2009).

General Background Knowledge

Consider the following passage taken from Oakhill and Garnham (1988; cited in Stuart, Stainthorp, & Snowling, 2008):

> Jane was invited to Jack's birthday. She wondered if he would like a kite. She went to her room and shook her piggy bank. It made no sound.

This seems like a passage most first graders could easily understand. Yet, despite its simplicity, the reader must have sufficient background knowledge to fully understand it. Much in this short passage is presumed and not explicitly stated. The reader must know that when invited to a birthday party, one is expected to bring a gift. Also, one is normally expected to buy a present rather than make one; thus the reference to the piggy bank. The reader must know the function of piggy banks and to understand why it would be expected to rattle. Little bits of general world knowledge are routinely required to comprehend spoken and written language.

We gave 50 typically developing second graders and 57 typically developing fifth graders the Wechsler Intelligence Scale for Children (WISC-III) Information subtest along with the reading comprehension subtest from the original Wechsler Individual Achievement Test. The correlation between these two tasks was highly significant at $r = +.60$ (Kilpatrick, Byrnes, Randall, & Isler, 2015). Working with adults, Shapiro (2004) found that background knowledge was so significant in determining reading comprehension performance that she argued that any assessment of reading comprehension should take background knowledge into account. Kamhi (2009) and Catts (2009) both reviewed studies demonstrating the importance of background knowledge for children's language comprehension and by extension, reading comprehension. Nation (2005) cited research indicating that children with the hyperlexic pattern not only lack sufficient general background knowledge, but they also fail to apply the background knowledge they do possess. General knowledge and vocabulary accounted for correct answers to reading and listening comprehension tasks among fifth graders even beyond specific topical knowledge (Compton, Miller, Elleman, & Steacy, 2014).

Specific Topical Knowledge

Further support for the importance of background knowledge comes from studies that examined readers' specific content knowledge. Poor comprehending fourth- and fifth-grade boys with a good knowledge of baseball understood and recalled more information when the passage they read concerned baseball than when reading about a different topic. The nonbaseball passages were constructed with an equivalent level of difficulty in terms of vocabulary and sentence structure (Gaultney, 1995). College students with greater prior knowledge of biology understood and recalled more of a basic passage that related to biology than those with less prior biology knowledge (Ozuru, Dempsey, & McNamara, 2009). Typical fourth-grade readers understood and remembered more from passages on familiar topics compared to unfamiliar ones (Marr & Gormley, 1982), even when text difficulty was controlled. Miller and Keenan (2009) found that topical knowledge directly influenced the reading comprehension scores of fourth and fifth graders after controlling for general intelligence, word reading, and text difficulty. Specific topical background knowledge is so important that poor word readers outperform good word readers when they happen to know more about the specific topic than the good word readers (Kahmi, 2009, 2012).

Constructing a Situation Model

There is both experiential/intuitive and experimental evidence that as we read or listen to something read to us, we create a situation model of what is occurring (Kintsch & Rawson, 2005; Oakhill et al., 2015). The story of Jack's birthday party illustrates this. This involves an integration of background knowledge, experience, and vocabulary. Poor comprehenders seem to have a more difficult time constructing a situation model (Compton et al., 2014; Nation, 2005; Oakhill et al., 2015). "Failure to construct situation models during reading is an acute symptom associated with reading comprehension disability" (Compton et al., 2014, p. 64). Greater background knowledge helps build a more accurate situation model and may decrease the demands on working memory (Compton et al., 2014).

Knowledge of Story Structure

An additional background factor is knowledge about various aspects of story structure and types of literary genre (Clarke, Truelove, Hulme, & Snowling, 2014). In a longitudinal study of 8- to 10-year-olds, Cain, Oakhill, and Bryant (2004) found that knowledge of story structure accounted for unique variance in comprehension beyond other key factors influencing comprehension. Knowledge of story structure can begin in the home as parents read to their children.

An Illustration of Poor Comprehension Due to Lack of Background

To illustrate some of the factors that influence comprehension, and to get a sense of what it might be like to struggle with comprehension, consider the following:

> The procedure is actually quite simple. First you arrange things into different groups. Of course, one pile may be sufficient depending on how much there is to do. If you have to go somewhere else due to lack of facilities that is

the next step, otherwise you are pretty well set. It is important not to overdo things. That is, it is better to do too few things at once than too many. In the short run this may not seem important but complications can easily arise. A mistake can be expensive as well. At first the whole procedure will seem complicated. Soon, however, it will become just another facet of life. It is difficult to foresee any end to the necessity for this task in the immediate future, but then one never can tell. After the procedure is completed one arranges the materials into different groups again. Then they can be put into their appropriate places. Eventually they will be used once more and the whole cycle will then have to be repeated. However, that is part of life. (Bransford & Johnson, 1972, p. 722)

The adult participants who read this paragraph as part of a study not only had difficulty understanding it, but they also displayed great difficulty recalling any of the details. This illustrates what reading comprehension is like without adequate background knowledge, without a situation model, and without the ability to draw inferences from what is in the text. However, because you are a good comprehender, simply learning the title of the paragraph can immediately rectify your poor comprehension of it: "Doing Laundry." With that key, the situation model and relevant background information immediately become clear, and you can make inferences about things not explicitly stated (e.g., ways in which a mistake can be expensive). This illustrates how significant background knowledge is for comprehending text.

Working Memory

Although not as important as language skills (Goff, Pratt, & Ong, 2005), working memory appears to be a "core process" (Fletcher et al., 2007) in comprehending language generally, as well as in reading comprehension. One needs to temporarily capture and maintain the specific words and grammatical constructions in memory in any given sentence or group of sentences in order to comprehend that information (Gathercole & Galloway, 2008). In a longitudinal study, Cain, Oakhill, and Bryant (2004) found that working memory accounted for unique variance in reading comprehension at

> **DON'T FORGET**
> ....
> General background knowledge and specific topical knowledge are important for understanding written and spoken language. A direct test of background knowledge should be a routine element in an evaluation of students with reading comprehension difficulties.

ages 8, 9, and 10, after vocabulary/general language skills had been accounted for. Cain, Oakhill, and Lemmon (2004) found that 9- to 10-year-old students who were poor comprehenders had more difficulty learning the meaning of novel vocabulary from context than their typically developing peers. The major determining factor in whether readers could learn the meaning of novel vocabulary from context was the degree of proximity in the text between the novel words and the information relevant to understanding the meaning of those novel words. This suggests that when the relevant information was not in close proximity to the novel words, it did not remain cognitively available, as the length of the intervening text exceeded working memory span. These authors concluded that working memory played an important practical role in deriving meaning from context.

Attention

Attention is an executive function that is required for comprehending oral and written language (Cain & Bignell, 2014; Kendeou, van den Broek, Helder, & Karlsson, 2014; Kieffer, Vukovic, & Berry, 2013; Miller et al., 2013). Some students with poor attention have listening comprehension scores that are lower

CAUTION

Students with attentional difficulties may have stronger receptive language skills than what is reflected on tests of listening comprehension.

than their reading comprehension scores (Aaron et al., 2002; Cain & Bignell, 2014). Presumably, they are more likely to mentally "wander" during a passive listening task than an active reading task. Also, there appears to be an interactive relationship between reading development and inattention. One study followed students for 7 years and found that students who experienced early and continued reading difficulties were more likely to develop inattentive behaviors compared to their typically developing peers (Prochnow, Tunmer, & Chapman, 2013).

Inferencing

Inferencing is a language skill required for both oral and written language comprehension (Oakhill et al., 2015). Some poor comprehenders can correctly respond to reading comprehension questions requiring literal answers, whereas others do not. Yet it is common for poor comprehenders to fail to draw inferences from text (Fletcher et al., 2007; Johnston, Barnes, & Desrochers, 2008; Kendeou et al., 2014; Nation, 2005). The birthday party passage presented above illustrates that inferencing is needed to supply the information not explicitly stated in the text. This typically requires the application of relevant background knowledge that a student brings to the text. Poor inferencing not only interferes with reading comprehension, it also hinders oral language comprehension. Hua and Keenan (2014) found that one of the sources of inferencing difficulties is text memory. When poor comprehenders remembered sufficient information from text, their inferences were accurate. When they did not remember relevant details, their inferences were not accurate. Most cognitive and achievement batteries do not have tests that directly assess inferencing, though reading comprehension subtests may have questions that require inferences. Some speech–language batteries directly assess inferencing skills.

Comprehension Monitoring

Comprehension monitoring refers to a reader's ability to recognize whether he understands what he is reading (Fletcher et al., 2007; Hulme & Snowling 2009, 2011; Johnston et al., 2008; Nation, 2005). Problems with comprehension monitoring commonly occur among poor comprehenders. It is unclear, however, whether it is a cause or consequence of poor comprehension. Poor comprehenders are not as likely as their typically developing peers to notice when they do not understand, and they continue reading without going back and clarifying any misunderstandings. While a recurring factor in the research literature, it is not something that is easy to assess formally in school settings, but teachers can do this informally in small groups (see Chapter 9).

Nonverbal, Visual–Spatial–Perceptual Skills

Studies have shown that visual–spatial–perceptual (VSP) skills are related to both oral and written language comprehension. Some early studies demonstrated this (Stroud, Blommers, & Lauber, 1957; Weaver & Rosner, 1979), even though they found no such relationship between VSP skills and word-level reading (Swanson, 1978; Vellutino, 1979; Vellutino, Steger, DeSetto, & Phillips, 1975). While not a heavily researched topic, there has been more recent empirical support for a connection (Adlof, Catts, & Lee, 2010; McCallum & Moore, 1999; Stothers & Klein, 2010). Adlof et al. (2010) found that nonverbal IQ measures taken in kindergarten were key predictors of eighth-grade reading comprehension, but not of word-level reading. Fuchs et al. (2012) found that nonverbal skills in first grade predicted fifth-grade reading comprehension. Also, some types of visual imagery training have provided benefits for both listening and reading comprehension (Center, Freeman, Robertson, & Outhred, 1999; Joffe, Cain & Marić, 2007; Johnson-Glenberg, 2000; Oakhill & Patel, 1991). Oakhill and Patel (1991) found that the reading comprehension of poor comprehenders improved after visual imagery training, but no such improvements were found in average comprehenders.

The precise nature of the relationship between VSP and language/reading comprehension is not clear. A possible connection may be found in an illustration by Samuels (2006; cited in Sadoski, McTigue, & Paivio, 2012):

> In order to understand the sentence "The executive ate his steak in the corporate dining room," the reader may form a mental image of a scenario that goes beyond the text information. For example, the reader may form an image of a well-dressed man who is wearing a business suit and holding a fork in his left hand and a knife in his right hand while cutting the steak on a plate that sits atop a white tablecloth. (pp. 489–490)

Perhaps students with weaker VSP skills are less able to effectively use visual imagery in creating their situation model than those with average VSP skills. This connection, however, remains speculative. The studies demonstrating a connection between VSP and reading comprehension and the studies showing reading comprehension improvements with visual imagery training have been largely independent lines of research. Further studies are needed to clarify this issue.

DON'T FORGET

There appears to be a definite link between reading comprehension and visual–spatial–perceptual skills. However, at this time, the precise nature of that relationship has not been adequately studied.

TEXT FACTORS

Text factors include genre, text structure, readability, text clarity, interest level of content, and so on. While it may be easy to distinguish text factors from reader abilities in principle, it is not always easy to distinguish them in practice. All of these text factors interact with many of the reader factors previously described. Poor comprehenders are not as sensitive to differences between genres as their typically developing peers, they struggle to become aware of text structure, and they have a difficult time reading texts that are considered to be at an appropriate level of readability for their grade level. Much research has gone into these text factors (Deane, Sheehan, Sabatini, Futagi, & Kostin, 2006; Fletcher et al., 2007;

Hulme & Snowling, 2009; Miller et al., 2013; Westby, 2012). Most of the reading comprehension subtests used in individualized assessments do not allow for a careful analysis of these factors. But in a general classroom situation, all of these factors can affect reading comprehension performance.

TASK FACTORS

Task factors include a student's instructional environment, response expectation during reading instruction, responses on classroom-oriented reading assessments, and types of responses expected on individualized reading evaluations. Does the student read silently and respond silently to multiple-choice questions such as on the Test of Reading Comprehension–Fourth Edition (TORC-4)? Does the student read silently and respond orally, as on the KTEA-3 or WIAT-III? Does the student read orally and respond orally, as in the Gray Oral Reading Tests–Fifth Edition (GORT-5)? Does the response involve filling in the blank, as in the cloze procedure on such tests as the Woodcock Reading Mastery Test–Third Edition (WRMT-III)? Does the student have the passage available while answering the comprehension questions (e.g., TORC-4) or is the student not allowed to look back (e.g., Peabody Individual Achievement Test–Revised [PIAT-R])? Research has shown that different reading comprehension tests, using different task expectations, are associated with different underlying skills (Cutting and Scarborough 2006; Keenan, Betjemann, & Olson, 2008; Nation & Snowling, 1997). This will be covered in detail in Chapter 9.

STUDENTS WHOSE FIRST LANGUAGE IS NOT ENGLISH

Most ELL students are at a distinct disadvantage when it comes to language comprehension compared to their peers whose first language is English. Such difficulties with language extend to reading comprehension. The simple view of reading framework applies to the reading comprehension development of ELL students in the same way that it applies to the reading comprehension development among native speakers of English. The progress of ELL students in reading comprehension is directly related to their abilities to comprehend spoken English as well as their abilities to quickly and efficiently read English words (Farnia, & Geva, 2013; Li & Kirby, 2014; Sparks, Patton, Ganschow, & Humbach, 2012). Their special difficulties stem from the fact that their vocabulary, possibly syntax, and sometimes cultural background knowledge are not as well developed as those of their native English-speaking peers. All of these factors affect comprehension.

SUMMARY

Reading comprehension requires a variety of skills above and beyond reading the words (see Rapid Reference 5.1). A deficiency in any of these skills can hinder reading comprehension. Many of these skills can be assessed in routine school-based evaluations. Others cannot be assessed formally, but an informal evaluation may be possible (e.g., comprehension monitoring, knowledge of genre). Students whose first language is not English are typically compromised in several of the key skills needed for reading comprehension. Chapter 9 reviews both reading comprehension subtests and also tests of the skills described above that contribute to reading comprehension. Chapters 10 and 11 describe ways of preventing and correcting reading comprehension difficulties.

≡ Rapid Reference 5.1 Skills Associated With Skilled Reading Comprehension

Language Skills

- Vocabulary–semantic knowledge
- Grammatical–syntactical knowledge
- General background knowledge and specific topical knowledge
- Inferencing

Text Skills

- Knowledge of genre and text structures

Cognitive Skills

- Working memory
- Visual–spatial–perceptual skills

Executive Functioning Skills

- Attention
- Comprehension monitoring

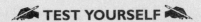

TEST YOURSELF

1. **All of the following are possible reasons a child may do poorly in reading comprehension. However, which of the following is the most common?**
   (a) Poor instruction
   (b) Poor attitude
   (c) Poor word-level reading
   (d) Poor motivation

2. **Specific reading comprehension impairment is most likely the result of**
   (a) Poor instruction.
   (b) Poor motivation.
   (c) Weak language skills.
   (d) Poor word-level reading.

3. **All of the following are identified as factors that affect a student's reading comprehension except**
   (a) Vocabulary knowledge.
   (b) Type of material a student selects to read (e.g., books, comic books, Internet).
   (c) Background knowledge and specific topical knowledge.
   (d) Working memory.
   (e) All of the above.

4. **What seems to be the relationship between attention, reading comprehension, and tests of listening comprehension?**
   (a) Inattentive students often do more poorly on tests of listening comprehension than reading comprehension.
   (b) Inattentive students often do more poorly on tests of reading comprehension than listening comprehension.
   (c) Inattentive students always do poorly on tests of both listening comprehension and reading comprehension.
   (d) Inattentive students typically do well on tests of both listening comprehension and reading comprehension.

5. **What has research indicated about ELL students and reading comprehension?**
   (a) They typically do not display difficulties with reading comprehension.
   (b) They have generally similar concerns as native speakers of English who have below-average language skills.
   (c) Reading comprehension has not been studied in ELL students because the focus has been on word-level reading.
   (d) Even following improvements in language comprehension and word-level reading, reading comprehension does not improve in ELL students.

6. What is a situation model?

(a) A mental picture students develop about what is going on in a text by integrating their vocabulary and background knowledge with the elements in the text.

(b) A character in a story being read that provides positive modeling to students.

(c) When teachers openly talk about the thinking process they use as they interpret text, which models for students how to comprehend the text.

(d) A theoretical formulation of all of the key factors that influence reading comprehension.

7. Why would general background knowledge or specific topical knowledge be so important in understanding what is read?

(a) It is more fun to read about things you know about.

(b) Reading comprehension requires inferencing, and research shows you can make better inferences about things you know about.

(c) Background knowledge correlates with general intelligence and general intelligence correlates with reading comprehension, so the relation between background knowledge and reading comprehension is indirect.

(d) None of the above.

8. Reading comprehension and word-level reading are similar in the sense that they can be boiled down to a few simple factors.

(a) True

(b) False

9. What might be the relationship between comprehension monitoring and reading comprehension?

(a) Students with poor reading comprehension may get accustomed to not understanding what they read, so they don't check back and reread and, therefore, it appears they are not properly monitoring their comprehension.

(b) Poor monitoring of comprehension results in poor comprehension.

(c) Poor comprehension monitoring could simply be a reflection of executive functioning skills, which, like attention and working memory, could influence reading comprehension.

(d) Given that researchers do not have a clear understanding of the relationship between comprehension monitoring and reading comprehension, any or all of the three above could be involved.

10. Why are good inferencing skills needed for reading comprehension?

(a) Because not everything in the text is explicitly stated and some things need to be inferred.

(b) Because one needs a high degree of intelligence to comprehend text, and inferencing is a reflection of intelligence.

(c) Because tests specifically incorporate inferencing questions even if most of what one reads does not involve inferencing.
(d) Inferencing is actually problematic because it causes the reader to interpret things within her own framework rather than the author's.

Answers: 1. c; 2. c; 3. e; 4. a; 5. b; 6. a; 7. b; 8. False; 9. d; 10. a

Six

ASSESSING PHONOLOGICAL PROCESSING SKILLS

AN INTRODUCTION TO INTERVENTION-ORIENTED ASSESSMENT OF READING

Because this is the first of four chapters addressing the assessment of reading-related skills, some introductory comments are in order. Chapters 6 through 9 focus on *intervention-oriented assessment*. The goal of intervention-oriented assessment is to acquire a better understanding of a child's reading difficulty in order to guide intervention. It is not intended for the purpose of making special education identification decisions (however, see Chapter 13). Intervention-oriented assessment attempts to base reading evaluations on our empirically derived understanding of reading acquisition and reading difficulties.

CAUTION

Although reading-related psychoeducational evaluations that incorporate the research presented in this book may lead to more valid specific learning disability diagnostic decisions, the specific purpose of this approach to determine *why* a child is struggling in order to identify the most effective approaches to intervention.

The Issue of Subtest Reliability

Individual subtest reliabilities are not considered strong enough to form the basis of important educational decisions. Yet in the following chapters, there will be an emphasis on interpreting subtest scores. There are two ways this issue is addressed in the context of intervention-oriented assessment. One is to administer more than one subtest of the same skill, preferably during different testing sessions. When a single subtest is administered, it is impossible to know for sure whether that score accurately represents the student's skill, given that particular subtest's reliability. If an equivalent subtest from a different battery yields similar results, it becomes more difficult to argue that *both* scores inaccurately represent the student's skill. However, if similar subtests yield different results, a third subtest might be administered to determine which of the other two more likely reflects the student's skills (McGrew & Flanagan, 1998). For example, although two low scores and one average score may decrease one's confidence that the two low subtests accurately represent the student's skill, it is still more likely that the outlier is the less accurate score, unless there are factors to suggest otherwise.

While an imperfect solution, administering multiple subtests of the same skill is more likely to yield information useful in forming a reasonable hypothesis about why a student is struggling in reading. One concern with this approach is the additional assessment time involved. However, except for reading comprehension subtests, the types of subtests used in intervention-oriented assessment for reading range between 45 seconds to 5 minutes to administer. Most take fewer than 2 or 3 minutes each. The time invested in administering "duplicate" subtests is brief and leads to increased confidence in the assessment results.

The second way the subtest reliability issue is addressed is through the acknowledgment that this approach does not involve long-term diagnostic decisions. Rather, the goal is to develop a working hypothesis about why the student struggles in order to design well-targeted interventions. A cautious approach to test score interpretation is to err in the direction of providing additional instructional support, which could result in too many false positives. However, this is unlikely to be an issue if schools implement the K–1 prevention research described in Chapter 10. If such prevention practices were implemented, there would be a substantial decrease in the number of students who struggle with reading in the first place. Also, with progress monitoring, false-positive students would be quickly discontinued from such help.

The Problem With Composite Scores

The conventional solution to the subtest reliability issue is to combine two or more subtests into a composite score because composite scores have greater reliability. For intervention-oriented assessment, however, composite scores are not typically recommended. The problem with composite or cluster scores is that they often combine different constructs or skills. For example, the Broad Reading Cluster of the Woodcock-Johnson IV Tests of Achievement (WJ-IV ACH) combines three different skills: word

---

CAUTION

In intervention-oriented assessment, composite and cluster scores are discouraged. They often mask the weaknesses we are trying to detect. The use of multiple subtests of the same skills from different batteries is recommended.

identification, fluency, and reading comprehension. Weak readers are often weak in one of these but strong in another, and the weakness is masked by any strengths. It is thus advisable to administer multiple subtests of the *same* skill from different batteries.

Gaps in the Assessment Research

There are many gaps in the reading research in terms of practical assessment issues. Despite hundreds of studies on reading, there is no body of "best practice" research that provides recommendations for how to apply the findings presented in Chapters 3, 4, and 5 to school-based reading assessments. It will become clear in Chapters 6 through 9 that we do not always have ideal test instruments to directly answer all reading-related referral questions. Two examples should suffice.

First, despite hundreds of studies investigating the relationship between phonemic awareness and learning to read, there has been no concerted effort to determine which of the many phonological awareness *tasks* is most useful for assessing the phonological skills that underlie reading (Kilpatrick, 2012a, 2012b). Second, in previous chapters, a distinction was made between word identification and word recognition. Yet most of our word-level reading tests confound the two.

Because the available tests are not always ideally suited for assessing the various components of reading, the best reading assessment tool is the evaluator's knowledge of research on reading acquisition and reading difficulties. The commercially available assessments are simply tools. A skilled carpenter can produce quality work without having the optimal set of tools. Similarly, with a solid knowledge base, we can generate quality reading assessments with our currently available tests.

> **DON'T FORGET**
>
> The best reading assessment tool is having a solid knowledge base regarding the research on reading acquisition and reading difficulties.

Due to the limited research on applying the findings described in Chapters 3, 4, and 5 to school-based evaluations, the assessment chapters will include some first-person descriptions of experiences and impressions from my efforts to apply this research over the past 15 years to my school-based practice. Such descriptions and impressions are reserved for when the research provides little or no guidance. These descriptions also serve to model the statement made above that the best assessment tool we have available is our knowledge of the empirical findings regarding reading development and reading difficulties.

Applying Reading Research to Psychoeducational Assessment

Chapters 6 through 9 will not provide a technical review of all of the tests on the market that assess reading-related skills. Most readers are able to evaluate the technical merits of the tests they use. The tests described in the following chapters have adequate or better reliability and validity. The goal in these chapters is to demonstrate how to apply the reading research to the evaluation process. Such assessments can generate information leading to better learning outcomes. Many specific tests will be described in the next four chapters, some in detail. However, assuming good reliability and validity, the actual test instruments are secondary to the knowledge base used to design the assessment and interpret the results.

> **DON'T FORGET**
> ....
> Assuming that the tests used have good reliability and validity, the actual test instruments are secondary to the knowledge base used to design the assessment and interpret the results.

(Re)interpreting Norms in Intervention-Oriented Assessment

There is an important caution in interpreting normative scores on reading-related tests. Traditional qualitative descriptors that accompany standard scores indicate any score within a standard deviation of the mean is in the "average range." Such a descriptor is statistical in nature and about a century old. Yet a quarter to a third of students struggle in reading, making the traditional descriptors problematic in interpreting reading-related standard scores. While a score of 90 is considered average, it is still at the 25th percentile. Students at the 25th percentile nationally are weak readers. A standard score of 86 is in the 18th percentile and is traditionally considered average or low average, but a student reading at that level based on national norms is reading poorly.

We need to think differently about how to interpret normative scores on reading-related tests. For example, a scaled score of 8 on a CTOPP-2 subtest would be considered average or low average using our conventional descriptors, implying there is no problem that needs attention. However, that scaled score of 8 represents only the 25th percentile for that skill, and the 25th percentile is within the range of the population of students who display weak reading skills. It is quite likely that this level of performance on that subtest is one of the reasons the student is struggling.

Consider how unusual our century-old practice is compared to analogous situations. For example, let's say that 30% to 34% of the adult population had poor enough vision that they would benefit substantially from glasses or contact lenses. What if the optometry field, based on 100-year-old practices, only prescribed glasses to those 1 standard deviation below the mean!

We should work backward from the actual data on how common reading problems are, rather than rely on 100-year-old descriptive terms that ignore *base rates* (i.e., how common a phenomenon occurs in a population). A scaled score of 8 (standard score of 90) on a reading-related test or subtest should never be considered average or low average and therefore dismissed as of no concern. This should apply regardless of intellectual ability. Even if a scaled score of 8 on a phonological awareness test or a nonsense word reading test was a student's highest

> # CAUTION
>
> Because one quarter to one third of students struggle in reading to some degree, a scaled score of 8 (standard score of 90) should not be dismissed as average or low average. Any scores in the bottom third of the distribution should receive some further attention because the skills that are likely problematic (letter-sound skills, blending, and phonemic analysis) are correctable with Tier 2 interventions.

score in the entire test profile, it should be addressed. Word-level reading and its underlying skills (e.g., letter-sound knowledge and phonological awareness) are quite correctable even among those with IQs in the 60s to 80s. Low IQ has a very large influence on reading comprehension (Gresham & Vellutino, 2010), but it need not affect word-level reading skills because the skills required for word-level reading are not substantially correlated with IQ test scores.

An administrator once commented to me: "There's always going to be a bottom third." While that is true, it misses an important point about reading difficulties. Roughly speaking, approximately 30% to 34% of fourth graders in the United States are reading at or below a second-grade level nationally, and the bottom 5% to 10% are reading as low as a kindergarten to first-grade level. If we apply the research presented in Chapters 10 and 11, we can re-envision this so that the bottom 25% of fourth graders read at a third- or fourth-grade level, with the bottom 5% reading no lower than a second-grade level. Also, rather than have our students with the most severe reading disabilities leave high school with a second- or third-grade reading level, they could be leaving with a fifth- or sixth-grade reading level. Such a reading level is far more functional as an individual enters the world of adulthood in our society. There is ample research demonstrating that this re-envisioning is entirely possible. While there will always be a bottom third, students in that bottom third can dramatically improve their reading proficiency compared to their current level.

Some might express apprehension about intervening with students who perform in 20th to 30th percentiles, especially in the early grades. However, schools that base their RTI approach on the kinds of prevention measures described in Chapter 10 are likely to experience 50% to 80% fewer students struggling in reading (NICHD, 2000; Shapiro & Solity, 2008). This will allow for more flexibility and resources to serve the remaining students who continue to struggle even after receiving excellent Tier 1 instruction (or students who transfer into the school who did not receive that Tier 1 prevention). Again, we must distinguish between intervention-oriented assessment and the traditional "test and diagnose" approach. The latter approach only allows individuals who are below a certain predetermined cutoff to qualify for special education services. This discussion of scaled scores has nothing to do with determining an educational disability. Rather it has to do with identifying the skills that require attention to improve a student's reading abilities. Thus, even a scaled score of 9 on a CTOPP-2 subtest should be considered borderline. This is because a scaled score of 9 is at the 37th percentile, which is only marginally above the bottom third. This means that any student who scores an 8 or lower on any of the CTOPP-2 phonological awareness subtests (Elision, Blending Words, or Phoneme Isolation) should be considered a potential candidate for Tier 2 remedial instruction.

ISSUES IN ASSESSING PHONOLOGICAL SKILLS

Phonological awareness plays a central role in word-level reading development (see Chapter 4). Given that deficiencies in phonological awareness are responsible for most word-level reading problems, it follows that an assessment of phonological awareness should be a central element of any evaluation of a student who displays word-level reading difficulties. Other phonological skills that should be evaluated include phonological working memory and rapid automatized naming (RAN).

> **DON'T FORGET**
> ....
> Because of its central role in reading development, an assessment of phonological awareness should be included in any evaluation of a student who displays word-level reading difficulties.

Phonological Awareness Tasks and Tests

We cannot directly observe phonological awareness. We can only observe students' responses to a variety of tasks intended to estimate a child's proficiency with that skill. None of these tasks is a perfect representation of phonological awareness. However, there is reason to believe that some phonological awareness tasks are better than others at measuring the underlying construct of phonological awareness as it pertains to reading development.

Researchers have measured the construct of phonological awareness/ analysis in many ways, including rhyming, segmenting, isolating, categorizing, and manipulating sounds in words (Anthony, Lonigan, Driscoll, Phillips, & Burgess, 2003; Chafouleas, Lewandowski, Smith, & Blachman, 1997; Høien, Lundberg, Stanovich, & Bjaalid, 1995; Lenchner, Gerber, & Routh, 1990; Lundberg, Olofsson, & Wall, 1980;

> **CAUTION**
> ....
> Phonological awareness is a latent ability that is estimated through various tasks. However, not all types of phonological awareness tasks are equally capable of reflecting the phonological underpinnings of word-level reading.

Stanovich, Cunningham, & Cramer, 1984; Yopp, 1988). Rhyming, as the name suggests, involves having children perform tasks involving rhyming or rhyme recognition. Segmentation consists of breaking a word into segments. Isolation involves determining the position of a sound within a word. For example, a student may be asked where the /d/ sound is in *dog* or *bed*. Categorization is most commonly represented by the *oddity task*, an example would be: "Which word ends with a different sound than the others: *bike, brush, truck?*" Research seems to suggest that phonological manipulation tasks are the best measures of the phonological awareness skills needed for reading because they are the best predictors of word-level reading proficiency (Caravolas et al., 2005; Kilpatrick, 2012a, 2012b; Kilpatrick & McInnis, 2015; Swank & Catts, 1994). Phonological manipulation involves deleting, substituting, or reversing sounds in spoken words (Caravolas et al., 2005; Kroese, Hynd, Knight, Hiemenz, & Hall, 2000; Lundberg et al., 1980; McInnis, 1999; Wagner et al., 1999).

Judging from its inclusion in most phonological awareness batteries (e.g., DIBELS, Aimsweb, easyCBM, PALS, Yopp-Singer), phonological segmentation is arguably the most widely used phonological awareness assessment in schools. One might assume that the decision to use segmentation rather than one of the other methods of assessing phonological awareness was based upon a body of best-practice research. This is not the case. While many studies have incorporated multiple phonological awareness tasks (e.g., Anthony et al., 2003; Høien et al., 1995; Schatschneider et al., 1999, 2004; Seymour & Evans, 1994; Stahl & Murray, 1994; Vloedgraven, & Verhoeven, 2009; Wagner, Torgesen,

Laughon, Simmons, & Rashotte, 1993; Wagner, Torgesen, & Rashotte, 1994; Yopp, 1988), unfortunately, these studies made no attempt to directly compare phonological tasks for clinical utility. Rather, they used multiple measures of phonological awareness to determine the factor structure of phonological awareness or to create a phonological awareness factor that is then used to study its relationship with reading. There have been rare instances in which specific tasks were directly examined for clinical utility (Kilpatrick, 2012a; Swank & Catts, 1994). These studies indicated that for first and second graders, segmentation provides no useful information beyond what is provided by blending and manipulation tasks, while these latter tasks provide useful information about a student's level of phonological awareness development not provided by segmentation.

These findings parallel a pattern that has existed in the phonological awareness literature for many years. While this fact has gone largely unnoticed (Kilpatrick, 2012a; Kilpatrick & McInnis, 2015), numerous research reports include data to show that from first grade onward, manipulation tasks display higher correlations with reading measures than segmentation tasks (Backman, 1983; Kroese et al., 2000; Lenchner et al., 1990; Perfetti, Beck, Bell, & Hughes, 1987; Swank & Catts, 1994; Wagner et al., 1993). Authors rarely mention this difference; one must discover these differences by examining their correlation tables. Exceptions include Catts, Fey, Zhang, and Tomblin (2001), who said phonological manipulation "ranks highly among phonological awareness tasks in predicting reading achievement" (p. 40), and Lenchner et al. (1990), who stated that their manipulation task had a higher correlation with phonic decoding ($r = .78$ and $r = .74$) than any segmentation task reported in the literature.

An informal task analysis may reveal why this is the case. Phonological manipulation incorporates the skills tapped by the other tasks. To do a deletion task (e.g., to change *sneak* to *seek*) or a substitution task (e.g., to go from *roof* to *room*), a student must be able to segment, isolate, and blend. For example, to delete the /n/ sound from *sneak*, a student must separate the sounds (phonological segmentation), determine where the /n/ sound is located in the word (phonological isolation), delete it (phonological manipulation), and combine the resulting sequence of sounds to arrive at *seek* (phonological blending). This suggests that manipulation tasks capture more of the metalinguistic underpinnings associated with the construct of phonological awareness (Kilpatrick, 2012a).

In addition to the evidence previously presented, there is some indication that training in phonemic segmentation appears to have limited long-term impact on reading (Fox & Routh, 1983), whereas training in phonemic manipulation has substantial long-term impact on reading (see Chapter 11). When this intervention evidence is combined with the correlational and regression analyses mentioned above, it becomes reasonable to assume that manipulation tasks, rather than segmentation tasks, should be relied upon to assess phonemic awareness.

Manipulation Tasks

As mentioned, the manipulation tasks are deletion, substitution, and reversal. The deletion task appears to be the most popular phonological manipulation task, having been used in countless research studies. Commercially it is included on CTOPP-2 (the Elision subtest; note that *elision* rhymes with *collision*). Such deletion tasks tend to correlate between $r = .50$ and .70 (in some cases as high as .84; see Rosner & Simon, 1971) with word-level reading. By contrast, segmentation tasks

> **DON'T FORGET**
> ....
> Phonological manipulation tasks are more sensitive to reading development than other phonological awareness tasks. This is likely because one must be able to use the skills tapped by those other tasks (i.e., segmentation, isolation, and blending) to respond correctly to phonological manipulation tasks.

tend to correlate with word reading between $r = .29$ (e.g., the CTOPP Segmenting Words subtest; Wagner et al., 1999) and about .47 (Kilpatrick, 2012a). Less common are substitution tasks, although substitution items are included in some phonological awareness or reading batteries, such as the Phonological Awareness Test-2 (PAT-2; Robertson & Salter, 2007), the Woodcock-Johnson Tests of Cognitive Abilities–Fourth Edition (WJ-IV COG), the WRMT-III (Woodcock, 2011), the KTEA-3, and the Differential Ability Scales-II (DAS-II).

The original CTOPP included a supplemental subtest called Phoneme Reversal that is not included on the CTOPP-2. My experience was that Phoneme Reversal was not helpful with younger students (grades 2 to 4) because of its difficulty level. However, it appears to be quite sensitive to reading problems for students in middle school and high school, even more helpful than the Elision subtest from the standard battery. Those who have the original CTOPP may want to retain it in order to administer Phoneme Reversal to upper-level students. Obviously, it uses older norms than the CTOPP-2. However, within the context of intervention-oriented assessment, the issue is to determine whether the student needs remediation in phonological awareness. This subtest would not be given in isolation, but would supplement one or two other phonological awareness subtests. This use of older norms is not inconsistent with the ethical guidelines of the American Psychological Association or the National Association of School Psychologists because no updated version of the Phoneme Reversal subtest exists.

Perhaps a future revision of the CTOPP-2 may reinstate this subtest with a focus on older students.

A problem in interpreting results from a phonological reversal task (such as Phoneme Reversal) is that it appears to confound phonological awareness with working memory. As a result, a low score may be interpreted differently depending on a student's working memory performance. If a student has a scaled score of 9 or higher on working memory subtests, one may assume that a poor Phoneme Reversal score is likely a reflection of poor phonological awareness. If the student did poorly on working memory subtests, one must consider the possibility that a poor Phoneme Reversal score could be partially or wholly accounted for by the poor working memory. Nonetheless, I have found that with middle school and high school students with adequate working memory, Phoneme Reversal was more sensitive to reading difficulties than Elision. A likely reason is that older students with poor phonemic awareness can "cheat" on a task like Elision and create the impression they have better phonemic awareness than they actually do (see the next section). With Phoneme Reversal, however, this is much more difficult to do successfully.

How Students "Cheat" on Phonological Awareness Tests

A problem with many phonological awareness tests is that they are untimed. DIBELS, Aimsweb, and easyCBM are timed, but the potential benefit of this is lost due to their use of a segmentation task. The comprehensive batteries such as the CTOPP, the CTOPP-2, and the PAT-2 use untimed phonological awareness tasks. Without a timing element, it is difficult to interpret phonological awareness test results because students can use an alternative strategy that circumvents phonological awareness to get an item correct, but it takes longer to respond in such cases (Caravolas et al., 2005; Kilpatrick & McInnis, 2015). For example, if a student is asked to change the /p/ in the spoken word *pat* to a /b/, students weak in phonological awareness can mentally spell the word *pat*, swap the *p* for *b*, and read back what they mentally spelled. This may require a few seconds to accomplish, but their answer is scored as correct. By contrast, students with good phonological awareness generally respond instantly,

> ## CAUTION
> ....
> Students can "cheat" on phonological deletion and substitution tasks via a mental spelling strategy. It is difficult to prevent this with untimed phonological awareness tasks. However, with timed tests, we can distinguish between proficient phonological awareness and the use of a compensating mental spelling strategy.

in 1 second or less. Given their instant responses, such students are not likely to have used mental spelling but rather relied on their proficient phonological awareness. If a student has very basic spelling skills (which many third, fourth, and fifth grade weak readers do), they are perfectly capable of converting a phonological awareness task into a mental spelling task. As a result, phonological awareness difficulties can be overlooked in some students due to the untimed nature of the tasks.

This threat to validity of phonological awareness assessment can be avoided with a timing element. On the PAST, the evaluator uses a 2-second silent count after presenting an item. Correct responses in 2 seconds or less are scored as "automatic." Correct responses longer than 2 seconds are scored as "correct." There is reason to believe that the faster responses represent greater phonological awareness proficiency. In using the PAST with several hundred students in research projects, I have found that typically developing readers respond to items up to their developmental level in an instantaneous manner (Kilpatrick & McInnis, 2015). When poor readers get items correct, their responses are typically longer than 2 seconds.

A concern that has been raised about phonological manipulation tasks is that they appear to confound phonological awareness with working memory (WM). Although this may be a valid concern with phonological reversal tasks (as described above), it is not likely a valid concern for the more common manipulation tasks of deletion and substitution. This is because students with average or better phonemic awareness skills typically respond to manipulation items instantly (Caravolas et al., 2005; Kilpatrick & McInnis, 2015). Such instant responding does not appear to require any effortful activity within WM. Indeed, if a student requires a substantive amount of working memory allotment to successfully complete a deletion or substitution task, it is very likely that the student has weak phonemic awareness skills. Under timed/automatic scoring conditions, such as on the PAST, it appears that manipulation tasks are not confounded by WM, unless one can explain how an instantaneous response in 1 second or less is affected by WM.

Another way to prevent a student from using a mental spelling strategy is to use orthographically inconsistent words in phonological tasks. For example, it would be much easier to use a mental spelling strategy to delete the /d/ in *card* to get *car* than to delete the /d/ in *word* to get *were*. The second substitution involves orthographic inconsistency and is presumably more difficult if using a mental spelling strategy. Orthographically inconsistent prompt words put the focus on the *sounds* in words rather than on the word's spelling. They are likely to be more "pure" assessments of phonological awareness. While the CTOPP-2 Elision has a mixture of orthographically consistent and inconsistent items, most are consistent. This makes the use of a mental spelling strategy easier for students with weak phonological awareness. It would seem that the combination of a timing element and the use of orthographically inconsistent items would provide a more rigorous test of phonemic awareness, uncontaminated by an alternative strategy. The PAST (included free in this book's supplemental materials) has five alternative forms, and four out of the five use orthographically inconsistent items. Plus, to facilitate use for universal screening, a shorter screening form is included.

Nonsense Word Spelling

Nonsense word spelling tasks have been used in various research studies (Manis, Custodio, & Szeszulski, 1993; Swank & Catts, 1994). They are highly correlated with both phonic decoding and phonemic awareness. Nonsense word spelling is not commonly found on achievement batteries. The Spelling of Sounds subtest from the extended battery of the WJ-IV ACH is a welcome exception. To correctly spell nonsense words, students must have good letter-sound knowledge and phoneme segmentation skills. Because it only requires phoneme segmentation, scores from such tests should be interpreted with caution. Low scores are indicative of a problem with phonological awareness and/or letter-sound knowledge, but an average score does not rule out phonological awareness difficulties (one would need a timed manipulation task for this). Yet as a quick assessment of *both* letter-sound knowledge and phonological segmentation, nonsense word spelling can provide additional data on a student with word-level difficulties, so long as it is not used as a substitute for either nonsense word reading or a phonological manipulation test.

Other Phonological Manipulation Tasks

The WJ-IV COG, KTEA-3, WRMT-III, and the DAS-II have manipulation subtests. These might be considered, but with important reservations. The WJ-IV COG has a subtest called Phonological Processing that incorporates three sections. The first section starts with a first-sound matching task, then shifts to a task requiring the production of a word that begins with the sound provided by the examiner. The second section involves a student saying as many words as possible that begin with a certain sound within a time limit. The third section is a substitution task. Students swap sounds in words (e.g., from _sat_ to _hat_ or _flip_ to _drip_). On the positive side, this test has norms that go up to adulthood. On the negative side, these three sections get merged into a single raw score. This is unfortunate because a more verbally astute child with a phonological awareness difficulty could do very well on the first and second sections but poorly on the third section. These performances may result in an overall average raw score.

This would mask the student's more advanced phonological awareness skills that would likely be identified by the manipulation task if it were a stand-alone subtest. The KTEA-3 is similar, except it merges items that involve rhyming, segmentation, phoneme matching, blending, and deletion, and only the latter is a manipulation task. This also has norms up to adulthood. The WRMT-III combines first-sound matching, last-sound matching, rhyme production, blending, and deletion into a single score. It only goes up to grade 2, however. The DAS-II combines items involving rhyming, blending, manipulation (deletion), identification, and segmentation. Because the scores from these phonological awareness tests combine manipulation tasks with other tasks, they should not be considered as a replacement for the CTOPP-2, the PAT-2, the LAC-3, or the PAST, though they may be used to supplement those batteries.

The Need to Supplement Universal Screenings

The insensitivity of segmentation tasks suggests the need to replace (or at minimum supplement) the segmentation tasks on the universal screening batteries with a manipulation task. Conventional wisdom has been that phonological manipulation tasks are too difficult for kindergartners and first graders (Rosner & Simon, 1971; Wagner et al., 1993). However, that only appears to be the case for manipulating *phonemes*. In contrast, when manipulation tasks begin with deleting *syllables* (e.g., "Say *cowboy* without saying *cow*"), typically developing kindergartners have no difficulty with such manipulation tasks. Adlof et al. (2010) found that a manipulation (deletion) test administered in kindergarten predicted eighth-grade reading skills. Bridges and Catts (2011) found a deletion task with kindergarteners was more predictive of reading skills than the DIBELS Initial Sound Fluency. The PAST predicted Aimsweb's kindergarten Nonsense Word Fluency better than Aimsweb's Phoneme Segmentation Fluency (Kilpatrick & McInnis, 2015).

> **CAUTION**
>
> Despite their inclusion in the universal screeners, segmentation tasks are not sensitive enough to identify many of the students with poor phonological awareness. Universal screenings should include a phonological manipulation test.

So whether dealing with kindergartners (Kilpatrick & McInnis, 2015), first graders (Kilpatrick, 2012a; Swank & Catts, 1994), or older struggling readers (Caravolas et al., 2005; Torgesen et al., 2001), a manipulation task is more likely to uncover phonological awareness problems than a segmentation task. A short form of the PAST is included with the supplementary materials.

It cuts administration time to facilitate its use with universal screeners. It can supplement the universal screeners' phonological awareness tasks in K–1 and provide a screening of phonological awareness for second grade on. The universal screeners discontinue their phonological awareness task after first grade. Given that the PAST is free and the short form involves a 1- to 4-minute administration, it is a good candidate to supplement a universal screening. However, once administered, it would not need to be re-administered as part of ongoing screenings for students in second grade and beyond who do well on it the first time.

Best Practice in Phonological Awareness Assessment

The foregoing allows us to suggest a best practice given current knowledge and available instruments. Phonological manipulation appears to be the phonological awareness task that most closely captures the phonological underpinnings of word-level reading. Phonological segmentation appears to be less sensitive to the degree of phonological proficiency needed to be a skilled reader. Figures 6.1 and 6.2 provide scatterplots that compare four phonological awareness subtests administered to 67 lower-middle-class first graders between January and March of first grade (Figure 6.1) and 50 second graders in that same school during those same months (Figure 6.2) (Kilpatrick & McInnis, 2015). These data included all students in their respective classrooms and therefore reflect a range of word-reading skills. The correlations between these subtests and the WRMT-R Word Identification for first grade were: Segmenting Words, $r = .47$; Blending Words, $r = .65$; Elision, $r = .60$; and the PAST, $r = .79$. For second grade, they were: Segmenting Words, $r = .31$; Blending Words, $r = .64$; Elision, $r = .56$; and the PAST, $r = .76$. However, these scatterplots reveal something important that is not reflected in the correlational coefficients. Both the segmentation and blending tasks have a high degree of false negatives in first grade (Figure 6.1). On each of these tests, there were students who performed at or above the median on the phonological test, yet were in the bottom third on the reading test. This questions the use of segmentation or blending tasks for screening purposes. When using the more sensitive manipulation tasks, first and second graders on the lower end of the distribution in reading were also on the lower end on these phonological awareness tasks. In

> **DON'T FORGET**
> ....
> In terms of selection of assessment instruments, it appears that tests of phonological manipulation, such as deleting and/or substituting sounds in words, represent best practice in phonological awareness assessment.

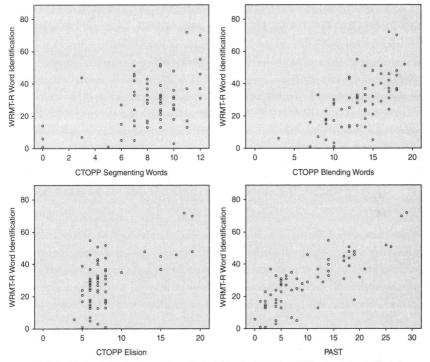

Note: WRMT-R = Woodcock Reading Mastery Test - Revised (Woodcock, 1998); CTOPP = Comprehensive Test of Phonological Processing (Wagner, Torgesen, & Rashotte, 1999); PAST = Phonological Awareness Screening Test (Kilpatrick & McInnis, 2015).

Figure 6.1 A Comparison of Four Phonological Awareness Subtests with 67 Students in the Winter/Spring of First Grade

Source: Kilpatrick and McInnis (2015).

addition, none of the stronger readers did poorly on the PAST, but some of the stronger readers did poorly on the Elision subtest due to the shift in task demands on the Elision subtest (described later in the chapter).

One way to judge the clinical utility of a screening test is to examine its sensitivity and specificity. *Sensitivity* means the test will correctly identify individuals with a target characteristic. *Specificity* means that those without the given characteristic will not be falsely identified. Sensitivity refers to true positives and specificity refers to true negatives. The Elision subtest was highly sensitive to lower reading skills and was more sensitive than Segmenting Words and Blending Words, even though Blending Words had a higher correlation with reading than Elision. This demonstrates that a group statistic such as a correlational coefficient can sometimes be misleading. However, the Elision has a "task shift" problem

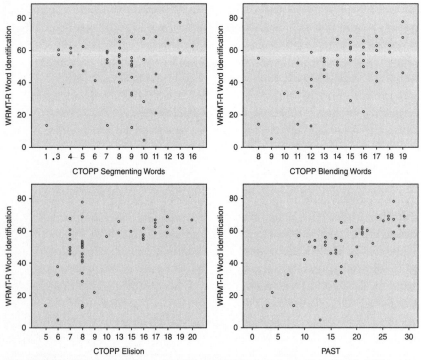

Note: WRMT-R = Woodcock Reading Mastery Test - Revised; CTOPP = Comprehensive Test of Phonological Processing; PAST = Phonological Awareness Screening Test

Figure 6.2 A Comparison of Four Phonological Awareness Subtests with 50 Students in the Winter/Spring of Second Grade

Source: Kilpatrick and McInnis (2015).

(described later in the chapter) that negatively affected its specificity. As a result, some students with average or better reading did not do well on Elision. Segmenting Words and Blending Words both had a high degree of specificity in first grade. Good readers did not do poorly on those tests. The only students who did poorly were the weaker readers (with a single exception on Segmenting Words). However, both of those subtests had poor sensitivity. Many readers in the bottom third did well on those tests. The PAST displayed good sensitivity *and* specificity at both grade levels. If the Elision subtest fixed the "task shift" problem, it would likely display sensitivity and specificity comparable with the PAST.

It seems reasonable to suggest that manipulation tasks represent best practice in phonological awareness assessment. Manipulation tasks have higher correlations with reading than other tasks, have better sensitivity and specificity than other tasks, and appear to incorporate the skills assessed on other phonological awareness tasks. Also, they account for unique variance beyond other phonological awareness tasks, whereas those other tasks do not account for unique variance beyond manipulation. Additionally, manipulation tasks appear to be the best way to assess the advanced phonological awareness skills described in Chapter 4, whereas segmentation and blending tasks only assess basic phonological awareness skills. Finally, phonological manipulation training was found to be far more beneficial in correcting reading difficulties than segmentation or blending training (see Chapter 11). Manipulation tasks include the Elision subtest from the CTOPP-2, the Phoneme Reversal subtest from the original CTOPP, the Deletion and Substitution subtests from the PAT-2, the Lindamood Auditory Conceptualization Test–Third Edition (LAC-3; Lindamood & Lindamood, 2004), and the PAST.

PHONOLOGICAL AWARENESS ASSESSMENT

The two major phonological awareness batteries are the CTOPP-2 and the PAT-2. A good stand-alone test used in many studies is the LAC-3. The Process Assessment of the Learner–Second Edition (PAL-II) has phonological awareness items, but there are few items at each grade level. The CTOPP-2 is recommended over the PAT-2, although practitioners may want to consider acquiring both (to address the subtest reliability issue previously described). An advantage of the CTOPP-2 over the PAT-2 is that the former has norms up to age 24, while the latter only goes to age 9. Also, the CTOPP-2 has tests of phonological short-term memory and RAN. Finally, the CTOPP-2 norm tables are more useful than those of the PAT-2. The standard scores in the PAT-2 norm tables do not consistently align with the percentile rankings. This is likely due to ceiling effects of different subtests at different age levels. However, evaluators are likely to be uncertain about how to interpret a subtest when the standard score is substantially different from the percentile ranking. The PAT-2 has good face validity in that the kinds of tasks found in the battery parallel the kinds of tasks that have been shown by research to be valid, such as deletion and substitution tasks. Also included are simple nonsense word reading subtests based upon different syllable types.

There are concerns about the CTOPP-2 as well. As mentioned, it is not timed, which means that examinees with weak phonemic awareness may use a mental spelling strategy to circumvent their weak phonological awareness and receive an average score. Another significant issue, highlighted in Kilpatrick (2012a), is the shift in task demands that occurs on the Elision subtest. Up until item 8 on the original CTOPP, students are asked to delete a sound from single syllable words. Starting with item 9 (item 19 on the CTOPP-2), students are asked to delete a sound from within a two-syllable word without prior explanation or practice (e.g., "Say *stormy* without saying /m/" → *story*). Once introduced, there are three consecutive items that are similar. No feedback is provided, and the subtest is discontinued when three consecutive items are incorrect. In clinical practice with hundreds of students, I have found many children got all three of these items incorrect, apparently because they did not understand the shift in task demands. For example, on an item like *stormy*, they would respond with *store*, leaving out the rest of the word after the deleted sound. This clinical impression was confirmed in a subsequent study displayed in Figures 6.1 and 6.2. In these figures, a "spike" occurs at items 7 and 8. Many students in this sample (primarily typically developing readers in the winter/spring of first and second grade) scored either 7 or 8 out of 8 before arriving at item 9, where the shift in task expectations occurs. The next three items were apparently unclear because they differed from what had been practiced and administered up to that point. They then got three in a row incorrect and the subtest was discontinued. Testing of limits with many of these students indicated that they usually got some of the items beyond those three correct (monosyllabic words following those multi-syllabic items). This is in contrast to this same group's performance on the other three subtests, which do not shift task demands without explanation and which demonstrated a much smoother spread across items (i.e., no similar "spike" in the other subtests).

Despite these caveats, the CTOPP-2 is highly recommended. It is arguably the most useful normed assessment of phonological awareness available. It should be a "default" element in virtually any evaluation of a student who presents word-level reading difficulties. While the PAST has shown consistently higher correlations with reading (Kilpatrick & McInnis, 2015), it is not a normed test. The CTOPP-2 and the PAST can both be administered due to the brevity of each. They also complement each other, as each has strengths that the other does not. Also, based on the concerns regarding subtest reliability, getting similar results from both the PAST and the CTOPP-2 will strengthen confidence in those results.

Interpreting the CTOPP-2 and the PAST

My first few years of administering the PAST to K–6 students indicated that nearly every student with word-level reading difficulties did poorly on that test. Because it was not normed and it had only been used with weak readers, there was the possibility it was simply a difficult test. Perhaps skilled readers would do poorly also. I field-tested it in 2003 with over 20 typically developing third graders. Their responses were fast and accurate. This prompted several studies of individuals ranging from kindergarteners to college students, average readers, and struggling readers (Kilpatrick & McInnis, 2015). These studies confirmed that typically developing readers do not experience difficulty with the PAST. The Elision subtest and the PAST usually provide similar results given that they are both manipulation tasks.

A cautious approach would be to provide phonological awareness training if either the PAST or the Elision subtest score is low. The PAST has five alternate forms to facilitate progress monitoring. A student's response to high-quality, short-term phonological awareness intervention with progress monitoring is likely to provide a better index of the student's phonological awareness proficiency than a single administration of either Elision or the PAST.

As of this writing, the CTOPP-2 is still fairly new. Thus, not much can be said based on personal experience. However, the test's norms suggest that the amount of phonological awareness skill required to be successful on the Phoneme Isolation test ceilings out earlier than the Elision subtest. One can determine this by looking at the raw scores in the age- and grade-based tables in the manual. This may mean that Elision likely provides a better assessment of advanced phonological awareness skills. This is, however, speculation based upon the CTOPP-2 norm tables.

Interpreting CTOPP-2, PAST, and PAT-2 Performance

As previously discussed, one can increase confidence in the estimate of a student's phonological awareness by administering more than one subtest. The well-equipped evaluation team will have at their disposal the CTOPP-2, the PAST, and one or more other phonological awareness assessments (e.g., PAT-2, LAC-3). The CTOPP-2 has four subtests of phonological awareness/analysis, though typically only three are applicable at any given age range. It also has two blending subtests (Blending Words and Blending Nonwords). It is suggested that at least two of the phonemic awareness/analysis subtests of the CTOPP-2 be given, which can be supplemented with the PAST. This will produce three data points, all generated in a matter of minutes. The PAST has a special role because of the timing element and the orthographic inconsistency of the items, which makes it difficult to compensate via mental spelling. These features of the PAST will influence the possible interpretations of the results. If all three tests are low or high, one can be reasonably confident that the student has weak or strong phonological awareness. However, when the subtest scores are inconsistent, further consideration will be needed.

CAUTION

The PAST is a criterion-referenced test. To avoid practice effects on normed phonological awareness tests, the PAST should be administered *after* any normed phonological awareness tests have been administered.

Before offering suggestions regarding interpreting a "mixed" profile, it must be stated that the PAST should be administered *after* the CTOPP-2, PAT-2, or LAC-3, or the phonological awareness subtests from the achievement batteries. This is because the PAST is not normed while those other tests are. The students in the normative sample of those other tests did not receive another phonological awareness task prior to being administered those subtests. The idea is to avoid a practice effect on the normed tests. Clearly, this is also an issue if one uses both the CTOPP-2 and another normed phonological awareness subtest. Doing them across different sessions does not completely eliminate the possibility of a practice effect, but may diminish it. There is much less concern about the influence of those batteries on the PAST. The PAST is criterion referenced, and the presumption is that because phonological awareness typically develops over months and years, a student with poor phonological awareness is not going to demonstrate good phonological awareness after a previous, 5-minute exposure to another phonological awareness test. However, subtle practice effects could boost performance by a few items and this could potentially affect a scaled score on a normed subtest.

Some students display a mixed profile of scores on phonological awareness subtests. Clinical judgment and hypothesis testing will be needed to interpret these cases. First, if two of the three subtests have a scaled score of 8 or lower, it is recommended that the student receive at least short-term Tier 2 phonemic awareness instruction. However, if only one of the three subtests is weak, one must do a little detective work. If the low subtest was the CTOPP-2 Elision with a younger student, it will be important to examine the "task shift" items. With older students (about third grade on), poor performance on those items suggests a problem. Also, with older students who do average on Elision but poorly on one or two other phonological awareness subtests, an estimate of response time should be made to see if the responses were immediate. Immediate responses likely rule out "mental spelling," whereas delayed responses do not. Also, a mixed profile on phonological awareness tests can be followed up with additional assessments (e.g., PAT-3, LAC-3, or subtests from an achievement battery) or with a short-term trial of Tier 2 phonological awareness instruction with progress monitoring.

Due to the timing element (Caravolas et al., 2005; Vaessen & Blomert, 2010) and its higher correlation with word reading than the original CTOPP subtests

(Kilpatrick & McInnis, 2015), the PAST appears to provide one of the best estimates of a child's level of phonological awareness proficiency. Also, the timing element and the orthographic inconsistency effect of the PAST make it less likely to yield misleading results due to the use of a mental spelling strategy. Also, the PAST involves corrective feedback on every incorrect item, and it presumably would be given after a normed phonological awareness test. These factors give the PAST the advantage that it is unlikely that a student did poorly due to not understanding the nature of the task. Any practice effect would benefit PAST performance; therefore, a poor score on the PAST is all the more significant. Thus, the PAST may be a somewhat more "pure" assessment of phonological awareness, not as likely affected by unfamiliarity with task expectations or by a mental spelling strategy.

Much of the same kind of reasoning would apply to interpreting the PAT-2. However, not much weight should be given to the PAT-2 Segmentation subtest due to the poor sensitivity of phoneme segmentation. However, the Isolation, Deletion, and Substitution subtests of the PAT-2 are all worth considering if one is able to reasonably interpret the norms (i.e., the standard scores align correctly with the percentile rankings). The PAL-II Phonemes subtest also uses deletion items, so if an examiner has access to the PAL-II, the Phonemes subtest is worth considering. As mentioned, the phonological awareness subtests from the achievement batteries must be interpreted with caution because they combine multiple tasks. Low scores on those tests suggest poor phonological awareness, but an average score does not necessarily rule out poor phonological awareness. This is because those scores are based upon multiple phonological awareness tasks, some with relatively low sensitivity to reading difficulties (e.g., segmentation and blending).

Universal Screening of Phonological Awareness After First Grade

The segmentation tasks used on the universal screenings reflect a basic level of phonological awareness. They have a ceiling effect by the end of first grade, but advanced phonological skills develop until third to fourth grade. Some students with milder phonological-core deficits, particularly those with early enriched language and literacy opportunities, may develop early and basic phonological awareness skills at a normal level but fail to develop advanced phonemic skills. For such students, reading difficulties may not surface until second or third grade, or sometimes later. But if a more sensitive phonological awareness screening test is used, one that continues beyond the basic level of phonological awareness, many such difficulties can be caught early, before reading problems become obvious. The CTOPP-2 and the PAT-2 each have only one form, and should therefore be reserved for individual evaluations, not universal screenings. The PAST has five alternate forms, so it is well suited for universal screenings. The drawback is that the PAST takes much longer to administer (3–6 minutes) than most universal screening subtests, though the PAST short form may be useful here.

The Phonological Awareness Screening Test (PAST)

The PAST is provided with this book's supplemental materials. There are six resources included to assist the reader in using it. The first is a research article in preparation that provides validity data from six studies. The results indicate that the PAST consistently yields validity results as strong as, or stronger than, the CTOPP Elision, Blending Words, and Segmenting Words subtests and the Aimsweb Phoneme Segmentation Fluency subtest. Second is a copy of a form of the PAST, the one used in five of the six studies. This form of the test does not have the "orthographic inconsistency" feature previously described. Third is Chapter 11 of *Equipped for Reading Success*, which provides details on administering, scoring, and interpreting the PAST. This information is critical because the PAST is not normed. Rather, it is aligned with typical phonological awareness development from kindergarten through the mastery of sophisticated phonological manipulations, which usually reaches a ceiling around third or fourth grade. Kilpatrick and McInnis (2015) showed that while there were substantial raw score improvements between kindergarten, first grade, second grade, and fifth grade, the profiles of fifth graders who were skilled readers were quite similar to the profile of college students. Fourth, Appendix C in the *Equipped for Reading Success* book contains four alternate forms of the PAST, all of which have the orthographic inconsistency feature. The PAST has been used with typically developing kindergartners, first graders, second graders, fifth graders, and college students. In addition, it has been used with students referred for reading difficulties from kindergarten through 12th grade. Fifth, a short form of the PAST is included for universal screening. Finally, an audio demonstration of the PAST is included.

PHONOLOGICAL BLENDING ASSESSMENT

The nature of phonological blending was presented in Chapters 3 and 4. Many children who display phonological awareness/analysis difficulties achieve average or higher scores on blending subtests, but the reverse is almost never true. Figure 6.1 illustrates this. The CTOPP-2 has a combined phonological awareness composite score that includes the Elision, Blending Words, and Phoneme Isolation subtests. This composite can be misleading if the Blending

Words subtest score is higher than the other two (Marshall, Christo, & Davis, 2013). As mentioned earlier, it is best to avoid composite scores in the context of intervention-oriented assessment. This is especially true here. Marshall et al. (2013) found that struggling readers generally displayed average standard score performance on the Blending Words subtest of the CTOPP (scaled score mean of 9.3) and significantly lower performance on the Elision subtest (mean of 7.5). The correlation between the Blending Words and Elision subtests among the 48 weak readers they assessed was $r = .21$ and was not statistically significant. They point out that the CTOPP manual reports that while the Blending Words subtest displays a moderate correlation with word identification in the general population, the correlation between Blending Words and word identification is very low and not statistically significant among weak readers ($r = .16$; Wagner et al., 1999). As a result of their findings and the data from the CTOPP manual just described, Marshall et al. (2013) do not recommend the use of the CTOPP Phonological Awareness Composite Score with students who display average (or better) performance on the Blending Words subtest and lower performance on the Elision subtest. The CTOPP-2 now has three subtests that make up that phonological composite, rather than two, but continued caution is in order.

The assessment of phonological blending is straightforward. The CTOPP-2 and the PAT-2 have blending subtests, and some cognitive or achievement batteries include a blending subtest (e.g., WJ-IV). Blending is required for successful responses on many deletion tasks (e.g., "Say *sly* without the /l/" → *sigh*) and all substitution tasks (e.g., "Say *sly* but instead of /l/ say /p/" → *spy*), so blending is "embedded" in those tasks. Doing a phonological blending task is no substitute for doing a phonological awareness/analysis task.

Figure 6.1 also illustrates that blending has very strong specificity. A poor score on a blending task provides a strong indication that a student has significant phonological difficulties. Poor blending will inhibit phonic decoding (Chapter 4). If a student displays poor blending performance, this suggests there is a phonological difficulty, and Tier 2 instruction in phonological awareness is recommended. However, in Chapters 10 and 11 it will become clear that phonological blending does not necessarily need to be trained on its own. Phonological awareness training programs that are based on phonological manipulation have phonological blending training built into them.

A Key to Blending: *T* Does Not Say /Tuh/

When giving phonological awareness tests, evaluators must skillfully enunciate phonemes in isolation. For example, the letter *t* does not say /tuh/, it says /t/, which is difficult to pronounce in isolation. When pronouncing the consonant phonemes, there is a common tendency to add a vowel sound (e.g., /buh/, /kuh/, /puh/, /tuh/). However, when doing phonemic awareness or phonics instruction, it is important to pronounce consonants without adding a vowel sound. The word *cat* is not pronounced *kuh-ah-tuh*, so we should not be pronouncing *c* as /kuh/ or *t* as /tuh/. Pronouncing phonemes in isolation requires practice and careful attention. Chapter 12 of the *Equipped for Reading Success* book (included in the supplemental materials) provides detailed guidance on how to properly enunciate the phonemes associated with every letter of the alphabet in isolation. An audio file is also included in the supplemental materials to assist with this.

THE RATIONALE FOR ASSESSING RAPID AUTOMATIZED NAMING AND WORKING MEMORY

Based on current knowledge, there remains uncertainty about the precise relationship between word-level reading and either RAN or WM. This is despite hundreds of studies associating these factors with reading. There are, however, at least six reasons why an assessment of RAN and WM should be a part of a comprehensive evaluation of students with reading difficulties or even a supplement to Tier 1 universal screenings (Catts et al., 2001; Nevo & Breznitz, 2011).

Before describing the importance of evaluating RAN and WM, it is noteworthy that the administration time involved in RAN and WM tests, including instructions and practice, is 1 to 2 minutes each. Thus, for a total of 4 to 5 minutes of assessment time, evaluators can obtain information about two factors that appear to have a substantive impact on reading development.

First, RAN and WM are good predictors of later reading difficulties (Lervåg & Hulme, 2009; Nevo & Breznitz, 2011; Norton & Wolf, 2012; Preßler, Könen, Hasselhorn, & Krajewski, 2014). Second, these skills

> **DON'T FORGET**
> ....
> Tests of rapid automatized naming and working memory require minimal assessment time. For a total time investment of 4 to 5 minutes, evaluators can obtain information about two factors that appear to have a substantive impact on reading development.

> **DON'T FORGET**
> ....
> Tests of both RAN and WM are good predictors of later reading skills. Also, they are good predictors of how well a student is likely to respond to Tier 2 reading interventions.

are good predictors of how well students respond to reading interventions (Al Otaiba & Fuchs, 2006; Stage, Abbott, Jenkins, & Berninger, 2003). When one considers the importance of catching reading difficulties early (a major goal of RTI), these first two advantages of WM and RAN assessment could be combined to suggest that students with WM or RAN deficits may start at a higher intensity of Tier 2 or Tier 3 intervention than Tier 2 candidates without WM or RAN deficits. This means that the brief amount of time invested in the assessment of WM and RAN can yield benefits for intervention planning.

A third benefit would be to determine if RAN or WM deficiencies can account for why a student is not responding well to Tier 2 remedial efforts. This differs from the previous item in that it applies to students receiving Tier 2 for whom there is no previous data on their WM or RAN skills. Weaknesses in RAN and/or WM would suggest a greater intensity of intervention and would clarify that the poor response to intervention cannot simply be accounted for by factors such as effort or the fidelity of the intervention (unless there is evidence to suggest otherwise).

Fourth, knowing that a student has difficulties with WM or RAN changes the equation when interpreting other reading-related scores. For example, it was previously noted that a scaled score of 9 is a borderline score for a phonological awareness subtest. Let's consider a first grader with a 9 on a phonological aware-ness subtest, standard scores in the low 90s on tests of word identification and nonsense word reading, and who has a scaled score of 6 on RAN and a 7 on WM. Such a student does not have the same potential growth trajectory as a stu-dent with the same phonological awareness and word-reading scores but who has a 10 on RAN and 11 on WM. The low RAN and WM scores should lead to a recommendation to strengthen the student's phonological awareness and phonics skills to push these well above the 50th percentile. This would reduce the impact of RAN or WM difficulties since the student would have other strengths to draw upon that are central to the word-reading process. The 37th percentile (i.e., a scaled score of 9 or standard score of 95) does not represent a strong enough skill to minimize the negative effects of poor WM or RAN. By contrast, the student with the same 9 on the phonological awareness subtest and word-reading scores in the mid 90s but good RAN and WM scores would likely need no additional reading help.

Fifth, knowing that a student has a deficit in one of these two skills may affect general teaching strategies when working in a small group or when trying to dif-ferentiate instruction in a large group setting, particularly for students weak in WM. For example, the strategy of breaking down instructions and tasks into smaller units would likely be more beneficial for a student with difficulties in

WM than for a student whose WM is average or better, all other things being equal (e.g., language skills). Using visual prompts and cues, another classic teaching technique, may also provide greater benefit to students with WM difficulties than those with typical WM capacity. For example, phonological manipulation training activities may be accompanied with blocks to represent phonemes, a technique quite unnecessary for most students without WM difficulties. It seems that a large number of the classic special educational techniques are helpful when instructing students with WM difficulties. However, one cannot use *all* of the classic techniques of effective remedial instruction in the same lesson, and many such techniques can slow the pace of instruction for those students who do not need them. Therefore, having knowledge about the WM skills of students in Tier 2 or Tier 3 instruction would help a teacher more effectively plan lessons and select students for small groups. For example, a teachers may want to group together students who would benefit from teaching approaches that work around poor WM and group separately students who would not need such approaches (and whose pacing would be unnecessarily slowed by incorporating such techniques).

A sixth advantage to assessing WM and RAN strays outside intervention-oriented assessment. Even though research shows we can dramatically decrease the number of struggling readers, there is no research to suggest that the percentage of students with reading disabilities will ever reach zero. As a result, even with optimal multitiered intervention, a small percentage of students will be "treatment resistors" (Torgesen, 2000). Because of the pervasive presence of WM and RAN among students with reading disabilities (Fletcher et al., 2007; Hulme & Snowling, 2009; Swanson et al., 2009), having data to indicate the presence of one or both of these may strengthen the validity of a learning disability identification in the area of basic reading (see Chapter 13).

The impact that RAN and WM have on reading is not as pronounced as the impact phonological awareness can have (Pennington, Cardoso-Martins, Green, & Lefly, 2001). There is actually no evidence that they *prevent* children from learning to read, but everything points to the idea that both WM and RAN make learning to read more difficult. The advantages of assessing WM and RAN previously mentioned should justify the 4- to 5-minute time investment to determine whether students struggle with these skills.

Assessing Rapid Automatized Naming

Poor RAN is associated with reading problems (Fletcher et al., 2007; Norton & Wolf, 2012; Pennington et al., 2001; Wagner & Torgesen, 1987; Wolf & Bowers, 1999), though good RAN does not ensure the development of skilled reading.

As mentioned, the precise manner in which RAN affects reading continues to be a source of uncertainty (de Jong, 2011; Lervåg & Hulme, 2009). Some researchers believe that it represents the speed with which one can access rote information from memory; some believe that a more subtle, deficient timing mechanism is involved; still others believe it affects orthographic development (for reviews, see de Jong, 2011; Norton & Wolf, 2012; Lervåg & Hulme, 2009).

Despite uncertainty regarding its relationship to reading, there are three to four general findings in the literature that are widely accepted (de Jong, 2011). First, while RAN for all stimuli (letters, digits, objects, and colors) displays moderate correlations with reading, RAN for letters and digits correlates somewhat more strongly with reading skill than RAN for objects and colors. Second, while moderately correlated with phonological awareness and WM, RAN contributes variance to explaining reading skill independently of phonological awareness and working memory. Third, RAN difficulties are more closely related to word-reading speed than to word-reading accuracy (de Jong, 2011). Additionally, it appears that the relationship between RAN and reading development is unidirectional. In a large, longitudinal study, RAN measures administered prior to the onset of reading instruction (RAN objects and colors) predicted reading growth independently of letter-sound knowledge and phonological awareness, but early reading development did not predict later RAN skills (Lervåg & Hulme, 2009). This narrows the possibilities of the relationship between RAN and reading. Either (a) poor RAN disrupts reading development in some manner not yet determined, or (b) RAN does not disrupt reading development, but problems with RAN and problems with reading are both caused by a third, undetermined factor. However, it appears that RAN problems are not the result of reading problems.

There is no body of research demonstrating that *training* RAN improves reading. However, several studies have demonstrated improvements in RAN following phonological awareness training and substantial improvements in reading (Kerins, 2006; Krafnick et al., 2011; Torgesen et al., 2010; Vaughn et al., 2003; Vukovic & Siegel, 2006; Wolff, 2014). So, while RAN is something that we should assess for the reasons outlined above, it is not a factor that we would attempt to address instructionally. It seems that with intensive phonological awareness training and reading improvements, problems with RAN partially resolve themselves. This is not necessarily inconsistent with the previous comment about the unidirectional relationship between RAN and reading because that longitudinal study (Lervåg & Hulme, 2009) took measures of RAN and reading prior to the onset of reading instruction while the latter set of studies showing RAN improvements involved students who already had reading instruction and demonstrated reading difficulties.

Assessing RAN is quick and straightforward. As illustrated in Figure 3.6 in Chapter 3, a student simply names digits or letters. Students in kindergarten and first grade name colors and objects so as not to confound RAN with delays in letter-name knowledge. The CTOPP-2 has RAN tasks for digits, letters, colors, and objects. The PAL-II has RAN for numbers, letters, and words, as well as what is called a *rapid alternating stimulus* (RAS). An RAS task involves rapidly naming alternative presentations of different categories of stimuli; digits and letters. The PAL-II uses numbers and words (e.g., 8, hop, 67, tree). The DAS-II uses colors, then objects, then a combination of both (blue cat, red horse), each with its own score. The KTEA-3 uses objects then letters (a mix of uppercase and lowercase). The Wechsler Intelligence Scale for Children–Fifth Edition (WISC-V) now has a RAN task. There are additional tests and test batteries on the market that also assess RAN.

Earlier in the chapter, the reader was cautioned to avoid composite scores. However, the RAN composite score from the CTOPP-2 is a notable exception. My experience with hundreds of students has been that the Rapid Digits and Rapid Letters yield very similar scaled score results, typically not differing by more than one scaled score point. Examiners can feel confident about the more reliable composite score than the individual subtest scores.

Assessing Working Memory

There is no consensus regarding the precise manner in which poor WM relates to word-level reading. One possibility is that working memory difficulties disrupt phonic decoding. For example, if a weak reader sounds out the word *institution*, by the time she gets to the ending *-tion*, she has already forgotten the beginning (*in-*). While there may be something to this, it cannot explain why poor WM is associated with problems of basic word reading generally, including short, single-syllable words. A second possibility is that there is no direct, causal relationship between WM and word-level reading. Rather, they are both "symptoms" of weaknesses in phonological skills mediated by the left temporal lobe, or metacognitive skills mediated by the frontal lobes, or both. A third possibility is that while children are reading and encountering new words, they require WM to map the sequence of letters in the written word to the sequence of phonemes in the spoken word, and poor WM involves a limited "work space" for doing that. As a result, those with poor WM are less likely to progress in their word-reading skills than those with adequate WM skills. Although this last possibility is speculative, it is consistent with research on sight-word learning (Ehri, 2005a; Share, 1995).

Currently there is no way to directly remediate WM problems that result in improvements in reading skills. The Cogmed program has a growing body of empirical evidence supporting improvements on WM tasks (e.g., Holmes, Gathercole, & Dunning, 2009), including new, unpracticed WM tasks. However, thus far, generalization to reading-related tasks has not been demonstrated, at least in the short term (Dunning, Holmes, & Gathercole, 2013; Gray et al., 2012), although it may improve math (Dahlin, 2013). Long-term follow-up studies are needed to see if over time, reading acquisition in the presence of improved WM may eventually improve. In other words, it may be unreasonable to expect that WM improvements would result in *immediate* reading improvements. Orthographic mapping suggests that time and exposure to thousands of words are required to build the sight-word lexicon. If WM disrupts the orthographic mapping processes, students may need a fair amount of time using their improved WM capacity to map words as they are encountered in text. However, there has not yet been research to examine this.

On the other hand, this lack of generalization seems to support the view that WM plays an associative but not causal role in reading development. In that view, one would not expect to see reading improvements as a result of WM improvements because there is no causal relationship between the two.

Swanson and colleagues (2009) did a meta-analytic review of the research on working memory and reading. They found that WM, which has an executive functioning aspect, could be distinguished from the more passive phonological short-term memory (STM). Other findings included: (a) students with reading disabilities display difficulties in WM and STM; (b) there is a strong association between verbal/phonological WM/STM and reading disabilities, but a much weaker relationship between visual–spatial WM/STM and reading disabilities; (c) WM and STM difficulties in students with reading disabilities persist over time; (d) while WM and STM correlate strongly with global IQ scores in the general population, there is very little correlation between WM or STM and IQ scores among students with reading disabilities; and (e) WM relates more directly to reading comprehension while phonological STM relates more directly to word-level reading.

The CTOPP-2 Memory for Digits subtest involves digits forward, which seems to be a phonological STM task. In contrast, the Digit Span task from the WISC-V combines digits forward, digits reversed, and digits sequenced into one score. On the surface, digits forward appears to be an STM task, while digits reversed appears to be a WM task. However, the review by Swanson et al. (2009) indicates that both are STM tasks. Digits reversed is not a true WM task (the new digits sequenced aspect of the WISC-V Digit Span was not available for their

2009 review). Thus, the Memory for Digits and Digit Span subtests are roughly comparable when one wants to give two similar tasks. My clinical impression is that the Digit Span score from the WISC-III and WISC-IV more closely aligns with reading and phonological skills than the Wechsler Letter-Number Sequencing subtest. The sentence imitation/memory tasks from some language batteries also measure phonological STM and yield scores consistent with a digit task, though sometimes the additional language demands of a sentence memory task result in discrepancies between sentence memory and digit memory tasks.

An important finding from the Swanson et al. (2009) meta-analysis is that while WM and STM can be distinguished, this distinction is quite small. Although the difference shows up in the statistical analyses of large groups of students, it appears that the size of that difference is too small to be reliably distinguished in individual evaluations. As a result, a common STM type of task such as the Digit Span subtest will likely provide a valid approximate of WM skills in most circumstances.

> ## DON'T FORGET
> ....
> Because phonological processes are central to reading, the assessment of phonological skills should have a correspondingly central role in both universal screenings and in evaluations of students with reading difficulties.

In addition to Memory for Digits, the CTOPP-2 also has another STM subtest, Non-Word Repetition. It involves repeating nonsense words of increasing length. While clearly an STM task, it also appears to measure how well a student can represent a new and unfamiliar phonological sequence in memory. This is not the case with the Memory for Digits subtest, which uses familiar digits as stimuli. As a result, a student's performance on these two CTOPP-2 STM tasks may differ. In such cases, the Phonological Memory Composite score should be avoided.

≡ Rapid Reference 6.1 Key Points About the Assessment of Phonological Skills
....

- Any students demonstrating word-level reading difficulties should have their phonological skills assessed.
- Composite scores of phonological skills should be avoided or interpreted with great caution because they can mask important information about a student's skill profile.

- Scores in the 25th percentile should not be dismissed as "average," but should be addressed because nearly the bottom third of the population struggles in reading.
- Phonological manipulation tasks appear to represent "best practice" compared to other phonological awareness tasks such as rhyming, blending, or segmenting.
- A student's speed of responding to phonological tasks can help judge whether that student is circumventing phonological awareness via a mental spelling strategy.
- There are several good reasons to invest the few minutes needed to assess the RAN and WM of struggling readers.

SUMMARY

Phonological skills play a central role in the development of word-level reading. As a result, the assessment of phonological skills should have a correspondingly central role in both universal screenings as well as in comprehensive evaluations of students with reading difficulties. While the currently available universal screenings have many useful subtests, their phonological awareness assessments are inadequate. As a result, universal screeners should be supplemented by a more sensitive task, such as a phonological manipulation task. The assessment of RAN and WM is also recommended. These could be included on a universal screener because of their brevity and their strong track record of predicting reading difficulties and also predicting responsiveness to reading interventions. The two major phonological awareness batteries on the market at the time of this writing are the CTOPP-2 and the PAT-2. Both have strengths and weaknesses, and school evaluation teams may want to consider acquiring both.

✍ TEST YOURSELF ✍

1. **What is intervention-oriented assessment?**
   (a) A way to improve the identification of educational disabilities.
   (b) A way to make better instructional decisions without needing formalized testing.
   (c) A way to assess children by intervening first and then creating hypotheses based upon their responses to intervention.
   (d) A way to determine why a child is struggling in the first place in order to design better intervention plans.

2. **What is the issue with subtest reliability that kept coming up in this chapter?**
   (a) Individual children routinely show wide ranges of discrepant performances on the same type of subtest from day to day, so subtest results can never be trusted.
   (b) While subtests are reliable in group comparisons because students generally do similarly from one testing of a particular skill to another, occasional variations in this overall pattern decrease confidence in making any important decisions based on a single subtest.
   (c) There are too many skills that need to be evaluated for which there is only one subtest available.
   (d) Subtests from IQ tests can be trusted, but those from achievement tests cannot.

3. **What is the issue with the traditional way normative performance has been labeled?**
   (a) Norms should not be used in the first place.
   (b) Traditional labels of "average" or "low average" have represented such a wide range and have not acknowledged that the bottom third of the population struggles in reading to one degree or another.
   (c) Traditional norms have considered even many typical readers as "below average."
   (d) Norms vary so much from test to test that it is hard to tell what is average.

4. **Why should phonological manipulation tasks be included in a reading-related evaluation rather than simply phonological segmentation or blending?**
   (a) Manipulation tasks can best assess advanced phonemic awareness.
   (b) Manipulation tasks are easier to administer than the other tasks.
   (c) Manipulation tasks are more fun for the students so they try harder.
   (d) All of the above are reasons to include manipulation tasks.

5. **How can students "cheat" on phonemic manipulation tasks?**
   (a) By peeking at the answers on the examiner's answer sheet.
   (b) By speaking with other students who already completed a similar evaluation.
   (c) By using a mental spelling strategy rather than phonemic awareness.
   (d) You cannot cheat on phonemic manipulation tasks.

6. **What is the problem with the phonemic awareness tests on the universal screeners?**
   (a) They rely on phonemic segmentation.
   (b) They do not assess advanced phonemic awareness.
   (c) They discontinue phonemic awareness assessment after first grade.
   (d) All of the above.

7. **What reason was given to justify assessing rapid automatized naming and working memory, even though these cannot be directly remediated?**
   (a) Both predict reading skill development.
   (b) Both predict response to intervention.
   (c) They both take only a few minutes to give.
   (d) All of the above are reasons to assess these skills.

8. **Given that it is not normed, what benefits are there for giving the Phonological Awareness Screening Test (PAST)?**
   (a) It correlates more strongly with reading than most commercially available assessments.
   (b) It has a timing element to further assess phonological proficiency.
   (c) It is free.
   (d) It has five alternate forms.
   (e) All of the above.

9. **Why are the more dedicated phonological awareness tests or batteries (CTOPP-2, PAT-2, LAC-3, PAST) recommended over the phonological awareness subtests found on achievement batteries (e.g., WJ-IV, KTEA-3)?**
   (a) The achievement battery subtests don't use real phonological awareness tasks.
   (b) While the other subtests on achievement batteries are normed, they did not norm the phonological awareness subtests.
   (c) The achievement tests only test segmentation and blending.
   (d) The achievement tests merge multiple tasks into one score, which may mask important details about a student's performance.

10. **All of the following are findings from the meta-analysis on WM and STM by Swanson et al. (2009) except which one?**
    (a) STM is more closely related to word reading and WM is more closely related to reading comprehension.
    (b) STM and WM are so closely related that an STM subtest can be used to estimate WM.
    (c) Digits Forward is an STM task while Digits Reversed is a WM task.
    (d) Students with reading difficulties tend to have difficulties with both STM and WM.

Answers: 1. d; 2. b; 3. b; 4. a; 5. c; 6. d; 7. d; 8. e; 9. d; 10. c.

Seven

ASSESSING PHONICS SKILLS

C hapter 3 indicated that cipher skills are comprised of letter-sound knowledge along with phonological awareness/analysis and blending skills. Cipher skills are a prerequisite for reading any alphabet-based written language. They are essential for both phonic decoding and for developing word-specific knowledge. Aside from rare cases of adults who acquired dyslexia as a result of a stroke or head injury, it appears that all skilled readers can successfully read nonsense words, such as *blem, prupe,* and *strobber.* This means that regardless of whether they were explicitly taught the cipher (via a phonics instructional approach), they have acquired the cipher.

> ### CAUTION
> ....
> Cipher skills are not optional for developing skilled reading in an alphabet-based written language.

Researchers have been aware of the necessity of the cipher for decades. In an article from 1956, Carroll reviewed various studies indicating that even when students were taught to read words as whole units and without instruction in phonics, they still developed letter-sound knowledge (Carroll, 1956). More recent studies have also shown that children taught in kindergarten and first grade by a nonphonic, whole-word method develop phonics and phonemic awareness (Dixon, 2011; Thompson, McKay, Fletcher-Flinn, Connelly, Kaa, & Ewing, 2008; Treiman, Goswami, & Bruck, 1990). Adults who had never been taught phonics can easily sound out nonsense words (Thompson, Connelly, Fletcher-Flinn, & Hodson, 2009). Even when college students were trained on nonsense words in a whole-word fashion using artificial characters for letters, they figured out the sound values of the novel characters and could sound out newly presented, nontrained nonsense words using the artificial characters

(Bitana & Karni, 2003). Also, aside from adult-acquired dyslexia, the research literature appears to lack any cases of fluent readers who cannot correctly pronounce basic nonsense words (Burt, 2006). Thus, regardless of the method used to teach beginning readers, all individuals who become skilled readers eventually develop phonic knowledge simply by interacting with written words (Liberman & Liberman, 1990; Tunmer & Chapman, 2002). This raises the question as to why so many school districts have used methods that do not explicitly and systematically teach the code early in a student's reading development. The classic whole-word and whole-language instructional approaches have placed very little emphasis on learning the code, preferring rather to teach it incidentally, on an as-needed basis (Goodman, 2005). This incidental approach has been shown to be significantly less effective than explicitly teaching the code (Adams, 1990; Brady, 2011, Christensen & Bowey, 2005; Foorman et al., 1998; NICHD, 2000; Share, 1995; Stahl & Miller, 1989).

Even though basic phonics/cipher skills are necessary for skilled reading, they are insufficient for developing skilled word-level reading. There are many reading-disabled "graduates" of various phonics programs who still lag behind their peers in reading. It was mentioned in Chapter 2 that the Wilson and Orton-Gillingham approaches substantially improve phonic decoding skills but do not consistently lead to substantial improvements in sight-word development or fluency. Sight-word learning and fluency require orthographic mapping, which is based on both letter-sound knowledge and more advanced phonemic awareness skills. Neither the Wilson approach nor the Orton-Gillingham approach provides training in the more advanced phonemic awareness/analysis skills. Yet despite the fact that letter-sound knowledge alone is insufficient for skilled word-level reading, it cannot be emphasized enough that phonic knowledge is a necessity for reading an alphabet-based writing system.

ORTHOGRAPHIC KNOWLEDGE

Orthographic knowledge functions on two levels. First, children learn what are permissible or impermissible strings of letters in English (e.g., *nat* is permissible while *tna* is not). This is referred to as *orthotactic awareness* or *graphotactic awareness*. Second, *orthographic knowledge* refers to the accumulation of familiar sequences,

DON'T FORGET

Orthographic knowledge is comprised of (a) *orthotactic* or *graphotactic awareness*, the process by which children surmise what letter orders are permissible and which ones are not, and (b) a data bank of familiar word parts that do not easily yield to letter-by-letter phonic decoding (e.g., -ould, -ing, -tion; kn-, wh-).

whether whole words or word parts. This parallels the concept of word-specific knowledge from the simple view of reading and can be called *pattern-specific knowledge*. Whether rime units (*-ip, -et, -ent, -ist*) or affixes (prefixes: *re-, con-, de-;* suffixes: *-ed, -tion, -ment*), common multiletter units become familiar sequences. As described in Chapters 3 and 4, parts of words such as rime units and affixes become mapped in long-term memory as if they are words (Bowey & Underwood, 1996; Kilpatrick & Cole, 2015).

Orthographic Tasks

Two common experimental tasks that are used to test orthographic skills are the wordlikeness task and the homophone or pseudohomophone task. The *wordlikeness task* assesses the orthotactic awareness aspect of orthographic knowledge. Children are presented with two nonwords and asked to identify which nonword is closer to how a real word would be spelled (e.g., *lmk* vs. *nop* or *ppoun* vs. *pounn*). The *homophone* or *pseudohomophone tasks* assess familiarity with word-specific knowledge. The student must identify a correctly spelled word from one or more foils (e.g., Which is a flower: *rose* or *rows?*). A *pseudohomophone* is a nonsense word that sounds like a real word. For example, a student may be asked: "Which of the following is a part of our bodies: *brain, brane,* or *braine?*"

The Nature of Orthographic Knowledge

Throughout the 1990s and early 2000s, many researchers considered orthographic knowledge to be an additional reading subskill, distinct from phonological awareness and letter-sound knowledge (e.g., Cunningham, 2006; Holmes, 1996). This was based on the finding that tasks that assess orthographic knowledge explained additional variance in word-level reading beyond phonemic awareness and nonsense word reading (Cunningham, 2006; Cunningham et al., 2002). However, more recent research has suggested that orthographic knowledge is better characterized as an advanced form of letter-sound knowledge based upon reading experience (Burt, 2006; Deacon, Benere, & Castles, 2012).

> **DON'T FORGET**
> ....
> Orthographic knowledge appears to be the *product* of learning to read and the reading experience, not a causal factor in learning to read. Thus, any assessment of orthographic knowledge is an assessment of reading development rather than an assessment of reading-related subskills independent of other such skills.

In a longitudinal study, Deacon and colleagues (2012) took an index of orthographic skills from students in February/March of their first-grade year, along with a battery of other reading-related tests. Students used both a wordlikeness test (they had to indicate the "best way" to spell a spoken nonsense word, e.g., *brill* vs. *bbril*) and a pseudohomophone test (they had to indicate which was the correct spelling of a real word (e.g., *boal* or *bowl*). There was a substantial amount of variability among the first graders on these tasks. Deacon and colleagues repeated their assessment in second and third grade (also in February/March of each year) and found that reading skills in first grade predicted third-grade orthographic skills, but orthographic skills in first grade did not predict third-grade reading skills. This is inconsistent with the idea that orthographic knowledge is a distinct reading-related skill that plays a causal role in reading development. Rather, as suggested by Vellutino et al. (1994), orthographic knowledge appears to be a *product* of reading development rather than a causative factor. They considered it a reflection of one's reading skill and reading experience. Bowey and Underwood (1996) supported this suggestion. They found that weaker second-grade readers pronounced *nalk* to rhyme with *talc*, consistent with basic phonic regularities. More advanced second graders, however, pronounced *nalk* to rhyme with *talk*, just like the fourth and sixth graders in the study did. It seems that with more reading experience, typically developing readers begin to notice these common orthographic patterns that are not phonically regular and map them to long-term memory. A comprehensive review of the orthographic research literature by Burt (2006) provides convincing evidence of this conclusion. This conclusion is also consistent with orthographic mapping. Orthographic mapping suggests that readers accumulate unitized memories of common sub-word letter sequences, which would explain performance on orthographic tasks found in experimental studies. Orthographic mapping would predict that reading experience is needed to provide extensive exposure to words so that common letter patterns are perceived and remembered. This is precisely what researchers have found. The amount of exposure readers have to print is related to how well students perform on orthographic tasks (Burt, 2006; Cunningham & Stanovich, 1990). Thus, the additional variance explained by orthographic tasks beyond phonological and phonic tasks may be a function of reading experience (Cunningham & Stanovich, 1990). Not all skilled readers in elementary school read a lot on their own. Two skilled readers can have the same phonological awareness and phonics skills, while one is an avid reader, and one reads far less. Based upon the studies connecting reading experience with orthographic skills (see the review by Burt, 2006), it seems that the unique variance in reading associated with orthographic tasks may be a function of that additional practice and exposure to words, rather than indicating it is a separate reading-related skill, alongside letter-sound knowledge, phonemic awareness, or vocabulary.

It seems that orthographic knowledge is a hybrid between cipher knowledge and word-specific knowledge. Word-specific knowledge could include various kinds of word parts, including spelling patterns that may not necessarily be phonically regular (e.g., *kn-, wh-; -ight, -alk, -ing, -ould, -mb*). Based upon the research just described, orthographic knowledge will not be considered as an additional reading-related skill, but as "advanced" letter-sound knowledge based upon reading experience.

Testing Orthographic Knowledge

Until recently, the orthographic tasks that were used by researchers were not found on commercially available tests, with two exceptions. In the Spelling subtest from the Peabody Individual Achievement Test–Revised (PIAT-R), students do not actually spell words. Rather, they select the correct spelling of a word from among four possible choices, some of which sound the same when pronounced and some of which look similar to the correct word. Also, the PAL-II Word Choice subtest is similar but has two distractor items rather than three.

Presumably to fill this void, the Test of Orthographic Competence (TOC; Mather, Roberts, Hammill, & Allen, 2008) was developed. The TOC is a normed test that allows evaluators to more directly assess orthographic skills using tasks that previously were found only in research studies. The TOC is comprised of several subtests, including tests to assess a student's familiarity with punctuation (e.g., " ", ?, !), abbreviations (e.g., USA, Mr., 3:00), and various printed symbols (e.g., #, &, $, %). The TOC contains two variations of the homophone choice task, which has been shown to correlate with reading skill.

Leading up to the time the TOC was developed and released, most researchers assumed that orthographic knowledge represented its own separate reading skill. As mentioned, more recent research suggests that this may not be the case, so some of the potential usefulness of the TOC might be diminished. However, the TOC may provide an additional index of a child's reading development above and beyond our standard tests. It also has many subtests that may provide an index of early reading experience. It may thus be useful in a comprehensive reading assessment.

Spelling and Orthographic Knowledge

Spelling is an index of orthographic knowledge. It demonstrates that a student knows the correct orthographic representation of a given word. Spelling tests found on most achievement batteries provide the evaluator with a rough estimate of a student's overall orthographic knowledge. They should be interpreted with some caution, however, since other experiential factors can influence how well students spell the specific words on a given subtest (e.g., their parents helped prepare them for spelling tests).

While a student's spelling and word-level reading generally are within a few standard score points of each other, there are times at which students will display spelling performance in the average range when their word-level reading scores are below average. An average spelling score does not rule out that a student has orthographic difficulties because of the multiple reasons why a student may score higher in spelling than in reading. Thus, any such discrepancy should be interpreted cautiously. However, very poor spelling is often an indicator of phonological and orthographic weaknesses, even if reading tends to be average or low average. Poor spelling is often a good indicator of the phonological-core deficit, though average spelling does not rule it out. This tendency must not be interpreted rigidly, because the poor spelling of some students may be more a function of poor motivation or minimal reading and writing experience outside of school. Nevertheless, spelling can sometimes be a window into a student's phonological and orthographic skills. Spelling should thus be included in any reading-related evaluation.

ASSESSING PHONICS SKILLS

The term *phonics* does not have a singular definition, and it is used to refer to a variety of different skills and instructional practices. Instruction in phonics can be divided into different types (synthetic, analytic, and embedded) as well as different levels (basic, simple rules, advanced analysis). More will be said about the types and levels of phonics instruction in Chapters 10 and 11. Most of the commercially available normed tests of phonics skills use nonsense word tasks, which do not presume any particular type or level of phonics instruction.

Nonsense Word Reading Tasks

Nonsense words, also called *pseudo-words*, are pronounceable letter strings that are not English words (e.g., *mib, brust, smand, plibber*). Sometimes the term *nonword* is used, but this is less precise because many nonwords used in experimental tasks

DON'T FORGET

Nonsense word tasks appear to be the best way to evaluate a student's phonics skills. In essence, all unfamiliar words a student encounters are functionally "nonsense" words until they are correctly identified.

are unpronounceable (e.g., *tmk* and *lpba* are not words and are thus *nonwords*). The nonsense word task has been studied extensively, appearing in hundreds of research studies. The correlation between nonsense word reading and real-word reading (including irregular words) varies somewhat with age, but it is consistently high, between $r = .70$ and .90 (Gough & Walsh, 1991; Share, 1995). Nonsense word reading provides a good approximation of a student's phonic decoding skills. A moment's reflection will reveal that all unfamiliar real words children encounter in text are functionally nonsense words until they are correctly sounded out (Ehri & Saltmarsh, 1995; Share, 1995). Also, proficiency in nonsense word reading in fall and winter of first grade is associated with better oral reading fluency in spring of first grade (Harn et al., 2008).

In addition to providing an index of the cipher skills needed for phonic decoding, nonsense words may estimate how well a student is prepared to successfully make use of the self-teaching mechanism described in Chapter 4. Recall that the self-teaching hypothesis is a well-supported theory that states that students who are able to phonically decode words in connected text are able to interact with the orthographic pattern in such a manner that it allows them to encode those patterns in long-term memory for later, instant retrieval. Thus, nonsense word reading tests are some of the most useful tests at our disposal for understanding students' reading skills, as well as for estimating their trajectory of reading progress.

A practical benefit of using nonsense word tests with students in kindergarten through second grade is that in some circumstances, scores on a word identification test may be artificially inflated. Some students with a mild form of the phonological-core deficit have had a great deal of early enriching language and literacy opportunities at home and/or in preschool. As a result, on the basic word identification tasks in first and second grade, such students seem to be on track for typical reading development. But these students are not able to sustain their average word identification over time, as reading increasingly relies on phonic decoding to facilitate the self-teaching phenomenon, which promotes sight-word development. Therefore, when there is a discrepancy between real and nonsense word subtest performance, scores on nonsense word tests may be a more accurate reflection of a student's reading development.

This may even hold true for fourth graders. Spear-Swerling (2004) tested 95 fourth graders on multiple tests of word reading and reading comprehension. She defined low word readers as students who had WRMT-R Word Attack standard scores below 90 but language scores greater than 97 to distinguish them from students who were low overall. Eleven students met those criteria and most of them had word identification scores that were 5 to 19 points higher than their nonsense word reading scores. Eight of these 11 students displayed below-average reading comprehension on one or both of two reading comprehension tests. She concluded that even in fourth grade, nonsense word tests "may be more sensitive indicators of word-level reading difficulties than are measures involving real words" (Spear-Swerling, 2004). Thus, the nonsense word reading test results should not be dismissed when real-word reading subtest scores are average. Typically, students with lower nonsense word reading than real-word reading also show difficulties on phonological manipulation tasks such as the CTOPP-2 Elision subtest or the PAST. With such students, a combination of weaknesses on nonsense word reading and phonological manipulation suggests that an average word-reading score will be very difficult to maintain over time.

Nonsense Word Reading Tests

Over the years, test developers have added nonsense word reading subtests to their achievement test batteries. These subtests provide useful information in reading-related evaluations. The appearance of nonsense word subtests on multiple batteries is particularly advantageous because of the value of using more than a single subtest to evaluate a skill, given the concern with subtest reliability discussed in Chapter 6. The following is not intended to catalog all of the nonsense word reading tasks on the market. However, some general comments are provided.

Timed Versus Untimed Nonsense Word Tasks

Nonsense word reading tasks can be timed or untimed, which has ramifications for interpreting a student's performance. While the three major academic achievement batteries all include tests of nonsense word reading (WIAT-III, KTEA-3, and WJ-IV ACH), as does a classic reading battery (WRMT-III), only the KTEA-3 has a subtest with a timed administration. It is highly recommended that practitioners use the Test of Word Reading Efficiency–Second Edition (TOWRE-2) to supplement the other nonsense word tasks. Adding this to an evaluation involves an extremely minimal time investment. The TOWRE-2 includes two 45-second subtests. One of the subtests involves reading a list of real words (Sight Word Efficiency; see Chapter 8) while the other subtest involves reading a list of nonsense words (Phonemic Decoding Efficiency). The latter appears to be an excellent assessment of a student's proficiency in cipher skills. This is also true of the KTEA-3 Decoding Fluency subtest. This is much like the TOWRE-2 Phonemic Decoding Efficiency subtest in that the student reads nonsense words under timed conditions. There are two differences. On the KTEA-3, there are two 15-second "trials" for a total of 30 seconds of timed nonsense word reading. Second, the words get more challenging much earlier on the KTEA-3 compared to the TOWRE-2, which may be expected given the shorter 15-second time frame for each trial. But the most challenging words from the KTEA-3 are far more difficult than the most challenging words from the TOWRE-2.

Timed nonsense word reading, such as in the TOWRE-2 and the KTEA-3, is arguably a better assessment of a student's cipher skills than the traditional, untimed nonsense word reading tasks. Students who correctly pronounce nonsense words slowly and with effort are not as proficient in their cipher skills as students who pronounce nonsense words quickly and accurately (Harn et al., 2008). Poor proficiency with the cipher not only negatively affects phonic decoding, but also slow and laborious access to letter-sound knowledge is likely to affect the efficiency of orthographic mapping. Orthographic mapping occurs as students encounter words in text. But if the phonological features of those words are not identified rapidly and efficiently, the proper connections in long-term memory are less likely to occur before moving on to the next word.

DON'T FORGET

....

Timed nonsense word reading tests may provide a better assessment of a student's level of proficiency with cipher skills than untimed tests.

There is a practical issue when administering a timed nonsense word subtest. Many students pronounce the words very quickly, and it can be difficult to determine if the pronunciation was correct. Recording student responses for later review (e.g., on your smartphone) seems to be a convenient solution.

Addressing the Subtest Reliability Issue With Nonsense Word Tests

Although it is advisable to use two nonsense word subtests to address the issue of subtest reliability, it is not advisable to use a timed and an untimed subtest as comparable tests for such purposes. Timed and untimed tests can often yield very different scores because these two types of tests likely assess two different levels of cipher skill development. Untimed tests determine how well a student can apply letter-sound skills and blending to pronounce nonsense words in a situation in which phonic decoding is their only focus. A timed test more directly addresses a student's proficiency with the code of written English. In a real-life reading situation, cipher proficiency allows a student to quickly determine phonically regular words and irregular words with the help of context and the set for variability (see Chapter 8). This quick, accurate determination of unfamiliar words does not appreciably detract from comprehension to the degree that slow, laborious phonic decoding might. Also, the instant access to the phonic properties of words facilitates orthographic mapping in real reading situations. The greater the proficiency in phonemic awareness and phonic decoding, the more likely it is that a student will make connections between orthography and phonology and thus expand the sight vocabulary. As a result, timed phonic decoding tasks are preferred over untimed tests.

This means that to properly address subtest reliability, an evaluator would need to administer two untimed nonsense word tests and two timed nonsense words tests. This may seem like a cumbersome practice, but it is not. The TOWRE-2 Phonemic Decoding Efficiency is a 45-second test and the KTEA-3 Decoding Fluency involves two 15-second trials. Untimed nonsense word reading tests typically take 1 or 2 minutes each. Because letter-sound proficiency is essential for both phonic decoding and sight-word memory, the total time investment of 6 to 9 minutes to administer two of each type of test is well justified. For students with word-level reading difficulties, these tests will often represent some of your most valuable assessment information.

In the context of intervention-oriented assessment, it seems that best practice would be to administer both timed and untimed nonsense word reading tests. If both types of test yield low standard scores, then that gives you helpful information in understanding why a student is struggling in reading. However, if the untimed standard score is average, this suggests that a student is farther along in skill development than a student whose scores are low in both. The student low on both needs direct and explicit work with basic phonics and phonemic awareness before one can reasonably expect reading gains. The student with an average untimed score but a low timed score likely requires more practice with phonic decoding. A weak reader with average scores in both (recall that we are considering "average" anything above the bottom third) likely has weaknesses in advanced phonemic awareness. Such a student does not have a problem with the letter-sound portion of orthographic mapping. This leaves the advanced phonemic awareness component as the likely problem. On the other hand, a student who displays good advanced phonemic awareness and a weakness in untimed and/or timed nonsense word reading is likely a student who has had inadequate instruction and/or practice with the cipher skills. Such a student needs work on phonics skills.

As of this writing, there appears to be only three ways to address the subtest reliability issue with timed nonsense word tests. The first is to administer the TOWRE-2 Phonemic Decoding Efficiency and the KTEA-3 Decoding Fluency tests. The second would be to use two of the alternate forms of the TOWRE-2.

A third is to use a timed nonsense word reading subtest from one of the universal screeners along with either the TOWRE-2 or KTEA-3.

It is recommended that any timed nonsense word reading task be administered after an untimed task, and not before. My experience has been that if the timed test is given first, students perform in a rushed manner on the untimed test, despite being told it is untimed.

Given all of these considerations, it is important to reemphasize that the context here is intervention-oriented assessment, not special education diagnosis. While this should not function as an excuse for using inadequate testing practices, it is an acknowledgment of the imprecision of the tests that we use and that the best we can expect from any test is an approximation of the skill level we are evaluating.

Individual Evaluations Versus Universal Screenings

Many schools have nonsense word reading data on all of their students. An advantage of these universal screenings is that they are timed, which likely provides a more accurate estimate of proficiency in phonics skills. Another advantage is that weak nonsense word reading scores may identify at-risk students earlier than most other types of screening measures. It may be tempting to not give much credence to a low nonsense word reading score if the child's other universal screening results are all average. However, particularly for kindergartners and first graders, the nonsense word reading score is typically more sensitive to future reading problems than most of the other screening measures, and therefore it should not be ignored. This does not mean that every student with a low nonsense word reading score needs intensive intervention. However, any such low score should be recognized as a sign of being at risk for a reading difficulty and thus should be addressed, either through more individualized testing or through a trial of Tier 2 intervention with progress monitoring.

> **DON'T FORGET**
> ....
> Timed nonsense word reading subtests, such as on the TOWRE-2 and the KTEA-3, are likely to provide a more valid estimate of a student's letter-sound and blending proficiency and are highly recommended for students struggling in reading.

As mentioned, the nonsense word subtest score from a universal screening can provide a second data point for estimating a student's skills. When a student who scores poorly on the nonsense word portion of a screener is referred for an individual evaluation, a similarly weak performance on a nonsense word subtest from an achievement battery may provide additional evidence of the difficulty.

In such cases, two subtests from different achievement batteries may not be necessary. However, if the nonsense word score is higher on the achievement battery than on the universal screener, it may be due to the fact that the former is untimed and the latter is timed. As already indicated, timed nonsense word tests appear to more

> **DON'T FORGET**
> ....
> Nonsense word reading subtests from universal screenings can supplement commercially available nonsense word tests administered as part of a comprehensive reading evaluation.

accurately estimate proficiency in phonic decoding. In these cases, the evaluator may want to administer the TOWRE-2 to confirm whether the student is weak on timed measures of nonsense word reading.

Nonsense Word Spelling Subtests

While not common on achievement batteries, nonsense word spelling tests (e.g., the Spelling of Sounds subtest from the WJ-IV ACH) provide an estimate of both letter-sound knowledge and phonological segmentation skills. Nonsense word spelling tasks have been used in various research studies (Manis et al., 1993; Swank & Catts, 1994) and they highly correlate with spelling, phonic decoding, and phonemic awareness. However, as Sprenger-Charolles, Siegel, and Bonnet (1998) have pointed out, nonsense word spelling is actually easier than real-word spelling because there is often more than one correct answer (e.g., /mōk/ could be correctly spelled *moke* or *moak*). Thus, nonsense word spelling is an index of basic phonic knowledge and phonemic awareness, but not orthographic knowledge, since the latter is concerned with the precise spelling of specific words or sub-word letter patterns.

Although nonsense word spelling tests are highly correlated with nonsense word reading and phonemic segmentation, they should never replace nonsense word reading or phonological awareness testing. Yet because such tests appear to rely upon skills that overlap with both letter-sound knowledge and phonemic awareness, they can provide evaluators with additional information.

Interpreting Norms on Nonsense Word Reading Tests

The discussion in Chapter 6 about interpreting norms on phonological awareness tests applies equally to nonsense word reading. Because the lowest one quarter to one third of students display reading skills substantially below curricular expectations, we must avoid using the traditional norm-referenced "cutoff" scores regarding what is considered "average." Rather, any student whose nonsense word reading is consistently in the bottom third when given multiple tasks, particularly on a timed nonsense task, should be considered at risk. So, for example, if the student receives a standard score of 88, 90, or even 92, traditionally these would be considered average or low average because they are within a standard deviation of the mean. However, these scores represent the 21st through 30th percentiles, which is consistent with the range routinely identified by national assessments as representing reading below a basic level. There is no suggestion here that the cutoff for designation for special education services should be more lenient. Rather, in the context of intervention-oriented assessment, the goal is to get a more accurate idea of which children should be receiving additional Tier 2 intervention.

Phonics skills are quite correctable, so there is no reason for allowing a student to struggle in reading when the student could perform much better with effective, short-term interventions. However, it will be seen in Chapter 11 that some students get "stuck" in their progress in phonics. These students have inadequate phonemic awareness. When the phonemic awareness issues are addressed, students then make very strong gains in phonics skills. Also, as previously mentioned, one should not assume that a large portion of students would require Tier 2 intervention if the school district is carefully implementing the Tier 1 prevention approaches described in Chapter 10.

Nonsense Word Reading and Phonological Awareness Skills

CAUTION

Nonsense word reading should never be used as a substitute assessment for phonological awareness skills. For students who struggle in reading, nonsense word reading and phonological awareness should both be assessed.

Nonsense word reading is not an adequate substitute for phonological awareness assessment, even though nonsense word reading is often considered to be one of the phonological processing skills. Although there is a close relationship between nonsense word reading and phonological awareness, when nonsense word reading is weak, providing only additional phonic decoding instruction is not likely to achieve the desired results (see Chapter 11). The most common reason a student struggles in nonsense word reading is due to poor phonological awareness and blending skills, although factors such as reading experience and motivation can also play a role. Nonsense word reading and phonemic awareness assessment are both essential for readers who struggle with word-level reading. A student who has strong phonemic awareness performance, even when rigorously assessed, but has poor phonic skills, is likely to be a student who has had limited code-based reading instruction and/or inadequate practice.

The most obvious phonological skill that affects performance on nonsense word reading tasks is phonological blending. Students with poor blending skills will not be able to efficiently blend isolated letter sounds into correct pronunciations of nonsense words. Data from the CTOPP-2 or PAT-2 blending subtests can help determine whether phonological blending deficiencies are interfering with nonsense word test performance.

Phonics Assessment and the Subtypes of Reading Difficulties

Students with the hyperlexic pattern typically perform average or better on reading nonsense words. Students with the dyslexic, mixed, and compensator patterns are all likely to display nonsense word reading scores in the bottom third of the normative distribution. Some will have extremely low scores at or below the 2nd percentile. This is because most of these students have varying degrees of the phonological-core deficit, and poor nonsense reading is one of the common symptoms of that deficit. Kilpatrick (2014b) found that timed nonsense word standard scores were, on average, 8 to 9 points lower than untimed subtests in the 22 compensating students studied. Students with the dyslexic pattern may also have higher untimed nonsense word reading scores than timed scores, particularly if they have received additional phonics help. Thus, timed nonsense word reading seems to be an indispensable element of a reading assessment.

Nonsense Word Reading and Reading Comprehension

There is a substantial correlation between nonsense word reading and reading comprehension, particularly in the early grades (Nation, 2005; Perfetti & Hogaboam, 1975). In the context of the research on the self-teaching hypothesis and orthographic mapping (Chapter 4), this is not surprising. Nonsense word tests may shed light on the source of reading comprehension difficulties not apparent from word identification tests. Recall that in the simple view of reading, reading comprehension is a function of oral language comprehension and word-level reading. Some students with strong oral language comprehension may have adequate word identification scores, suggesting that word-level reading is not the source of their weakness in reading comprehension. However, in some of these cases, the nonsense word subtest (and/or a phonemic awareness subtest) may indicate otherwise. If a student has an average word identification score (e.g., a standard score of 95 to 105) but a lower nonsense word reading score (e.g., below 90), this suggests that the word identification process may be effortful. This type of student fits the compensator pattern of reading difficulty and typically has a strong verbal IQ score. Because of the effort that goes into identifying the words, reading comprehension is compromised. This is precisely what Spear-Swerling (2004) found with a group of fourth graders. Students who struggled with reading comprehension on state-mandated tests had nonsense word reading scores that were between 5 and 19 standard score points below their word identification scores.

Phonics Assessment and Phonics Instruction

The foregoing discussion presumes that the educational evaluation is intended to determine why a student is struggling in reading. The types of assessment described all provide general information regarding a student's skill level in phonics. The value of these assessments is to identify whether phonics skills are affecting a student's reading difficulties and to estimate the severity of any such problem. However, these normed tests do not provide much information about the specifics of what elements of phonics skills are weak or missing. By contrast, there are many criterion-based assessments of very specific elements of phonic knowledge. Some are commercially available assessments and others are free online. These criterion-referenced assessments will index the particular letter-sound combinations that the student knows, such as the various letters, blends, digraphs, and diphthongs, which can aid instructional planning.

≋ *Rapid Reference 7.1 Key Points About the Assessment of Phonics Skills*

- Nonsense word reading tests appear to be the best way to assess phonics skills.
- Timed nonsense word reading tests likely provide a better index of a student's proficiency in phonic decoding than untimed tests.

SUMMARY

Like phonemic awareness, the assessment of phonics skills should be a central component of any assessment of struggling readers. Nonsense word reading tasks appear to be the most efficient way to assess phonics skills. There are several test batteries on the market that contain a nonsense word reading subtest. It would be easy to administer two of these so that practitioners can get a reliable index of a student's skill. Timed nonsense word reading tasks are likely to provide a more valid assessment of a student's phonic decoding proficiency. Nonsense word reading tasks, particularly timed ones, can sometimes uncover a difficulty or potential difficulty in reading that may not be obvious from word identification tasks, particularly for the compensating type of student.

🐾 TEST YOURSELF 🐾

1. **All of the following are true about phonic knowledge except:**
   (a) Typically progressing readers develop phonic knowledge even if not directly taught.
   (b) Phonic knowledge is not essential for skilled readers, even if it is helpful for weak readers.
   (c) Phonic knowledge is best assessed with nonsense word reading tests.
   (d) Some basic phonic knowledge is a necessary prerequisite for reading in an alphabet-based orthography.

2. **All of the following are true about orthographic knowledge/skills except:**
   (a) Orthographic skills strongly correlate with word-level reading skills.
   (b) The most recent research suggests orthographic knowledge/skills to be an independent reading subskill largely unrelated to phonics and phonemic awareness.
   (c) Common ways to assess orthographic knowledge are with homonym-based tasks and wordlikeness tasks.
   (d) There is now a test of orthographic knowledge/skills on the market.

3. **All of the following are features of orthographic knowledge except:**
   (a) Knowledge and awareness of common patterns in written English (e.g., -alk, -ight).
   (b) Good spelling skills.
   (c) Having a good understanding of the meanings in words with familiar spelling patterns.
   (d) An awareness of which spelling patterns are permissible and which are not (e.g., *bbrin* is not acceptable but *brinn* is).

4. **All of the following are true about using nonsense word subtests except:**
   (a) They provide a direct assessment of which type of phonics instruction a child has received (i.e., synthetic, analytic, embedded).
   (b) They help assess letter-sound knowledge.

(c) They help assess phonic decoding skills.

(d) They help predict likely progress in real-word reading.

5. **Timed and untimed nonsense word reading tests pretty much assess the same thing, so both do not need to be given.**

(a) True

(b) False

6. **Though it is highly recommended, what is the one caveat when using the TOWRE-2 Phonetic Decoding Efficiency subtest?**

(a) The test is too short to get any reliable information.

(b) The test has too many unusual words.

(c) Many children read nonsense words so fast, evaluators should consider audio recording student responses to check later.

(d) All of the above.

7. **What does a nonsense word spelling subtest (e.g., WJ-IV Spelling of Sounds) evaluate?**

(a) Phoneme segmentation and letter-sound knowledge.

(b) Phoneme blending and letter-sound knowledge.

(c) Phoneme segmentation and phoneme blending.

(d) Phoneme manipulation and letter-sound knowledge.

8. **What level of performance on nonsense word reading tests would indicate there is no concern with phonic decoding so no additional help in that area would be recommended?**

(a) Any score above the 16th percentile.

(b) Any score above the 20th percentile.

(c) Any score above the 25th percentile.

(d) Any score above the 34th percentile.

9. **If children get stuck in their development of phonic skills**

(a) They are not likely to make much progress until any underlying phonological awareness deficits are addressed.

(b) They should be encouraged to shift to a whole-word approach.

(c) They should continue with the same regimen of phonics instructions until they finally get it.

(d) They should be encouraged to rely on contextual guessing.

10. **Commercially available tests that involve timed nonsense word reading include**

(a) WJ-III ACH and PIAT-R.

(b) WIAT-III and WRAT-4.

(c) TOWRE-2 and KTEA-3.

(d) All of the above have timed nonsense word reading subtests.

Answers: 1. b; 2. b; 3. c; 4. a; 5. False; 6. c; 7. a; 8. d; 9. a; 10. c.

Eight

ASSESSING WORD IDENTIFICATION AND READING FLUENCY

Word-level reading skills are foundational to reading comprehension. The correlation between isolated word-level reading and reading comprehension is quite high (Fletcher, Lyon, Fuchs, & Barnes, 2007; Hulme & Snowling, 2009; Hoover & Gough, 1990; Nation, 2005; Perfetti & Hogaboam, 1975). Three of the four patterns of reading problems (dyslexic, mixed, and compensating) involve word-level reading difficulties. It is only hyperlexics who do not struggle with this aspect of reading.

Reading fluency is also highly predictive of reading comprehension (Desimoni, Scalisi, & Orsolini, 2012; Fletcher et al., 2007; Hulme & Snowling, 2009; Nation, 2005). It may not be surprising that isolated word reading, such as the kind assessed on traditional word identification tests, correlates strongly with fluency (Fletcher et al., 2007; Hulme & Snowling, 2009; Nation, 2005). This appears to support the view described in Chapter 4 that fluency is generally a byproduct of having a large sight vocabulary of instantly accessible words. In a longitudinal study from first to third grade, Eldredge (2005) found that the development of phonics skills preceded the development of skilled word recognition, which in turn preceded the development of reading fluency. This chapter focuses on the assessment of both isolated word reading and reading fluency.

THE ASSESSMENT OF WORD-READING SKILLS

Currently, there are no word-level reading tests that were developed based on the concept of orthographic mapping. However, for evaluators who are familiar with how word-level reading works (see Chapters 3 and 4), as well as how word-level reading does *not* work (see Chapter 2), the available crop of word-reading tests can be used to help develop reasonable hypotheses about why a child struggles in word-level reading. Also, in the last two decades, more tests and subtests have become available that can help evaluators distinguish between word recognition and general word identification.

Nearly all of the traditional context-free word identification tests confound instant word recognition, phonic decoding, and guessing. This means that students can identify unfamiliar words on such tests via phonic decoding and guessing. They receive the same score whether they guess or instantly recognize the words from memory. Clinical impressions may help here, as we watch the student respond to the words. However, due to the inherent confound on these tests, the actual scores generated may be limited in what they tell us about why a student struggles in reading.

> **CAUTION**
> ....
> Nearly all of the traditional context-free word identification tests confound instant word recognition with phonic decoding and/or guessing.

Phonic Decoding on Word Identification Tasks

The obvious way to provide a correct response to an unfamiliar word on a word identification task is through phonic decoding. A student can develop decent phonic decoding skills and still have a limited sight vocabulary. Such a student may achieve a fairly normal word identification score because many items on a word identification task can be sounded out. The Word Identification sub-test from the WRMT-R (Woodcock, 1998) has some words that illustrate this point. Many students mispronounce the words *passage* and *yardage* as *pass'-āge'* and *yard'-āge'* stressing both syllables in these words and inappropriately making the *a* in the second syllable a long *a*. If these were familiar words to those students, this rigid application of phonic decoding would not be necessary, and they would be pronounced properly. Another example is a common phenomenon in which items 65 to 69 (which are not easy to sound out: *urgent, mechanic, wounded, zenith,* and *petroleum*) are all mispronounced, and students are about to hit the ceiling of six items in a row incorrect. When they come to numbers 70 and 71, which are the words *stigma* and *spectacular*, students often correctly identify both of these. These words are easy to phonically decode, and they have no obvious competitors (i.e., words that look similar). In cases like this, students are not instantly recognizing familiar words but are using phonic decoding to arrive at the correct answer. This illustrates how standard word identification tests do not distinguish between correct responses based on known words versus correct responses to unknown words that are phonically decoded during the test.

Guessing Correctly Without Context

Most word identification tests consist of a graded word list, so any guessing is not based on context. But there are two factors that can influence a student's guessing. First, a child can correctly guess a word that has been partially decoded phonically (Share, 1995; Tunmer & Chapman, 1998, 2012). Recall the concept of the set for variability described in Chapter 4. This allows students to determine unfamiliar words that are either irreg-

> **CAUTION**
> ....
> Students can correctly determine many unfamiliar words on traditional word identification subtests via phonic decoding and the set for variability. The use of timed tests helps minimize this concern, and these are likely better estimates of the size of a student's sight vocabulary.

ular or are regular but that the student did not accurately decode phonically. Tunmer and Chapman (2012) found that those with better oral vocabularies were better at determining words based upon the set for variability. This has important significance for both older dyslexics and compensators. As children grow older, their oral vocabularies increase and they are presumably more able to correctly determine unfamiliar words based upon the set for variability. Also, compensating students tend to have strong vocabulary skills and are thus more capable of using the set for variability for determining words presented on untimed word identification tests.

The second factor overlaps with the first. Words that have few or no "competitors" in the child's phonological or semantic lexicons are more likely to be correctly guessed than words with more competitors. A *competitor* is a word that looks or sounds similar to the target word. If a word has few (or no) competitors, the child's choices for guessing are narrowed considerably. Examples from the WRMT-R Word Identification illustrate this (Woodcock, 1998). The word *beautiful* is phonically irregular. However, in a young child's phonological or semantic lexicon, there are few words that are likely to come to mind while trying to phonically decode the word *beautiful*. Other words from that test have a similar property, in that they do not have many competitors in the lexicon of an elementary-level student. Many words on word identification subtests do not easily yield to phonic decoding. It may thus be tempting to assume that if a student correctly pronounces these irregular words, they must be known words. By contrast is a word such as *expert* from the WRMT-R. This word is phonically regular, but students weak in phonic decoding may not be able to completely sound it out. A common response to the word *expert* is the word *expect*. The word *expect* is more common in the vocabulary of an elementary school student than *expert* (Zeno, Ivens, Millard, & Duvvuri, 1995) and is thus a strong competitor.

Low scores on a word identification test can reliably indicate that a student has a weak sight vocabulary. However, a low average or average score on a word identification subtest does not provide us with confidence that a student has a good sight vocabulary. The use of phonic decoding, the set for variability, and the presence of words with few or no competitors can combine to help students correctly identify many unknown words on these tests.

> ## CAUTION
>
> Low scores on a word identification test can reliably indicate a student has a weak sight vocabulary. However, low average and even average scores on word identification subtests do not guarantee a student has an adequate sight vocabulary. Students can use phonic decoding and the set for variability to identify unknown words on these tests.

UNTANGLING THE CONFOUND BETWEEN WORD RECOGNITION AND WORD IDENTIFICATION

It should be clear, then, that phonic decoding and instant word recognition are inherently confounded in our traditional word identification subtests. Why is this a concern? Recall from Chapter 4 that reading fluency appears to be based primarily upon the size of the student's sight vocabulary. Typically developing students can often read words three times faster than students with reading disabilities, regardless of whether they are reading from a list or reading in context (Jenkins et al., 2003). As a result, word-level reading fluency is a key factor that distinguishes skilled readers from struggling readers. There are two approaches to avoiding the inherent confound between sight-word recognition and correctly identifying unfamiliar words in reading tests. If combined, these two approaches could effectively eliminate this confound. Unfortunately, it appears that there are no tests currently available that use both of these approaches.

The first way to distinguish between instant word recognition and on-the-spot phonic decoding is with a timed, graded word list. A reader's verbal response to a familiar word typically begins in less than a second. So, if a student requires a longer initial response time, such as a full second or longer, to correctly identify a word, it suggests that the word is not in the student's sight-word vocabulary. Recall that we have no evidence that words in a student's sight vocabulary may be accessed slowly. As mentioned in Chapter 4, the difference in speed of access to *known* words can vary based upon a variety of factors. But this speed difference requires specialized timing equipment because it only involves about 1/10th of a second. Because we cannot notice such subtle speed differences, all sight words appear to come out in a fairly similar, instantaneous manner. This suggests that words correctly responded to within a second are likely to be sight words, and those with slower responses are not likely to be sight words. Rapid Reference 8.1 highlights informal ways to determine whether a word a student is reading is a sight word. These can be passed along to teachers, though experienced teachers will be familiar with many of these.

≡ Rapid Reference 8.1 Informal Indicators That a Word a Student Reads Is Not in the Student's Sight Vocabulary

Although none of the following are 100% reliable, they provide a good general idea about which words a child has in his or her sight vocabulary and which ones are being phonically decoded or guessed on the spot.

- The child can get the word correct in context, but not in isolation.
- The child pronounces a particular word inconsistently.
- It takes the child 1 second or longer to begin a response to the word.
- The child pronounces the word slowly.
- The child self-corrects.
- The child pauses during the correct pronunciation of the word.
- The child puts the stress/accent on the wrong syllable.
- The child pronounces the word with at least one unusual sounding vowel or consonant, different from how the child would say the word orally.

A word is in a student's sight vocabulary when the word is consistently pronounced correctly, instantly, and effortlessly, without benefit of context.

A second approach would be for the word identification test to include only irregular words. This is not as powerful of a solution as a timed test because of the phenomenon of the set for variability.

The Test of Irregular Word Reading Efficiency (TIWRE; Reynolds, & Kamphaus, 2007) uses only irregular words. This test has three forms for multiple administrations, and the student's protocol is designed to accommodate all three forms of the test (i.e., three protocols are not required for three administrations). Unfortunately, the TIWRE is untimed, so students can use the set for variability to identify words correctly, even though the words are not in their sight vocabularies. My only experience with this test was at the middle school level. It seems that there is a rather hard shift midway through the test from relatively easy and common irregular words to relatively difficult and uncommon irregular words. I used this for triennial evaluations and a few initial evaluations and found that middle school students tended to respond correctly to most of the easy items and missed most of the more difficult items. The result was that almost all of these middle schoolers received a standard score between about 88 and 94, regardless of how well they did on other word identification tests. If the TIWRE was a timed test and did not have the apparent hard shift in task difficulty, it could be one of the best tools available for reading-related evaluations. Because of its use of only irregular words, it would likely be a much more valid index of a student's sight vocabulary than conventional subtests that mix regular and irregular words. However, in its current form, it is unclear how it adds to existing word identification tests, at least with secondary students. The easier items mentioned might not be so easy for first through third graders who are struggling readers and who can make less use of the set for variability. At those levels, I suspect that the TIWRE may provide useful information about sight-word development to supplement standard word identification tests. Also, it is very brief to administer.

Estimating Word Recognition With Timed Measures

One of the best tools we now have available for reading-related assessments are timed, context-free, word-level reading tasks (Clements, Shapiro, & Thoemmes, 2011; Compton & Carlisle, 1994; Constantinidou & Stainthorp, 2009). Since 1999, the Test of Word Reading Efficiency (TOWRE) has provided evaluators with such a timed measure (now the TOWRE-2). Also, for nearly as long, the Test of Silent Word Reading Fluency (TOSWRF, now the TOSWRF-2) has also provided a timed word-reading measure in a very different format than the TOWRE/TOWRE-2. The KTEA-3 also has a timed word-reading test. There are other timed tasks that will be discussed later under the topic of fluency. Here the discussion is limited to timed, context-free word identification tests.

The TOWRE-2
The TOWRE-2 has two subtests, the second of which was described in Chapter 7 (Phonemic Decoding Efficiency). The first subtest, Sight Word Efficiency, is a 45-second test in which a student reads from a list of words of increasing difficulty. Only correct items make up the total score. Thus, if one student got the first 50 items in a row correct in 45 seconds (i.e., 50/50) and another student

attempted 60 but got 10 of those incorrect (50/60), each student would receive the same score of 50. Because of the timing element, students who rely on sounding out words will get a lower score, with lower scores suggesting a weaker sight vocabulary. Often, the standard score from the TOWRE-2 is fairly close to the standard score of an untimed test. However, with a substantial number of weak readers at the elementary level, their TOWRE-2 scores will be 5, 10, or even 15 standard score points below their untimed word identification.

The TOWRE-2 is not suitable for pairing with an untimed test to address the issue of subtest reliability. Another timed test would be needed for that, such as the TOSWRF-2, the KTEA-3 Word Recognition Fluency, or one of the alternative forms of the TOWRE-2 administered on a different day.

TOWRE-2 Caveat

From my 13 years using the TOWRE with hundreds of students in school-based evaluations and in research studies, I have found that the TOWRE has not been as useful at the middle school and high school levels as it is with elementary students. This appears to be due to the construction of the test. Whether students are in grade 1 or grade 12, they all start at

> **CAUTION**
>
> Because there are so many fairly basic words in the TOWRE-2 Sight Word Efficiency subtest and only a 45-second time limit, it appears to be a good estimate of sight vocabulary for younger students but not older students.

the same place and are allotted the same 45-second time limit. The problem is that 45 seconds does not allow older students to reach the challenging words. In fact, compared to most word identification subtests, even the most difficult items on the TOWRE-2 do not appear to be particularly difficult for average secondary level students.

It was mentioned in Chapter 4 that after a large number of exposures, even weak readers eventually map words to long-term memory. Because they are so inefficient at this, however, they have a limited sight vocabulary. Yet the limited sight vocabularies of middle school and high school students with reading problems appear to include most of the easier words on the TOWRE/TOWRE-2. As a result, they respond to the many easy words on the test very quickly, and not much slower than their typical peers (i.e., once a word is "mapped" to permanent memory, they read that word as quickly as a typically developing reader). It is not uncommon for weak, older readers to achieve a scaled score that is 5, 10, or more points *higher* than their untimed word identification. This pattern is the opposite of the pattern mentioned with the elementary students. With the elementary students, the TOWRE-2 pushes up against the limits of their sight vocabularies. However, for older students, this does not appear to be the case. While my experience has been with the TOWRE, and only more recently with the TOWRE-2, the item difficulty appears to be similar in the revised edition. It would seem that the TOWRE-2 would be much more useful with older students if either: (a) the test went to a full minute with the older students and had more difficult items toward the end, or (b) if older students had a different set of words and did not have to go through so many easy words before getting to more challenging words. As it is, the TOWRE/TOWRE-2 does not appear to do an adequate job assessing the sight vocabulary of older students, unless their reading difficulties happen to be very severe.

Nonetheless, the TOWRE-2 is highly recommended, particularly with K–5 students. It has a very brief administration time, it has alternative forms, and it was co-normed with the CTOPP-2. For elementary-level students, it is one of the best ways to estimate the relative size of a student's sight vocabulary.

KTEA-3 Word Recognition Fluency

The Word Recognition Fluency subtest from the KTEA-3 is similar to the TOWRE-2 Sight Word Efficiency test. Both involve a timed, graded word list. Word Recognition Fluency has two sections, A and B, both involving two 15-second "trials" of reading context-free words. Section A is for grades 1 and 2 only and uses very basic words and does not get more difficult as the test progresses. The average first grader should be able to read most or all of these words, so the assessment is more like a RAN task with words and does not provide an estimate of the size of the sight vocabulary. Section B works the same way but begins with very basic words and quickly progresses to more difficult words. It goes from grades 3 to adulthood. The words toward the end of each 15-second trial are much more difficult than the most difficult words on the TOWRE-2. This appears to provide a resolution to the caveat regarding the TOWRE-2 previously described. For older students, Word Recognition Fluency appears to provide a better estimate of the size of a student's sight vocabulary. However, this is a new test at the time of writing, so any comparisons with the TOWRE-2 represent speculation based on their relative properties, particularly the difficulty level of the words on each test.

The TOSWRF-2

The TOSWRF-2 is an unconventional reading test. The task used in the TOSWRF/TOSWRF-2 has existed for decades in research studies, and it is very fortunate to now be available as a normed, commercially available test. With instructions and practice, the total test administration takes about 5 or 6 minutes

Table 8.1 The Type of Lines a Student Sees on the TOSWRF-2 Representing Three Levels of Difficulty (None Are Actual Lines From the Test)

Location on Page	Text Line Seen by Student
Line toward the top of page	catwhofunpopandseewhytreehandbackwashnowtab
Line toward the middle	windowstandhelperapplemodernwatermessagecapture
Line toward the bottom	incapacitatenonethelesstraversesubstantialrealistic

and can be administered individually or in a group. The test itself is 3 minutes. Students are given a sheet of paper with many lines of words, and the words do not have spaces between them (see Table 8.1 for examples). The student is required to put a slash mark in between each of the words. To be able to do this, the student must either recognize these words as familiar or sound them out to determine where the word breaks are. This task appears to be very sensitive to the size of an individual's sight vocabulary. As a side note, teachers strongly influenced by whole language might consider this task to be "inauthentic." While this may not satisfy their concerns, it could be pointed out that spacing between words is a late invention in alphabetic scripts. One need only look at ancient Greek and Latin inscriptions, as well as letters and documents written from ancient times. All of the words ran together without spaces between them. Trivia aside, a key feature of words in our sight vocabulary is that they effortlessly pop out at us. Therefore, students with extensive sight vocabularies have very little difficulty with this task. Students with limited sight vocabularies have far fewer words that pop out at them, so this task is difficult. The timing element appears to effectively separate students with large sight vocabularies from those with limited sight vocabularies.

TOSWRF-2 Caveats

I found a similar difficulty with the TOSWRF as I found with the TOWRE. It seems that within the time allotted, many struggling middle school and high school students do not get to the more challenging words. They are able to quickly recognize the easier words, because those words are in their limited sight vocabularies. As a result, the TOSWRF-2 seems better suited for elementary-level students. However, others may have a different experience with this test than I have had. Also, it is unclear why the TOSWRF-2 test has a 3-minute time limit. It seems that the test could easily be between 1 and 2 minutes, with fewer easy words toward the beginning. A final comment is that this test presumes normal fine motor skills, particularly motor speed. Granted, motor skills would not commonly be an issue, yet it is something that evaluators may need to consider in those cases in which fine motor skills may be a factor.

With these caveats, the TOSWRF-2 is also a highly recommended test, particularly at the elementary school level. Like the TOWRE-2, the TOSWRF-2 is one of the very few normed tests available that directly examines the scope of the child's sight vocabulary, uncontaminated by the confounding factors on standard word identification subtests. As long as there are no fine motor issues, particularly motor speed, the TOSWRF-2 can provide examiners with valuable information about whether a student has an adequate sight vocabulary relative to her peers.

> **DON'T FORGET**
> ....
> The TOWRE-2 Sight Word Efficiency test, the KTEA-3 Word Recognition Fluency test, and the TOSWRF-2 test are all recommended ways to assess the size of a student's sight vocabulary. As timed tests, they reduce the confound between word recognition (accessing known words) and identifying unknown words via phonic decoding and the set for variability.

WIAT-III Word Reading

On the Word Reading subtest from the Wechsler Individual Achievement Test–Third Edition, the examiner can mark whether a student responded in less than 3 seconds. However, that allows plenty of time to correctly respond to an unfamiliar word. Thus, this aspect of the WIAT-III Word Reading does not appear to have much usefulness. Instant recognition of known words involves a response that begins in under a second.

WORD IDENTIFICATION SUBTESTS

Little needs to be said about the traditional word identification subtests because they are familiar to those doing educational evaluations. These tasks/subtests are standard on almost every achievement battery that assesses reading. This type of word-reading task has been used in hundreds of research studies. Based upon group statistics, such subtests display a great deal of validity in terms of strong and predictive correlations with reading fluency and reading comprehension. However, when interpreting the test profile of an individual student, caution must be taken because of the confounding factors inherent in these traditional word identification subtests, discussed earlier. Before moving on to interpreting word-reading tests, there are other formats for word-level reading tests that should also be considered. For example, the WJ-IV ACH has three word-level reading subtests in addition to the Word Identification and Word Attack subtests, two of which are new to this edition of the WJ-IV ACH.

Word-Level Reading in Context

New to the WJ-IV ACH is Oral Reading, a word-level reading test that assesses word-reading accuracy in the context of sentences. While presented as a list of isolated sentences, each sentence follows from the other, and the theme continues from one section to the next. Although the description of this subtest in the manual suggests it has a fluency component ("fluency of expression"; Mather & Wendling, 2014, p. 16), there is no timing element, which is a central aspect of fluency. Nor is it a reading comprehension task, because there are no comprehension questions. Rather, it is an assessment of oral word-reading *accuracy* in sentence contexts. If a student does much better normatively on Oral Reading relative to context-free word reading, it would suggest that the student is able to make good use of sentence context in identifying words. For example, if a student's performance on a traditional untimed word identification subtest is 87 and his nonsense word reading is 83 but his Oral Reading is 94, this suggests the student may have the compensator-type reading pattern. It is difficult to notice compensating students in typical classroom situations because, in classroom reading situations, words are read in context. But for this student, it is likely that reading is more effortful than for a student who also had a 94 on Oral Reading but whose word identification and nonsense word scores were also around 94. So, in situations in which there is a substantial normative difference between the WJ-IV ACH Oral Reading and other word-level reading tests, this subtest could be informative.

WJ-IV ACH Word Reading Fluency

Another new subtest on the WJ-IV ACH is Word Reading Fluency. It is a timed test of single-word reading. However, it differs in format from the single-word reading fluency tests described earlier. Students see rows of words on a page with four words per row. They must look at the four words in each row and determine which two go together. For example, if the words are *banana, truck, house, car,* the student would put a line through *truck* and *car* because they are related. This subtest can only be considered as marginally similar to tests like the TOWRE-2 or TOSWRF-2. There is a language component and possibly a metacognitive component in terms of needing to know the meaning of the words as well as making connections, skills not found in those other tests. It is not clear how much this influences the outcome. The items do not appear to be particularly challenging, assuming average or better verbal skills. However, for students who cannot quickly make connections between verbal/categorical concepts, this test may underestimate their actual word-reading speed.

WJ-IV ACH Reading Vocabulary and WRMT-III Word Comprehension

A subtest that goes by two different names in the WJ-IV ACH (Reading Vocabulary) and WRMT-III (Word Comprehension) has been in those batteries through multiple editions. It involves reading isolated words and providing a synonym or antonym for those words (WJ-IV ACH, WRMT-III) or making a verbal analogy (WRMT-III). Students are required to read the words themselves before providing the response. A parallel task is the Oral Vocabulary subtest from the WJ-IV COG battery. The examiner presents the words orally and asks for a synonym or antonym, but the student is not required to read any words. This latter subtest appears to be a good indication of a student's vocabulary skills and is recommended (see next chapter). However, because the Reading Vocabulary/Word Comprehension subtest requires students to read the words, it has an inherent confound between vocabulary knowledge and word-reading skills. The WJ-IV ACH manual acknowledges this.

As a result of the confound between word reading and vocabulary, students who struggle with word-level reading may not do well on this subtest due to inaccurate word identification. Those with the hyperlexic-type pattern may correctly identify the words but lack the vocabulary knowledge to provide accurate responses. Thus, two individuals could achieve the exact same low score for different reasons. This limits the value of this subtest in a reading evaluation. This particular subtest has been a part of those batteries for decades, and it is not the kind of task that researchers typically use to get a better understanding of the skills underlying reading. As a result, it is unclear what information this subtest offers evaluators who are trying to understand why a student is struggling in reading. When looking for a way to shorten an evaluation, this would be a good candidate to skip.

Interpreting Word-Reading Test Results

Word identification subtests should be interpreted alongside timed word-reading tests and nonsense word reading tests. These represent three different types of data that the evaluator can use to get a better understanding of a child's word-reading skills. Often, all three of these types of word-reading tasks yield scores that are similar to one another. In these cases, an evaluator can feel confident about estimating a student's skills. However, equally often, students will display a mixed profile among these three different types of word-reading tests. This requires additional thought and hypothesis generation.

There is no direct, research-based guidance on how to integrate information from tests of phonemic awareness/analysis, phonological blending, rapid automatized naming (RAN), working memory (WM), nonsense word reading, and context-free timed and untimed word reading. As a result, this task of interpreting skill profiles is more of an art than a science. But this "art" is founded on an empirical base of knowledge about reading acquisition and reading difficulties. Any of the four phonological skills just mentioned can be considered a potential threat to word-reading skills. Thus, weaknesses in one or more of those skills would result in a working hypothesis that those skills could be inhibiting the student's word-reading growth. Rapid Reference 8.2 provides sample profiles along with provisional hypotheses about those profiles. Due to space limitations, the descriptions in Rapid Reference 8.2 are simplistic because it is not always easy to categorize a given skill as weak or strong. All such skills fall along a continuum. Clinical judgment will always have to be a part of those "in between" cases. Also, the interpretation of those profiles can vary by age and the characteristics of specific tests used (e.g., the discussion of the age considerations of the TIWRE and TOWRE-2 earlier in the chapter). Nonetheless, this table should at least illustrate the kind of thinking that may occur when interpreting a student's word-level reading skill profile.

≡ *Rapid Reference 8.2*

Sample Word-Reading Skill Profiles and Possible Hypotheses About Them

Test Results	Hypothesis	Reading Difficulty Pattern	Potential Action
Nonsense Words: Weak Timed Words: Weak Untimed Words: Weak PA Skills: Weak	Limited phonics skills and sight vocabulary due to phonological-core deficit	Dyslexic or mixed pattern	Train PA and phonics skills
Nonsense Words: Weak Timed Words: Weak Untimed Words: Average PA Skills: Weak	Limited sight vocabulary due to phonological-core deficit	Compensator or mild dyslexic	Train PA and phonics skills

(continued)

(Continued)

Test Results	Hypothesis	Reading Difficulty Pattern	Potential Action
Nonsense Words: *Average* Timed Words: *Weak* Untimed Words: *Weak/Average* PA Skills: *Weak*	Incomplete PA skills; has enough for phonic decoding but not for efficient sight-word acquisition	Mild dyslexic pattern	Train more advanced PA; increase exposure to readable connected text
Nonsense Words: *Average* Timed Words: *Weak/Average* Untimed Words: *Weak* PA Skills: *Average*	Inadequate instruction or experience	Reading problem not likely	Improved instruction and greater reading opportunities
Nonsense Words: *Weak* Timed Words: *Average* Untimed Words: *Average* PA Skills: *Average*	Inadequate phonics instruction	Reading problem not likely	Additional phonics instruction to prevent limitations on reading progress
Nonsense Words: *Average* Timed Words: *Average* Untimed Words: *Average* PA Skills: *Average*	Any word-reading difficulties likely due to attentional, motivational, or anxiety issues	Reading problem not likely	Further investigation of attentional and motivational issues

Note: PA = phonemic awareness.

THE ASSESSMENT OF WORD-READING FLUENCY

There is ample evidence in the research literature consistent with the notion presented in Chapter 4 that word-reading fluency is largely a byproduct of the size of a student's sight vocabulary (Eldredge, 2005; Goff et al., 2005; Nation, 2005; Snowling & Hulme, 2011; Torgesen, 2000, 2004a). Other factors have been shown to affect fluency, such as RAN (Lervåg & Hulme, 2009), reading experience (Mol & Bus, 2011), and prosody (Whalley & Hansen, 2006). Prosody has to do with voice intonation while speaking or reading. Thus, if reading fluency is based primarily on the size of a student's sight vocabulary, then all assessments of fluency are, on some level or another, an assessment of a student's sight vocabulary.

Students for whom most or all of the words effortlessly "pop out" at them are able to read more quickly and accurately than students for whom many words are unfamiliar. Further support for this comes from the kinds of reading profiles we find among students. Some students can display average or better skills both in word identification and fluency, while others may be weak in both. A third profile involves students with average word identification but poor fluency. The pattern we do not see is a fluent reader with limited word identification skills.

What we take from all of this is that efforts at addressing fluency should be directed toward building a large sight vocabulary. It also helps explain the results from research on the popular technique of repeated readings. The *repeated readings* technique attempts to directly improve reading speed by practicing the same passage multiple times. The repeated readings approach seems to presume that reading speed can be improved with practice much like one might improve typing speed or free-throw shooting with practice. There is plenty of research showing the repeated readings technique improves the speed

> **DON'T FORGET**
>
> The largest factor that determines a child's fluency appears to be the size of the child's sight vocabulary. This means that efforts at addressing fluency should be directed toward building the student's sight vocabulary.

> **DON'T FORGET**
>
> Sight vocabulary is foundational for reading fluency. This means that on some level, assessments of fluency are assessments of a student's sight vocabulary.

> **CAUTION**
>
> Repeated readings involve opportunities to use context and prior knowledge of a passage to identify unfamiliar written words without interacting with the precise orthographic sequence of those words. There is thus little reason to believe this approach will help students with poor orthographic mapping skills remember unfamiliar words for later, instant retrieval in a different context. Techniques that do not promote orthographic mapping have limited value in promoting fluency.

and accuracy of *practiced* passages. However, generalization to unpracticed passages is very limited (for a review, see Chard, Ketterlin-Geller, Baker, Doabler, & Apichatabutra, 2009). Also, in those studies of repeated reading that report gains on normative reading tests, there are only modest improvements of about 3 to 5 standard score points in word identification, nonsense word reading, and reading comprehension (O'Connor, White, & Swanson, 2007). (Chapter 11 highlights interventions of 12–25 points.) This finding makes sense because there is little reason to assume that the words in these practiced passages are being added to a student's sight vocabulary. The repeated readings approach does not appear to derive from an empirically based theory on how words are remembered, aside from simple exposure and practice, which presumes memory based upon paired-associate learning.

Assuming they have had adequate instruction and reading opportunities, students with limited sight vocabularies are students who are not skilled in orthographic mapping. Students who are not skilled in orthographic mapping are not likely to efficiently turn unfamiliar words into familiar words via the repeated readings approach. When reading predictable passages, it is not necessary to attend to the detailed orthographic sequence and note how that sequence maps onto the phonemic sequence stored in long-term memory. Words read correctly in practiced passages that are not mapped to permanent memory will not likely be instantly recognized when encountered in an unpracticed passage. It is true that simple exposure to words and reading practice boosts the sight vocabularies of typical readers. But that is because they are skilled at orthographic mapping. However, simple exposure to words is not a sufficient means to build the sight vocabularies of students who are poor at orthographic mapping.

TYPES OF FLUENCY TASKS

There is no attempt to provide here a definitive categorization scheme of fluency tasks. The purpose here is rather practical. We can define at least four functional types of fluency tasks: (1) RAN (digits, letters, objects or colors); (2) word-level fluency (real words and nonsense words); (3) sentence-level fluency; and (4) passage-level fluency. RAN was covered in Chapter 6, and real-word and nonsense word fluency tasks were covered earlier in this chapter and in Chapter 7. Here, the focus is on sentence-level and passage-level fluency tests.

Sentence Fluency

Tests that use timed sentence reading to assess fluency include the WJ-IV ACH Sentence Reading Fluency (called Reading Fluency in WJ-III), the Test of Silent

Reading Efficiency and Comprehension (TOSREC), the Test of Silent Contextual Reading Fluency–Second Edition (TOSCRF-2), and the KTEA-3 Silent Reading Fluency.

WJ-IV ACH, TOSREC, and KTEA-3

The WJ-IV, TOSREC, and KTEA-3 all make use of a similar task. Under timed conditions, the student reads sentences and indicates whether they are true or false. Thus, this task assesses basic reading comprehension along with fluency. I have extensively used the earlier, WJ-III version of the WJ-IV ACH Sentence Reading Fluency subtest in high school evaluations and have concerns about its value at that level. The WJ-IV ACH subtest is focused on speed, and the items do not get much more difficult as the test progresses. I would suspect that this is potentially a better test of fluency at the elementary level than at the high school level. Ardoin and colleagues (2004) support its value with younger students. With 77 general education third graders, they found that the WJ-III Reading Fluency subtest (WJ-IV ACH Sentence Reading Fluency) correlated with a curriculum-based passage fluency test $r = .70$. However, the reason it does not appear to be helpful at the secondary level is that most of the words in the simple sentences are presumably in the sight vocabularies of high school students with mild to moderate reading difficulties. It does not seem that this subtest was developed to get a fine-tuned understanding of the child's sight vocabulary development. Rather it appears to be a direct measure of fluency for easy sentences and, secondarily, the simple comprehension element is to ensure that the sentences are read correctly because the test involves silent reading. The comprehension element is extremely basic for older students; it does not tell us much about the student's comprehension abilities (see Chapter 9). I have not had experience with the KTEA-3 or TOSREC sentence fluency tests. The KTEA-3 Silent Reading Fluency test is nearly identical in nature to the WJ-IV ACH Sentence Reading Fluency test, though a cursory look at the items suggests that the words become slightly more difficult as the test progresses, though the comprehension level remains very basic. The TOSREC has a different version of the test for each grade level from kindergarten to 12th grade.

TOSCRF-2

The TOSCRF-2 is the companion to the TOSWRF-2 described previously. Like its companion, the TOSCRF-2 has no spaces between the words. The difference is that the TOSCRF-2 is made up of meaningful sentences that provide a context to assist the student in determining the words. Like the TOSWRF-2, fine motor problems could occasionally be an issue. The TOSCRF-2 seems marginally parallel to the other sentence-level fluency tasks mentioned. All four of these tests allow sentence context to help a student determine unfamiliar words. The TOSCRF-2 does not have a direct response comprehension component like the other two. However, at least some degree of comprehension is necessary in order for the context to be helpful in determining words.

It is unclear precisely what the TOSCRF-2 offers for an individualized reading evaluation beyond other types of reading-related assessment tasks. Its companion, the TOSWRF-2, is highly recommended because it can estimate whether a student has an adequate sight vocabulary. The TOSCRF-2 might compromise that somewhat by providing a sentence context. While the TOSCRF-2's promotional materials say that it is useful for individualized evaluations, it also says it could be used for whole-class screenings. I would suggest that it is better suited for the latter than the former. It seems to confound multiple aspects of reading, which may be advantageous for a brief screening. For students who do poorly on such a task, follow-up would be in order. Also, the TOSCRF-2 can be contrasted with its companion TOSWRF-2 to see how much boost in word identification a student gets from context. If a student's normative score is much higher on the context-based TOSCRF-2 than the context-free TOSWRF-2, that could be evidence of compensation. The latter is an index of the size of one's sight vocabulary while the former indicates how well one can read connected text by integrating available sight vocabulary with phonic decoding and set for variability.

Passage Fluency

Although they have been around for decades, passage fluency tasks have become very popular since the National Reading Panel highlighted fluency as one of the critical aspects of skilled reading (NICHD, 2000). Passage fluency tests have long been used in curriculum-based measurement (CBM) but have been appearing more often on standardized, norm-referenced batteries. Some of these passage fluency tasks include comprehension questions (e.g., GORT-5) while others do not (e.g., WRMT-III). Passage fluency appears to require the integration of multiple reading-related skills and be a facilitator of reading comprehension. Students who can effortlessly read the words in a passage can focus their attentional and working memory resources on the meaning of that passage. As proposed by the simple view of reading, if the word-level reading is truly fluent, then it is a student's receptive language skills and background knowledge—not word-reading skills—that will primarily determine the student's comprehension (Fletcher et al., 2007).

Illusory Fluency
Not all fluent reading is equivalent. There are two types of apparently fluent reading that are misleading, one of which is easier to notice than the other. In one

situation, a student may read quickly and accurately, but lack prosody. If you ask such students comprehension questions, they may do quite well. This situation could be the result of the student not thinking to read with prosody. Simple encouragement, modeling, and practice would likely correct this. Such students simply have not incorporated prosody into their reading habits.

Sometimes, however, lack of prosody may indicate that a student requires so much effort to read as quickly and accurately as he is used to hearing others read, that little attention or working memory is available for either prosody or comprehension. This pattern is found most commonly among compensators and some mild dyslexics. Compensators notice how quickly and accurately others read and try to do the same. They often have decent basic phonics skills, and typically their verbal skills are in the top third of the population. They supplement their limited sight vocabularies with strong language abilities, phonics skills, and set for variability to read with a normal rate and accuracy. However, it is effortful for them to maintain that pace. Their prosody and comprehension usually suffer because all of their mental resources are devoted to fast and accurate word reading.

Another variation of this is simply an extension of the first, and similar to the case just described. Because all reading-related skills fall along a continuum, some of these compensators function like the ones just mentioned except that their prosody is quite good. Students displaying this pattern have been some of the most puzzling cases I have evaluated. They have great verbal language skills and seem to read with fluency—and even prosody—yet they display reading comprehension well below their oral language comprehension. This seems in direct contradiction to the simple view of reading, which would predict that good language skills and fluent word reading result in good reading comprehension. But if we go deeper into the subskills within the simple view (see Chapter 3), we find this type of case presents no contradiction. In each of these cases, the students had weaknesses in advanced phonemic awareness/analysis. Thus, their orthographic mapping was not extremely poor, but it was not average, either. They had mildly limited sight vocabularies, so they knew more words than in the scenario described above. This allowed them more working memory allotment to which they could add prosody to their oral reading repertoire.

CAUTION

Compensating students can sometimes mimic fluent reading, but at the cost of compromising their reading comprehension. Without displaying the great effort involved, they can combine their limited sight vocabularies with phonic decoding and typically strong set for variability (due to strong verbal skills) to produce what sounds like a fairly normal level of fluency.

Because compensators who require much effort to display such fluency can mimic fluency—even fluency with prosody—we should not automatically consider fluency as a more accurate representation of a student's reading skill compared to word-level reading tests. All aspects of reading must be considered, from phonological skills (awareness/analysis, blending, RAN, and WM), to word reading (real and nonsense words), to fluency, to comprehension. We must also take seriously the comments students (or their parents) make to us about how reading is difficult for them or that they don't like reading.

Passage Fluency Tests and Subtests

Passage fluency subtests are found in commercially available tests (e.g., GORT-5, WIAT-III, WRMT-III). The major universal screeners (e.g., DIBELS, Aimsweb, easyCBM) also have oral reading fluency (ORF) tests. These ORF measures appear to be good screeners and can be used alongside the normed tests. If there are existing ORF data on a student that suggests weaknesses, a single normed passage fluency test with similar results is all that is likely needed to feel confident in that particular outcome.

An attractive feature of the ORF subtest from the WRMT-III is that it has a separate rating of elements of fluency beyond speed and accuracy, such as smoothness, phrasing, and expression. These three factors each get a rating of 1 to 4. A student's total can range from 4 to 12. Unfortunately, this is a qualitative rating, with no norms available. Norms would be helpful, especially in identifying a student who reads quickly and accurately but with much effort.

Reading Fluency Tests in the Context of the Simple View of Reading

While the administration and scoring of most fluency-related subtests are straightforward, interpreting where they fit in to the bigger picture of reading acquisition and reading difficulties is not always clear. What do we make of good fluency or poor fluency? Poor fluency signals a problem, but what precisely is the problem? There is no clear evidence in the research literature to suggest that fluency represents its own problem unrelated to other aspects of reading. One might think fluency represents its own reading subskill because it is typically treated that way. While poor fluency indicates a breakdown in the process somewhere, it does not indicate the nature of that breakdown. A hypothesis must be developed regarding why a given student displays poor reading fluency.

While it would seem that a good fluency test score needs no further interpretation, this is not necessarily the case. As mentioned, some children sound fluent but require effortful compensation in order to display what appears to be fluent reading. Some compensators may not be identified using a fluency test, whereas others may. Also, students with the hyperlexic pattern may display good reading fluency, but that does not translate into skilled reading comprehension. In essence, performance on fluency-related tests provides a limited, though important, piece of information. Some compensators and mild dyslexics may show a weakness in fluency but have good reading comprehension performance. The hyperlexic student may show the opposite pattern. While reading fluency is the bridge between word-reading skills and reading comprehension, it is what lies on either side of that bridge that will ultimately determine a child's reading skill.

≡ Rapid Reference 8.3 Key Points About the Assessment of Word Identification and Fluency

- Standard word identification tests confound the reading of familiar and unfamiliar words. Students can use phonic decoding and the set for variability to correctly read unfamiliar words.
- Timed word identification tests provide a better estimate of the size of a student's sight vocabulary.
- Some timed word-reading tests and sentence fluency tests appear to be more useful with elementary-level students than middle school and high school students due to the preponderance of elementary-level words on those tests.
- Passage fluency tests generally provide a good index of reading proficiency, but they require follow-up testing to understand the reasons for poor fluency.
- Some compensators can sound fluent, but they put forth great effort to do so.

SUMMARY

At the risk of oversimplification, it could be said that the route to reading fluency goes like this: letter-sound knowledge and phonological blending produce phonic decoding, phonic decoding skills combined with advanced phonemic awareness produce a sight vocabulary, and a strong sight vocabulary produces instant and accurate word reading, which in turn produces passage fluency (Eldredge, 2005).

Tests of reading fluency represent an important piece of information that can assist evaluators in gaining a better understanding of a student's reading skills. This chapter deliberately combined the assessment of word reading and the assessment of reading fluency because of the apparent direct relationship between the two (Torgesen, 2004a). While reading fluency may be the gateway to reading comprehension, skilled word-level reading, particularly a large sight vocabulary, appears to be the gateway to reading fluency.

TEST YOURSELF

1. **All of the traditional context-free word identification tests confound instant word recognition with phonic decoding and/or guessing.**
   (a) True
   (b) False

2. **What are ways that students can correctly identify unfamiliar words on word identification tests?**
   (a) Phonic decoding
   (b) Set for variability
   (c) Guessing at a word with few "competitors"
   (d) Any or all of the above

3. **Which of the following may help reduce the likelihood that students correctly guess unfamiliar words on word identification tests?**
   (a) By using timed word identification tests
   (b) By asking students not to guess when they don't know a word
   (c) By only using tests that involve some sort of sentence context
   (d) By using non-normed tests

4. **All of the following suggest that a student is sounding out a word "on the spot" rather than identifying a familiar word except:**
   (a) The child identifies the word in a quick, rushed manner.
   (b) The child self-corrects.
   (c) The child puts the stress or accent on the wrong syllable.
   (d) The child pronounces the written word differently than he might normally say it.

5. **Why do timed word-reading subtests provide a better estimate of the size of a student's sight vocabulary than untimed tests?**
   (a) There are more words for them to read than on most untimed measures.
   (b) Sight words are instantly accessible so the more words instantly read on a timed test, the larger the sight vocabulary.
   (c) If they have to sound out more words, they get fewer correct within the time limit.
   (d) All of the above.
   (e) Both b and c are correct.

6. **Though highly recommended, what is the one drawback to the TOWRE-2 Sight Word Efficiency subtest?**

   (a) It is too short to provide an accurate assessment.

   (b) It has too many unusual words.

   (c) It does not seem as useful with middle school and high school students.

   (d) It does not seem as useful with elementary school students.

7. **What is a drawback to sentence fluency–type tests?**

   (a) They take too long and are tedious for students.

   (b) They are too brief to validly assess this skill.

   (c) Because the words do not get more challenging, they do not seem as useful with middle school and high school students.

   (d) Because the words are too challenging, it does not seem as useful with elementary school students.

8. **What is a drawback to passage fluency tests?**

   (a) They are all unreliable.

   (b) They don't have established validity.

   (c) They don't ask comprehension questions, making the tests inauthentic.

   (d) They cannot, by themselves, indicate *why* a student has poor fluency.

9. **An advantage of fluency tests is that high scores rule out reading problems.**

   (a) True

   (b) False

Answers: 1. True; 2. d; 3. a; 4. a; 5. e; 6. c; 7. c; 8. d; 9. False

Nine

ASSESSING READING COMPREHENSION AND RELATED SKILLS

The simple view of reading, presented in Chapter 3, provides a starting point for untangling the factors involved in reading comprehension difficulties. A student may struggle in reading due to (a) poor word-level reading skills, (b) poor language skills, or (c) both. Based on this, the four patterns of reading difficulty emerge: dyslexic, hyperlexic, mixed, and compensator (see Rapid Reference 9.1). These four patterns are just that: *patterns*. They are not diagnoses. Displaying one of these patterns does not mean a student has an educational disability, although a large percentage of students identified with educational disabilities (e.g., SLD, SLI, ID, ED) fit one of these patterns. Rather, these patterns provide an organized way to understand the underlying source of the reading comprehension problems so that effective interventions can be identified and implemented.

The dyslexic and compensator patterns presume average or better language skills. Such students understand passages that are read to them, but display comprehension difficulties when they read text themselves. By contrast, the hyperlexic and mixed patterns have difficulty comprehending even when a passage is read to them. Students with the mixed pattern typically have the greatest challenges because they have difficulty with both the word-reading and the language skills necessary for reading comprehension.

⚏ Rapid Reference 9.1 A Review of the Four Patterns of Reading Difficulties

Dyslexic The student has word-level reading difficulties but average or better language skills. Word-reading skills, reading fluency, and reading comprehension are substantially below the student's language comprehension skills.

Hyperlexic The student displays good word-level reading but weak language skills. Reading comprehension skills are substantially below the student's word-level reading and reading fluency.

Mixed The student has poor word-level reading skills and weak language skills.

Compensator The student displays a mild form of the dyslexic pattern but compensates to some degree with strong language skills, making this problem more difficult to recognize.

Various ways of assessing the construct of reading comprehension will be examined in this chapter. Comprehension of text requires a complex set of interrelated skills as described in Chapter 5. Any score from a reading comprehension test cannot possibly provide the information needed to understand why a student struggles in understanding what is read.

In addition to discussing reading comprehension tests, this chapter will examine listening comprehension tests, along with tests of other skills related to reading comprehension, such as vocabulary, background knowledge, and attention. The focus of this chapter is on the skills that affect reading comprehension apart from word-level reading. However, the role of word-level reading must always be considered as a potential source of reading comprehension difficulties.

READING COMPREHENSION ASSESSMENT

In this section, commercially available tests of reading comprehension will be discussed in light of the reading comprehension research using the simple view of reading as an interpretive framework. This discussion will be limited to standardized, normed measures specifically intended to assess reading comprehension. Before examining these tests, however, an important issue will be addressed that has arisen in the research regarding what tests of reading comprehension actually test.

Not All Reading Comprehension Tests Are Created Equal

Standardized, norm-referenced reading comprehension tests use different methods for assessing the construct of reading comprehension. British researchers Nation and Snowling (1997) appear to be the first to formally study whether different types of reading comprehension tests evaluate the same skills. They gave 184 third and fourth graders tests of nonsense word reading, real-word reading, passage reading, listening comprehension, and two different reading comprehension tests. One test (Neale Analysis of Reading Ability–Revised) involved reading passages orally and answering verbal questions. The other (Suffolk Reading Scale) was a written, multiple-choice sentence-completion task similar to the traditional cloze-type task. They found that the oral passage reading with verbal responses was more influenced by students' listening comprehension skills than by their word-reading skills. By contrast, the multiple-choice sentence-completion task was more influenced by word-reading skills than by listening comprehension.

DON'T FORGET

A cloze task can be oral or written. Cloze reading involves the examinee providing a word that makes sense in a blank space in a sentence; the student must understand the sentence to do this correctly. There are multiple ways of administering a cloze task, including fill in the blank and multiple choice.

Fill in the blank: Thomas pulled a diamond ring from his pocket and asked Anna if she would _____ him.

Multiple choice: Out on the lake he was disappointed that the wind died down. His canoe/sailboat/motorboat was now going very slowly.

The oral form of the cloze task is read by the examiner rather than by the student. Wilson Taylor first introduced the cloze technique and the term *cloze* in 1953. He said, "It is pronounced like the verb 'close' and is derived from 'closure.' The last term is one Gestalt psychology applies to the human tendency to complete a familiar but not-quite-finished pattern" (Taylor, 1953, p. 415).

Cutting and Scarborough (2006) in the United States had similar findings as Nation and Snowling (1997). They used the WIAT reading comprehension subtest, the GORT-3, and the Gates-MacGinitie. The WIAT reading comprehension test required the student to silently read a short passage and answer one or more questions about it, with the text still in front of the student. On the GORT-3, students are asked to orally read a passage quickly and then are asked five questions with the text no longer in view. The Gates-MacGinitie is a timed test involving reading passages and answering written, multiple-choice questions with the passage still in view. These researchers found that the WIAT was more influenced by word-reading skills than the GORT-3 or the Gates-MacGinitie, which were more influenced by language skills. Eason, Sabatini, Goldberg, Bruce, and Cutting (2013) studied the relationship between single-word reading efficiency and oral reading rate. Both of these skills affected reading comprehension.

They used multiple reading comprehension measures: the Stanford Diagnostic Reading Test–Fourth Edition (SDRT), the Gates-MacGinitie Reading Tests, the Diagnostic Achievement Battery (DAB), and the GORT-4. The SDRT involves timed silent reading with written multiple-choice questions, and the DAB involves silent reading followed by open-ended oral questions. Eason et al. (2013) found that the relationship between word-reading efficiency and oral reading rate varied significantly depending on the reading comprehension task.

Keenan, Betjemann, and Olson (2008) administered four reading comprehension tests to 510 children between the ages of 8 and 18. They administered the GORT-3, the Qualitative Reading Inventory–Third Edition (QRI-3), the Passage Comprehension subtest from the Woodcock-Johnson Tests of Achievement–Third Edition (WJ-III), and the Reading Comprehension subtest from the Peabody Individual Achievement Test (PIAT). This selection of tests allowed them to include multiple reading comprehension test formats. Two tests involved oral reading and two involved silent reading. Two used a paragraph reading format and two required reading only one or two sentences at a time. Each test used different response formats: (a) pointing to a correct picture (PIAT), (b) a cloze procedure (WJ-III), (c) multiple choice (GORT-3), (d) open-ended questions (QRI-3), and (e) story retell (QRI-3). The students were also given tests of listening comprehension, word identification, and nonsense word reading. The only two reading comprehension subtests that were highly correlated with one another ($r = .70$) were the PIAT and WJ-III. All other correlations were moderate to low, suggesting that these various tests are not interchangeable, even though they all purport to test reading comprehension. The WJ-III and PIAT correlated much more strongly with word identification and nonsense word reading than with language skills (listening comprehension), while the QRI-3 and GORT-3 correlated more strongly with language skills than word-reading skills. They also found significant patterns among various ages. For younger students, word-level reading skills accounted for a very large portion of the variance in the WJ-III and PIAT performance but for very little variance among the older students. By contrast, word-reading skills accounted for limited variance on the QRI-3 and GORT-3, regardless of age. So even on the same test, different aspects of reading/reading comprehension are being tested at different age levels.

These findings have significant implications for the validity and interpretation of reading comprehension tests among younger readers and poor readers. If younger readers do well on a reading comprehension test that is primarily influenced by word reading, this may not be a good predictor of future reading comprehension skills. Also, students with reading difficulties may appear to have weaker comprehension skills on tests more heavily dependent on word identification. If those students were given one of the tests more dependent on language skills, their reading comprehension scores might be substantially higher.

Keenan et al. (2008) point out that word-reading tests are rather interchangeable, and it is common for them to correlate very strongly with one another (often between $r = .88$ and .92). They suggest that many researchers appear to assume that reading comprehension tests are also equivalent and interchangeable. They note that most research studies include a single test of reading comprehension, often with no explanation as to why that particular test was selected. Yet apart from the $r = .70$ correlation between the PIAT and WJ-III, the correlations among the five reading comprehension tests were far lower, ranging between .31 and .54 (the QRI-3 had two response formats generating two comparisons). Keenan et al. (2008) also indicated that the GORT-3 had many "passage independent" questions, suggesting that students could answer the questions correctly from general knowledge, even if they could not accurately read the passage. This is also what Keenan and Betjemann (2006) previously found. They gave the GORT-3 test questions (identical questions as the GORT-4) to children and adults who had not read the passages, and they were able to correctly answer the questions above chance level. Among students who read the passage, they found that the best predictor of correct answers was how easily the questions could be answered without reading the passage, not how accurately the passage was read. To the credit of the authors and publisher of the GORT, these findings prompted them to redesign and re-norm the test. The GORT-5 eliminated passage-independent questions, thus increasing its validity in assessing the construct of reading comprehension.

Keenan et al. (2008) provided two additional informal analyses to help explain their findings. The first pertained to why the different tests correlated more or less strongly with word-reading skills. They pointed out that the formats of the PIAT and WJ-III typically involved reading one or two sentences and the correct response was often based on accurately identifying one key word. They created an illustration of the WJ-III Passage Comprehension (i.e., not an actual item):

> I thought that the painting was too enormous. I did not, however, feel like arguing about the _____.
>
> —*Keenan et al. (2008, p. 296)*

If the student correctly identifies *enormous,* Keenan et al. (2008) suggest he would correctly respond with the word *size.* But if he was not able to read the word *enormous,* they suggest the likely response would be *painting.* They cite other research supporting the hypothesis that the cloze procedure is more influenced by word-reading skills than language comprehension skills. Keenan et al. (2008) note that in the PIAT, as in the WJ-III Passage Comprehension, the correct answer typically hinges on identifying a single word. They speculate that this is a reason why these two tests are so heavily influenced by word reading. They also suggest that length is another related feature of these two tests that influences the role of word reading. Because these tests involve reading only one or two sentences, there is not sufficient context to aid comprehension if the student cannot identify one or more key words. Keenan et al. (2008) suggest, for example, if a student could not phonically decode the word *magician,* a longer passage may provide clues to indicate the passage is about a magician and the child can "revise" a previous word identification failure using help derived from the lengthier context.

At least two studies appear to provide direct support for the view of Keenan et al. (2008). Spear-Swerling (2004) examined the performance of 95 fourth graders on two state-mandated reading comprehension tests, one was a cloze test and the other used a question-and-answer format. She also administered tests of listening comprehension, vocabulary, word identification, and nonsense word reading. The cloze test differed from most cloze tests because it involved reading paragraphs rather than isolated sentences. The paragraphs had multiple blank spaces requiring a response. Spear-Swerling (2004) found an $r = .76$ correlation between the cloze task and the question-and-answer task. Also, the vocabulary and listening comprehension scores accounted for the same amount of variance on both reading comprehension tests, which contrasts with cloze tasks that use isolated sentences.

Gellert and Elbro (2013) also used a similar paragraph-based cloze procedure with over 200 Danish-speaking college students who were receiving remedial reading help. The 10-minute cloze test with lengthier text correlated $r = .84$ with a 30-minute reading comprehension test that used a question-and-answer format. Also, only a small portion of the variability in performance was accounted for by word-reading skills, which contrasts with most cloze tasks that use isolated sentences.

Keenan et al. (2008) also considered how the different kinds of tests might influence test performance of specific students. For example, if a student with the dyslexic pattern was administered the WJ-III or PIAT, the student is likely to be perceived as having weaker reading comprehension skills than he would on a test with longer passages. We could extend their thinking to suggest that hyperlexics might appear to have good reading comprehension on the WJ-III or PIAT (at least during the younger grades). Compensators are likely to perform average on the WJ-III and PIAT because of their resourcefulness at figuring out unfamiliar words based upon the set for variability (see Chapter 7). Perhaps only students with the mixed type of reading difficulty are likely to do poorly on all types of reading comprehension tests Keenan et al. (2008) studied.

Story Retell

Another format for assessing comprehension is to have students retell a story they just read (Roberts, Good, & Corcoran, 2005). This has been used in the context of curriculum-based measurement (CBM) for many years (Fuchs, Fuchs, & Maxwell, 1988). Story retell has strong face validity. Roberts et al. (2005) say it was incorporated into CBM to address a concern often expressed by teachers that oral reading fluency does not directly assess reading comprehension. However, numerous difficulties have been raised about using story retell to assess reading comprehension, summarized by Reed and Vaughn (2012).

First, Reed and Vaughn (2012) indicate that story retell has had multiple formats. Some require silent reading whereas others use oral reading. Some expect an oral retell while others expect a written response. Some provide prompts and others are open-ended. These wide variations may lead to differing outcomes. Second, reading research has indicated that retelling, recalling, summarizing, and paraphrasing all represent distinctly different comprehension-related skills, yet story retell tests treat them interchangeably. Third, students with learning disabilities perform more poorly on story retell than students without learning disabilities, even when matched for vocabulary knowledge. Fourth, this type of approach does not easily allow examiners to determine if poor performance on a story retell task is based upon problems with input, retrieval, or oral expression skills. Fifth, there are problems with the psychometric properties among the various retell tests (see also Reed, 2011).

Despite these problems, there are reasons why evaluators may consider using retell. First, most of the psychometric problems are resolved by the recent release of a normed, standardized story retell subtest, the WJ-IV ACH Reading Recall. It would be problematic if story retell were the only formal assessment of reading comprehension administered. However, the WJ-IV ACH Reading Recall subtest is not intended to be a stand-alone reading comprehension subtest. Indeed, it is on the extended portion of the battery and thus assumed to be supplemental to other subtests on the battery. Based upon the findings of Keenan et al. (2008) described previously, it seems that Reading Recall may provide a potential "corrective" to the WJ-IV Passage Comprehension subtest, which is likely more influenced by word-level reading skills than language comprehension. In turn, the Passage Comprehension provides a "corrective" to the Reading Recall, which is likely influenced more by language skills than word-level reading. Also, the Story Recall subtest in the WJ-IV COG is an oral parallel to Reading Recall and forms an interesting point of comparison from the standpoint of the simple view of reading.

It must be noted, however, that Keenan et al. (2008) found that not only did the story retell test have only a moderate correlation with tasks using short sentences (PIAT, $r = .45$, and WJ, $r = .48$), but it also correlated only moderately with the question–answer format of the GORT-3 or QRI-3 ($r = .31$ and .41, respectively). Thus, to span the full range of reading comprehension tasks assessed by Keenan et al. (2008), an evaluator would need to administer an additional test, one that uses the question–answer format (e.g., GORT-5). A problem with using multiple reading comprehension subtests is the time-consuming nature of such tests. Administering multiple reading comprehension subtests would thus be reserved for cases of students for whom reading comprehension is a major focus of the evaluation (i.e., not for those with the dyslexic or compensator patterns). However, other comprehension-related tasks, discussed later, might provide more insight into a student's reading comprehension difficulties.

Is There a Best-Practice Reading Comprehension Test?

In light of the findings that different reading comprehension test formats do not measure the same construct in the same way (Cutting & Scarborough, 2006; Eason et al., 2013; Keenan & Betjemann, 2006; Keenan et al., 2008; Nation & Snowling, 1997), it is not possible to recommend any single reading comprehension subtest as "best practice." Best practice in reading comprehension assessment will involve multiple subtests and the assessment of the key skills that underlie reading comprehension and general language comprehension.

The proposed solution to the subtest reliability issue assumes that two tests are measuring the same skill. While this is typically the case for tests of word identification and nonsense word reading, it is not the case with reading comprehension. Given the moderate correlations between different reading comprehension subtests, one would not expect the scores on two different types of subtests to be consistent with each other. Cutting and Scarborough (2006) recommend using multiple reading comprehension tests to address the differences among tests. However, this does not resolve the issue of subtest reliability since these tests are measuring somewhat different skills. As a result, it becomes very difficult to confidently estimate a student's reading comprehension using traditional reading comprehension subtests.

Three types of tests emerged in the study by Keenan et al. (2008): (1) those with one or two sentences that are more closely aligned with word-reading skills, (2) those with a question–answer format that are more closely aligned with

DON'T FORGET

Given the moderate correlations between different reading comprehension subtests, one would not expect the scores on two different types of subtests to be consistently similar, even if subtest reliability were not an issue.

language skills, and (3) those with story retell that are also more closely aligned with language skills, but not strongly correlated with the question–answer format. As a result, an evaluator would need to administer six reading comprehension subtests, two of each type, in order to address both the concerns with subtest reliability and the issue of differing test formats. This does not seem like a practical situation, especially since reading comprehension subtests are among the lengthiest subtests on most achievement batteries. Also, when one considers that a reading evaluation would include an assessment of many other skills beyond reading comprehension, it is clear that a comprehensive assessment of reading comprehension skills can be a cumbersome undertaking.

A potential solution for a comprehensive evaluation of reading comprehension that is consistent with the goals of intervention-oriented assessment would be to administer one subtest of each type and interpret these results (a) in the context of the findings about the differing test formats, and (b) in the larger context of other evaluation data, such as the various skills described later in this chapter. This approach may compromise the solution to subtest reliability proposed in this volume, but there are two points to consider in this regard. One is to acknowledge that current reading comprehension tests, by their very nature, are not capable of capturing the broad spectrum of skills and processes that are required for children's ability to comprehend text. The other is to recognize that with intervention-oriented assessment, the goal is to determine the reasons why a student struggles in reading comprehension, not to establish IDEA eligibility. Many reading comprehension subtests may be able to provide a "level" of performance, relative to peers. But they do not provide sufficient help in pinpointing why a student struggles in reading comprehension. As a result, the issue of the disparity in skills assessed among reading comprehension subtests is more of a challenge for IDEA identification than for intervention-oriented assessment.

If a student does poorly on a reading comprehension subtest, what should be done to improve reading comprehension? Most reading comprehension subtests do not provide an answer to that question (the GORT-5 and QRI-5 being partial exceptions). An intervention plan will have to be designed to address the reason or reasons why a student did poorly on the reading comprehension test in the first place. Intervention-oriented assessment, drawing upon the simple view of reading, seeks to determine how much (a) word-level reading skills and (b) language comprehension and related skills contribute to a student's reading comprehension performance. Then, an intervention plan would be established to address the specific skills that are negatively affecting reading comprehension.

The problems with reading comprehension subtests that are raised by researchers that were described above provide a strong argument for evaluating the skills that contribute to reading comprehension. As mentioned, most reading comprehension subtests do not do this. Before examining various measures of the components of reading comprehension, we will look at some of the more popular reading comprehension tests.

> **DON'T FORGET**
> ....
> If a student does poorly on a reading comprehension subtest, what should be done? Most reading comprehension subtests do not provide an answer to that question. An intervention plan should be designed to address the reason or reasons why a student struggles in reading comprehension.

TESTS OF READING COMPREHENSION

Some commercially available assessments only measure reading comprehension, such as the GORT-5 or TORC-5 (see Rapid Reference 9.2 for a list of acronyms), and others are subtests from larger achievement or reading batteries (e.g., KTEA-3, WIAT-III, WJ-IV). Several subtests use the cloze procedure (WJ-IV ACH, WRAT-4, WRMT-III), and at least one subtest involves reading a single sentence followed by a pointing response (PIAT-R). Based upon the studies described above, scores on these tests are likely to be influenced disproportionately by word-reading skills compared to language comprehension skills, especially in the younger grades. These tests may underestimate the real-world reading comprehension skills of students with the dyslexic and compensator patterns. By contrast, they may overestimate the reading comprehension skills of students with the hyperlexic pattern and some ELL students who are making good progress with word-reading development but whose vocabulary skills continue to lag. The only reading disability pattern that is likely to be consistently represented accurately by these reading comprehension subtests would be the mixed pattern. Students with the mixed pattern typically have neither the word recognition skills to accurately read the sentences nor the higher-level language skills to compensate for any word-reading inaccuracy.

≡ Rapid Reference 9.2 Acronyms for Common Reading Comprehension Tests

DAB-4: Diagnostic Achievement Battery–Fourth Edition (2014)

GORT-5: Gray Oral Reading Tests–Fifth Edition (2012)

KTEA-3: Kaufman Test of Educational Achievement–Third Edition (2014)

PIAT-R: Peabody Individual Achievement Test–Revised, Normative Update (1997)

QRI-5: Qualitative Reading Inventory–Fifth Edition (2010)

SRI-2: Standardized Reading Inventory–Second Edition (1999)

TORC-5: Test of Reading Comprehension–Fifth Edition (2009)

WIAT-III: Wechsler Individual Achievement Test–Third Edition (2009)

WRAT-4: Wide Range Achievement Test–Fourth Edition (2006)

WJ-IV ACH: Woodcock-Johnson Tests of Achievement–Fourth Edition (2014)

WRMT-III: Woodcock Reading Mastery Test–Third Edition (2011)

Most of the remaining reading comprehension tests and subtests consist of either oral or silent reading of longer passages followed by either verbal or written questions, some open ended, some multiple choice. These longer selections are more likely to accurately reflect the reading comprehension performance observed by classroom teachers among students with the compensating or dyslexic patterns. They are also likely to "flag" students with the hyperlexic or mixed patterns, as well as ELL students with limited vocabulary.

Because tests with longer passages appear to provide a more accurate representation of a student's reading comprehension, it might seem that they would be recommended over the other types of reading comprehension tests. However, this may not always be the case. For students with the dyslexic or compensator patterns, it would be easy to conclude that they do not have reading difficulties if their passage reading scores are average or better. But these types of tasks do not directly assess the degree of effort that goes into generating correct responses on such tests. Students with the compensating and dyslexic patterns require a great deal of effort to comprehend what they read, yet they are able to comprehend what they hear with relative ease.

This discussion is not intended to suggest the abandonment of reading comprehension tests. Such assessments provide us with a reference point for interpreting a student's reading skills. Examining discrepancies between reading comprehension subtest scores and the level of reading comprehension skill reported by teachers or parents may shed light on the nature and source(s) of a student's struggles. Contrasts between tests of reading comprehension and tests of listening comprehension (discussed below) can also be instructive. In addition, reading comprehension subtests can help track progress. Although nationally normed assessments are generally not helpful for short-term progress monitoring, they can be used to track longer-term progress (e.g., semi-annual or annual) to determine if a child is closing the gap with same-aged peers.

Reading comprehension subtests must be integrated into the larger picture of a student's skill profile. Such a profile would include (a) word-level reading proficiency, particularly the size of a student's sight vocabulary; (b) comments by teachers, parents, and the students themselves; (c) listening comprehension, vocabulary, and other language-related test performance; (d) other factors that are likely to influence reading comprehension (background knowledge, working memory, knowledge of genre and text structure, etc.); and (e) issues such as motivation, previous learning opportunities and instruction, as well as reading experience outside of school.

TESTS OF LISTENING COMPREHENSION

A skill closely related to reading comprehension is listening comprehension. In theory, reading comprehension and listening comprehension represent similar skills except that with the former, the student reads language rather than listens to it. However, recall from Chapter 5 that the correlation between measures of listening comprehension and reading comprehension are not as strong among students with attentional difficulties (Aaron et al., 2002; Cain & Bignell, 2014). With such students, listening comprehension scores often underestimate their potential for reading comprehension. Scores from language-related assessments besides listening comprehension generally provide a more accurate estimate of potential for reading comprehension among inattentive students.

Attentional issues aside, comparisons between listening comprehension and reading comprehension can yield useful information. Such a comparison provides an estimate of the degree to which word-level reading is affecting reading comprehension, because word reading is not involved in listening comprehension. Thus, a discrepancy between listening comprehension and reading comprehension will be most pronounced among those displaying the dyslexic and compensator patterns. Various combinations of performance, the patterns they represent, and suggested hypotheses are described in Rapid Reference 9.3.

≡ Rapid Reference 9.3

Sample Listening Comprehension and Reading Comprehension Performance Profiles and Possible Hypotheses About Them

Test Results	Hypothesis	Reading Difficulty Pattern	Potential Action
LC score: *Weak* RC score: *Weak* VIQ score: *Weak*	General language skills are hindering reading comprehension	Hyperlexic or mixed	1) Develop language skills; 2) Address word-level reading skills in students with mixed pattern
LC score: *Weak* RC score: *Average or better* VIQ score: *Average or better*	Poor listening comprehension skills relative to general language skills	Possible attentional or anxiety issues*	Address attentional (or anxiety) issues
LC score: *Average or better* RC score: *Much lower than LC* VIQ score: *Average or better*	Word recognition skills are likely effortful and drawing attention from reading comprehension	Dyslexic or compensator pattern	Address word-level reading skills

Note: LC = listening comprehension; RC = reading comprehension; VIQ = performance on verbal portion of traditional IQ assessments or other language assessments.
*Anxiety has not received adequate attention in the reading comprehension research.

It is fortunate that multiple achievement batteries have both listening comprehension and reading comprehension tests. The subtests in some batteries (e.g., KTEA-3, WIAT-III, WJ-IV COG/ACH) are designed so that the nature of the listening comprehension and reading comprehension tasks are parallel to one another in every respect other than who reads the passage, the examiner or the student. Not all batteries are like this, however. For example, the WRMT-III uses the cloze procedure for reading comprehension and a question–answer format for listening comprehension. An advantage of having both a listening comprehension and a reading comprehension subtest in the same battery is that both subtests are normed on the same students. An assessment of listening comprehension is highly recommended for any student who displays difficulties with reading comprehension.

When combined with reading comprehension subtests and word-level reading subtests, listening comprehension can distinguish among the four types of patterns of reading difficulties. As a result, while reading comprehension test results do not tell us much about which skills are deficient and need intervention, a listening comprehension subtest takes a step in that direction. However, like reading comprehension subtests, listening comprehension subtests do not offer specific information about why a student performed poorly on the listening comprehension test. Was it weak vocabulary? Limited background knowledge? Poor attention? The remainder of the chapter is intended to address this.

ASSESSMENT OF SKILLS THAT CONTRIBUTE TO READING COMPREHENSION AND LISTENING COMPREHENSION

A variety of skills that contribute to reading comprehension and listening comprehension were described in Chapter 5. The following discusses the assessment of these skills. While a comprehensive evaluation of reading will not always require every one of these (or two of each to address the subtest reliability issue), many of them will be critical to understanding why a child struggles in reading comprehension independently from word-level reading.

Vocabulary–Semantic Knowledge

The National Reading Panel review validated the intuitively strong notion that vocabulary knowledge has a strong influence on reading comprehension (NICHD, 2000). More recent research has added further support to this (e.g., Lervåg & Aukrust, 2010; Nation, 2005; Yesil-Dagli, 2011). Indeed, vocabulary is arguable the biggest factor affecting the reading comprehension of many ELL students (Farnia & Geva, 2013; Li & Kirby, 2014), and it is also an issue for students whose first (or only) language is English (Catts et al., 2006; Nation, 2005).

Reading researchers have routinely used the same commercially available tests educational evaluators use to assess vocabulary–semantic knowledge. Most commonly, they use the verbal portion of one of the Wechsler scales (VIQ or VCIQ) or a single subtest from that scale (typically the Vocabulary subtest). Also, they may use the Peabody Picture Vocabulary Test (PPVT) or occasionally portions of language batteries typically administered by speech–language pathologists.

If the goal is to determine which aspects of language functioning are affecting reading comprehension, then language batteries are the best alternative. For students with reading comprehension difficulties beyond any word reading deficiencies, it is advisable to include a speech–language pathologist in the evaluation process. The traditional verbal portions of IQ tests confound multiple aspects of language, such as receptive and expressive vocabulary, and provide no index of grammar or listening comprehension. Language batteries typically take account of all of these skills, and often more. As a result, to better understand a student's language functioning in terms of how it impacts reading comprehension, a language evaluation appears most appropriate.

With that said, the verbal portions from the traditional IQ batteries can function as screeners for language skills in circumstances in which one or two such subtests can be conveniently used early on in the evaluation process if screening by a speech–language pathologist is not as practical (again, the issue here is hypothesis generation, not IDEA identification). These verbal subtests have an extensive history of being used in this manner in the empirical research literature on reading comprehension, with extensive support for their validity in being used this way. While they are no substitute for a more comprehensive language battery, they can be a fairly quick way of determining whether language skills are likely contributing to weak reading comprehension performance. This would be unnecessary if a school has sufficient resources such that a speech–language pathologist can routinely provide a language screening for students referred due to concerns about reading comprehension. If not, students with low reading comprehension performance could receive the Vocabulary and Similarities subtests from one of the Wechsler scales or the Oral Vocabulary subtest from the WJ-IV. Those displaying weak performance on those screenings would be referred for further language evaluation. There is no intent to make decisions about language skills based on this limited data. Rather, these would be used to screen students who already displayed weaknesses on reading comprehension subtests from nationally normed assessments. The goal is to develop a hypothesis about whether language is a likely contributing factor to the reading comprehension difficulties and thus whether it should be addressed in order to remediate the reading difficulty.

There are at least two potential concerns with using some portion of a traditional IQ test as a screener for vocabulary functioning. First, the whole concept of IQ has a mystique it does not deserve, and some teachers and parents may perceive IQ as immutable. It would be important to communicate the limited and "screening" nature of such subtests to teachers and parents when presenting results. Second, one may question the treatment validity of such subtests. However, there are treatment implications of varying outcomes, particularly if they are followed up with a full language evaluation. Knowing whether language is a contributing factor to low reading comprehension performance can help distinguish between the dyslexic and mixed patterns of reading difficulties. Addressing the needs of these two types of weak readers would involve different treatment protocols. The former may require little or no additional work in vocabulary, while the latter would. However, it is assumed that decisions are not made simply based upon these subtests, as their best function would be for screening for weak language skills. Rapid Reference 9.4 provides a real case illustration of how this usage was helpful.

≡ Rapid Reference 9.4 A Case Example of a Vocabulary Screening

The semantic lexicon has two levels (see Chapter 5). The first consists of the 2,000 to 3,000 words routinely used in daily social communication. The second represents the tens of thousands of additional words that are less commonly heard, read, or spoken. Some older students can master the former and still struggle with the latter. Anna had struggled in reading comprehension since third grade, and by seventh grade the problem could not be ignored, so she was referred to me for an evaluation. Anna's reading comprehension difficulties were puzzling to her teachers and parents because she was very verbally and socially adept, her word reading was strong, and she was a hard worker. The evaluation confirmed the weak reading comprehension and strong word-reading skills. My interactions with her also confirmed she was verbally and socially average or better. Despite her ostensibly good verbal skills, I administered the Vocabulary and Similarities subtests from the Wechsler Abbreviated Scale of Intelligence (WASI). She performed below average on both, which none of us anticipated. The speech–language pathologist then conducted a full language evaluation, which indicated Anna had weak vocabulary skills. Thus, absent the vocabulary screening, her poor reading comprehension would have likely remained a mystery. No one had considered her to be a candidate for a full language evaluation because her daily vocabulary lexicon was essentially mastered.

Validity of IQ Measures for Reading Comprehension

This limited, screening function of traditional verbal IQ measures in lieu of an available, formal language screening must not be confused with use of the classic IQ–achievement discrepancy model for diagnosing reading disabilities. This model has been shown to be invalid on multiple levels (Gresham & Vellutino, 2010; Stuebing et al., 2002). It may be tempting to assume from the invalid nature of the IQ–achievement discrepancy approach to learning disability determination that traditional IQ tests have no place in the assessment of reading difficulties. However, even Gresham and Vellutino (2010), who argue strongly against the IQ–achievement model, state that IQ tests may have value for understanding students' reading *comprehension* abilities. They state that

> the expectation of positive and significant correlations between measures of intelligence and measures of reading ability has never been in dispute when reading ability is defined as the ability to comprehend the meanings embodied in connected text in children who have acquired enough facility in word decoding and word identification . . . . Indeed, knowledge and skills assessed by most tests of intelligence are important for language and reading comprehension. (p. 199)

They go on to say that

> reading disability has traditionally been defined as a significant deficiency in word decoding and word identification that adversely affects reading comprehension and has never been defined as a significant deficiency in reading comprehension in children who have acquired adequate facility in word decoding and word identification. (p. 199)

Thus, IQ tests have little or no value in assessments of word-level reading problems but may provide insight when reading comprehension difficulties exist in the presence of skilled word reading. These statements by Gresham and Vellutino (2010) are supported by many empirical studies. There is no suggestion here that these authors would endorse the specific screening function of verbal IQ subtests just described. However, this practice appears quite consistent with their statements. Nonetheless, evaluation teams should defer to formal language screenings or full language evaluations administered by speech–language pathologists. Only when such screenings are not available or practical would the use of these coarser-grained vocabulary subtests from traditional cognitive batteries be recommended for screening purposes.

Summary

A student's vocabulary knowledge should be assessed when there is a concern about reading comprehension that cannot be easily accounted for by a word-reading problem. Best practice would involve a language screening and potentially a full language evaluation by a speech–language pathologist. Vocabulary subtests from traditional cognitive tests can provide a screening that would then require a more extensive language assessment as a follow-up if a student performs poorly on such screenings.

Syntactical–Grammatical Knowledge

The reading assessments used by school psychologists, reading specialists, and special educators do not typically evaluate grammar and syntax directly. It was mentioned in Chapter 5 that students do not ordinarily have grammatical and syntactical problems in the absence of vocabulary problems. Thus, if a student's vocabulary–semantic skills are average or better, it is likely that grammatical–syntactical skills are average as well. The reference here is not to poor *spoken* grammar or syntax; it is to receptive understanding of other people's spoken language, that is, *receptive* grammatical and syntactical skills. It is possible for a student to display poor expressive grammar skills yet have no difficulty understanding the spoken language of others. If either grammar or syntax appears to be an issue, a language evaluation by a speech pathologist is recommended.

Background Knowledge

Background knowledge is a multifaceted phenomenon as it pertains to reading and language comprehension. The following represents some of the more significant types of background knowledge that can influence reading.

General Background Knowledge

There are subtests available that evaluate general background knowledge, the briefest being the WISC-V Information subtest. The PIAT-R General Information subtest is lengthier, and would provide a good second assessment of background information to corroborate the WISC-V Information subtest. The WJ-IV COG has one assessment of general background knowledge (General Information) and the WJ-IV ACH has three: Science, Social Studies, and Humanities. The kinds of questions found on these subtests roughly parallel the kinds of questions found on the WISC-V and PIAT-R subtests. Any of these WJ-IV subtests could also function as a second assessment of background knowledge in order to address the issue of subtest reliability. In fact, any two of the four subtests from the WJ-IV can function as a second subtest for another. While it is true that three of the four WJ-IV assessments of background knowledge cover particular topical areas, each is still a reflection of how much a student has absorbed from her environment, including the school environment. No doubt there may be some individual differences based on interest (i.e., strong on one of these subtests and weak on another), but the strong intercorrelations between these subtests suggest that they all reflect general background knowledge.

Because of the length of the four WJ-IV background knowledge subtests, one may want to reserve them for students for whom background knowledge appears to be a genuine concern. By contrast, the WISC-V is the briefest and could be used as a routine screening for any student who displays reading comprehension concerns, even if one is not administering the full Wechsler battery.

Specific Topical Knowledge

There do not appear to be subtests available on standard assessment batteries for specific topical knowledge. The four WJ-IV subtests mentioned are too wide ranging in the material covered to be considered tests of specific topical knowledge. As a result, we cannot assess this element through standardized tests. However, the student's background knowledge needs to be considered when evaluating performance on specific reading comprehension and listening comprehension subtests.

Constructing a Situation Model and Knowledge of Story Structure

Like specific topical knowledge, we do not have formal assessments that directly evaluate a student's ability to construct a situation model or the student's knowledge of story structure or literary genre. There are subtests on language batteries that may overlap somewhat with these areas. However, teachers can assess these important areas of reading comprehension informally. If teachers are aware of issues like knowledge of story structure, genre, and the building of situation models, they may be able to informally pose questions to students related to developing a situational model or regarding students' knowledge of story structure or literary genre. While these elements fall under the broad category of background knowledge, they are specific factors related to an individual's background knowledge. It is difficult to create a situational model, as we saw in Chapter 5, if one does not have a good understanding of the background factors that go into a particular passage.

Working Memory

According to the meta-analytic review of WM and short-term memory by Swanson et al. (2009), digits forward and digits reversed are both phonological short-term memory (PSTM) tests, not WM tests. They also found that students with reading difficulties struggle with both, though WM is more associated with reading comprehension and PSTM is more correlated with word-level reading. However, sophisticated statistical analyses were used to arrive at these conclusions, and this does not easily translate into individual profile interpretation. For our purposes, the fact that WM and PSTM are so highly intercorrelated means that simple PSTM tasks can function as a proxy for WM tasks, and this is routinely done in the research literature. As a result, information derived from the WISC-V Digit Span, the CTOPP-2 Memory for Digits, the WJ-IV COG Memory for Words, or sentence imitation/memory tasks from speech–language batteries can all provide an estimate of a student's WM. Nonword repetition tasks, such as from the CTOPP-2 or WJ-IV COG, also assess PSTM. However, they involve a heavier phonological component and may not be considered as a similar subtest to the simpler digit-memory tasks.

If scaled scores on these PSTM tasks are low (e.g., scaled score of 8 or lower, i.e., bottom quartile), then WM may be at least one contributing factor to poor reading comprehension. While there is currently no known way to correct WM problems in such a manner that it impacts reading comprehension, knowing that a student is not strong in this area may have instructional implications. For example, the teacher might stop more often and ask questions to assess a student's comprehension to that point, or teach the student to break up sentences or paragraphs into smaller units of meaning (e.g., main ideas and supporting details) to help the student better comprehend and mentally organize the information.

Attention

Because attention appears to have a substantial impact on reading comprehension, it may be good practice to assess the attention of students who present with poor reading comprehension. This assessment could be informal and simply involve speaking with the student's teacher about his ability to sustain attention during various tasks, not just reading. Another option is to have the teacher do a brief attention-related rating scale. Many years ago, Russell Barkley (1991) designed an informal assessment in which he listed each of the criteria for ADHD from the *DSM-III-R* on a list with a rating of 1 through 4. A rating of 1 meant this symptom never occurred, 2 meant sometimes, 3 meant often, and a 4 indicated almost always. Rapid Reference 9.5 describes how to construct a similar informal rating scale using the DSM-5. This assessment is quick and informative, though not normed. A third alternative would be to use a formal ADHD rating scale. The goal here is not to diagnose ADHD, but to determine if difficulties with attention might be affecting a student's reading comprehension performance. While students with attentional difficulties tend to have reading comprehension skills lower than their peers (Prochnow, Tunmer, & Chapman, 2013), there are students with attentional deficits with strong reading comprehension skills, so having attentional difficulties does not automatically mean that such difficulties are responsible for a student's reading comprehension problems. However, attention should be considered as a possible contributing factor.

≡ Rapid Reference 9.5   Creating Your Own Informal Attention Rating Scale

One can create an informal attention rating scale that can be used profitably in the context of a reading evaluation. List the nine criteria from the *DSM-5* with the four ratings of 1, 2, 3, or 4 next to each item (the first of the nine items appears here with the scale as an example):

	Never 1	Sometimes 2	Often 3	Almost Always 4
Fails to give close attention to details or makes careless mistakes in schoolwork, at work, or during other activities (e.g., overlooks or misses details, work is inaccurate).*				

This rating scale takes teachers about 2 minutes to complete. To score, ignore all 1s and 2s because they represent a typical level of occurrence. Score each 3 and 4 as 1. Total the number of items (i.e., score range is 0 to 9). This provides an informal estimate of attentional concerns. While not normed, most students will score between 0 and 2. The *DSM* requires at least six of the nine criteria to be present to be considered for a diagnosis of ADHD. Students who score 6 or higher on this informal scale may or may not have ADHD, but as mentioned, such a diagnosis is not the goal of this scale. Rather, students with such high scores are likely to have attentional issues, and these issues may be negatively influencing reading comprehension. A student with a score of 4 or 5 may also have milder attentional issues that could be considered as a possible source of weak comprehension performance. Incidentally, students with high scores on this informal screening should also receive a comprehensive evaluation for ADHD as required by the Child Find Mandate in IDEA.

*Adapted from American Psychiatric Association. (2013). *Diagnostic and statistical manual of mental disorders* (5th ed.). Washington, DC: Author.

Inferencing and Comprehension Monitoring

Most cognitive and achievement batteries do not have tests that directly assess inferencing, though some reading comprehension questions require inferences. However, some speech–language batteries assess inferencing skills. The Qualitative Reading Inventory (QRI) is a non-normed test that provides two types of comprehension questions with each passage: text explicit and text implicit. The answers to the former are located in the text, whereas answers to the latter are not and thus require an inference. Text-implicit questions are related to the passage, and answers cannot be inferred solely from background knowledge.

While a recurring factor in the literature, comprehension monitoring is not easily assessed in schools other than through informal means. When a student is reading (or listening to someone else read), the teacher can frequently stop to ask the student questions to determine whether the student understands what has been read thus far. In a sense, the teacher is doing the comprehension monitoring for the student. Another possibility would be to stop and ask, "Who understands what was just read?" A raised hand does not guarantee understanding and should be followed with queries to check. A nonraised hand may be a teachable moment about comprehension monitoring and can be used to suggest a strategy, such as rereading, to address the lack of understanding. Another informal way to check this is for a teacher to insert an inconsistent element into a text and determine whether students notice the incongruity.

Nonverbal Visual–Spatial–Perceptual (VSP) Skills

Chapter 5 cited research to show a clear correlation between nonverbal VSP skills and long-term reading comprehension outcomes. Chapter 11 will cite studies that indicate that some visualization techniques provide a modest boost in comprehension among poor comprehenders. But these chapters draw from unrelated sets of research. The studies that show VSP skills are related to reading comprehension involved no intervention. The studies of visualization training do not assess the VSP skills of the weak comprehenders. Therefore, we do not know if VSP-related intervention techniques work only with poor comprehenders that have poor VSP skills or if they work for all poor comprehenders. At the present time, there is no evidence of a benefit for testing VSP skills as part of an evaluation of a student with poor reading comprehension. This may change based upon future research.

≡ Rapid Reference 9.6 Key Points About the Assessment of Reading Comprehension and Related Skills

- Different reading comprehension test formats yield different results; some are more influenced by word-reading skills and less by language skills, and other tests show the opposite pattern.

- Tests of listening comprehension can provide a rough estimate of what a student's reading comprehension would be like if word reading was not an issue.
- Assessments of vocabulary level, general background knowledge, working memory, and attention may help develop hypotheses about why a student struggles in reading comprehension.
- A student whose reading comprehension performance appears to be affected by language skills should receive a language evaluation.

SUMMARY

Reading comprehension is a complex construct not easily assessed with demonstrated validity because researchers have shown that different kinds of reading comprehension test formats yield different kinds of outcomes. While such tests should be given to students with reading comprehension difficulties, we must pay attention to test format and incorporate that into our hypothesis about why a child struggles. Reading comprehension tests cannot, by themselves, tell us *why* a student is struggling. This requires other types of assessments.

Listening comprehension assessments can potentially help us understand reading comprehension performance. Yet if students struggle with listening comprehension, one must ask *why* they struggle. To answer this question, we must examine some of the skills that are needed to be successful at both listening comprehension and reading comprehension. These include vocabulary, grammatical and syntactical skills, background knowledge, working memory, inferencing ability, and attention. Further, there are important skills related to reading comprehension that are not easily assessed formally, such as comprehension monitoring and knowledge of genre. Any one of these factors can partially explain why a student may struggle in reading comprehension, independently of word-reading skills. Many children with reading comprehension difficulties display low scores in more than one of these skill areas. While there is no certainty that a low score on assessments of any of these skills means that that particular skill is contributing to reading comprehension difficulties, the research suggests that the probability is fairly strong. Examining the probable factors for poor reading comprehension allows evaluators and teachers to plan for the most appropriate type of intervention, based upon skills with which students struggle. Intervention for reading comprehension difficulties will be addressed in Chapter 11.

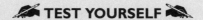
TEST YOURSELF

1. **Which two patterns of reading difficulties have reading comprehension difficulties that cannot simply be the result of poor word reading?**
   (a) Dyslexic and hyperlexic
   (b) Dyslexic and mixed
   (c) Compensator and mixed
   (d) Hyperlexic and mixed

2. **What have researchers found about commercially available reading comprehension tests?**
   (a) They do not necessarily assess the same underlying construct.
   (b) They are simply a reflection of word-reading skills.
   (c) They are simply a reflection of language skills.
   (d) Most of them have context-independent questions.

3. **Why do reading comprehension tests with one- or two-sentence passages (WJ-IV, PIAT-R) seem to correlate more with word reading than language skills?**
   (a) The words on those tests are easier.
   (b) The questions on those tests are less sophisticated.
   (c) There is not enough context to figure out unfamiliar words.
   (d) Research has not suggested any good possibilities to answer this question.

4. **If a reading comprehension test relies more on word-reading skills than language skills, then all of the following are likely *except*:**
   (a) It will overestimate the reading comprehension skills of hyperlexics.
   (b) It will underestimate the reading comprehension skills of dyslexics.
   (c) It will overestimate the reading comprehension skills of the mixed type.
   (d) It will underestimate the reading comprehension skills of the compensator type.

5. **All of the following can be said about using story recall for reading comprehension *except*:**
   (a) The WJ-IV now has a normed version of this type of subtest.
   (b) This type of subtest is the best way to assess reading comprehension, with the fewest technical or conceptual problems.
   (c) It does not correlate strongly with other types of reading comprehension tasks.
   (d) It correlates more with language skills than word-reading skills.

6. **Based on research on reading comprehension tests, which of the following is likely the best reading comprehension subtest available?**

   (a) WIAT-III, KTEA-3, and similar tasks with similar formats
   (b) WJ-IV Passage Comprehension and similar cloze-type tasks
   (c) WJ-IV Story Retell and similar tasks
   (d) Current research has not established a "best practice" type of reading comprehension test format.

7. **Listening comprehension subtests can often provide a good estimate of a student's potential for reading comprehension if word reading is not an issue.**

   (a) True
   (b) False

8. **If there is a suspicion that a student may be struggling in reading comprehension as a result of subtle language problems, what may be the best assessment option?**

   (a) The verbal portion of a conventional IQ test
   (b) A listening comprehension subtest from an achievement battery
   (c) Select verbal subtests from various cognitive and achievement batteries
   (d) A language battery administered by a speech–language pathologist

9. **For which of the following comprehension-related skills are there limited opportunities for formal assessment?**

   (a) Vocabulary and grammar
   (b) Background knowledge
   (c) Attention and working memory
   (d) Inferencing and comprehension monitoring

Answers: 1. d; 2. a; 3. c; 4. c; 5. b; 6. d; 7. True; 8. d; 9. d.

Ten

EFFECTIVE APPROACHES FOR PREVENTING READING DIFFICULTIES

The goal of this chapter and the next is to present the most effective, empirically validated approaches for preventing and correcting reading difficulties. The primary focus will be on word-level reading problems, but there will also be discussion of preventing reading comprehension difficulties. The exciting news, as described in Chapter 1, is that we can prevent a large proportion of the reading problems that we now encounter.

PREVENTION: REMOVING THE HURDLES BEFORE THE RACE BEGINS

"The components of effective reading instruction are the same whether the focus is prevention or intervention" (Foorman & Torgesen, 2001, p. 203). Both require an understanding of the prerequisite skills needed for a child to become a good reader. Prevention efforts are designed to ensure that children have those skills in place as they begin the process of learning to read. To return to the analogy in Chapter 1, if a child arrives at the starting line of reading instruction and already has hurdles in her lane, those hurdles will need to be removed before the race begins. In sum, we must begin with an understanding of how phonic decoding, orthographic mapping, and higher language skills develop so that we can be sure that each component of the reading process is in place when the child begins the process of learning to read. "Any well-founded educational intervention must be based on a sound theory of the causes of a particular form of learning difficulty, which in turn must be based on an understanding of how a given skill is learned by typically developing children" (Snowling & Hulme, 2011, p. 1).

CAUTION

Much of the material in this chapter on prevention and the next chapter on remediating reading difficulties is based upon the information found in Chapters 3 through 5. Readers are strongly encouraged not to skip ahead to this chapter and the next without having first read those chapters.

This chapter is based upon the description of typical reading development and reading difficulties presented in Chapters 3 through 5. It will be important that readers of this volume not skip ahead to this chapter without first having a solid grasp of the material in those chapters. Without an adequate understanding of that information, it will be difficult for readers to fully understand and apply the preventive and remedial approaches offered in this chapter and the next. Thus, if you have not yet read Chapters 3 through 5, it is strongly recommended you read those chapters prior to reading this chapter and the next.

The Simple View of Reading and the Prevention of Reading Difficulties

In keeping with the comments by Snowling and Hulme (2011), we can approach prevention based upon an empirically validated model of reading. With direct support from over 100 studies and indirect support from hundreds more, the simple view of reading (see Chapter 3) is a useful framework for approaching the task of preventing reading difficulties. The simple view of reading says that reading comprehension is the product of word-reading and language comprehension. More specifically, our understanding of word reading acquisition involves a combination of phonic decoding and the development of a large and expanding sight vocabulary, the latter being based on orthographic mapping. Phonic decoding and orthographic mapping are both based upon strong letter-sound skills, phonological blending, and phonemic proficiency. Language comprehension requires vocabulary knowledge, background knowledge, working memory, syntactical skills, as well as other discourse-level skills. The goal of preventing reading problems will be best served when the skills required for each reading-related skill (word-level reading and comprehension) is directly addressed in our prevention efforts.

Prevention in English Language Learners

The skills needed for ELLs to be successful in reading are no different than the skills needed for students whose first language is English (see Chapters 4 and 5). Greater care must be taken to help build the language skills needed for ELL students to be successful, but the same skills are involved. As a group, ELL students have a greater challenge due to their level of English proficiency compared to their non-ELL peers. For students who learned to read first in another language, additional help may be needed for transitioning to the English letter-sound relationships. Nonetheless, the basic tenants of the simple view of reading apply to ELL students as well as native speakers of English (Lesaux & Siegel, 2003).

The Origins of RTI

Recall from Chapter 1 that RTI originated as an attempt to "capture" some highly successful research results from the 1980s to the early 2000s. These findings related to both the prevention and the remediation of reading difficulties. The National Reading Panel (NICHD, 2000) reviewed the prevention research up to the late 1990s. They found that training kindergarteners and first graders in phonemic awareness skills, along with explicit and systematic phonics instruction, substantially reduced the percentage of students who displayed reading difficulties. Previous reports had similar findings (Snow et al., 1998), as have comparable reading panel reviews in Canada (Ontario Ministry of Education, 2003), the United Kingdom (Department for Education and Skills, 2006), and Australia (Australian Government, 2005). In this chapter we will explore what made those prevention efforts so successful.

The prevention studies reviewed by the National Reading Panel prompted the creation of what we now call Tier 1 of RTI. Even though there has been much discussion about the findings of the panel's report since its release, it is uncertain how commonly schools are implementing the panel's Tier 1 prevention recommendations in their K–1 classrooms. At the time of writing, a literature search using multiple keywords in three databases (PsycINFO, Academic Research Complete, and ERIC) did not turn up any studies that examined how common is formal training in phonological awareness as a Tier 1 general education practice. Anecdotally, it would seem this practice is *not* common. Through informal surveys at presentations I have done to groups of teachers and school psychologists in numerous school districts in a few different states, it seems that

> **DON'T FORGET**
> ....
> RTI was prompted by the positive results from the studies described in this chapter and the next. However, when RTI was translated into a process and a framework, the actual intervention techniques that produced these great results were left behind. These approaches are described in this chapter and in Chapter 11.

Tier 1 phonological awareness training in kindergarten is the exception, not the rule. There are several whole-class phonological awareness programs on the market, and no doubt some teachers are using them. But currently, there does not appear to be any clear evidence that in Tier 1, whole-class phonological awareness instruction is common practice, with the apparent exception of some states that have included it in their statewide guidelines. But even these are guidelines with a great deal of latitude ranging from a careful systematic presentation to something touched upon in a cursory manner to satisfy state standards. Indirect evidence for the perception that systematic phonological awareness has not been a routine part of Tier 1 general education instruction comes from the fact that we have not seen a substantial drop in the percentage of students with reading difficulties in the United States since the release of the National Reading Panel report in 2000. If phonological awareness training was common in Tier 1 kindergarten and first grade instruction, we would have expected to see such a drop, given the sheer number of research studies displaying that effect (for reviews, see Foorman et al., 2001; Hatcher, Hulme & Snowling, 2004; NELP, 2008; NICHD, 2000; Shapiro & Solity, 2008; Snow et al., 1998). Until this question is studied directly, it is uncertain how widespread is formal, systematic phonological awareness training in K–1.

The Importance of Prevention

There seems to be a window of opportunity for reading acquisition. Students who are "ready" to read progress normally when reading instruction begins, whereas a sizeable minority who are not ready lag behind their peers right from the start. The top 70% of readers do not wait around for the bottom 30% to become ready or to mature (*mature* being a misnomer because students typically do not outgrow their reading difficulties without direct intervention).

DON'T FORGET

Being *ready* for word-level reading means having the letter-sound knowledge and phonological awareness skills needed to acquire and apply the alphabetic principle. Without explicit instruction in these skills, most at-risk students will not spontaneously become ready to read.

Based upon our understanding of early reading acquisition (see Chapter 4), being *ready* means having adequate letter-sound knowledge and phonological awareness skills to acquire and apply the alphabetic principle. These skills are responsible for both phonic decoding and sight-word acquisition. Studies suggest that it takes between 6 months and a year to become a competent, word-level reader in consistent orthographies like Spanish and Italian and about 1 to 2 years in English (Seymour et al., 2003; Ziegler & Goswami, 2005). That time frame represents a fairly limited window when one considers the years of reading comprehension development and vocabulary development that continue through high school and into adulthood. Students who develop typically during this window go on to become skilled readers. This is also true for at-risk readers who receive the kinds of prevention discussed in this chapter. Torgesen (2004a) points out that when reading problems are prevented in at-risk readers, performance is often very typical across all domains of reading. However, for students who miss that early window of opportunity, even if they receive one of the highly effective approaches described in the next chapter and they normalize their performance in word-level reading and reading comprehension, they typically do not catch up in reading fluency. This suggests that a few months of prevention in kindergarten and/or first grade is critical.

Tier 2 as Prevention

Tier 2 is often conceptualized as "intervention." While true, Tier 2 can be conceptualized as either intervention *or* prevention, depending on whether a student is an at-risk reader or a struggling reader. A struggling or weak reader generically refers to any student who is displaying reading skills below his peers. This may include students with reading disabilities or milder reading problems. At-risk readers, by contrast, are students who have not yet been expected to read, such as

> **DON'T FORGET**
> ....
> In this volume, Tier 2 is considered *prevention* when working with at-risk students who have not yet demonstrated reading failure (e.g., kindergartners). Tier 2 is considered *intervention* when it is applied to students who have already demonstrated reading difficulties (i.e., students in mid-first grade and beyond).

kindergartners or beginning first graders. Students are considered at risk when they display signs that they are likely to have reading difficulties in the future, such as difficulties with letter-name knowledge, letter-sound knowledge, phonological awareness, working memory, rapid automatized naming, or vocabulary. Students with difficulties in any of these skills are at an increased risk for later reading difficulties. If a school provides at-risk kindergarteners with additional Tier 2 instruction based upon results from a Tier 1 universal screening, that Tier 2 extra help can be considered preventive instruction rather than an intervention, since "reading failure" has not yet occurred. These kindergarteners are at risk based on weaknesses in skills prerequisite for reading acquisition, even though they are not yet expected to read. In this volume, Tier 2 is considered to be a preventive measure when it is used with kindergarteners and also with students in the first months of first grade. However, by mid-first grade, students are expected to demonstrate a fair amount of basic reading skills. At that point, if a student is demonstrating difficulties acquiring beginning reading skills, then Tier 2 efforts are considered *intervention*. Thus, Tier 2 will be discussed in both this chapter on prevention and also the next chapter on intervention.

CAUTION

There appears to be no universally accepted model of multitiered RTI. Some models have three tiers and some have four. In some three-tiered models, Tier 3 represents special education, but that is not the case in others. There is no intention in this volume to promote one particular RTI framework over another. Rather, the goal is to present the highly effective reading-related instructional and intervention content that prompted RTI in the first place. Such content will make any reading-related, multitiered RTI service delivery model successful. For simplicity, in this volume, the following guidelines will be used:

Tier 1 will refer to general educational instruction that all students receive. Such instruction may be delivered either in a whole group or a small group context.

Tier 2 will refer to the additional general educational instruction provided only to students who are at-risk readers or who demonstrate reading difficulties. This is presumed to supplement Tier 1 instruction.

Tier 3 will refer to a more intensive level of instruction than Tier 2, such as more instructional time and smaller group size. It is provided only to struggling students, typically those who have not demonstrated adequate response to Tier 2 intervention (however, see Chapter 13 for an alternative). Any reference to Tier 3 in this volume makes no presumption about whether it is delivered as a general educational or special educational service.

These very broad descriptions can be easily adapted to virtually any of the current multitiered frameworks.

The preventive benefits of developing good letter-sound knowledge and phonological awareness have been studied extensively. In the next section, the research supporting the preventive benefits of phonological awareness training will be presented, followed by the preventive benefits of teaching basic letter-sound skills. Neither of these alone has the preventive benefits of both of these together.

EXPERIMENTAL SUPPORT FOR PHONOLOGICAL AWARENESS INSTRUCTION

Jerome Rosner, an optometry professor from the University of Pittsburgh, appears to be one of the first researchers to examine the impact of phonological awareness training on reading (Rosner, 1971). Wallach and Wallach (1976) and Williams (1980) also conducted early training studies. All of these early studies suggested that phonological awareness training in kindergarten and/or first grade produced a substantial benefit for early reading acquisition. However, Oxford University researchers Bradley and Bryant (1983) are typically credited with the first experimentally rigorous phonological awareness training study related to reading development. They provided 40 supplemental lessons, delivered one-on-one, to 65 students considered at risk for reading difficulties. The 65 students were divided into four carefully matched groups, all of whom received the school's general education literacy program. The first group received only phonological awareness training, the second received phonological awareness training plus letter-sound training, the third was given some conceptual/vocabulary type training, and the fourth received no treatment beyond the standard classroom literacy instruction.

Bradley and Bryant (1983) found significant differences in outcomes between the intervention and comparison groups. On average, the "phonological awareness only" group outperformed the two comparison groups by 4 to 8 standard score points on the two reading measures. The group that received phonological awareness training coordinated with letter-sound learning outperformed the comparison groups by 8 to 15 standard score points on the two word-level reading tests. A drawback to this study was that the phonological awareness training used was sound categorization. Other approaches that train segmentation, blending, and/or phoneme manipulation have had better success (NICHD, 2000; Shapiro & Solity, 2008). Regardless, the study by Bradley and Bryant (1983) was groundbreaking in that it provided a more rigorous design (multiple experimental and comparison groups) than previous studies, and students were tracked for a much longer period (3 years rather than several months).

A report that same year by Swedish researchers Olofsson and Lundberg (1983) demonstrated that phonemic awareness could be taught in kindergarten, even before children were expected to read. However, they did not examine the impact of phonological awareness improvements on reading, leaving that for their later studies. Important contributions from the Olofsson and Lundberg (1983) study included: (a) they used whole group kindergarten instruction for all students rather than one-on-one tutoring for at-risk students; (b) they demonstrated that systematic instruction in phonemic awareness improved these skills while informal, nonsystematic phonological awareness displayed no such improvements; and (c) they showed that phonological awareness can be trained prior to reading acquisition. These researchers followed the students and tested them at the end of the first and second grades. They found that the students who had received the early phoneme segmentation instruction significantly outperformed a comparison group in reading and spelling at the end of second grade (Lundberg, Frost, & Peterson, 1988).

Ball and Blachman (1988) in the United States replicated Olofsson and Lundberg's (1983) work, demonstrating that phoneme awareness skills can be developed in prereaders. However, since kindergarteners in Sweden are a year older than in the United States, Ball and Blachman (1988) showed that even prereading 5-year-olds are capable of developing phoneme segmentation skills when given systematic instruction. They also replicated Olofsson and Lundberg (1983) in that their study was not limited to at-risk students. A difference was that they delivered the phonological awareness training in small groups rather than to the whole class.

Ball and Blachman (1988) made additional contributions to our understanding of phonological awareness instruction and reading acquisition. They randomly assigned 151 kindergarteners to one of three conditions. One condition received phonemic segmentation training and letter-sound instruction. The second received the identical letter-sound instruction as the first, but no phonemic awareness training. Instead, they received additional language activities not related to phonological awareness. The third was a no-intervention comparison group. After their 7-week instructional trial, Ball and Blachman gave all three groups of kindergarteners two word identification tests. The group that received the combined phonemic awareness and letter-sound instruction read significantly more words than both the no-treatment group and the letter-sound plus language activities group. The difference between the latter two groups did not reach statistical significance. Thus, doing additional, explicit letter-sound instruction supplemental to the classroom curriculum did not significantly improve word-level reading skills in the children in this study. However, supplementing the classroom letter-sound instruction with a combination of explicit, phonemic segmentation activities and additional letter-sound activities had a substantial impact on early reading acquisition. Others have also found a substantial benefit of training phonological awareness along with letter-sound knowledge in kindergarten compared to simply training letter-sound knowledge (Foorman et al., 2001; Haddock, 1976; O'Connor, Jenkins, & Slocum, 1995). One of the most striking aspects of the findings from Ball and Blachman (1988) is that these results occurred after only 7 weeks of small-group kindergarten instruction for 20 minutes, four times per week.

Another finding from Ball and Blachman (1988) was that all three groups performed similarly on letter-name knowledge before and after the study. However, both the experimental group and the letter-sound plus language activities comparison group showed significantly more growth than the no-treatment group in the development of letter-sound knowledge during that 7-week period. Yet this increase in letter-sound knowledge did not automatically produce improved phonological segmentation skills or better reading skills than the comparison group. The letter-sound plus language activities and the no-treatment comparison groups performed similarly at post-test on phonological segmentation, but the group trained in phonological awareness robustly outperformed both groups in segmentation and word reading after the 7-week training. Given that phonological awareness in prereaders strongly predicts later reading skills, this finding is noteworthy.

Cunningham (1990) further clarified the role of phonological awareness in reading acquisition. She examined three groups of kindergarteners and first graders, all of whom received the same classroom instruction. One group received phonological awareness instruction, a second group received the same phonological awareness instruction combined with explicit instruction in applying the phonological awareness skills to reading, and a third group was a treated comparison group that did language activities. Both phonological awareness groups significantly outperformed the comparison group in word reading in kindergarten and first grade. However, the group taught to apply their phonological awareness to reading outperformed the group that was taught phonological awareness alone.

The studies just described by Bradley and Bryant (1983), Ball and Blachman (1988), and Cunningham (1990) appear to yield an interesting pattern (see Table 10.1). First, all three studies found that the combined phonological

Table 10.1 Comparisons of Groupings in the Bradley and Bryant (1983), Ball and Blachman (1988) and Cunningham (1990) Studies

Study	PA Training Only	Letter-Sound Training Only	PA and Letter-Sound Training	Treated Comparison	Untreated Comparison
Bradley an Bryant (1983)	X		X	X	X
Ball and Blachman (1988)		X	X		X
Cunningham (1990)	X		X	X	

Note: PA = phonological awareness.

awareness plus letter-sound learning groups fared the best. Second, phonological awareness without explicit phonics yielded better results than treated and untreated comparison groups, but lesser results than when phonological awareness was combined with letter-sound instruction (Bradley & Bryant, 1983; Cunningham, 1990). Third, additional letter-sound instruction without phonological awareness training did not result in performance higher than an untreated comparison group (Ball & Blachman, 1988). All of this suggests that the key ingredient in these three studies was the phonological awareness training. Given the alphabetic nature of the English writing system, which bases its written characters (i.e., the letters) on phonemes, this result should not be surprising.

Throughout the 1990s, similar studies were conducted. In a study reported in *School Psychology Review*, Lennon and Slesinski (1999) intervened with at-risk students in five elementary schools who were tutored in the spring of kindergarten. The teacher–student ratio was 1:2. The groups met daily for 10 weeks with the possibility of an additional 10 weeks for those not making sufficient progress. The at-risk students scored in the bottom 25% of their school's November screenings of letter knowledge. A sample of not-at-risk students in the middle of the distribution and a sample at the top of the distribution also received the same battery of tests. The intervention was based on the program used by Vellutino et al. (1996; described in Chapters 1 and 11) and provided training in phonemic awareness and letter-sound knowledge, along with opportunities to read appropriate leveled text. At the end of kindergarten, those who received this Tier 2–type preventive instruction outperformed the typically developing students in the middle range group and matched the skills of a third, top group.

Since the Reading Panel's report in 2000, further studies on the effectiveness of Tier 1 phonological awareness training have been conducted (Foorman et al., 2001; Hatcher et al., 2004; Shapiro & Solity, 2008), but the pace of these studies appears to have slowed considerably since "the 1980s and 1990s when training of phonological awareness was new and fashionable" (Kjeldsen, Kärnä, Niemi, Olofsson, & Witting, 2014, p. 454). Since the reading panel reports in the United States (NICHD, 2000; NELP, 2008), Australia (2005), the United Kingdom (2006), and Canada (2003) were published, it seems the importance of early phonological awareness training in kindergarten is viewed as a settled issue, and fewer such studies have been appearing in recent years. A notable study subsequent to these major reviews was that of Shapiro and Solity (2008). They trained over 250 kindergarteners in phonological awareness and letter-sound skills and compared them to a matched group of 213 students receiving their standard kindergarten curriculum (which included the same letter-sound learning). At the end of first grade, 20% of the comparison group was deemed by the school district to have reading difficulties. Using the same criteria, only 5% of students in the experimental group had reading difficulties. Thus, the Tier 1 training in phonological awareness and letter-sound skills reduced the number of struggling readers by 75%.

Also since the National Reading Panel report, several long-term studies of the impact of phonological awareness training have appeared (Byrne, Fielding-Barnsley, & Ashley, 2000; Elbro & Klint Petersen, 2004; Kjeldsen et al., 2014; Snowling & Hulme, 2011). Generally speaking, the findings from grades 5, 7, and even 9 indicate that students who received phonological awareness training in kindergarten fared better then their untrained counterparts in various aspects of reading. A recent study (Kjeldsen et al., 2014) indicated that phonological awareness training in kindergarten resulted in better reading comprehension in ninth grade. Not every longitudinal study had positive findings on every reading outcome (e.g., word identification, phonic decoding, fluency, reading comprehension). However, all of these longer-term longitudinal studies of the kindergarten phonological awareness training have shown positive outcomes on one or more of those reading skills compared to matched controls who did not receive such training. Also, long-term benefits are expected primarily in at-risk students, not in all students (some of these longitudinal studies involved all students, e.g., Kjeldsen et al., 2014) given that these skills develop naturally in most children but do not naturally develop in students with phonological-core deficit (see Chapter 4). Thus, the finding of any long-term effect in a general population of students is noteworthy.

Measurable Benefits of Phonological Awareness Training in Kindergarten

When one examines the various studies of phonological awareness instruction in kindergarten, the benefit of such instruction on word-level reading for typically developing students appears to be about 5 to 10 standard score points. The National Reading Panel's meta-analysis estimated the average improvement in reading among the studies they reviewed at about 8 standard score points (i.e., an effect size of .53; NICHD, 2000). These were immediate benefits following training. Follow-up studies at the end of first or second grade did not consistently demonstrate continued benefits of phonological awareness instruction on word-level reading among students who were *not* at risk for reading difficulties. This is not

> **DON'T FORGET**
> ....
> In general, at-risk students trained in phonological awareness in kindergarten outperform comparison at-risk students in reading by about 13 or more standard score points.

surprising because the typically developing members of the comparison groups in these studies would be expected to naturally develop phonemic awareness throughout first and second grade, even without being directly taught. Comparison groups would thus be expected to catch up.

By contrast to typically developing readers, there appear to be substantial, ongoing benefits of kindergarten phonological awareness instruction for at-risk readers (Hatcher et al., 2004). For example, the National Reading Panel's meta-analysis found that the average benefit of trained versus untrained at-risk students was 13 standard score points (an effect size of .86) immediately following training. At a longer-term follow-up (typically 6 months to 2 years later), the gap between trained and untrained students' word-level reading was equivalent to nearly 20 standard score points (effect size 1.33). By contrast, the National Reading Panel reported an average gap in word-level reading performance between trained and untrained *typical* readers of about 7 standard score points (effect size .45) at the end of training and 4 to 5 standard score points at follow-up (effect size .30).

The two interesting findings here are that: (1) the trained at-risk readers display a much larger benefit than not-at-risk students, and (2) with time, the gap between trained and untrained at-risk students widened, while the gap between trained and untrained typically developing readers narrowed. While this pattern was not found in every study, it did represent a significant trend in the National Reading Panel's meta-analysis.

This pattern can be interpreted within the context of our understanding of reading development described in Chapter 4. Students who progress at a typical pace in reading develop phonological awareness skills simply by being exposed to reading instruction. When such students receive phonological awareness training, they get an early "jump" on their peers and initially show faster reading gains compared to nonphonologically trained peers. But their untrained, typically developing peers eventually develop phonological awareness skills as a natural byproduct of learning to read, and as a result, they come close to catching up. The picture is quite different for students who are at risk for reading difficulties. Most of them have the phonological-core deficit, so they do not naturally develop phonemic awareness as a result of beginning reading instruction. For them, direct training of phonological awareness skills is necessary. At-risk readers who receive phonological awareness training make substantially more progress in reading than untrained comparison students, and these untrained at-risk comparison students do not catch up as a natural consequence of reading instruction. Thus, there are lasting word-level reading benefits displayed by phonologically trained at-risk students. The phonological awareness skills they develop via direct training have a positive influence on their reading—skills that they would not have developed on their own.

It must be noted that most of the standard score point differences described previously, which are estimated based on the reported effect sizes, represent differences between experimental and comparison groups. They do not necessarily represent standard score point gains on nationally normed tests. This issue will be addressed more fully in Chapter 11. Nonetheless, the contrast between those who do and do not receive these early prevention efforts is quite pronounced.

For RTI to succeed, Tier 1 needs to be effective. It is difficult to have effective Tier 2 and Tier 3 instruction with small group sizes when a very large proportion of students require Tier 2 or Tier 3 help. Effective Tier 1 instruction and early Tier 2 preventive instruction with at-risk students should reduce the number of students who struggle in the first place, so fewer students will require Tier 2 or Tier 3. This means that Tier 1 phonological awareness instruction in kindergarten and Tier 2 kindergarten prevention are foundational for the whole enterprise of reading-related RTI. Most whole-class Tier 1 instruction takes a few minutes a day. Because our screening instruments are not perfect, we cannot be certain which students may have phonological awareness difficulties. Providing whole-class instruction can help a wider range of students and provide a "double dose" to students identified by universal screeners as at risk who receive small group Tier 2 phonological awareness training.

Tier 1 Instruction: Whole Class or Small Group?

Most studies of phonological awareness doing Tier 1–type training with not-at-risk students use small group instruction (NELP, 2008). The National Reading Panel's meta-analysis showed a large advantage of small-group phonological awareness instruction over whole-group instruction. However, none of the studies directly compared whole-class versus small-group instruction. Comparing the results of whole- versus small-group instruction by comparing differing studies involves multiple confounds, so it is thus difficult to feel confident in their finding. Indeed, Shapiro and Solity (2008) reduced the number of students with reading difficulties by 75% using whole-class phonological awareness instruction. Not all of the studies with small-group phonological awareness instruction reviewed by the National Reading Panel can boast results that strong. Yet multiple successful studies used whole-group instruction (Lundberg et al., 1988; Olofsson & Lundberg, 1983; Schneider, Ennemoser, Roth, & Küspert, 1999; Schneider, Küspert, Roth, Vise, & Marx, 1997; Shapiro & Solity, 2008), though such studies are far fewer in number than studies with small-group instruction.

Given that there are several studies showing that whole-group instruction in phonological awareness can yield substantial benefits for later reading and spelling skills, it would seem that implementing Tier 1 phonological awareness training as whole class instruction is a defensible option. One may feel more comfortable deferring to the opinion put forth by the National Early Literacy Panel (2008) and use small-group Tier 1 instruction. However, this may present practical difficulties in many schools. Yet because whole-class phonological awareness instruction has been shown to have tremendous potential (Shapiro & Solity, 2008), it should be seriously considered.

Is Best Practice a Combination of Tier 1 and Tier 2 in Kindergarten?

Many of the studies mentioned involved Tier 2 prevention activities with at-risk readers. There have been limited efforts at combining whole-class Tier 1 phonological awareness instruction with additional small-group Tier 2 phonological awareness instruction for at-risk students. If both were used, at-risk students would get a double dose of phonological awareness instruction. Olofsson and Lundberg (1983), whose study involved successful whole-class phonological awareness instruction, appear to come close to this practice. Their program in kindergarten deliberately moved at a slow pace (6 months compared to some 7- to 10-week programs such as Ball and Blachman, 1988). They believed this slow pace would allow for the weaker students to keep pace with the activities. However, they did not report providing at-risk students with additional help.

DON'T FORGET

Given the minimal time investment involved in phonological awareness training relative to its potential benefits, it seems to make the most sense to provide whole-class or small-group Tier 1 instruction to all students and supplement that with additional Tier 2 small-group instruction for at-risk students.

It seems reasonable to assume that combining Tier 1 whole-class phonological awareness instruction with additional Tier 2 phonological awareness instruction for at-risk students would improve the likelihood of reducing reading difficulties compared to the standard single-dose approaches. Indeed, this double-dose approach seems to be how RTI is supposed to work: Effective Tier 1 instruction using approaches shown to promote skilled reading and Tier 2 supplemental instruction shown to benefit at-risk students. Phonological awareness has strong research support for Tier 1 and Tier 2 instruction.

The goal of Tier 1 and Tier 2 phonological awareness training in kindergarten is for students to arrive at first grade ready to benefit from the reading instruction provided. Children with poor phonological awareness do not benefit from first-grade reading instruction as much as their typically developing peers. The proverbial clock is ticking during the kindergarten year, and in order to improve the outcomes for at-risk students, it is essential that age-appropriate phonological awareness and letter-sound skills are developed on time. Doing a double dose would presumably provide greater assurance that this will happen.

Another potential benefit of Tier 1 phonological awareness instruction is the prevention of the compensating reader pattern. Such students have poor phonological awareness but compensate due to strong verbal skills. These students tend to fly under the radar. But with Tier 1 phonological awareness instruction for everyone, they would receive the training they need to avoid later struggles.

Using Letters to Teach Phonological Awareness

Based upon Cunningham (1990) and several other studies (including Bradley & Bryant, 1983, described previously), the National Reading Panel emphasized the importance of helping students make connections between phonological awareness instruction and reading. A variety of studies reviewed by the panel indicated that when phonemic awareness is taught as an isolated skill, it improves reading outcomes but not as effectively as when students are also instructed on how to apply phonemic awareness skills to letters and written words.

Unfortunately, the manner in which the National Reading Panel expressed this finding has caused confusion. Many have interpreted the panel's statements to mean phonemic awareness should be taught using letters as prompts, rather than using oral prompts or tokens (without letters on them). For example, a student may have the word *sat* in front of her spelled out in magnetic letters. She is told to remove the letter that makes the /s/ sound and replace it with a letter that makes the /b/ sound, then asked to say the word that results from this. Another example would be when a student is asked, "What letter

> **CAUTION**
>
> Phonemic awareness is not required for correct responses to tasks and activities that use letters. While letters or tokens can be used in the early stages of phonological awareness training, skilled phonemic awareness is displayed by instant, oral-only responding to phonological awareness prompts.

makes the /t/ sound in *cat*?" when the word *cat* is sitting in front of her in letter tiles. These activities may *mimic* oral phonological awareness activities, but because the letters are being displayed for the student, these are actually phonics activities and are not phonemic awareness activities. A student can correctly respond to all such activities using letter-sound knowledge. Phonemic awareness is not required for correct responses to tasks and activities that use letters. The answer to the question the teacher poses can be determined with little or no recourse to an awareness of the oral phonemes.

To illustrate the importance of integrating phonemic awareness training with letter-sound instruction, the National Reading Panel highlighted a single study from their meta-analysis to exemplify their point (Cunningham, 1990). Yet that prototypical study did *not* use letters to train phonemic awareness. "The letter-sound correspondences were specifically not included in the training sessions for either of the experimental groups [i.e., the two groups receiving phonological awareness training], instead subjects always used the wooden chips to represent each sound" (Cunningham, 1990, p. 435). Thus, when emphasizing the importance of integrating phonemic awareness and letter-sound knowledge, the National Reading Panel illustrated their point using a single study, and that single study involved teaching phonological awareness *without* the use of letters. The National Reading Panel categorized 48 experimental comparisons of phonological awareness training they reviewed as having "manipulated letters" and 42 that did not. Yet of the 48 studies the panel categorized as "manipulating letters," about 5 actually *used* letters to teach phonemic awareness. Rather, like Cunningham (1990), phonological awareness in those studies was almost always taught without letters. However, these studies differed from the 42 "phonological awareness without letters" studies in that letter-sound learning was done in parallel or children were shown how their developing phonological awareness applied to letters or written words. Thus, the notion that phonemic awareness training is more effective when letters are used to teach phonemes does not represent the findings of the National Reading Panel.

None of this discussion should obscure the point the National Reading Panel intended, which is that phonemic awareness training is most effective when it is not taught as an isolated skill. Phonemic awareness instruction has its greatest impact when it is integrated at some point with the learning of letters and written words. To illustrate how this could be done, let's say a kindergarten teacher is introducing the written word *me* to her students. Before showing them the word, she may ask the students to identify each sound they hear in the spoken word *me* (phoneme awareness). Then, she may ask them to guess what letters might be used to spell the word *me* (phoneme awareness integrated with letter-sound knowledge). Finally, she displays the printed word *me* and points out how the sounds in the spoken word (phonemic awareness) align with the letters in the written word (letter-sound knowledge). Such activities integrate phonemic awareness and letter-sound knowledge while maintaining the distinction between the two.

The National Early Literacy Panel (2008) also did a meta-analysis and included some studies published since the National Reading Panel's report. Their findings led them to emphasize the same point: Phonemic awareness training has its best results if at some point it is applied to letters and written words (NELP, 2008). However, they made no statements that could be misinterpreted to suggest that phonemic awareness is best taught using letters as prompts.

> ## CAUTION
>
> Some have misinterpreted statements by the National Reading Panel to suggest that phonological awareness training works best when letters are used as prompts. This does not reflect the studies they reviewed. Their point was that phonological awareness should not be taught as an isolated skill. At some point, it should be applied to letters and written words.

How Letters Can Be Useful for Phonemic Awareness Training

The point is not that letters should *never* be used during phonological awareness instruction. For students with basic letter-sound knowledge, letters can be used *to illustrate* a phonological task that is too difficult for a student to do orally (Kilpatrick, 2015a). For example, many students struggle segmenting consonant blends (e.g., *bl, cr, fl, sp*). If a student is unable to delete the /s/ from the word *slip* to get /lip/, despite attempts orally or with tokens, a good next step would be to demonstrate this manipulation using letters. With letters in front of the student, removing the letter *s* in the written word makes it very clear where the break should be made in the oral word. Once understood, the letters are removed and the teacher transitions to tokens or to a strictly oral task. However, if the teacher *only* uses letters that mimic phonological awareness tasks, it is quite possible that the student will not develop phonemic awareness. Rather, the student may continue to use letter-sound knowledge to correctly respond to the phonics task that has been misconstrued as a phonemic awareness task. Then, if the student becomes proficient at responding to this letter-based task, the teacher may assume the student has developed phonemic awareness, when in fact this may not be the case. Nonetheless, when instructing a child in phonological awareness who seems stuck on a particular oral manipulation, anything that will get the student to understand that manipulation is acceptable, including the use of letters. But in order for a child to show genuine phonemic awareness, the child must be able to demonstrate the task without additional multisensory prompts, whether they are letters or nonlettered tokens (Kilpatrick, 2015a). "A good way to remember the difference ... is that *phonemic awareness can be done with your eyes closed while phonics cannot*" (Kilpatrick, 2015a, p. 15).

Tokens are a great teaching tool and have been used to train phonological awareness in numerous studies. However, responding correctly to phonemic awareness activities using nonlettered tokens should be viewed as a step along the continuum of phonological proficiency. Ultimately, a student who can only do phonological awareness tasks with tokens is not likely displaying the level of phonological proficiency needed for orthographic mapping/sight-word learning. Kilpatrick (2015a) displays a developmental teaching hierarchy of phonological awareness instruction that goes from the easiest type of task to most difficult, with each step on the continuum representing a technique/approach that has been drawn from one or more studies that successfully taught phonological awareness. This developmental teaching hierarchy is displayed in Figure 10.1.

	Step/Type of Activity	Type of Assistance Provided	Skills Developed or Reinforced
Easier	1. Use letter-sound cues to illustrate phonological awareness concepts	Visual-spatial, oral, plus letter prompts	• Letter-sound skills • Understanding the nature of phonological awareness task expectations
	2. Use visual-spatial cues (tokens) to illustrate phonological manipulations	Visual-spatial and oral (no letters)	• Phonological manipulation • Segmentation • Isolation • Oral blending
	3. Use clapping or tapping to reinforce segmentation	Visual-sequential and oral (no visual-spatial prompts)	• Segmentation • Isolation
More Difficult	4. Use stretching, repeating, or other verbal emphasis to assist in phonological isolation	Oral only (no visual prompts)	• Phonological manipulation • Isolation • Oral blending
	5. Oral manipulation activities (deleting or substituting sounds)	None	• Phonological manipulation • Segmentation • Isolation • Oral blending

Figure 10.1 Developmental Teaching Hierarchy for Phonological Awareness Skills

Source: Adapted from Kilpatrick, 2015a.

Thus, letters can be used to *illustrate* phonemic awareness, so long as it is understood that any such usage is ultimately a phonics activity and does not necessarily represent genuine phonological awareness. Then, teachers should transition to nonlettered tokens and eventually to oral-only prompts.

Letter-Sound Instruction Is Not Enough

Another important point drawn from the previous discussion of phonological awareness research in kindergarten and first grade is that letter-sound learning does not automatically prompt improved phonemic awareness (Ball & Blachman, 1988; O'Connor et al., 1995; Piasta & Wagner, 2010; Schneider et al., 1999). This means that providing at-risk kindergarteners with additional letter-sound learning is no substitute for doing explicit phonemic awareness training. Phonemic awareness must be taught as a discrete, oral- and auditory-based skill, whether or not tokens are initially used as prompts. As phonological awareness skills develop, they must be integrated with letter-sound knowledge and word reading (O'Connor et al., 1995).

Practical details about phonological awareness training will be presented later in the chapter.

> **CAUTION**
> ....
> Providing at-risk kindergarteners with additional letter-sound learning is no substitute for doing explicit phonemic awareness training.

EXPERIMENTAL SUPPORT FOR EXPLICIT AND SYSTEMATIC LETTER-SOUND INSTRUCTION

Teaching the code of written English (i.e., basic phonics) in a systematic and explicit manner has been empirically shown to have superior results compared to methods that do not explicitly and systematically teach the code (for reviews, see Brady, 2011; Ehri, Nunes, Stahl, & Willows, 2001; NELP, 2008; NICHD, 2000; Share, 1995). The classic whole-word approach puts little emphasis on explicitly teaching letter-sound relationships, instead focusing on the whole word as a unit. Whole language (or literacy-based instruction) which uses the three cueing systems approach tends to teach letter–sound relationships in an informal, "as needed" manner. Numerous studies have demonstrated that the classic whole-word approach and the three cueing systems approach are less effective compared to an explicit phonics approach. In general, children taught through an explicit phonics approach display scores on word-level reading tests that are

6 or 7 standard score points higher than students that are taught phonics skills more informally (effect size of .44; NICHD, 2000). More importantly, the positive impact of explicit and systematic phonics on at-risk readers is much greater, with standard score equivalents being 11 points higher than at-risk readers who are taught through nonsystematic phonics approaches. That difference is large enough that it may prevent some students from future reading difficulties.

Foorman, Francis, Fletcher, Schatschneider, and Mehta (1998) examined the impact of classroom instruction on 285 first and second grade readers who displayed reading skills in the bottom 18th percentile. Whole classes were taught via one of three approaches. The first instructional approach was the "direct code" approach, which involved the explicit teaching of both phonics and phonemic awareness. The second was an "embedded code" approach, which taught phonemic awareness only to the onset-rime level and focused on reading and spelling "word families" (e.g., *sat, cat, mat, hat*). The third was an "implicit code" group in which phonemic awareness was not explicitly taught, and phonics skills were taught only on an as-needed basis while doing authentic reading. In addition to their whole-class instruction, all of these at-risk first graders received either small group or one-on-one instruction as part of their school-based Title I support. This extra help for all students was based on the implicit code approach and had little or no impact on the outcome because it was "overshadowed by the strong effects of classroom instruction" (Foorman et al., 1998, p. 52).

Foorman et al. (1998) found that the students in the direct code classrooms developed word-level reading skills at a much faster pace than students taught via the other instructional approaches. The at-risk first graders in the direct code classrooms had an average end-of-year standard score for word reading (96), whereas the other two groups' standard scores remained in the bottom quartile (88 and 89). They found that of these at-risk readers who all started in the bottom 18th percentile, 44% in the embedded code group and 46% in the implicit code group made little or no reading progress across their first grade year. By contrast, only 16% of those in the direct code group displayed little or no progress. If one were to roughly estimate the number of "treatment resistors" in the direct code instructional group, that would be 16% of students starting out in the bottom 18th percentile, which represents less than 2% of the general population (see Foorman & Al Otaiba, 2009 and Vellutino et al., 1996, for similar estimates).

Also, in all instructional groups, the amount of phonological awareness skill these students displayed at the beginning of the study influenced their progress in reading. Those who started with greater phonological awareness in the embedded code and implicit code groups were better word-level readers at year's end than those starting with weaker phonological awareness skills. This was true of the direct code group as well, yet with an important difference. Because the direct code students received direct instruction in phonological awareness, those in the direct code group who began with the weakest phonological awareness displayed more reading growth than those in the other groups who began with a similar level of phonological awareness skills. This demonstrates the potential value of teaching phonological awareness and phonics as whole-group, Tier 1 instruction.

Taught or Not, Letter-Sound Skills Are Essential

Tunmer and Chapman (2002) conducted a longitudinal study from first to third grade with students in New Zealand taught using a whole language approach. They were not taught phonics in an explicit or systematic way. They asked students at the end of first grade: "When you are reading on your own and come across a word that you don't know, what do you do to try to figure out what the word is?" (p. 48). They divided the children's responses into word-based strategies and text-based strategies. Word-based responses included comments such as "sound it out" or "think of the sounds," whereas text-based responses included comments such as "read it over again," "look at the picture," and "skip it and go on and come back to guess a word that makes sense." They found that 52% reported using word-based strategies, 34% used text-based strategies, and the remainder did not articulate a strategy. By the middle of third grade, students who used a word-based strategy outperformed those who used a text-based strategy on every reading measure, including reading comprehension. Surprisingly, those who used a word-based strategy also outperformed the text-based students in their ability to benefit from context to determine an unfamiliar word. The students in both groups developed the ability to sound out nonsense words, although the word-based group was superior in this regard. In other words, even students who were not systematically *taught* phonic decoding learned phonic decoding, and those who made more use of it comprehended more of what they read as third graders.

Given evidence like this (see also citations in Chapter 7), it is clear that phonics skills are acquired in typically developing students, regardless of whether they are taught. Also, being skilled in phonics provides a reading advantage over those less skilled in phonics, including better reading comprehension. From results like these, it is easy to understand why systematic, explicit phonics is recommended for Tier 1 instruction. If such instruction is delivered with integrity, we should expect a decrease in the number of struggling readers.

What Is Meant by Explicit and Systematic?

Two catchwords often used to describe research-based phonics instruction are *explicit* and *systematic*. These terms are often used but rarely defined. *Explicit* instruction means the teacher provides clear and precise instruction regarding the letter-sound relationships and directly teaches phonic blending. In nonexplicit instruction, the student has greater responsibility for inferring this information from the examples and opportunities provided. *Systematic* instruction means that the teacher has a specific plan or sequence for introducing letter-sound relationships. Traditional phonics instruction tends to be systematic and explicit, whereas the classic whole-word and three cueing systems approaches generally take nonexplicit and/or nonsystematic approaches to phonics instruction. Because the explicit and systematic approach is more successful with most students, the terms *explicit* and *systematic* are often used to distinguish more effective approaches to phonics instruction from less effective ones.

The Impact of Phonics Instruction on Reading Comprehension

The classic whole-word approach and the three cueing systems approaches (i.e., whole language, balanced instruction, and the literacy-based approach) are considered to be meaning-based approaches, whereas phonics is considered to be a code-based approach. The former puts its focus on reading comprehension, and the latter focuses on word-level reading. Ironically, by the end of first grade, students taught by a code-based approach perform, on average, the equivalent of 7 to 8 standard score points higher on tests of reading comprehension than students taught with the meaning-based approaches (NICHD, 2000). This finding is likely because in first grade, what stands between most students and the meaning of a passage are the actual words in that passage. If children cannot read the words, they cannot comprehend the passage. So if a systematic phonics approach results in superior word reading, it should also result in superior reading comprehension (Nation, 2005).

However, explicit phonics instruction tends not to have the same degree of impact on reading comprehension beyond first grade. In the later elementary grades, research results are mixed. In some studies, there is no significant difference in reading comprehension scores between students taught via an explicit phonics approach versus students taught through informal phonics approaches (NICHD, 2000). This finding provides evidence for the notion that most students will learn to read regardless of the approach (Liberman & Liberman, 1990; Tunmer et al., 2002). However, the picture is different after first grade for at-risk and struggling readers. Those taught to read via an explicit phonics approach continued to show, on average, about a 5 standard score point comprehension benefit compared to at-risk and struggling readers not taught through an explicit phonics approach. So, early, explicit phonics instruction provides long-term reading comprehension benefits to children at risk for reading difficulties.

PRACTICAL CONSIDERATIONS REGARDING TEACHING LETTER-SOUND SKILLS AND PHONICS

Phonics instruction can be categorized in the following three ways, based on the depth of information or rules taught:

1. *Letter-sound knowledge with blending.* This refers to knowing letters and their corresponding sounds, as well as digraphs, blends, and diphthongs (discussed later). There are no rules here, only information about the associations between the letters and the most common sounds they make. These should be taught very explicitly and systematically throughout kindergarten and reinforced throughout first and second grades.

2. *Basic phonics rules.* This goes a step beyond the regularities of individual letter-sound correspondences and teaches some basic patterns or rules. For example, knowing about the silent-*e* rule allows a student to know that the word *tape* uses the long *a* sound and the *e* is silent, and *tap* has the short *a* sound in the absence of the silent *e* marker. Another common rule is that when two vowels appear together, the second vowel is typically silent while the first vowel presents its long sound (e.g., *seem, boat, paid*). The most common and helpful rules are very few in number. It seems best to teach these in first grade, once the individual letter sounds have become established.

3. *Elaborate rules phonics.* Considered by some to be the gold standard in responding to poor word-level readers, the Orton-Gillingham approach and its popular derivatives (e.g., Wilson) involve teaching fairly elaborate phonic rules. Students learn the six syllable types of written English (open, closed, silent *e*, vowel digraph, *r*-controlled, and the -*le* type). Teaching these six syllable types may be useful in first and second grade, and with older struggling readers. It is an organized way to present the basic phonic rules. However, these approaches typically teach the exceptions to each of these syllable types, and then the exceptions to the exceptions. This is a complex approach for students with learning difficulties. It will be argued in Chapter 11 that this approach is unnecessarily difficult and does not

directly address the source of the student's reading problem, so the results are often limited.

Most skilled readers cannot name the six syllable types, and if presented with them, they cannot easily list all of or most of the exceptions. Thus, the information trained in these elaborate rules phonics approaches is clearly not a requirement for skilled reading. By contrast, average and above-average readers are skilled in phonemic awareness, while weak readers using Orton-Gillingham and Wilson are not. This should give us clues as to where remedial energies should be directed (see more in Chapter 11).

Teaching the Sounds of the Letters: *T* Does Not Say /Tuh/

Recall from Chapter 6 that it is important that teachers carefully enunciate consonants without an extraneous vowel sound after them (i.e., not /tuh/, /buh/, /puh/). Not only do teachers need to enunciate these consonants correctly, they should teach students how to enunciate them correctly. This will facilitate both phonemic awareness instruction and phonics instruction.

Teaching the Sounds of Letters: Teach Letter Names First

There has been research accumulating to indicate that letter names are useful in helping students learn letter sounds (Cardoso-Martins, Mesquita, & Ehri, 2011; Share, 2004b, Treiman, Weatherston, & Berch, 1994). But not all letter sounds are equally easy to learn. Letters that contain their sound in the initial position in their names (*b, d, j, k, p, t, v, z*; i.e., *bee, dee, jay, kay, pee, tee, vee, zee*) are more easily learned than those whose sounds are second in the letter's name (*f, l, m, n, r, s, x*; i.e., *ef, el, em, en, ar, ess, ecks*) or those whose sound is not contained in the letter's name at all (*h, w, y*) (Cardoso-Martins et al. , 2011; Share, 2004b; Treiman et al., 1994; Treiman et al., 1996). The educational implications of this seem to be that in order to provide an easier path to learning letter sounds, schools should teach the easier-to-acquire letter sounds first—those letters whose sounds are the first phoneme in the letter's name, followed by those letters whose sounds are embedded within the letter's name—leaving for last those letters whose sounds are not found in their letters' names. Most children will learn their letter sounds regardless of the order in which they are taught. However, students with weak phonological skills may benefit from a more gradual, careful sequencing of letter-sound instruction. It is presumed that these students will also be receiving basic phonological awareness training as well, particularly training on recognizing initial sounds in words (Ehri, Defner, & Wilce, 1984).

Teaching the Sounds of Letters: Distributed Practice and Multisensory Learning

In Chapter 4, research was cited that indicates that from first grade on, typical readers only require between one and four exposures to new words before those words become part of their permanent sight vocabulary. However, learning letter names and letter sounds has a very different learning curve. While sight-word learning is based on orthographic memory and requires one to four learning trials, letter-sound knowledge is based on visual–phonological paired-associate learning. This means that students require dozens or even hundreds of exposures to letters and their corresponding names and sounds before they become permanently stored and automatically accessible. For students with the phonological-core deficit, the phonological half of the equation is less efficient than in typically developing peers. Such students often take much longer to learn letter names and letter sounds, which is why these two skills are good predictors of later reading proficiency (i.e., slow learning of letter names and sounds indicates the likely presence of the phonological-core deficit).

For decades, both general and special education teachers have relied heavily on multiple practice opportunities and on multisensory input. A good example of these was the Assured Readiness for Learning (ARL) program (McInnis, 1981, 1999). In that program, kindergartners and even first graders would write letters with their fingers in 9-by-9-inch pans filled with rice or sand, write letters in shaving cream or whipped cream, form the letters out of clay or pipe cleaners, write the letters very large using gross motor skills using either chalk on a board or on the sidewalk, or "paint" them on the blackboard with a large art brush and water. They would even walk around a large version of the letter taped to the floor (with prior approval of the custodian!). This was all in addition to the traditional flashcards and fine motor tasks of writing letters (McInnis, 1999). Both letter names and letter sounds can be learned this way.

Another effective approach to learning paired-associate material is the use of distributed practice. Shapiro and Solity (2008) review research that shows that when information is presented at multiple points of the day in small chunks, it becomes more well established in memory compared to a singular, more lengthy learning experience. An example of distributed practice is when a teacher provides letter-sound instruction and practice in 5-minute mini-sessions, four times a day, compared with covering that same material in a single, 20-minute instructional session. In the ARL program just mentioned, at numerous points throughout the day, the teacher would randomly point to various letters of the alphabet on the alphabet chart listed above the chalkboard, sometimes asking for letter names and at other times the letter sounds. Both manuscript and cursive alphabets were always present from the first day of kindergarten so students would be exposed to both forms of writing from the beginning. The research presented in Chapters 2 and 4 helps us understand why this practice makes good sense: Students develop an abstract representation of letters not tied to a particular script. ARL rigorously implemented distributed practice and multisensory learning, and exemplified good, research-based Tier 1 instruction in letter knowledge long before RTI was developed.

Teaching the Sounds of Letters: Embedded Picture Mnemonics

An additional approach that has received research support over the last few decades is the use of embedded picture mnemonics. These are drawings of letters that are embedded in a picture. The items in each picture begin with the sound of the letter embedded within it. The prototypical example would be a snake shaped like the letter *s*. Ehri, Deffner, & Wilce (1984) taught prereading, at-risk first graders five letter sounds that were unfamiliar to them. Students were randomly assigned to training with embedded picture mnemonics, training with the same picture but with the letter not embedded within it, or just exposure to the letter alone. Students with the embedded picture mnemonics learned the letter sounds much more quickly than the other two groups, which did not differ from each other. Thus, a keyword picture by itself may not be more helpful than learning the letter without a keyword picture. However, using pictures in which the letter can be logically or meaningfully embedded appears to be more effective than learning letters by themselves or with nonembedded keyword pictures. It should be noted that students were trained in basic phonemic awareness along with the embedded picture mnemonics. This phonemic awareness training was limited to teaching students to notice the initial sounds in words. Without the ability to notice the first sound in a word, any picture mnemonic is unlikely to have the associational benefits. Without an awareness of initial phonemes, it would not be clear to the child as to why that particular picture is associated with that particular letter. Several studies subsequent to Ehri et al. (1984) have provided further confirmation of the embedded picture mnemonic approach (Agramonte & Belfiore, 2002; DiLorenzo, Rody, Bucholz, & Brady, 2011; Fulk, Lohman, & Belfiore, 1997; Shmidman & Ehri, 2010).

Most of the sets of embedded mnemonic picture letters that have been used in the various studies are not commercially available. However, an Internet search on "embedded picture mnemonics" will turn up a few sets of embedded mnemonic alphabets, as well as websites that provide embedded picture mnemonic crafts for kindergartners. If one searches for such embedded picture mnemonic sets, it will become clear that some of them are very elaborate and visually complex, while others are very basic and involve simple line drawings. Most of the studies of embedded picture mnemonics used very simple line drawings, so it will be important to select a set in which pictures do not "get in the way." One set that proved successful in a research study (DiLorenzo et al., 2011) is called Itchy's Alphabet. It is one of the few full sets commercially available.

Teaching the Sounds of Letters: Early Spelling Instruction Boosts Early Reading

Spelling, including invented spelling, is an excellent way to instruct and reinforce letter-sound knowledge and phoneme awareness and to establish secure orthographic representations (i.e., sight words). A recent meta-analysis indicated that spelling instruction improved spelling, phonological awareness, and reading (Graham & Santangelo, 2014). Beginning reading and spelling both require letter-sound knowledge and phoneme-level awareness. Invented spelling in kindergarten encourages students to attempt to spell words on their own that they have not yet learned. This reinforces phonological awareness because students must think about the sounds they hear when they say the word. It also develops letter-sound skills because students must select the letter that best represents a given sound. At some point, however, teachers must provide corrective feedback to ensure the learning of accurate spelling. Not only is feedback critical for improving spelling, but it also ensures that a student has the correct spelling of words in order to help establish those words in long-term memory for reading.

Teaching the Sounds of Letters: Letter-Sound Skills Involve More Than Just Letters

Letter-sound knowledge goes beyond simply knowing the correspondences between individual letters and their sounds. Students must also become familiar with digraphs, blends, and diphthongs.

Digraphs

There are several consonant digraphs in English that children must learn, just like they learn individual letters. *Digraphs* are two-letter combinations that represent a single phoneme. The most common English digraphs are *ch, ph, sh,* and *th.* For each of these, the sound they produce is not affiliated with either of the individual letters that make up the digraph. For example, we do not hear the sounds

/t/ or /h/ in *th*. There are other consonant digraphs as well. These preserve the typical sound of one of the letters while the other letter is silent, such as *gh* (e.g., *ghost*), *kn* (e.g., *known)*, *wh* (e.g., *what)*, and *-mb* (e.g., *comb*). There are also vowel digraphs such as *ai, ay, ea, ee,* and *oa*. Some of these vowel digraphs have consistent pronunciations such as *oa* (e.g., *coat, toad*) and *ee* (*free, sleep*). Unfortunately, one of the most common vowel digraphs in English is *ea,* which is also the least consistent.

Generally speaking, vowel digraphs follow this classic rule: "When two vowels go walking, the first one does the talking." For example, in the words *boat, seen,* and *paid,* the first letter in the digraph represents the long vowel sound and the second letter is silent. Because digraphs represent a single phoneme just like individual letters, they should be treated like letters instructionally. After children learn all the letter sounds in the alphabet in kindergarten, it seems judicious to continue beyond the alphabet to introduce the digraphs toward the end of kindergarten, even if it is only the most common consonant digraphs (*ch, ph, sh, th*) and some of the most consistent vowel digraphs (e.g., *ee, oa*). Throughout first and second grade, these should be systematically taught and reinforced.

Blends

Blends are common consonant patterns of two and sometimes three letters that preserve the typical letter-sound relationships. For example, in the word *spent,* there are two blends, one at the beginning (*sp*) and one at the end (*nt*). In the blend at the beginning of *spent,* we hear the pronunciation of both the *s* (/s/) and the *p* (/p/). Likewise, we hear the sounds associated with both of the last two letters. There are some blends that involve three letters (e.g., *burnt; first*). Beginning three phoneme blends always start with the letter *s* (e.g., *splash, string*). Some blends include a digraph (e.g., *shred; twelfth, chrome; bench*). There are many blends in English, but only a small number of digraphs. However, like digraphs, children need to become familiar with the blends because they are so common in English. Blends may be rather difficult in kindergarten, but should be taught and reinforced throughout first and second grades.

Diphthongs

Diphthongs are vowel combinations that when pronounced, produce a continuous vocal output in which the mouth, lips, and/or tongue position change midway through the pronunciation. Common diphthongs include *oi* and *oy*. Also, *ow* is a common diphthong when it is pronounced as in the word *cow,* but not as in *grow*. Notice that when pronouncing the word *grow* slowly, there is a continuous (long) /ō/ sound, yet when the word *cow* is pronounced slowly, there is a change in the vowel sound part way through its pronunciation.

In Chapter 4, it was indicated that it takes longer to learn to read English than the more consistent orthographies (Seymour et al., 2003), in large part due to the many irregular words. In addition, the most transparent languages (e.g., Turkish, Swahili, Spanish, Italian) have very few, if any, digraphs, blends, or diphthongs. These letter sound mappings present additional challenges to students, particularly those with the phonological-core deficit.

THE CENTRALITY OF PHONOLOGY IN WORD READING

Recall from Chapter 4 that phonological skills play a central role in every aspect of word-reading development. The early phonological skills are critical for learning letter names and sounds. The basic phonemic awareness skills of blending and segmenting promote phonic decoding and basic spelling skills. Advanced phonemic proficiency is necessary for efficient sight-word memory. So phonological processes are central at every stage of a student's word-level reading development, from learning letter names at age 3 to 5 all the way to highly proficient word-reading fluency years later. However, since most students with intact phonological skills naturally develop and integrate those skills into reading acquisition, the central nature of phonological awareness is not obvious. But for most students in the bottom third of the population, this does not happen naturally and requires direct instruction in these key skills.

The necessity of good phonological skills for the efficient development of word-level reading means that phonological awareness must be a central element of a school's Tier 1 kindergarten instruction. If it is not, there is little reason to expect the kind of strong preventive benefits that prompted RTI in the first place. As mentioned, RTI originated in large measure from research findings showing that whole-class and/or small-group phonological awareness and explicit phonics instruction in kindergarten prevented a large portion of reading difficulties. Thus, if explicit phonics instruction and formalized phonological awareness training are not central to a school's Tier 1 instruction in reading, then that school is not doing RTI as

> **DON'T FORGET**
> ·······································
> Phonological skills are central to every phase of a student's reading development. Thus, if phonological awareness is not a central element of a school's Tier 1 kindergarten instruction, there is little reason to expect the strong preventive benefits that prompted RTI in the first place. If phonics and phonological awareness instruction are not foundational to a school's K–1 ELA reading curriculum (Tier 1), then that school is not doing RTI as originally intended.

originally intended. RTI demands the use of research-based general educational instructional practices, and there are no general educational teaching practices for reading that even remotely approach the effectiveness of providing phonological awareness training coupled with explicit phonics instruction. The combination of explicit phonics and phonological awareness training for all students in kindergarten and first grade provides far greater results in word-level reading skills than any other teaching practice that has been studied. This combination of instructional elements is the very essence of research-based practice in early word-level reading and spelling skills.

PHONOLOGICAL AWARENESS TRAINING PROGRAMS

The clear implication of the research is that explicit phonics instruction coupled with formalized phonological awareness training should be central to any English language arts (ELA) curriculum in kindergarten and first grade. Formal and informal early phonics programs, activities, and materials are ubiquitous and will not be reviewed here. When it comes to phonological awareness programs, there are fewer that are available or are well known. Some of the available programs have been directly researched and demonstrated to be effective. However, most of the successful training programs in the research literature were "experimenter designed" and are not commercially available (NELP, 2008). There are phonological awareness programs available that draw their methods and techniques directly from the empirical research, though they have not been examined in any published studies. Such programs are likely to be successful, given that virtually every phonological awareness program studied has shown success when compared to not doing phonological awareness training. This is not to say that every program is as good as every other. It is reasonable to assume that some are better than others. However, there exists no body of research that does a *Consumer Reports*–style comparison between existing phonological awareness programs. We must thus rely on studies that indicate which features of phonological awareness training are superior to others. For example, earlier in the chapter, studies were cited that indicated that explicit and systematic phonological instruction is superior to nonsystematic, incidental approaches and that phonological awareness training alongside letter-sound training has superior results to phonological awareness or letter-sound training alone. But we are in no position at this point to suggest that any one of the programs discussed below will produce superior results to any of the others.

The following are options available for teachers to use for kindergarten and first grade Tier 1 and Tier 2 instruction and training. This is not intended to provide a comprehensive overview of every available program. It should be noted that the phonological awareness programs listed below for Tier 1 and Tier 2 prevention have limited overlap with the phonological awareness programs described in Chapter 11 for remedial purposes. This is because the latter requires that students develop skills to the advanced phonemic awareness level, and most of the programs discussed in this chapter are restricted to teaching early and basic phonological awareness skills. Schools will need to consider two different programs for the purposes of prevention and remediation, respectively (the two exceptions being the Rosner program and the Equipped for Reading Success program, both of which apply to Tier 1 prevention and Tier 2/Tier 3 intervention).

Florida Center for Reading Research Phonological Awareness Program

The Florida Center for Reading Research (FCRR) has a fairly complete phonological awareness program available for free. One can download each part of this program from www.fcrr.org. The various faculty and researchers behind the FCRR have made extensive contributions to our understanding of phonological awareness and reading development for over 20 years. For K–1, it would seem this program could be considered an excellent "go to" program given that it is free and it is based on decades of research. The FCRR materials are typeset in such a manner that a school district could easily print them either in full color or black and white.

Road to the Code

As mentioned, the majority of effective phonological awareness training programs in the research literature have been experimenter designed and are not commercially available. Road to the Code (Blachman, Ball, Black, & Tangel, 2000) is one of the exceptions. This program is essentially the same program that was developed and used by Benita Blachman and her colleagues in studies over the past three decades (Ball & Blachman, 1988, 1991; Blachman et al., 1994; Blachman, Tangel, Ball, Black, & McGraw, 1999; Tangel & Blachman, 1992). Some of these studies were highlighted by both the National Reading Panel (NICHD, 2000) and the National Early Literacy Panel (2008).

The Road to the Code is comprised of 44 structured phonological awareness lessons that are best delivered in small groups. While not a "scripted" approach, it provides very explicit details related to instruction. It is based upon the say-it-and-move-it segmentation approach in which tokens are used to represent syllables and phonemes. It trains phonological segmentation and blending.

The only cost is the manual for the teacher. Overall, for Tier 1 and Tier 2 K–1 prevention, this is a program that has a strong empirical track record and is therefore highly recommended.

Rosner Phonological Awareness Training Program

In 1974, Jerome Rosner published the Rosner Auditory-Motor Program, a fairly complete phonological awareness training program. It had been previously used in research studies (Rosner, 1971) with great effect. It begins with preschool-level exercises that include basic skills such as one-to-one counting (e.g., the teacher claps three times then asks the students to clap the same number of times) and proceeds to more sophisticated phonological awareness activities, including some manipulation activities. It is well laid out and easy to use. An advantage of this program is that it goes beyond simple segmentation and blending and uses phonological manipulation activities, particularly phonological deletion with syllables and phonemes. While a lot has been learned about phonological awareness since 1974, this program continues to have enduring value. A revised version of this program is available (Rosner, 1999).

Interactive Strategies Approach

This is the program used by Vellutino et al. (1996), which was one of the key studies that prompted RTI. The interactive strategies approach was originally a one-on-one tutoring program with first graders, but it has been adapted and developed since that time and used in additional studies (Lennon & Slesinski, 1999; Scanlon, Gelzheiser, Vellutino, Schatschneider, & Sweeney, 2008; Scanlon, Vellutino, Small, Fanuele, & Sweeney, 2005; Vellutino & Scanlon, 2002). It now has small-group and whole-class elements, and it can be used in kindergarten. Small-group and whole-class versions of this program in kindergarten have been shown to reduce the number of struggling readers (Scanlon et al., 2005, 2008), making it a good resource for preventing reading problems. After over 15 years of development, the interactive strategies approach has been released in book form (Scanlon, Anderson, & Sweeney, 2010). This program has much helpful information and practical resources on early reading well beyond the phonemic awareness training.

Phonemic Awareness in Young Children

Swedish researchers Åke Olofsson and Ingvar Lundberg were responsible for some of the earliest experimental studies on phonological awareness (Olofsson & Lundberg, 1983, 1985; Lundberg et al., 1988). Their program was adapted for American English students by U.S. researchers, with Lundberg being one of the co-authors (Adams, Foorman, Lundberg, & Beeler, 1998). It includes a wide variety of phonological awareness activities for kindergarten and first grade.

Ladders to Literacy

Ladders to Literacy (O'Connor, Notari-Syverson, & Vadasy, 1998b, 2005) has been shown to be effective in teaching phonological awareness and to have an impact on reading achievement (O'Connor et al., 1995, 1998a). Studies that used Ladders to Literacy were reviewed by the National Reading Panel (NICHD, 2000).

Words Their Way

While neither a phonological awareness program nor a reading program, Words Their Way supports the development of both of these. It is primarily a spelling program, but as mentioned, spelling instruction can improve letter-sound knowledge, phonological awareness, and reading skills. Regardless of which phonological awareness program is selected, Words Their Way would be an excellent supplement to any such program. With its emphasis on early spelling and orthographic skills, it would likely enhance the effectiveness of any phonological awareness program. Unlike most programs mentioned here, which are best suited for K–1, this program is appropriate beyond first grade.

Equipped for Reading Success

Equipped for Reading Success (Kilpatrick, 2015a) is a comprehensive phonological training program designed for whole class or small group Tier 1 instruction, appropriate for kindergarten through second grade. It is also designed for Tiers 2 and 3 from kindergarten through adulthood (see next chapter). Equipped for Reading Success is the most recent of the programs discussed here, and the only program that "works backward" from our understanding of orthographic mapping. It also appears to be the only program that specifically and programmatically develops automaticity of phonological awareness skills. While not yet used in a published study (it is currently under study at the time of writing), each aspect of the program was built upon elements from studies with highly successful outcomes (see next chapter).

Other Programs for Tier I Instruction and Tier 2 Prevention

There are other programs available that could be used for whole-class or small-group Tier 1 and/or small-group Tier 2 prevention. Most of the available programs have *not* been the specific subjects of research studies, even though the instructional approaches used in those programs have been shown to be effective in various studies.

Some effective phonological training programs are not mentioned here because they are more appropriate for intervention and are described in the next chapter. Other available programs that educators may want to consider include Sounds Abound, Phonological Awareness Training for Reading, and the Phonological Awareness Kit. An Internet search will turn up these and additional programs. Because so few programs have been directly studied, it is difficult to indicate which may be the best.

PREVENTING LITERACY-RELATED LANGUAGE DIFFICULTIES

The empirical research on preventing the language comprehension problems that affect reading comprehension is not nearly as extensive as the research on preventing word-level reading difficulties (McKeown & Beck, 2014; NELP, 2008). The National Reading Panel found an insufficient number of studies on literacy-related language enhancement programs (mostly vocabulary instruction) to conduct a meta-analysis (NICHD, 2000). The National Early Literacy Panel (2008) had more studies to analyze, yet they found that for most types of language-oriented literacy interventions, there was an insufficient number of studies to conduct a meta-analysis for many outcome measures (e.g., vocabulary, listening comprehension). Nevertheless, there are numerous studies that can guide both curricular decisions and intervention efforts (Kamhi, 2014), and both panels generated recommendations based upon the available studies.

Shared Book Reading

A topic covered by the National Early Literacy Panel (2008) that was not directly addressed by the National Reading Panel (NICHD, 2000) was the impact of shared book reading on literacy outcomes. A previous review of the literature (Scarborough & Dobrich, 1994) indicated that the research on the language and literacy benefits of reading aloud to preschoolers was surprisingly scant, mostly correlational, and suggested a modest impact. Fortunately, better studies have appeared since then and were reviewed by the National Early Literacy Panel (2008). The panel concluded that reading aloud to young children provides a substantial benefit for their language development.

Overall, the National Early Literacy Panel found a .57 effect size for shared book reading on oral language outcomes. This translates into an approximately

8 to 9 standard score point difference between those in the shared book reading interventions and their matched comparison groups. This magnitude of effect has educational significance, not just statistical significance. They found similar effects whether the book reading occurred during the preschool years or in kindergarten. Students who displayed typical development had stronger results than at-risk students, but the latter still averaged about 7 standard score points higher than matched comparison groups.

Programs implemented by preschool and kindergarten teachers fared better than at-home programs, though the latter at least showed a modest benefit and should be encouraged. What appeared to be the most successful approach in developing language skills was *dialogic reading* in which

> the adult reader asks the child or children questions about the story or the pictures in the book and provides feedback to the child or children in the form of repetitions, expansions, and modeling of answers. In dialogic reading, the adult tries to facilitate the child's active role in telling the story rather than foster passive listening. (NELP, 2008, p. 158)

Other Literacy-Oriented Language Programs

Based on 19 studies of programs designed to enhance literacy-related language skills such as vocabulary and listening comprehension, the National Early Literacy Panel found an average effect size of .63 (NELP, 2008). This translates into a standard score difference of about 9 points between students who received such instruction or intervention and those who did not. A 9 standard score point gain represents a substantial, educationally meaningful improvement. Most of the findings related to vocabulary improvement, and this finding paralleled the findings from the National Reading Panel several years earlier (NICHD, 2000). Interventions for children ages 3 and younger had nearly twice the impact as those for children from ages 4 to 6, emphasizing the importance of early intervention (NELP, 2008). Yet even among at-risk students in preschool and kindergarten, improvements relative to controls averaged 7 to 8 standard score points.

So what are these effective programs that can boost literacy-related language skills, such as vocabulary and listening comprehension? Unfortunately, most are experimenter designed and not commercially available (NELP, 2008). Also, they are typically not described in the research reports with sufficient detail to guide implementation. Most simply speak about providing a variety of language games and activities above and beyond the standard curriculum. It thus seems that conscientiously providing additional language enrichment appears to be effective,

> **DON'T FORGET**
> ....
> Providing deliberate, planned, additional language-oriented activities targeting vocabulary development, grammar, and other expressive and receptive language skills stimulates growth in these areas beyond the "business as usual" approaches of teaching preschool and kindergarten.

regardless of the details of the particular program. The National Early Literacy Panel (2008) concluded from their meta-analysis that "there seemed to be no key features to these interventions that consistently gave an advantage. All of these programs seemed to work" (p. 222). In essence, providing deliberate, planned, additional language-oriented activities targeting vocabulary development, grammar, and other expressive and receptive language skills stimulates growth in these areas beyond the "business as usual" approaches of teaching preschool and kindergarten. Providing such language enrichment requires careful thought and planning given that many preschool and kindergarten programs already provide language stimulation. Yet the research suggests that with greater language emphasis comes better results. Educators cannot assume that their state's curriculum or their school district's ELA program or reading series will be sufficient to provide optimal language development, particularly for at-risk students.

Vocabulary Development

Vocabulary is only one facet of language, yet it is a central element. There are many available strategies for teaching vocabulary. Numerous books, programs, and games are available to teachers for vocabulary development. Most of the available vocabulary programs have not been directly assessed via an empirical research study (NELP, 2008). Yet, the message to take away from the National Reading Panel (2000) and the National Early Literacy Panel's meta-analysis (2008) is that educators must make a contentious effort to systematically emphasize language development to the greatest degree possible. There are many resources available for this, but teachers must use careful judgment in terms of adopting these vocabulary or language programs, given that there is no database of comparison studies to help establish best practice.

In Chapter 5, it was mentioned that researchers are giving greater recognition to the central role that background knowledge plays in reading comprehension and oral language comprehension (Catts, 2009; Compton et al., 2014, Kamhi, 2009). Yet neither the National Reading Panel (NICHD, 2000) nor the National Early Literacy Panel (2008) specifically addressed this in their reviews. In some sense, schooling is all about providing background knowledge. The fact that so many children lack such knowledge indicates that what is typically covered in school does not sufficiently bridge the gap between children with high and low background knowledge. The vicious cycle is that as children grow older, reading provides greater background knowledge, but those who have lesser background knowledge and weaker reading skills are less likely to read. While there may not be as many formalized programs available for background knowledge development, preschool and kindergarten teachers need to be cognizant of the importance of background knowledge and provide a "background knowledge–enriched" learning experience, to the extent possible.

A Recommended Language Program

As mentioned, studies that successfully boosted language abilities in at-risk students did not provide sufficient detail in their reports to facilitate implementation of their successful practices. There is an important exception to this. A team of British researchers conducted a large-scale, comprehensive prevention study of both word-level reading and language comprehension difficulties. Results from different aspects of their study were published in scientific journals. In addition, the team produced a book titled *Developing Language and Literacy: Effective Interventions in the Early Years* (Carroll, Bowyer-Crane, Duff, Hulme, & Snowling, 2011). Unlike other successful studies, this program provides the information needed for implementation. *Developing Language and Literacy* provides details on all aspects of their highly successful project. This includes information ranging from training teachers to selection of specific language or literacy programs and activities. While it is not a curriculum, the authors describe the reasoning behind their selection of the instructional materials and activities they used. They also provide many practical details about how they implemented their study. To date, it appears to be the most well-developed resource for guiding preventive efforts for early literacy-related language acquisition.

SUMMARY

Most reading difficulties can be prevented with effective K–1 Tier 1 instruction in explicit letter-sound skills and phonological awareness. Follow-up with Tier 2 preventive instruction for at-risk readers will further support these efforts. Several easy-to-implement phonological awareness programs are available for both Tier 1 and Tier 2, all of which are inexpensive or free. Language development can be boosted by conscientiously adding further language enrichment activities or by implementing the *Developing Language and Literacy* program.

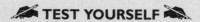

TEST YOURSELF

1. **What does research suggest about preventing reading difficulties in English language learners?**
   (a) There are no special considerations whatsoever.
   (b) Word-reading problems can be prevented but reading comprehension problems cannot.
   (c) Reading comprehension problems can be prevented but word-reading problems cannot.
   (d) While they may require more attention in terms of language development and converting to different letter-sound patterns (if they were exposed to a different orthography), most of the same principles of prevention are involved with English language learners as with native English speakers.

2. **How common is using phonemic awareness training as a Tier 1 general education instructional/preventive practice?**
   (a) It is very common.
   (b) It is very uncommon.
   (c) It is used in about half of kindergartens and first grades in the United States.
   (d) There does not appear to be any research upon which to answer this question.

3. **What might be the best way of conceptualizing a child being "ready" for reading instruction?**
   (a) The child is at least 6 years old.
   (b) The child has been to preschool.
   (c) The child's parents often read to the child at home before the child goes to kindergarten.
   (d) The child has age-appropriate letter-sound knowledge and phonological awareness.

4. **In the studies establishing effective prevention practices, which combination of instructional approaches was superior to all the others?**
   (a) Additional letter-sound training beyond the general kindergarten curriculum.
   (b) Phonological awareness training.
   (c) Phonological awareness training plus opportunities to apply phonological awareness to letters and words.
   (d) Additional letter-sound training plus additional vocabulary development.

5. **Which of the following has been the general finding about the benefits of early prevention efforts using phonological awareness and letter-sound instruction?**
   (a) All children benefit, but those with stronger skills benefit more.
   (b) Only children at risk seem to benefit.

(c) All children benefit, but at-risk children seem to benefit more in the long run.

(d) All at-risk children benefit except the weakest (i.e., those in the bottom 5%).

6. **What can we say about delivering Tier 1 phonological awareness instruction in either small groups or to the whole class?**

(a) The research is clear that whole-class Tier 1 instruction is superior.

(b) The research is clear that small-group Tier 1 instruction is superior.

(c) Research is somewhat mixed, but both seem to produce good results so schools should decide based upon available resources.

(d) The research suggests that whole group works best with typically developing students, while small group works best with at-risk students.

7. **What has research said about using letters to teach phonemic awareness?**

(a) Under no circumstances should letters be used when teaching phonemic awareness.

(b) Letters should always be used when teaching phonemic awareness.

(c) Phonemic awareness seems best taught at first without letters, but at some point, phonemic awareness needs to be applied to letters and words.

(d) Early letter-sound/phonics instruction focuses on letters and phonemes, so no explicit phonemic awareness training beyond this is necessary.

8. **Teaching explicit letter-sound relationships to kindergartners and first graders provides an advantage over approaches that do not explicitly teach those relationships.**

(a) True

(b) False

9. **The phonological awareness programs designed to prevent reading difficulties in kindergarten and first grade are also the same programs that are best suited for remediating older students.**

(a) True

(b) False

Answers: 1. d; 2. d; 3. d; 4. c; 5. c; 6. c; 7. c; 8. True; 9. False

Eleven

EFFECTIVE APPROACHES FOR OVERCOMING OR MINIMIZING READING DIFFICULTIES

The components of effective reading instruction are the same whether the focus is prevention or intervention: phonemic awareness and phonemic decoding skills, fluency in word recognition and text processing, construction of meaning, vocabulary, spelling, and writing.

—Foorman and Torgesen (2001, p. 203)

Any well-founded educational intervention must be based on a sound theory of the causes of a particular form of learning difficulty, which in turn must be based on an understanding of how a given skill is learned by typically developing children.

—Snowling and Hulme (2011, p. 1)

We call for the development of a new generation of reading interventions that target the fundamental knowledge structures and learning mechanisms known to support skilled reading development.

—Compton, Miller, Elleman, and Steacy (2014, p. 57)

The word-recognition skills of students with identified reading disabilities can be normalized with effective interventions.

—Foorman and Al Otaiba (2009, p. 257)

The premise of this chapter is simple: Intervention efforts should be based on an understanding of both typical reading development and on the factors that disrupt this process. With this foundational knowledge, intervention is based on a student's assessment data, which provides a hypothesis about why the student is struggling. Intervention efforts are then directed toward removing the hurdles that are preventing the student from making typical reading progress.

Closing the gap between struggling readers and their typically developing peers is difficult because the latter do not slow down and wait. They continually expand their pool of sight words as their reading develops. Reading remediation has typically been more a matter of trying to keep the gap from widening (Torgesen, Rashotte, Alexander, Alexander, & MacPhee, 2003). For weak readers to close this gap, they would have to accelerate their progress to a rate of growth that is faster than their typically developing peers (Torgesen et al., 2003), like a runner in a race who would have to run faster than those who are ahead, at least for a while, in order to catch up with them.

Three things must happen to accomplish the formidable task of getting weak readers to learn at such an accelerated pace.

1. Students need to develop good phonic decoding skills. This helps when they encounter unfamiliar words, which is quite often given their limited sight vocabularies. Yet poor phonic decoding is a common characteristic of weak readers, so this first item seems to be a major challenge.

2. Weak readers need to develop the capacity to easily remember the words they read. Weak readers have limited sight vocabularies because when they encounter new words, they do not remember them. This capability must be developed so they can efficiently build large and continually expanding sight vocabularies. Weak readers require dozens of exposures to words before they are permanently stored (Ehri & Saltmarsh, 1995; Martens & de Jong, 2008). This is highly inefficient compared to their typically developing peers who require only one to four exposures for new words to be solidly encoded into long-term memory. Reading progress cannot be accelerated unless readers develop the ability to quickly add words to their sight vocabularies.

3. Once the capacity to efficiently store new words has developed, students require a great deal of reading practice. Only words that have been encountered can be added to one's sight vocabulary. Wide exposure to words is necessary to build sight vocabulary. But reading practice is not an effective way to boost reading skills if the student is unable to phonically decode unfamiliar words or to remember the words being read.

It is only when all three of these components are in place that a student can possibly begin to "close the gap" in reading.

Those who have worked with poor readers know how difficult it is for these students to develop phonic decoding skills and to build their sight vocabularies. Fortunately, it is possible to "normalize" the reading skills of a large portion of weak readers (Foorman & Al Otaiba, 2009; Simos et al., 2002; Torgesen, 2005;

DON'T FORGET

In order for weak readers to catch up with their peers, they need to accelerate their learning at a faster pace than their typically developing peers. Fortunately, research has demonstrated that this is possible.

DON'T FORGET

Intervention researchers estimate that if the best prevention and intervention approaches were widely used, the percentage of elementary school students reading below a basic level would be about 5% rather than the current 30% to 34%.

Truch, 1994, 2003, 2004; Vellutino et al., 1996). Also, for those whose response to these highly effective approaches does not result in "normalized" performance levels, they still make a great deal of progress compared to those exposed to traditional remedial methods (McGuinness, McGuinness, & McGuinness, 1996; Truch, 1994).

The approaches described in the second half of this chapter have been empirically shown to make dramatic improvements in struggling readers, even those in the bottom 1% to 3% of readers. In their review of intervention research, Foorman and Al Otaiba (2009) point out that if broadly applied, our best interventions could take the number of strug-

gling readers from about 30% to 34% of the population down to about 5%, and the percentage of students with the more significant reading difficulties and disabilities could be closer to 1% to 2%. If the estimates by Foorman and Al Otaiba (2009) are truly possible, then why is this not happening? There are multiple answers to that question, many of which were presented in Chapter 1 and will not be repeated here. Rather, the focus of this chapter is on the highly successful approaches that would produce such results.

CAUTION

Before proceeding, it is important that readers have already read Chapter 4, which provides the foundational knowledge needed to best understand and apply the effective reading interventions described in this chapter.

The review of intervention research by Foorman and Al Otaiba (2009) focused primarily on word-level reading. The incredible success achieved in some of these studies suggests that three of the four types of reading problems can be successfully addressed, namely dyslexia, mixed reading difficulty, and the compensating type. All three of these involve word-level read-

ing difficulties. Only the mixed type involves language comprehension difficulties independently of the word-reading difficulties. Thus, if their word-level reading difficulties were normalized, these students with the mixed type pattern would then display the hyperlexic pattern because they would no longer have word-reading difficulties.

INTERVENTION WITH WORD-LEVEL READING DIFFICULTIES

Results from the intervention research studies on word-level reading have displayed a wide range of outcomes, from a mean of 0 standard score points on nationally normed tests (Vaughn, et al., 2012) to a mean of 25 standard score points (Simos et al., 2002). The following sections will review the likely reasons for this variability and then focus on presenting the approach that has had the best outcomes for struggling readers.

The Three Bodies of Intervention Research: Minimal Versus Moderate Versus Highly Successful Outcomes

The intervention research designed to correct word-level reading difficulties can be sorted into three categories, based on outcomes. The first represents a large proportion of the research. These studies report minimal improvements in word-level reading, with average gains on nationally normed word identification subtests ranging from 0 to 5 standard score points. Improvements in this range are not easily noticed in real-world reading activities. In this chapter, this will be referred to as the *minimal improvement* category. The second category also represents a large proportion of studies. These studies display improvements in reading that range from 6 to 9 standard score points. This represents a welcome level of improvement, because it means that more "acceleration" in the rate of learning has occurred, relative to peers. However, in all but the mildest cases of reading difficulties, an improvement of 6 to 9 standard score points typically falls short of closing the gap. This will be referred to as the *moderate improvement* group.

The third category represents a small minority of the intervention research studies, yet involves substantially better results. In this group, the improvements on nationally normed word identification tests range from 12.5 to 25 standard score points. This will be referred to as the *highly successful* category. What is the difference between these bodies of research that can account for such a disparity in outcomes? Factors like (a) SES, (b) group size, (c) age of students, (d) severity of reading difficulty, and (e) the amount of intervention time cannot account for the differences. A continuum of each of these variables is present in all three categories of studies.

The studies with the greatest outcomes displayed intervention approaches consistent with our understanding of reading development as outlined in Chapter 4.

In particular, every one of the most successful studies contained the following three elements:

1. They aggressively addressed and corrected the students' phonological awareness difficulties and taught phonological awareness to the advanced level.
2. They provided phonic decoding instruction and/or reinforcement.
3. They provided students with ample opportunities to apply these developing skills to reading connected text.

> **DON'T FORGET**
> ....
> Intervention research studies appear to fall into three general categories based upon their average standard score point improvements on normative tests of word identification: (1) minimal (0- to 5-point gains), (2) moderate (6- to 9-point gains), and (3) highly successful (gains or 12.5 to 25 points).

Found in every one of the highly successful studies, these three elements closely align with the three requirements for students to accelerate their progress described earlier in the chapter. By contrast, every one of the studies in the minimal group was missing one or more of these three essential elements. The studies in the moderate category included training in phonemic awareness, phonics, and opportunities to read connected text. However, they only taught phonemic awareness to the basic level. They trained phonemic blending and segmentation but did not teach the advanced phonemic awareness skills. Nearly all of the studies from all three categories provided systematic and explicit phonics instruction and reading opportunities, so it appears there is a direct relationship between the degree and nature of phonemic awareness training and the degree of improvement in the students' word identification skills: The minimal studies included no phonemic awareness training, the moderate studies only trained basic phonemic awareness, and the highly successful studies involved training phonemic awareness to the advanced level.

As a result of this distinctive pattern in the literature, we will refer to teaching advanced phonemic awareness skills, phonic decoding instruction, and reading connected text as the "key elements" of successful word-level reading remediation. Before presenting the studies with highly successful outcomes, a review of the research on some of the popular reading interventions will be presented. This is important because educational professionals should be well informed about the effectiveness of commonly used approaches for RTI or special educational reading instruction. The research on such approaches should guide instructional decisions.

An Important Caveat Regarding the Reporting of Intervention Effectiveness

There is currently no consensus regarding what constitutes the best way to gauge improvement in research studies. It is common to report an effect size. However, an effect size must be interpreted with a great deal of caution.

Effect sizes are based on the normal curve in which an effect size of 1.0 refers to 1 standard deviation. It is thus simple to convert reported effect sizes into standard scores by multiplying them by 15 (e.g., an effect size of .40 = 6 standard score points). However, effect sizes are most commonly reported in relation to a control group, not national norms. When this is the case, *the effect size does not necessarily indicate whether a given intervention helped students narrow or close the gap with their typically developing peers.* For example, Vaughn et al. (2012) report an effect size in word identification of .49 between experimental and comparison groups, which is equivalent to a 7.4 standard score point difference. However, the experimental group displayed no normative increase in standard score points. Their mean pretest and posttest standard scores were both 89. The .49 effect size difference was reported because the comparison group's posttest scores were substantially lower than their pretest scores.

While effect sizes may overestimate student progress, they may also substantially underrepresent large gains. For example, Torgesen, Wagner, Rashotte, Herron, and Lindamood (2010) showed extremely large standard score improvements of 21 and 23 points with the Read, Write, Type and the Lindamood LiPS intervention programs, respectively. Yet the comparison group that received the school's standard remediation program made a virtually unparalleled average gain of about 14 standard score points. This is highly unusual and is clearly an outlier in the research literature. Comparison groups typically make minimal normative gains in research studies, and the 14 point gain made in this particular study exceeds the gains made by intervention groups in well over 90% of intervention studies. The net result of this outlier performance of the comparison group in the Torgesen et al. (2010) study is that the effect size relative to the comparison group was modest, roughly similar in magnitude to the effect size reported in the Vaughn et al. (2012) study in which there was no normative improvement. Thus, normative gains of 21 to 23 standard score points and a normative gain of 0 points are both reported as having similar, modest effect sizes! These examples should make it clear that effect sizes alone can be a very misleading index of progress.

An unfortunate consequence of relying exclusively on effect sizes is that based on this single study (Torgesen et al., 2010), the bestevidence.org website lists the

> ## CAUTION
> ....
> Intervention effect sizes relative to control groups can be very misleading and may grossly overestimate or underestimate how much students have improved. Thus, standard score point gains on nationally normed reading tests appear to be the best way to determine if an intervention has helped weak readers narrow or even close the gap with their typically developing peers.

two programs that produced those large standard score point improvements as having limited effectiveness due to the reported effect size, with no reference to their outstanding 21 and 23 standard score point normative gains. Also, in its presentation of the LiPS program, which has many studies indicating very strong results (e.g., Alexander et al., 1991; Torgesen, 2004a, 2005; Torgesen et al., 2001, Truch, 1994), bestevidence.org only reports this single study to evaluate the effectiveness of the LiPS program while providing no explanation as to why they only used that single study to make their determination of effectiveness. By contrast, bestevidence.org lists programs as "effective" that display substantially smaller standard score point gains on nationally normed tests, almost exclusively single-digit gains. If researchers uniformly reported standard score point gains on normative assessments in addition to effect sizes relative to control groups, it would be much easier to judge the genuine efficacy of any given program.

> ## CAUTION
> ....
> Results can be statistically significant without being educationally meaningful. Very small normative improvements in standard scores (e.g., 2 to 4 points) may not be noticed in real-world reading situations and do not close the gap between weak readers and their peers. However, such minimal differences often reach "statistical significance" in research studies and may thus be described as "evidence-based" or "research-based."

A related issue of concern is that many intervention studies published in school psychology journals report "statistically significant" results, yet these results often translate into very small normative gains (e.g., Mitchell & Begeny, 2014). Some standard score gains of 2 to 4 points may be statistically significant depending on the number of participants in the study and the performance of the comparison group. Such gains are not educationally meaningful. When studies report statistically significant intervention gains, the approaches that produced such results are then termed "evidence-based" or "research-based" despite their very limited efficacy based upon nationally normed standard score gains. Therefore, in the following discussions, every attempt is made to represent growth relative to the population using normative scores from normed measures. This appears to be the best index for determining if students are closing the gap with their peers (Torgesen, 2004a; Torgesen et al., 2003).

POPULAR READING INTERVENTIONS WITH MODEST OR MINIMAL RESULTS

In addition to reviews of some of the popular reading interventions, some less popular approaches will be mentioned that are marketed to schools. Parents, teachers, and school psychologists should be aware of the research on their effectiveness. Parents are vulnerable because they want their children to improve in reading, which means they are willing to try anything. Also, they may not be relying on dependable sources of information about such programs. It is important to direct them to approaches that are likely to have the greatest benefit. All of the popular approaches in this section have displayed weak results for word-reading skills, ranging from 0 to about 6 standard score point improvements.

Orton-Gillingham, Wilson, and Related Elaborate Rules Phonics Approaches

Considered by many to be the gold standard for remediating word-level reading difficulties, the Orton-Gillingham and Wilson programs require learning a complex set of rules. They teach the six syllable types of printed English (open, closed, silent-*e*, vowel digraph, *r*-controlled, and the *le* type), the multiple exceptions to each of these syllable types, and finally the exceptions to the exceptions! This is a challenge for poor readers, many of whom have metacognitive issues. Most skilled readers cannot name the six syllable types, let alone their exceptions. It follows from this that it is not necessary to learn all these rules and exceptions in order to be a skilled reader. Skilled phonic decoding only requires letter-sound knowledge and phonological blending. A few simple rules can be very helpful, and the six syllable types approach may be a practical way to organize those simple rules (i.e., without all the exceptions and the exceptions to the exceptions). If a student develops letter-sound skills and blending but is still a weak reader, it does not logically follow that more complex and in-depth phonics rules are the answer.

These "elaborate rules" programs seem to assume it is necessary for students to accurately decode every decodable word in isolation. However, that is not how reading develops. Most new words are encountered in the context of reading connected text. The combination of basic phonic decoding (letter-sound knowledge plus blending with a few basic "rules"), the set for variability, and sentence context together allow students to identify most English words, including irregular words. With this combination of skills and strategies, there is no need for such an elaborate system of phonics rules.

Due to their emphasis on phonics, Orton-Gillingham and Wilson have long produced better results with poor readers than nonphonic remedial approaches. These programs can often dramatically boost phonic decoding skills but not necessarily real-word reading (Kuder, 1990; Ritchey & Goeke, 2006; Stebbins et al., 2012; Torgesen et al., 2007).

Some students "take off" in their reading skills with Wilson or Orton-Gillingham. These individuals likely had mild phonological awareness difficulties. For them, explicit interaction between letters and phonemes stimulated their phonological awareness development, which in turn allowed them to develop a sight-word vocabulary. But for students with more moderate to severe phonological awareness difficulties, such intensive phonics instruction does not produce the more advanced phonemic proficiency needed to become skilled at orthographic mapping. As a result, growth in sight vocabulary among many graduates of these approaches is often limited.

When students have mastered the basic phonics skills and this is not translating into better general word-level reading, this is a clear indication of a problem with phonemic proficiency. It is not a sign that the student needs to learn *more* complex phonics rules.

Evaluation: Based upon the three elements of successful reading intervention, Orton-Gillingham, Wilson, and similar programs do not teach phonemic awareness to the advanced level, which is necessary for sight-word development. They only train the basic phonological skills of blending and segmentation.

READ 180

READ 180 is a popular program designed for weak readers in grades 4 to 12. It teaches word reading and reading comprehension. Independent research studies on READ 180 report an average of a 3 standard score point improvement in word-reading skills on nationally normed tests (Kim, Samson, Fitzgerald, & Hartry, 2010; Papalewis, 2004; Slavin, Cheung, Groff, & Lake, 2008).

Evaluation: READ 180 lacks two of the three elements of highly successful interventions. It provides limited phonics instruction and virtually no phonemic awareness training to address the limited sight-word skills of the weak readers READ 180 is intended to help.

System 44

It is admittedly premature to include System 44 in this section because, at the time of writing, there were no available research studies on System 44 in peer-reviewed journals. It claims to be research-based and presumably justifies this claim because of its strong emphasis on phonics. In fact, System 44 appears to be a very well-implemented phonics program. However, beyond simple blending and segmentation, System 44 does not appear to directly address advanced phonological awareness skill deficits. As described earlier in the chapter, research studies using explicit phonics instruction have yielded average gains of between 0 and 25 standard score points. Thus, by itself, a program based upon systematic and explicit phonics instruction does not guarantee any particular level of outcome.

Evaluation: System 44 appears to address two of the three critical skills found in the studies with highly successful results. It does not provide training of advanced phonological awareness, but it provides phonics instruction with opportunities for reading connected text. This evaluation is based on the premises laid out in this chapter and the information on the System 44 website. The actual success rate of System 44 will be determined by future research.

Repeated Readings

Problems with the repeated readings approach were discussed earlier (see Chapters 4 and 8). To summarize, research on repeated readings has shown that while there are typically short-term improvements in word-reading accuracy and speed on practiced passages, there does not appear to be much generalization to unpracticed passages (for a review of research, see Chard, Ketterlin-Geller, Baker, Doabler, & Apichatabutra, 2009). In those studies reporting standard score point improvements on normative reading tests, there are only minimal to modest improvements (3 to 5 standard score points) in word identification, nonsense word reading, and reading comprehension (e.g., O'Connor, White, & Swanson, 2007) after 14 weeks of intervention. O'Connor et al. (2007) found that the results from a repeated readings intervention were equivalent to a parallel intervention in which the same amount of reading was done but without the repeated element. This suggests that the total amount of extra reading practice time made the impact rather than the specific method of repeated readings. Based upon limited standard score point improvements, there is little reason to believe that repeated readings closes the reading gap between weak and average readers.

While practice helps most skills, it is not so simple with word-level reading. Children with the phonological-core deficit display minimal benefit from reading practice. The repeated reading technique does not proceed from an understanding of why the child struggles in the first place. It seems to assume that the key to reading improvement is practice. This is not the case with poor word-level readers.

CAUTION

···

While practice helps most skills, it is not so simple with word-level reading. Children with the phonological-core deficit display minimal benefit from reading practice.

Evaluation: The repeated readings intervention provides extensive opportunities for reading connected text, but does not address the phonemic awareness difficulties or poor phonics skills that are causing the problem.

Flash Cards

Flash cards can be great tools, and there are ways they can be used within the context of highly effective interventions. However, flash cards can also be inefficient, in a similar manner to the repeated readings technique. Often flash cards are used under the assumption that written word memory is based on paired-associate learning. We now know that word reading is based on orthographic memory, not on paired-associate, visual-phonological memory. However, flash cards are a wonderful tool for learning letters, digraphs, and blends.

Evaluation: Flash cards typically provide reinforcement of reading skills and by their nature do not include all three ingredients found in successful studies.

Reading Recovery

Critiques of Reading Recovery from a scientific perspective are rather common (e.g., Foorman & Al Otaiba, 2009; Hempenstall, 2002; Tunmer, Chapman, & Prochnow, 2002). The best research outcomes have come from Reading Recovery advocates, but far more modest results come from independent researchers (Tunmer et al., 2002). This is partially due to the fact that students who do not appear likely to be successful are dropped from the program after several lessons and excluded from the effectiveness statistics. This is inconsistent with scientific practice and inflates the reported success rate. Also, Reading Recovery interventions are based on screening the bottom 20%, yet the practice is to first tutor the top half of that bottom 20%. There is often not enough time left in the school year to address the bottom 10%. The focus is therefore on the students who are naturally easier to remediate. Overall, independent studies have suggested that Reading Recovery, with all the expense involved in its one-on-one service delivery, results in about a 3 standard score point improvement (Slavin, Lake, Davis, & Madden, 2011). Even when stronger gains are found, the results often do not last (Foorman & Al Otaiba, 2009).

These outcomes should not be surprising given that Reading Recovery is based on the three cueing systems model of reading. Chapman, Tunmer, and Prochnow (2001) found that student success in Reading Recovery was directly based upon the degree of phonological awareness skills with which they started the program. Chapman et al. (2001) also found that Reading Recovery did not improve the phonological awareness skills of struggling readers. A big part of Reading Recovery is to teach word-reading strategies that are based on contextual guessing, which does not promote the skills needed to develop a sight-word vocabulary.

Evaluation: Reading Recovery provides extensive opportunities for reading connected text. It is more limited in its phonic decoding instruction and does not correct the poor phonemic awareness skills that are limiting struggling readers.

Leveled Literacy Intervention (LLI)

LLI is an intervention for struggling readers marketed as research-based. However, at the time of writing, there have been no research studies on LLI published in peer-reviewed journals. LLI appears to be a small group adaptation of the one-on-one Reading Recovery program, but it includes more phonics instruction than is typically found in Reading Recovery. As previously mentioned, outcomes based upon phonics instruction are highly variable, so simply adding additional phonics to a program does not allow us to confidently predict any particular level of results. Foundational to LLI is the three cueing systems approach, which has been shown to be problematic on multiple levels (see Chapter 2).

Evaluation: Relative to Reading Recovery, LLI is a step in the right direction because it incorporates more phonics instruction. However, as just mentioned, outcomes based upon phonics instruction are so variable that simply adding additional phonics to a program does not guarantee any particular level of results. Also, LLI does not adequately address the phonemic awareness deficiencies found in most struggling readers. Furthermore, it is based on the three cueing systems model, which focuses heavily on contextual guessing and therefore does not promote sight-word acquisition. The three cueing systems model has significant disadvantages for weak readers. Given the lack of published research on this program, it is unclear whether the additional phonics materials within LLI will counteract these disadvantages.

Fast ForWord

Fast ForWord was based upon a hypothesis that a subtle timing mechanism in the perception of language results in reading and language disabilities. This theory has not withstood the test of time (Gillam et al., 2008; Share, Jorm, MacLean, & Matthews, 2002), though it appears that the program continues to work from this premise. Fast ForWord claims to improve decoding and language skills. Research indicates that it does not provide any significant improvements in either of these areas (Gillam et al., 2008; Strong, Torgerson, Torgerson, & Hulme, 2011).

Evaluation: Fast ForWord is not based upon an empirically validated understanding of the nature of reading difficulties, is expensive, and research suggests it does not improve language or reading skills.

Failure Free Reading

On its website, Failure Free Reading is marketed as a "nonphonic" approach for making large reading gains in students who fail to learn using other methods. The website presents strong claims about the program's effectiveness. Touting its research base, downloadable PDFs of several studies are on its site. Interestingly, these studies are inconsistent with their strong claims of success. Many of the studies have no control groups and report no standard scores, so actual progress cannot be estimated (e.g., Algozzine, Lockavith, & Audette, 1997; Slate, Algozzine, & Lockavith, 1998). When standard scores are present, the results range from 1 to 5 standard score points on word-reading tests (Algozzine & Lockavith, 1998). The website accurately states that a study by Carnegie Melon neuroscientists showed changes in the white matter of the brain following the use of Failure Free Reading. However, that study showed an average improvement on the WRMT-R Word Identification subtest of 2.5 standard score points, 5.5 points on Word Attack, and 1.1 points on Passage Comprehension (Keller & Just, 2009). Torgesen et al. (2007) found less than 2 standard score points of growth in word reading in struggling third graders and 0 points in struggling fifth graders. The minimal gains from these studies followed the program's 100 hours of intervention.

Evaluation: Failure Free Reading provides extensive opportunities for reading connected text but no systematic opportunities for phonic or phonemic awareness development. It is a lengthy program that yields minimal results.

Great Leaps

This is a popular program that includes phonics and fluency elements. Its website refers to the program as "researched and evidence based." Independent studies of Great Leaps that used normative tests to evaluate progress report 0 to 2 standard score point gains (Begeny et al., 2010; Spencer & Manis, 2010).

Evaluation: Great Leaps does not address advanced phonemic awareness.

Irlen Lenses and Scotopic Sensitivity Syndrome

Strong claims have been made regarding dyslexia and colored overlays or the use of tinted glasses. However, research has provided very limited support for these claims. It appears that some people have more eyestrain when reading than others, and for approximately 5% of the population, such overlays improve reading (Wilkins, Lewis, Smith, Rowland, & Tweedie, 2001). However, this phenomenon appears to be independent of the phonological-core deficit and it occurs in typically developing readers, not just weak readers. There is no evidence that overlays or tinted glasses can close the gap between poor readers and their typically developing peers. However, this technique should not be dismissed if a student complains of eyestrain and could benefit from a colored overlay. It seems this technique addresses eyestrain, not reading difficulties (Whiteley & Smith, 2001; Wilkins et al., 2001).

Evaluation: Colored overlays or lenses are an accommodation for a presumed ophthalmological concern independent of reading level or instructional approaches.

Visual Tracking Training

Poor visual tracking has long been a presumed cause of reading problems. However, visual tracking difficulties cannot account for the fact that weak readers struggle in the identification of single words, apart from context, when visual tracking is not involved. While visual tracking problems cannot explain poor reading of single words in isolation, poor single-word reading skills can account for poor visual tracking while reading connected text. Students with poor word-reading skills do a lot of backtracking in their eye movements (Ahmed, Wagner, & Kantor, 2012; Adams, 1990; Crowder & Wagner, 1992; Rayner & Pollatsek, 1989). Because of their inaccurate word reading, they often go back and "revise" when they discover they did not get the meaning. Also, scanning the context occurs more in students with limited sight vocabularies who often get stuck on a word. Studies have been done in which skilled readers were given very difficult passages and weak readers were given easy passages (Ahmed et al., 2012). Under these conditions, the skilled readers displayed poor visual tracking and unusual eye movements while the weak readers displayed normal eye movements. Thus, erratic eye movements (i.e., "poor visual tracking") are more likely to be the *result* of poor reading skills, not the cause (Ahmed et al., 2012). Improving visual tracking is not likely to improve reading, with very rare exceptions of some sort of rare ocular condition. On the contrary, the general finding has been that visual tracking training improves visual tracking of non-alphabetic material, but does not improve reading (Ahmed et al., 2012). Because of the research findings, the American Academy of Pediatrics published a joint statement by various ophthalmology organizations discouraging visual tracking and similar therapies for correcting reading difficulties (American Academy of Pediatrics, 2009).

Evaluation: There is no evidence that the training of visual tracking skills addresses the cause(s) of reading problems. Ophthalmological organizations recommend against it.

Learning Styles

The learning styles approach to teaching divides students into visual learners, auditory learners, and kinesthetic learners, as well as students who are better at "left brain" and "right brain" skills. The whole enterprise is based upon intuition and observation, not on scientific inquiry (Kavale & Forness, 1987; Stahl, 1999; Stahl & Kuhn, 1995), though it is often presented with generic comments like "scientists tell us ... ." These intuitive categories of learners have not been informed by the major findings of reading research over the last three to four decades.

> **CAUTION**
> ....
> Independent studies have shown that some of the most popular and heavily marketed reading interventions display very minimal or modest gains.

Evaluation: The learning styles approach displays little understanding of the research on reading acquisition or the causes of reading difficulties.

Summary of Popular Interventions with Minimal Results

None of the approaches mentioned above includes all three of the key elements that are found in every one of the intervention studies that displayed highly successful outcomes, which will be presented later in the chapter. Furthermore, none of these approaches is consistent with our current understanding of reading development, particularly sight-word development. These popular remedial methods do not represent the kinds of approaches that were the impetus for RTI, which was developed based on the studies that displayed highly successful outcomes. Yet it seems that at least some of the approaches presented above (e.g., Repeated Readings, READ 180, Reading Recovery) are often used in the context of RTI, despite their limited efficacy.

READING INTERVENTION RESEARCH WITH MINIMAL TO MODEST RESULTS

While it may be true that many of the popular intervention programs used in schools have not been shown to produce highly successful results, what about researcher-designed interventions? In this section, we will examine the first two "categories" of research: those with minimal results and those with modest results.

Vaughn and colleagues intervened with sixth graders who fell below criterion on their state reading assessments. They used an RTI model that included phonics instruction and the teaching of reading comprehension strategies. Vaughn and colleagues followed these students for 3 years and provided outcome reports each year (Vaughn et al., 2010, 2011, 2012). At the end of the first year, all of the gains on the decoding and comprehension measures ranged from 0 to 4 standard score points (Vaughn et al., 2010). Students who were still below the state cutoff continued for a second year, with similar instruction but with a reduced group size. At the end of seventh grade, improvements ranged from 0 to 3 standard score points (Vaughn et al., 2011). Those still qualifying based on state test performance continued for a third year (i.e., eighth grade). Group size was further reduced while instruction remained similar, though it was more carefully catered to student skills than in the previous two years. At the end of the third year, the post-test data ranged from 0 to 4 standard score points on various normed reading measures. The authors expressed disappointment in the outcome, but pointed out that the intervention students outperformed the comparison group by a statistically significant margin, because the comparison group outcomes were lower than their pretest.

Lovett and colleagues (e.g., Frijters, Lovett, Sevcik, & Morris, 2013; Lovett et al., 1994; Lovett, Lacerenza, Borden, Frijters, Steinbach, & De Palma, 2000; Lovett, Lacerenza, De Palma, & Frijters, 2012) have published numerous intervention studies over the last three decades. Much of their research involved older students (late elementary through high school) often with more severe reading disabilities than found in the studies by Vaughn and colleagues (Vaughn et al., 2010, 2011, 2012). Lovett and colleagues found that two different approaches to word-level reading intervention were equally effective, so they combined them into a single, integrated intervention program (see Lovett, Lacerenza, & Borden, 2000). This combined intervention has been field tested across multiple studies and produced about a 7 to 8 standard score point improvement on normed tests of word identification (Frijters et al., 2013; Lovett et al., 2012). This is a welcome improvement, yet it often results in reading performance that is still below average.

> **DON'T FORGET**
> ....
> The majority of studies of reading interventions report minimal to moderate gains in reading, with average standard score point improvements typically in the 3- to 5-point range.

Rashotte et al. (2001) studied 115 first through sixth graders who received a small-group (1:3 to 1:5) intervention. Average pretest standard scores were 87 on Word Identification and 83 on Word Attack. The 8-week program consisted of daily 50 minutes of "instruction in phonemic awareness, phonics, and reading and writing for meaning" (p. 123). The phonological awareness instruction was limited to training segmentation and blending, but not the more advanced phonemic awareness skills. Students in grades 1 through 4 gained 8 standard score points on the Word Identification subtest, while students in grades 5 and 6 gained 7 points. By contrast, the Word Attack gains were far more sizeable, between 19.1 and 19.5 standard score points among all three grade-level groups. This should not be surprising given what was argued in Chapter 4, that skilled phonic decoding only required the basic phonological awareness skills of blending and segmentation. Once children developed these basic phonemic awareness skills, their progress in phonic decoding quickly accelerated. However, presumably due to the lack of training of the more advanced phonological awareness skills, they had more modest gains in real-word reading.

The examples of intervention studies just mentioned were selected because of the meticulous and well-designed nature of this research, conducted by three of the most well-respected teams of reading intervention researchers. Numerous other intervention studies with similar results from top researchers could be reviewed here as well, with similar results (e.g., Berninger et al., 2003; Blachman et al., 2004, 2014; see reviews by Flynn, Zheng, & Swanson, 2012, and Wanzek et al., 2013).

THE PHONOLOGICAL AWARENESS INTERVENTION CONTINUUM

These studies support the notion that there appears to be a direct relationship between the degree and nature of phonemic awareness training and the word-level reading outcomes in the existing intervention research. The studies by Vaughn and colleagues included no phonological awareness training, and their word-level reading improvements ranged from 0 to 4 standard score points. Lovett and colleagues as well as Rashotte and colleagues provided *basic* phonological awareness training (blending and segmentation), and their word-level reading results ranged from 4 to 8 standard score points. In contrast, the studies described in the following section intensively trained *advanced* phonemic awareness skills and their reading score increases ranged from 12.5 to 25 standard score points. Since all of the studies just referred to incorporated explicit, systematic phonics instruction and reinforcement, along with practice reading connected text, the differences in outcomes cannot be explained by differences in those elements. The one variable that differed across these studies was the nature and degree of the phonological awareness intervention.

DON'T FORGET

The degree of outcome in reading progress appears to be directly related to the presence and nature of phonemic awareness training. Studies with no phonological awareness element tend to have minimal outcomes. Studies that train phonemic awareness to the basic level have moderate outcomes. Studies that train phonemic awareness to the advanced level have very strong outcomes.

This proposed direct relationship between the degree and nature of phonological awareness training and word-reading outcomes can be explained with reference to the phases of reading development and phases of phonological awareness development outlined in Chapter 4 and, in particular, orthographic mapping. The basic phonological awareness skills of blending and segmenting appear to be critical skills for phonic decoding while more advanced phonemic awareness seems to be an important factor involved in efficient orthographic mapping. Orthographic mapping appears to require instantaneous access to the phonemic sequences in words as a student is reading connected text so that the spellings of unfamiliar words have an efficient way of "anchoring" in long-term memory. The studies with minimal outcomes did not train phonemic awareness and displayed very limited word-reading gains. The studies with the moderate outcomes included basic phonological skill training (segmentation and blending) and yielded somewhat stronger real-word reading outcomes along with very impressive phonic decoding improvements. However, studies in which advanced awareness was trained (discussed next) yielded superior real-word reading improvements, often normalizing word-reading skills. The studies with minimal to moderate outcomes did not train students to this higher level of phonemic proficiency and were thus unlikely to improve these students' abilities to quickly and efficiently add words to their sight vocabularies.

READING INTERVENTION STUDIES WITH HIGHLY SUCCESSFUL RESULTS

> **CAUTION**
> ....
> RTI was inspired by intervention findings with highly successful results, yet most interventions currently recommended and/or used in the context of RTI reading remediation do not incorporate these highly successful interventions.

Research has shown that even students with some of the most severe reading disabilities can make substantial progress in their word-level reading skills, with a considerable proportion developing word-reading skills to an average level. As previously mentioned, this was the type of research that prompted the development of RTI (e.g., Torgesen et al., 2001; Vellutino et al., 1996). The results of these studies were so substantial that RTI was originally conceived in order to "capture" this level of success. However, in developing RTI into a service delivery model the actual approaches and techniques that produced such impressive gains were apparently left out of the development and subsequent promotion of RTI. Educators have thus been left with the mandate to use research-based approaches for general educational reading instruction (Tier 1) and for remedial efforts among struggling readers (Tiers 2, 3/4), without being sufficiently informed as to what those research-based approaches are.

The Three Key Elements of Successful Intervention

It was previously stated that the studies in the highly successful category shared three common elements, and that not a single study in the minimal to modest groups of studies contained all three. To review, the three elements are:

1. Eliminating the phonological awareness deficits and teaching phonemic awareness to the advanced level
2. Teaching and reinforcing phonics skills and phonic decoding
3. Providing opportunities for reading connected text (i.e., authentic reading)

Following is an overview of several studies with highly successful outcomes. As mentioned, all involved the three key elements. Do not assume that one-to-one tutoring was an essential ingredient in their success, even though many of them involved one-to-one service delivery. It will be demonstrated below that studies incorporating the three key elements achieved equivalent results using small groups.

First Grade Remediation

One of the studies that prompted the development of RTI was Vellutino et al. (1996). These researchers intervened in the spring of first grade with 74 students who represented the lowest 9% on a kindergarten assessment of letter names and sounds. After 15 weeks of daily, one-to-one tutoring for 30 minutes, 67% of these students scored at or above the 30th percentile in word reading. Those who did not, received an additional 8 weeks of tutoring in the fall of grade 2. Post-testing at the end of grade 2 revealed that only 15% of the original group continued below the 30th percentile. Follow-ups showed that these results were maintained 2 and 3 years later (Vellutino, Scanlon, & Lyon, 2000; Vellutino, Scanlon, & Jaccard, 2003).

Vellutino et al. (1996) projected their results across the original population of students screened in kindergarten, from which these at-risk students were drawn. Assuming their intervention would work with less severe cases (and research suggests it would, given that reading difficulties fall along a continuum; Fletcher et al., 1994; Stanovich & Siegel, 1994), they projected that only 3% of the total population from which they drew their students would score below the (national) 30th percentile if such an intervention was available to all struggling students. Of those, only half (1.5%) would score below the 16th percentile. In the previous chapter, it was indicated that Lennon and Slesinski (1999) replicated Vellutino et al. (1996) using their same program. However, they used groups with a ratio of 1:2 and 10-week sessions. This suggests that the one-to-one service delivery was not the determining factor in their strong results.

> **DON'T FORGET**
> ....
> One of the reasons Vellutino et al. (1996) was a catalyst for RTI was because the intervention used in that study dramatically reduced the number of struggling readers to nearly 1/10th of the national average.

Second Grade Through Adulthood

Torgesen et al. (2001) provided an intervention with 60 students in third through fifth grades with extremely low word-reading skills (mean at the 2nd percentile) but average IQ (mean of 96). The 60 students were divided into two groups of 30. Half received the Lindamood Auditory Discrimination in Depth program (ADD) while the other half received an experimenter-designed program. Both programs included the three key elements of successful intervention. However, the experimenter-designed program involved far more reading of connected text.

DON'T FORGET

From a group of third to fifth grade readers whose average word-reading scores were in the second percentile, the two interventions used by Torgesen et al. (2001) resulted in 40% of those readers no longer requiring any special educational reading remediation.

The initial skills and the outcomes of the two groups were very similar. Students in both conditions received two, 50-minute, one-on-one tutoring sessions per day. At the end of the intervention, both groups gained an average of 14 standard score points in word identification. The experimenter-designed intervention gained 20 standard score points in nonsense word reading, and the Lindamood group gained 27. At 1- and 2-year follow-ups, standard scores for word identification for both conditions were 18 points above their pretest levels, showing further gains rather than a regression. Among these students who initially displayed severe reading disabilities, 40% required no ongoing special educational reading help following the 8-week intervention. Thus, two different programs using the same three elements yielded similar strong results.

Simos et al. (2002) replicated Torgesen et al. (2001) with a wider age range (7 to 17). They had fewer students in the study because all participants received MSI brain scans before and after the intervention. Eight students had reading disabilities and eight controls were typical readers, matched for age. They used two commercially available intervention programs that contained all three of the key elements of successful intervention. Three students received the Lindamood ADD program and six received Phono-Graphix (McGuinness et al., 1996). Of the eight poor readers, six scored at or below the 3rd percentile in word identification, while the remaining two scored at the 13th and 18th percentiles. Prior to the intervention, the areas in the brain activated during reading differed substantially between the groups. The intervention was comprised of 1 to 2 hours of daily tutoring for 8 weeks. Following the intervention, the brain activation patterns of the experimental group were indistinguishable from the comparison group. The word-reading performance in the tutored group ranged from the 38th to 60th percentiles. When their mean percentile rank improvement is translated back into standard scores, it represents an average gain of approximately 25 standard score points.

Torgesen et al. (1999) selected students from among those who scored in the bottom 12% on phonological skills in kindergarten. The students were divided into four groups. Three of the groups received approximately 80 hours of one-to-one tutoring from the spring of kindergarten until the end of second grade in one of three tutoring conditions. The fourth was a no-treatment control.

One experimental group used the Lindamood ADD program, the second used an experimenter-designed intervention with minimal phonological awareness training, and the third focused on supporting the classroom instruction, also with minimal phonological awareness training. The Lindamood group, whose instruction contained all three elements of effective intervention, had an average word identification score of 103 at the end of second grade. Nearly half of these students (47%) had standard scores above 100, and only 21% had scores below 85. This contrasts with the no-treatment control in which 55% of students had a standard score below 85 at the end of second grade. The two other groups, which were tutored for 80 hours with instruction that did not address all three elements of effective reading intervention, had 28% and 31% of students below 85. Following the rough-cut estimating procedure used by Foorman and Al Otaiba (2009) and Vellutino et al. (1996), we can project the percentage of students who would be below a standard score of 85 (16th percentile) if all at-risk students had access to the most successful intervention. Twenty-one percent of the original bottom 12% comes out to about 2.5% of students would be below an 85 standard score (16th percentile). This estimate is consistent with the estimates of Vellutino et al. (1996), Foorman and Al Otaiba (2009), and Torgesen (2004a).

Alexander, Andersen, Heilman, Voeller, and Torgesen (1991) found a 12.5 standard score point improvement on the WRMT-R Word Identification subtest in a group of 10 students who were 7 to 12 years old. They received an average of 65 hours of individual tutoring that provided all the key elements of successful intervention via the Lindamood ADD program. Their standard score improvement on the WRMT-R Word Attack subtest was 20 points.

> **DON'T FORGET**
> ....
> Truch (1994) found that among 281 weak readers from ages 5 to 55, only one did not make progress in phonological awareness. This suggests that well below 1% of those with phonological-core deficits were not responsive to explicit and systematic phonemic awareness instruction.

Truch (1994) presented data on 281 clients with word-level reading difficulties who received approximately 80 hours of intervention in the Lindamood ADD program at a Canadian clinic. The clients ranged in age from 5 to 55, with most being in the late elementary to middle school range. On average, students made a 17 standard score point gain on the reading subtest from the WRAT-R, and also 17 points on the spelling subtest. Considering the age range and the large sample size, it was noteworthy that only a single client failed to make progress in phonemic awareness. By contrast, 75% reached the ceiling on the phonological awareness post-test. Truch (1994) further analyzed results according to three age groupings: 6–12, 13–17, and 18+. The percentages of participants who improved their WRAT-R reading standard scores by 8 points to over 30 points were 88%, 90%, and 83% in each of the age groups, respectively. The percentages of participants who improved their standard score points by 16 to over 30 points were 55%, 59%, and 58%, respectively. Only two clients made no gains on the reading subtest. "As a group, students started almost two standard deviations below average, and ended up in the lower end of the average range for their respective ages" (Truch, 1994, p. 74).

Unfortunately, Truch (1994) only reported grade equivalents to measure growth on the WRMT-R Word Attack measure. Within his three age groups, the percentages of students who displayed more than 2 years of growth in their grade-equivalent scores were 70% (ages 6–12), 92% (13–17), and 94% (18–55). Of these, 37%, 72%, and 84% made 4 or more years of grade-equivalent progress. It is noteworthy that contrary to common experience with teaching phonics to older students with reading disabilities, Truch (1994) found that the older students made greater gains than the younger students. He argued that the reason older students with reading disabilities usually make so little progress in phonics is that they lack the phonemic awareness to develop such phonics skills. Truch (1994) suggested that once the phonemic awareness deficits were remediated, these "treatment resistors" became able to develop phonics skills. The large gains in the Word Attack subtest in the studies described in this section provide strong support for Truch's hypothesis.

McGuinness et al. (1996) achieved similar results following only 12 hours of one-to-one instruction with the Phono-Graphix program. They intervened with 87 students who were 6 to 16 years old with a mean WRMT-R Word Identification score of 86.4 and a mean Word Attack score of 88.6. These students showed a mean improvement of 13.7 standard score points on Word Identification and 19.5 points on Word Attack, essentially "normalizing" their word-reading performance (i.e., mean of 100.1 on Word Identification and 108.1 on Word Attack). Like Truch (1994), McGuinness et al. (1996) broke down their sample into three age groups: 6–7, 8–9, and 10–16. McGuinness et al. (1996) found that the older students made larger gains than the younger students in both real-word reading and pseudoword reading.

Truch (2003) replicated the study by McGuinness et al. (1996) using the same program they used (Phono-Graphix), but with a larger sample (*n* = 203). He found equivalent gains, but it required 80 hours rather than 12. Yet when Truch (2003) assessed the students after 12 hours of instruction (to coincide with the McGuinness et al., 1996 study), he noticed a sizable improvement on virtually every reading-related measure except fluency. For example, Truch (2003) found an average 7 standard score point improvement in word identification following 12 hours of intervention. While an impressive result, it was far shy of the 13.7 mean standard score point improvement found by McGuinness et al. (1996). He noted multiple reasons to account for the differences, including the fact that his clients began at a much lower reading level than the clients in the McGuinness et al. (1996) study. Nonetheless, Truch (2003) affirmed a phenomenon he called the "12-hour effect." He also demonstrated that the program used by McGuinness et al. (1996) was capable of producing a mean improvement of 15.3 standard score points in word identification in his clients, though after 80 hours of instruction. Truch (2003) hypothesized that other programs might also have a similar 12-hour effect of an initial boost, but researchers generally do not evaluate after 12 hours as did McGuinness et al. (1996) and Truch (2003).

Truch (1994, 2003) used two different, commercially available programs for his two large, clinical studies: the Lindamood ADD and Phono-Graphix. Both programs had similar results within the 80-hour tutoring timeframe. Even though these two programs had many different features and administration characteristics, they each made use of the three key elements of successful intervention, which Truch specifically acknowledges (Truch, 2003, 2004). Based on these three elements (and others he believed important), Truch (2004) developed another program to be used in that clinic. He called the program Discover Reading, and he examined the results of the program with 146 students. He replicated the 12-hour effect with the new program. On average, the students made a 6.5 standard score point improvement following the first 12 hours of instruction. Then, his result after 80 hours was a mean growth in word identification of 14.4 standard score points, with a final mean of 100, representing a normalized performance in word-level reading. Thus, in three different large clinical samples in the same reading clinic (Truch, 1994, 2003, 2004), using three different intervention programs, students with reading difficulties across the age span (all three samples ranged from age 5 or 6 through adulthood) made approximately a standard deviation improvement in word-level reading. All three programs emphasized the three key elements found in all of the studies with highly successful results.

Another important contribution of the studies by Truch (2003, 2004) and McGuinness et al. (1996) is that they demonstrated that phonemic awareness deficits can be remediated fairly quickly. In all three of those studies, the phonemic awareness skills began to "ceiling out" by the end of the first 12 hours of instruction. Thus, any reading gains that occurred after that were the likely result of applying their newly developed phonemic awareness skills to the processes of phonic decoding and orthographic mapping. In a sense, students had to learn to read all over again, now that they were better prepared to do so. These are encouraging results because they indicate that despite a large genetic/neurological component to the phonological-core deficit, the resulting poor phonological skills can be remediated. Such remediation is rapid and successful when the intervention provides explicit and systematic phonological awareness instruction on the full range of these skills (i.e., including the advanced phonemic awareness skills).

Among the studies by Vellutino et al. (1996), Torgesen et al. (2001), McGuinness et al. (1996), and Truch (1994; 2003, 2004), five completely different programs were used, all with similar results. Thus, the highly successful outcomes of these studies are not "program specific." However, these outcomes appear to occur only when all three of the "key ingredients" are present, which was the case with all five of the programs used in those studies. Three of those five programs are commercially available (presented later in the chapter).

Use of Comparison Groups

One concern about some of the studies reported above is the lack of treated comparison groups in order to control for potential placebo effects. While this is indeed a concern, two important factors need to be kept in mind. First, several studies that incorporated the three key elements of highly successful intervention included treated comparison groups and had equivalent outcomes. Some of these were already described (Lennon & Slesinski, 1999; Torgesen et al., 1999; Vellutino et al., 1996), whereas others will be discussed below (Torgesen et al., 2003, 2010). Second, one must postulate a reason why a placebo effect accounted for 12 to 25 standard score point gains in the studies described above yet produced only 0 to 8 point gains in the studies that did not incorporate all three key elements of successful intervention.

One-on-One Versus Small Group Instruction

> **DON'T FORGET**
> ....
> Contrary to long-standing assumptions, one-on-one instruction is not needed for optimal results. Similar results can be achieved from 1:2 to 1:4 groupings.

Although most of the studies just described provided one-on-one instruction, it is not likely that was essential to their success. It was previously indicated that Lennon and Slesinski (1999) replicated the one-on-one tutoring study by Vellutino et al. (1996) using one-on-two groups. Also, Torgesen et al. (2010) intervened with struggling first-grade readers using two programs that provided the three essential elements via a combination of teacher instruction and computer-aided instruction (CAI). One program was the Read, Write, Type program and the other was the updated version of the Lindamood called the Lindamood Phoneme Sequencing Program for Reading, Spelling, and Speech (LiPS). Each program was administered in small groups with a ratio of 1:4. Both programs had equivalent results with each other, and students made an average of 20 to 23 standard score point improvements in word identification and over 30 standard score points on nonsense word reading. These gains were maintained at the 1-year follow-up.

Torgesen et al. (2003) presented a series of five intervention studies, three of which provided small-group instruction (1:2 to 1:4). A fourth used one-on-one tutoring, and the fifth included a combination of 1:1 and 1:2. Among the five studies, different intervention programs were used, but they all featured the three key elements. There were also differences in initial skill levels between the studies, ranging from mild to severe reading difficulties, and there was also a wide range of SES levels among the studies. Standard score improvements in word identification across these five studies averaged about a standard deviation of improvement, with nonsense word reading test scores even higher. The authors indicated that group size did not affect the outcome of these studies. This supports the view that one-on-one service delivery was not an essential element in the strong results in the one-on-one studies described above.

Summary of Studies With Highly Successful Outcomes

There exists a body of research literature, much of it funded by the National Institute of Child Health and Development (NICHD) reading intervention initiatives and published in top journals, which demonstrates that large gains are possible in students with reading difficulties of all ages and levels of severity. Yet these studies represent a very small minority of the reading intervention studies. Most other studies produced far smaller improvements, typically between 3 and 5 standard score points. Even though normative standard score points do not fully capture reading gains, they are useful as a measure of improvement because they provide an index of the degree to which students are closing the gap with their typically developing peers (Torgesen et al., 2003).

The studies presented in this chapter suggest that there are clear dividing lines between three different categories of outcomes in intervention studies. One set yielded very substantial gains in word identification skills ranging from an average of 12 to 25 standard score points. Every study in this highly successful category contained the three key elements of (1) training phonemic awareness to the advanced level, (2) phonics instruction and reinforcement, and (3) opportunities for reading connected text. A second set of studies displayed more modest outcomes, with average gains in word identification ranging from

5 to 9 points. These studies only trained phonemic awareness to the basic level (i.e.., blending and segmentation). The third category did not involve explicit or systematic phonemic awareness training, and the standard score improvements in word identification in this category of studies ranged from 0 to 5 points. The implications of this categorization of studies seems clear and will be further elaborated upon below.

Phonemic Awareness Is Not Enough

While phonemic awareness skills are a powerful factor in determining word-level reading skills, improving phonemic awareness is no guarantee that older students will improve their reading skills. Bhat, Griffin, and Sindelar (2003) studied 40 sixth to eighth graders who were very weak readers, all with poor phonological awareness. They provided 18 sessions of phonological awareness training across a 4-week period and essentially eliminated these students' phonological awareness difficulties. These students went from an average standard score of 67 to a mean score of 96 on the CTOPP Phonological Awareness Composite, improving by nearly 2 standard deviations. These researchers used a commercially available program that was substantially modified by adding phonological manipulation activities such as those found in the studies with highly successful outcomes. However, these students showed no improvement in word-level reading. The authors acknowledged that this outcome was likely due to the fact that the intervention exclusively targeted phonemic awareness and provided no phonics instruction or additional reading practice. This finding supports the basic thesis of this chapter. Bhat et al. (2003) lacked two of the three key elements of successful word-reading intervention and was thus unsuccessful in demonstrating reading improvements.

> ### CAUTION
> ....
> While phonemic awareness appears to be a necessary ingredient in the highly successful interventions, unless it is integrated with phonics instruction and reading opportunities, it is not likely to produce the desired results.

Despite their poor reading results, the Bhat et al. (2003) study made two very important contributions to our understanding of effective intervention for students with severe word-reading difficulties. First, it provided additional confirming evidence beyond the studies by McGuinness et al. (1996) and Truch (2003, 2004) that advanced phonemic awareness skills can be successfully remediated over a short period of time in older, struggling readers. The sixth to eighth graders had been struggling in reading for many years, and the presumed underlying source of their reading difficulty was removed after only 4 weeks of targeted instruction. This finding is of great significance and should be a source of encouragement to those working with poor, older readers. Second, Bhat et al. (2003) incorporated phonemic manipulation activities (which trains the advanced phonemic awareness skills) without using any of the programs previously described. This provides further confirmation of the notion that positive results in phonological awareness development in older students are not program specific. Rather, they appear to support the idea that programs that require the training of advanced phonemic awareness is the key to addressing the phonemic awareness needs of struggling readers. In the case of Bhat et al. (2003), their training provided a nearly 2 standard deviation gain in phonemic awareness skills.

Is It Ever Too Late to Train Phonological Awareness to Impact Reading?

The term *treatment resistors* refers to students who do not respond to conventional reading interventions (Torgesen, 2000). Reviews of research conclude that poor phonemic awareness skills are typically associated with the treatment resistor phenomenon (e.g., Al Otaiba & Fuchs, 2002, 2006; Dukleth Johnson & Swanson, 2011; Torgesen, 2000). The studies that formed the basis of these literature reviews were drawn primarily from the studies in the "minimal" to "modest" categories of treatment outcomes. It is not surprising that these treatment resistors continued to struggle, since these studies do not appear to have adequately addressed their lack of advanced phonemic awareness.

The highly successful category of studies strongly suggests that training in advanced phonological awareness skills was instrumental in the large word-level reading gains those students made. These studies collectively resulted in an average of approximately 1 standard deviation of progress in word identification, along with even greater progress in nonsense word reading. In some of these studies, older students made more reading progress than the younger students.

The finding that older children appear to dramatically boost their reading skills as a result of eliminating their phonological awareness difficulties does not appear to be widely known, even among many reading researchers. For example, after reporting a limited benefit from 3 years of reading intervention that provided instruction in phonics and reading comprehension strategies (no phonemic awareness training), Vaughn et al. (2012) candidly said:

> We have been asked on numerous occasions when presenting these findings … to provide speculation or conjecture about what it would take to make a significant improvement in the overall reading success of students with significant reading difficulties. (p. 523)

They provided various suggestions, such as the use of computers, integrating reading into content area classes, improving the quality of instruction, or earlier intervention. None of their suggestions included addressing the phonological awareness deficits these weak readers presumably had.

In a chapter devoted to teaching older, struggling readers, O'Connor (2011) suggests that while phonemic awareness may be important for younger students in the early stages of reading, it may not play a role in reading among older students. The only study cited to support this view was Bhat et al. (2003), described above. O'Connor (2011) concludes from this study that because improvements in phonemic awareness did not result in improved reading, phonemic awareness training is not useful for older, struggling readers. We saw that Bhat et al. (2003) trained *only* phonemic awareness and provided no reading help, so this study does not support her assertion. The fact that O'Connor (2011) nowhere mentions any of the studies with highly successful outcomes described earlier in this chapter suggests that she was not familiar with those studies. Those who believe that phonemic awareness training is not helpful beyond the earliest stages of reading would need to explain why advanced phonemic awareness training appears to have played such a pivotal role in the most dramatic reading gains reported in the empirical literature.

Integrating orthographic mapping into our intervention efforts requires a shift in thinking. Conventional word-reading interventions either do not include phonological awareness training or only teach blending and/or segmenting. Such interventions work from the assumption that any phonological awareness development that occurs beyond first grade is of no consequence for reading. Most educators and many researchers (e.g., O'Connor, 2011; Shapiro & Solity, 2008; Share, 1995, 2011; Tunmer, 2011) assume that the role of phonological awareness in reading development is to help "young children beginning to decode one-syllable words with regular spellings" and is "irrelevant for older readers" (O'Connor, 2011, p. 381–382). While it is true that phonological awareness helps with phonic decoding, that represents only one of its roles in reading development. It was demonstrated in Chapter 4 that a substantial amount of evidence shows that phonemic awareness plays a central role in developing sight vocabulary (Dixon et al., 2002; Duff & Hulme, 2012; Ehri, 2005a, 2014; Kilpatrick, 2015c; Laing & Hulme, 1999; McKague et al., 2008; Torgesen, 2004b; Torgesen et al., 2003; van den Broeck & Geudens, 2012; van den Broeck, Geudens, & van den Bos, 2010). This makes phonemic awareness *very* relevant for older readers. After demonstrating an average word identification improvement of 17 standard score points in clients aged 5 to 55, Truch (1994) stated: "Recent work in phonological awareness makes it clear that more than phonics is required. There is a 'missing link' so to speak, at a more basic level of processing for many students" (p. 61). He identifies this missing link as phonemic awareness. The studies reported in this chapter suggest that advanced phonemic awareness is that "missing link."

The common assumption that limits the role of phonological awareness to the development of phonic decoding likely stems from the well-established fact that phonological awareness loses its power to predict reading outcomes among older students, although this varies somewhat by task (i.e., blending and segmentation lose their strong correlation with reading earlier than manipulation). This "decline" in the correlation between phonemic awareness and reading is analogous to failure of letter-name knowledge to predict reading outcomes past first grade. After first grade, all children know their letters, so therefore letter naming no longer correlates with reading skill. In a similar way, phonemic awareness "ceilings out" around third or fourth grade in most students. As a result, it provides limited additional explanatory power for reading acquisition in typically developing readers because such readers have all acquired the phonemic proficiency they need for skilled reading. However, phonemic awareness continues to be a strong predictor of reading outcomes for those on the bottom end of the reading continuum who have not adequately developed their phonological awareness skills. Intervention studies that allow students to complete their phonological awareness development (if accompanied by the other two key elements) produce very large gains in word-level reading skills. Studies that do not address phonemic awareness skills beyond the basic level (blending and segmentation), however, yield more limited results because their students have only partially completed their phonological awareness development.

Students with the phonological-core deficit do not learn phonological skills naturally. Most will only develop to the level that they are directly taught. If they are only taught to the level of segmentation and blending, that is where their development will likely stop. For them to develop the more advanced phonemic skills needed for efficient orthographic mapping, they will require direct remediation. Studies that trained these more advanced skills yielded very strong outcomes

CAUTION

There appears to be a common assumption among many educators and researchers that phonemic awareness training is not likely to be useful for older readers with the phonological-core deficit. However, the intervention studies reported in this chapter strongly suggest that advanced phonemic awareness is *essential* for older struggling readers to make substantial progress in their word-level reading skills.

of 12 to 25 standard score points (mostly 14 to 17). By contrast, the studies that failed to address these advanced phonemic skills had much more modest results.

The common assumption that the role of phonological awareness is complete once students can do phonic decoding is thus incongruous with two bodies of empirical research. First, it is inconsistent with "the most complete current theory of how children form sight word representations" (Torgesen, 2004b, p. 36), namely, Linnea Ehri's orthographic mapping theory (Ehri, 1998a, 2005a, 2005b, 2014). Orthographic mapping clearly indicates that phonemic awareness is a critical skill for developing one's sight vocabulary—it is not just for phonic decoding. Second, this common assumption is inconsistent with the intervention research reviewed in this chapter. Those studies that taught advanced phonemic awareness beyond the basic level needed for phonic decoding had the strongest outcomes reported in the literature.

The argument presented in this chapter is that the source of the dramatic results in the "highly successful" category of intervention studies is the combination of the three key elements: advanced phonemic awareness training, phonics instruction and reinforcement, and authentic reading opportunities. Many of the factors typically examined in intervention research, such as SES, group size, and total intervention time, did not appear to play a significant role in outcomes compared to the combination of these three key elements. This is because studies in all three categories of outcomes had a wide range of variation in SES, group size, and length of intervention, so they cannot account for the differing outcomes between categories. This is not to deny the importance of these other factors. Rather, it is to say that the relative contribution of SES, group size, and intervention length are not as significant as directly addressing the skills required for orthographic mapping.

It seems reasonable to conclude that the statute of limitations never runs out on phonemic awareness. While there appears to be an ideal window of opportunity to prevent reading problems from occurring in the first place, that window never completely closes and phonemic awareness can be trained at any age (Truch, 1994, 2003). Such training can make a substantial impact on word-reading skills.

Implications for RTI

The studies with highly successful outcomes provide a clear template for correcting word-reading problems, regardless of severity. The research on reading development (Chapter 4) provides the overarching theory for understanding what skills need to be in place to be a successful word-level reader. Skilled word reading requires a high degree of proficiency in basic and advanced phonological awareness and phonic decoding. These skills allow students to accurately determine unfamiliar words (phonic decoding) and, once read, to remember those words (orthographic mapping). This allows them to build large and continuously expanding sight vocabularies. As mentioned, fluent reading is built upon a large sight vocabulary.

Common But Bad Advice

In the thousands of research reports on reading, there exists no empirically supported alternative for efficiently developing the ability to acquire a large sight vocabulary. There are inefficient ways, such as visual memory tactics boosted by extensive drill and practice or by relying on contextual guessing. The inadequacies of these approaches were discussed in Chapter 2. Poor readers naturally gravitate to these ineffective solutions because they do not have the phonological skills needed to learn to read efficiently.

A common belief that continues to be recommended is that some students with severe reading disabilities simply cannot learn phonics and they should be shifted to a whole-word type of approach. This recommendation is inconsistent with the accumulated research on the nature of reading development and reading disabilities. Such advice is intuitive, not empirical. One would be hard pressed to find a single study in an empirical journal to show this whole-word strategy will significantly close the gap with typically developing peers. By contrast, several studies described above indicate that students get "stuck" in phonics due to weak phonemic awareness. Once that is addressed, average gains in phonics skills (displayed on the WRMT-R Word Attack subtest) range from 14 to 30 points.

> **CAUTION**
>
> The common recommendation that students not responsive to phonics instruction should be switched to a whole-word approach is without a solid research basis and is inconsistent with empirically validated theoretical understandings of reading development and reading difficulties. Better advice would be to train phonemic awareness to the basic and advanced levels, and students will become more responsive to phonics instruction.

Additional Techniques for Fostering Word-Level Reading Skills

Chapter 6 of the *Equipped for Reading Success* manual (included in this book's supplemental materials), provides 22 instructional techniques for building sight vocabulary based on orthographic mapping, so they will not be covered here.

SPECIFIC PROGRAMS USED IN HIGHLY SUCCESSFUL OUTCOME STUDIES

There was a wide variety of factors that varied among the studies reported above, including SES, age, beginning reading level, length of intervention, amount and nature of previous intervention, and the nature of the students' classroom reading instruction. As a result, there would be little basis for suggesting that one of the programs used in the highly successful category of studies is superior to any of the others. What was common to all of them was the use of phonemic manipulation activities (deletion, substitution, and occasionally reversal). These are more challenging than phonemic blending and segmentation, and therefore presumably result in a higher degree of phonemic proficiency. Every program in the studies that trained advanced phonological awareness via manipulation tasks proved successful. It may be reasonable to infer that other phonological awareness programs that train phonological manipulation in an explicit, systematic, and developmentally sequenced manner would produce similar results.

It is assumed here that most of the programs recommended in the previous chapter for preventing reading difficulties would not be as effective for correcting such difficulties. Most of the programs recommended in Chapter 10 do not train advanced phonemic awareness skills, but are limited to activities that teach basic phonemic awareness.

Lindamood Phoneme Sequencing Program (LiPS)

This program was previously called Lindamood Auditory Discrimination in Depth (ADD), and most of the studies described above used this program when it went by that earlier name. The ADD program was used more frequently in the highly successful studies than any other.

The LiPS first trains an awareness of sounds via a multisensory approach. Children learn to pay attention to the "articulatory gestures," that is, the position of the mouth, lips, and tongue while producing sounds. Picture cards are used to show drawings of mouths in position for the sounds. Students use a mirror for visual feedback while producing the sounds, and they learn a new vocabulary for speaking about categories of sounds (e.g., "lip poppers," "tip tappers"). In the next phase, students begin a careful sequence of paying attention to the phonemes in spoken words using colored blocks to represent sounds. Several letters of the alphabet are introduced, and students learn how letters represent the sounds in spoken language. Students then learn how to form words out of letters, spell, and then read texts designed for their level of reading and phonological awareness attainment.

Given its presence in multiple intervention studies with highly successful results, the LiPS appears to have the most extensive track record of any program discussed here. However, it requires extensive prior training for the teacher and it spends a fair amount of time initially teaching the articulatory gestures, which may not be a necessary component. A few studies compared the LiPS with other programs that also teach advanced phonological awareness, and they were as effective without the preliminary articulatory gesture training (Torgesen et al., 2001, 2003; Truch, 2003, 2004; Wise, Ring, & Olson, 1999; but see Castiglioni-Spalten & Ehri, 2003). The LiPS has been used in other studies, sometimes in a piecemeal fashion. As a result, reading outcomes are not as consistently strong as in the studies described above (www.lindamoodbell.com/programs/lips.html).

Phono-Graphix

A few studies provide support for the effectiveness of Phono-Graphix (McGuinness et al., 1996; Simos et al., 2002; Truch, 2003). This program does not teach the articulatory gestures. Not every study using Phono-Graphix has had results as strong as in the studies reported in this chapter (www.readamericaclinic .com/phonographix/phonographix.html).

Discover Reading

This is a proprietary program developed by Dr. Stephen Truch, who directs a reading clinic in Canada, after years of successful use of the Lindamood ADD (Truch, 1994) and Phono-Graphix (Truch, 2003) programs in that clinic. While it is not commercially available as an off-the-shelf program, they do offer training for teachers (www.readingfoundation.com).

Read, Write, Type

This program was investigated alongside the LiPS program, and both had excellent results (Torgesen et al., 2010). Read, Write, Type uses a mixture of 1:3 small group instruction and computer-based learning. The computer portion represents approximately half of the instructional time. While it has a heavy emphasis on phonemic awareness, it does not rely as much on manipulation activities as the other programs mentioned here. However, it does something that differs from traditional phonics that is very consistent with orthographic mapping and is likely a contributor to its effectiveness. While phonic decoding progresses from text to sound (i.e., starting out with an unfamiliar word and sounding it out), Read, Write, Type goes from sound to text, a skill that is critical for orthographic mapping. Before presenting a word in its printed form, the student's attention is directed to the individual phonemes within the spoken form of the word. Instruction then demonstrates how those sounds are represented in print. Based upon the orthographic mapping principle, this should facilitate sight-word acquisition. Indeed, the developer of orthographic mapping endorses the concept of doing phonological activities with oral words *before* they are presented to children in their printed form (Gaskins, Ehri, Cress, O'Hara, Donnelly, 1996/1997), consistent with Read, Write, Type (www.talkingfingers.com).

Equipped for Reading Success

Unlike the programs just mentioned, Equipped for Reading Success (Kilpatrick, 2015a) has not yet been the subject of a study in a peer-reviewed journal, though a longitudinal research project on this program was underway at the time of writing. The program goes from simple beginning kindergarten-level activities to advanced phonemic awareness activities using phoneme manipulation, the latter being a key feature in the studies with the highly successful outcomes. Equipped for Reading Success is the newest of the programs, incorporating findings not available when the other programs were developed. In addition to being a comprehensive phonological awareness development program, it is designed to actively promote sight-word development given it is the only program based on the findings regarding orthographic mapping. Chapter 6 from the Equipped for Reading Success program manual includes over 20 activities that directly promote sight-word development. That chapter is included in the supplementary resources available for this volume.

What About Rapid Automatized Naming (RAN) and Working Memory (WM)?

In Chapters 3 and 4, it was indicated that RAN and WM were important factors that affect word-reading development. It may have been noticed that these are missing from the discussions in this chapter. Students with poor RAN and WM respond less well to reading remediation than those with stronger skills (see Chapter 3). Unfortunately, none of the studies above specifically addressed these factors. But within those studies, there was variation in the amount of progress made within each group. It is likely these factors contributed to that variation. It was mentioned in Chapter 3 that there is no research to suggest that we can directly remediate RAN or WM in a manner that would affect reading. However, there is evidence that RAN and WM standard scores improve by as many as 5 to 10 points as a result of reading intervention (Kerins, 2006; Krafnick et al., 2011; Torgesen, 2010; Vaughn et al., 2003; Vukovic & Siegel, 2006; Wolff, 2014).

An awareness that a student struggles in WM or RAN may have an impact on how a teacher approaches specific learning tasks. If a student has a problem with WM, the teacher may more rigorously apply the classic intervention of providing things in small chunks. In addition, a teacher may check for understanding more frequently. There do not appear to be any obvious teaching adaptations for students with RAN difficulties. However, teachers may anticipate that these students may lag behind their peers in word reading fluency, despite the most effective word reading interventions available. This knowledge can help teachers to set reasonable expectations for the amount of time such students will need to complete reading assignments.

The Problem of Word-Reading Fluency

Even with large gains in word-reading skills using highly effective interventions, studies show modest gains in fluency (Torgesen, 2004a, 2005; Torgesen et al., 2001, 2003). This is not necessarily the case when reading problems are prevented altogether in at-risk readers (Torgesen, 2004a). It seems that when addressed at the earliest stages of reading, both word-reading accuracy and word-reading speed can become normalized.

The smaller gains in fluency in these studies with highly successful outcomes are not due to an inadequate emphasis on fluency. For example, Torgesen et al. (2001) had equivalent, highly successful results with two different intervention programs. In one intervention, 50% of the time was spent on reading connected text and fluency. By contrast, only 5% of the time was spent on these activities in the other program. Yet the fluency results of these two interventions were nearly identical.

DON'T FORGET

Even with the most highly successful interventions, there still appears to be a gap in reading fluency. This is a likely result of the fact that typically developing peers have a multiyear head start in acquiring large sight vocabularies, and a large sight vocabulary appears to be the basis of reading fluency.

While this fluency gap is not fully understood, three points must be considered. First, RAN is believed to be a source of fluency difficulties (e.g., Norton

& Wolf, 2012). Because RAN is common among weak readers, it may account somewhat for the fluency gap. Second, students in these studies actually made substantial improvements in fluency, measured in raw scores (Torgesen et al., 2003). But because their typically developing peers were also increasing their fluency, the degree to which these students closed the gap was much less in comparison to their gains in word reading or phonic decoding.

Third, consistent with orthographic mapping, Torgesen (2004a) builds the case that the fluency gap is related to sight-word acquisition. The typically developing peers of the remediated students had a "head start" of many years to encounter far more words, including less common words. Torgesen (2004a) argues that we should not be discouraged by this fluency gap. He suggests that such gaps will likely narrow further with time as students get older, assuming they increase the amount of reading they do.

ADDRESSING COMPREHENSION DIFFICULTIES

Research on word-level reading has been quite extensive and often very complex. Yet what has emerged from thousands of studies is relatively simple in terms of intervention. To be a successful word-level reader, individuals need to have a strong command of letter-sound knowledge and phonemic awareness. However, when we turn to intervention with reading comprehension difficulties, no such simplicity emerges. It seems the more that is learned about reading comprehension, the more complex the picture becomes.

Revisiting the Simple View of Reading

Recall that the simple view of reading proposes that reading comprehension is the product of word-level reading skills and language comprehension. The most common source of reading comprehension difficulties is poor word-level reading. This is the case with the dyslexic, compensating, and mixed types of poor readers. Only the hyperlexic's reading comprehension is unaffected by word-reading problems. Consistent with the simple view of reading, Torgesen et al. (2003) stated that "the ultimate goal" of word-level reading intervention "is to help children acquire the knowledge and skills necessary to comprehend printed material at a level that is consistent with their general verbal ability or language comprehension skills" (p. 278). In what follows, the focus will be on reading comprehension difficulties that are independent from difficulties with word reading.

Reading comprehension difficulties most commonly involve language comprehension difficulties (Catts et al., 2006; Nation, 2005; Nation, Clarke, & Snowling, 2002; Oakhill, Cain, & Elbro, 2015). There is very little about reading comprehension that is not directly influenced by language comprehension, once word recognition skills are removed from

> **DON'T FORGET**
> ....
> Reading comprehension difficulties usually involve difficulties in language comprehension. Aside from word reading skills, there is very little about reading comprehension that is not directly influenced by language comprehension.

the equation. We have learned in previous chapters that language comprehension involves an interaction of a wide variety of skills, including vocabulary, syntax, general background knowledge, specific topical knowledge, listening comprehension, knowledge of idioms and expressions, working memory, and attention. Even factors that tend to be specifically associated with *reading* comprehension may still be somewhat dependent on language comprehension and background knowledge, such as knowledge of genre, narrative structure, and inferencing. These not only influence what a person reads, but also what he understands when something is read to him (Clarke, Truelove, Hulme, & Snowling, 2014).

Research on intervention for reading comprehension represents a very large topic, or more accurately, a large set of topics. A full chapter would be inadequate, let alone a portion of a chapter. Indeed, the *Handbook of Reading Interventions* (O'Connor & Vadasy, 2011) devotes four chapters to four different aspects of reading comprehension: (1) vocabulary (McKeown & Beck, 2011), (2) determining main idea and summarization (Jitendra & Gajria, 2011), (3) metacognitive skills (Klingner, Morrison, & Eppolito, 2011), and (4) teaching narrative and expository text structure (Williams & Pao, 2011). Even these presentations are only able to survey the research in those specific areas and summarize some of the practical instructional and remedial approaches derived from the intervention literature. Fortunately, there are some helpful book-length resources that address the findings from reading comprehension intervention in very practical ways (e.g., Beck, McKeown, & Kucan, 2013; Carroll, Bowyer-Crane, Duff, Hulme, & Snowling, 2011; Clarke et al., 2014; Kamhi & Catts, 2011; Oakhill et al., 2015; O'Connor & Vadasy, 2011).

Reading comprehension intervention research has focused on directly addressing the kinds of skills that poor comprehenders lack, which were described in Chapters 5 and 9. Not every skill has received the same amount of attention.

The two most commonly studied aspects of reading comprehension have traditionally been vocabulary and reading comprehension strategies. Indeed, these were the two areas examined in the meta-analysis of the National Reading Panel (NICHD, 2000).

Vocabulary

Vocabulary is central to comprehension, and teaching vocabulary can improve comprehension (NICHD, 2000). Such training is most effective when new words are contextualized and reinforced (McKeown & Beck, 2011). Beck et al. (2013) provide a useful and practical guide for boosting vocabulary knowledge. The earlier version of their program (Beck, McKeown, & Kucan, 2002) was an influential part of a highly effective reading comprehension intervention program described later in the chapter (Clarke et al., 2014).

Background Knowledge

Teaching background knowledge has received less attention than vocabulary or reading comprehension strategies, despite its centrality for language and reading comprehension (Catts, 2009; Kamhi, 2009). Miller and Keenan (2009) discuss the "centrality deficit," in which poor comprehenders struggle to determine the difference between central and peripheral information. Yet when provided with relevant background information, this centrality deficit disappeared. Other studies have demonstrated the benefits of providing adequate background knowledge (see citations in Compton et al., 2014).

Inferencing

Inferencing has received substantial attention under the heading of "reading comprehension strategies." It is a language-dependent skill that is not unique to reading comprehension. However, studies have demonstrated that inference training can bring about measurable benefits in poor comprehenders within a short amount of time (Compton et al., 2014).

Working Memory and Attention

While working memory computer training can improve performance on working memory tasks (see Chapter 3), there is no evidence to date that such improvements influence reading comprehension. Thus, effective interventions for students with working memory or attention problems consist of strategies to work around these problems. One fruitful avenue has been the training of various metacognitive strategies, such as summarizing, self-questioning, and self-monitoring (Jitendra & Gajria, 2011; Klingner et al., 2011; Rapp, van den Broek, McMaster, Kendeou, & Espin, 2007). Students with such difficulties might benefit from teachers stopping more often to check for comprehension.

In addition, reading material and presentation methods that heighten interest and active participation are likely to engage such learners.

Comprehension Strategy Instruction

Directly teaching reading comprehension skills and strategies has demonstrated benefits for poor comprehenders (Fletcher, Lyon, Fuchs, & Barnes, 2007; Hulme & Snowling, 2009; NICHD, 2000). These include skills like inferencing, summarizing, comprehension monitoring, and identifying the main idea. As mentioned, these skills can yield benefits in a short amount of time (Compton et al., 2014). This is likely because of the fact that many children with learning disabilities and language difficulties lack metacognitive skills (Fletcher et al., 2007; Hulme & Snowling, 2009), so they need direction in terms of how to approach text in ways that come naturally to others. In addition, a variety of other techniques that have become popular in recent years can also assist poor comprehenders. These include prior teaching of text vocabulary and background information, instruction in genre and text structure, and the use of various graphic organizers, though the latter has weaker research support than most realize (Kim, Vaughn, Wanzek, & Wei, 2004). Another strategy that has shown some benefit is when some sort of movement or activity is involved, ranging from the use of puppets and figurines to acting out scenes in class (see citations in Marley, Levin, & Glenberg, 2007).

An Effective Comprehension Intervention Program

Again, the complexity of language comprehension and reading comprehension requires more attention than can be provided here. The Further Reading section in the back of this volume lists helpful resources for educators. One particular resource deserves special mention. *Developing Reading Comprehension* (Clarke et al., 2014) is a concise volume (193 pages) that provides a fairly detailed blueprint for addressing reading comprehension on a class-wide or school-wide basis. This volume was the result of the York Reading for Meaning project, a randomized control trial research study out of York University in England. Portions of the results of this project were published in peer-reviewed journals. *Developing Reading Comprehension* functions as a manual

DON'T FORGET

The manual for the Reading for Meaning project (Clarke et al., 2014) is an excellent resource for schools to provide a comprehensive way to address the needs of students with reading and language comprehension difficulties.

that integrates a large amount of research data into a practical implementation program. The authors provide a nontechnical overview of the theory and research behind the program. They discuss the reasons for their selection of specific instructional strategies and assessments. They also provide information on all of the practical aspects of implementing their project, including the training of teachers and teaching assistants. Their program was quite successful, with moderate to large gains on most reading comprehension and language measures.[1] The Reading for Meaning project was also cost effective because of its heavy reliance on trained teaching assistants. This program is available for schools to implement with the only cost being the manual and training. Since the training is described in the manual, in-house professionals can inexpensively provide training to paraprofessionals. Also, the authors have established a website for additional assistance with implementation: http://readingformeaning.co.uk.

MAKING IT WORK: PRACTICAL INTERVENTION ISSUES

In this section, a variety of practical implementation issues will be presented, drawn from various studies and supplemented by personal experience.

Group Size

One-on-one instruction should no longer be considered the gold standard for remediation (e.g., Elbaum, Vaughn, Hughes, & Moody, 2000; NELP, 2008; NICHD, 2000). Numerous studies with small groups have obtained results similar to one-to-one instruction, as long as the groupings did not exceed about 1:4 or, at most, 1:5 (Torgesen et al., 2003). However, it is important to group students with equivalent skills, so the instructor does not have to cater to multiple skill levels in the same group. Lennon and Slesinski (1999) were successful in grouping students by skill levels and regrouped them as needed when one student progressed faster than another (they used 1:2). Thus, teachers were always presenting the same material at the same level to each group member.

If a teacher is using the highly effective interventions described in this chapter, there are at least two ways to manage situations in which small group sizes are not very small (e.g., 5 to 10+ students). The first way is to split the group time and

---

[1] These British authors used the term "standard score" for a statistic that we in the United States would call "scaled score." Thus, the findings they report in their book appear to be only one third as strong as their actual outcomes. Their reported moderate to strong effect sizes clarify this.

group size in half and have the groups alternate between instruction and independent work. For example, 15 to 20 minutes with a group of four students is likely to be more productive than 30 to 40 minutes with a group of eight. The second way is with a "wait list" approach. Students receive small group instruction in waves of 10, 15, or 20 weeks in a school year. For example, given a 40-week school year, one could divide the year into three 12-week sessions. This would leave a week at the beginning and the end of the year, and a week in between each of the three sessions to allow for pre- and post-testing. Thus, rather than an unwieldy group of nine students all year, for example, remedial teachers could have three much more intensive (and likely productive) sessions with 1:3 groups. These and other creative scheduling approaches could alleviate some of the group size issues and provide greater intensity in terms of teacher–student ratio. Again, it is the *content* of the instruction that will provide most of the success. Using these creative scheduling approaches with traditional remedial methods will likely result in minimal outcomes. Conversely, even the most highly effective approaches would not likely be effective if small groups become too large. Anything over five students is likely to diminish results. Groups of two to four students would be best, assuming they are grouped according to similar skill levels.

Round Robin Reading

Most elementary school students have a 6-hour day and 90 minutes of English language arts. Traditionally, these are divided into three small group times, with eight in a group. Half the group time is spent with students taking turns reading ("round robin"), and the other half discussing the story or other small-group instruction. That's about 15 minutes of actual reading practice shared among eight students, or less than 2 minutes of actual reading practice per student, per 6-hour school day. Also, inattentive students may not pay attention when it is not their turn. One way to boost reading practice and focused attention in small groups is via choral-solo-choral-solo reading (McInnis, 1999). The teacher has a student read a line, then the entire small group reads the next line, followed by another student reading the third line, and the group reads the fourth line, and so on. Teachers develop a signal or simply say a student's name to indicate the next solo reader. Using this approach, students are more focused and engaged and they get more reading practice because their choral reading supplements their solo opportunities. Inattentive students are more engaged because they have to read every other line. Though awkward at first, it quickly becomes very natural for the students and the teacher. This approach can also be used in small remedial groups of two to four students.

Peer Tutoring

Peer tutoring has received a great deal of research support. By itself, it is not likely to "close the gap" between struggling readers and their fellow students. But it is a practical way to provide additional skill reinforcement. For example, a weak and strong reader can be paired, with the weak reader getting some additional oral reading practice with feedback.

Reading comprehension can also be improved via peer tutoring. A program called Peer Assisted Learning Strategies (PALS) has undergone numerous studies and has been shown to benefit reading skills in typically developing students, struggling readers, and ELL students (Fuchs et al., 2001; Sáenz, Fuchs, & Fuchs, 2005; Spörer & Brunstein, 2009). While the results from PALS do not approach the level of improvement found in the highly successful interventions already mentioned, PALS has demonstrated measurable reading improvements and therefore appears to be an excellent approach to supplement the remedial instruction provided by teachers or teaching assistants.

Reciprocal Teaching

Reciprocal teaching was originally developed to assist students with reading comprehension difficulties (Palinscar & Brown, 1984). Students are taught to approach text with four reading comprehension strategies in mind. After students are trained in this, they take turns functioning as teachers of the small group. Student leaders have students read and then ask them questions related to the trained strategies. By itself, reciprocal teaching may not close the gap (Greenway, 2002). However, it appears to be a practical and cost-effective supplement to other remedial efforts. Both reciprocal teaching and PALS involve a minimum of teacher involvement, but they have been shown to boost results, so for that reason they are recommended.

Spelling

Spelling requires a precise orthographic sequence, often more precise than is needed for reading. Any large-group or small-group opportunities for having students spell words they are learning can be helpful to reading development. Further, spelling of homophones (*their/there/they're; pear/pair/pare; sent/cent/scent; I'll/aisle/isle;* etc.) side by side helps students develop more precision in their word-specific orthographic development. Students are more likely to read words they have learned to spell than to spell words they have learned to read.

SUMMARY

There appear to be three critical instructional elements related to highly successful outcomes in word-level reading: (1) advance phonemic awareness skills, (2) explicit and systematic phonics instruction, and (3) opportunities to read real, connected text. A few programs were described that incorporate all three elements. Also, reading comprehension–specific problems are typically related to language development. The York Reading for Meaning program was recommended because it can produce substantial improvements in reading comprehension and language comprehension. Therefore, the most important instructional components for virtually all types of reading problems were described. It would be difficult to improve upon the summary provided by Foorman and Torgesen (2001), who concluded their article on reading remediation with the following:

> In summary, effective classroom reading instruction on phonemic awareness, phonemic decoding, fluency in word recognition and text processing, construction of meaning, vocabulary, spelling, and writing can maximize the probability that all but a very small percentage of children can learn to read on grade level. To address the needs of this small percentage we need to provide additional instruction on the same components in a small-group or one-on-one format. However, research shows that such instruction will need to be more explicit and comprehensive, more intensive, and more supportive than that typically provided by schools. (p. 210)

🐾 TEST YOURSELF 🐾

1. **Which of the following was *not* a key element present in the studies with the most highly successful word-reading intervention outcomes?**
   (a) Training advanced phonemic awareness skills
   (b) Phonics instruction/reinforcement
   (c) Training in reading comprehension strategies
   (d) Opportunities for reading connected text

2. **Of the studies that had minimal to modest intervention outcomes, which of the following key elements was most commonly missing?**
   (a) Training advanced phonemic awareness skills
   (b) Phonics instruction/reinforcement
   (c) Training in reading comprehension strategies
   (d) Opportunities for reading connected text

3. **Which of the following is likely to be the best way to determine if an intervention reported in the research literature is likely to help struggling readers close the gap with their same-aged peers?**
   (a) The demonstration of statistical significance between an intervention group and a comparison group
   (b) A demonstration of a moderate to large effect size when compared to a control group
   (c) Standard score point gains on normative reading tests
   (d) All the above are equally helpful.

4. **What is the likely reason that the classic gold standard reading disability remediation programs (i.e., Orton-Gillingham and Wilson) produce large gains in nonsense word reading but only modest gains in real-word reading?**
   (a) The intervention is not continued long enough.
   (b) They only train phonemic awareness up to the basic level and therefore do not foster orthographic mapping skills.
   (c) Too much time in these programs is spent sounding out nonsense words.
   (d) All of the above.

5. **What might be a reason that the repeated readings approach does not have a gap-closing impact on struggling readers?**
   (a) It does not directly address the phonic decoding deficiencies many of the struggling readers have.
   (b) It does not train phonemic awareness to the point where students can become good at orthographic mapping.
   (c) It does not involve activities that integrate phonemic awareness and letter-sound knowledge with the goal of promoting orthographic mapping.
   (d) All the above.

6. **Based on the studies by Torgesen et al. (2001) and Simos et al. (2002), what can we conclude about readers from third to fifth grade and older whose reading is in the bottom 2%–3% of the population?**
   (a) All of these students can reach grade level within 8 weeks using the right techniques.
   (b) Almost none of the students can be reasonably expected to read higher than the bottom quartile, regardless of intervention method.
   (c) With the right kind of intervention, a substantial percentage of these students can develop reading skills above the bottom quartile, with some even developing average scores.
   (d) While impressive gains were made in the studies, these interventions were so impractical that they could not be implemented in schools.

7. **Truch (1994, 2003, 2004) published results from large clinical samples of struggling readers, including readers from high school to adulthood. What can be concluded from Truch's clinical reports?**

    (a) Older students and adults do not make substantial progress in reading.

    (b) Older students and adults can make progress in reading, but at a substantially lower rate than younger students.

    (c) Older students and adults can make as much or more reading progress as younger students.

    (d) Older students and adults make progress in nonsense word reading, but it does not transfer to real-word reading.

8. **If a student just cannot seem to develop phonics skills, what might the research suggest should be done in such a situation?**

    (a) Chances are the student has phonemic awareness difficulties that will need to be corrected before progress in phonics skills can be expected.

    (b) Simply keep on course, because with enough practice and reinforcement, the student will develop the phonics skills needed.

    (c) It may be time to abandon phonics and switch to a whole-word approach.

    (d) There are multiple ways of teaching phonics, and it seems that alternative phonics approaches should be investigated.

9. **The research on intervention is clear: One-on-one instruction is the only reliable way to bring about substantial change in weak readers.**

    (a) True

    (b) False

10. **Which of the following commercially available programs have been shown to have the potential for very large and lasting gains in word-level reading in poor readers?**

    (a) Lindamood LiPS; Phono-Graphix; Read, Write, Type

    (b) READ 180; Fast ForWord; Great Leaps

    (c) Reading Recovery; Leveled Literacy Intervention; Failure Free Reading

    (d) All of the above have been shown to produce very large and lasting reading gains.

Answers: 1. c; 2. a; 3. c; 4. b; 5. d; 6. c; 7. c; 8. a; 9. False; 10. a

Twelve

CASE ILLUSTRATIONS

I n the following pages, several case examples are provided to illustrate some of the principles and concepts presented throughout this volume. With the exception of the PAST test (see Chapter 6), well-known commercially available tests are used, each of which has demonstrated reliability and validity. Table 12.1 provides explanations of abbreviations. All of these cases describe actual students I evaluated, with their names replaced. Note that older editions of tests are often referred to because these assessments occurred between 2003 and 2010.

Table 12.1 List of Abbreviations for Tests

Abbreviation	Test
ADDES-2	Attention Deficit Disorders Scale–Second Edition
CTOPP	Comprehensive Test of Phonological Processing
PAST	Phonological Awareness Screening Test
PIAT-R	Peabody Individual Achievement Test–Revised
TORC-3	Test of Reading Comprehension–Third Edition
TOWRE	Test of Word Reading Efficiency
WASI	Wechsler Abbreviated Scale of Intelligence
WDRB	Woodcock Diagnostic Reading Battery
WIAT	Wechsler Individual Achievement Test
WISC-III	Wechsler Intelligence Scale for Children–Third Edition
WRAT-3	Wide Range Achievement Test–Third Edition
WRMT-R	Woodcock Reading Mastery Test–Revised

MILD DYSLEXIC PATTERN

Eugene has weak word-level reading skills for both real words and nonsense words, both of which are poorer under timed conditions than when untimed (Table 12.2). This is a common pattern, particularly among brighter struggling readers whose parents "did all the right things" (i.e., early literacy learning opportunities at home). However, the phonological-core deficit makes it difficult for them to learn to read. When given enough time, they are able to correctly identify words. But they have neither a large enough sight vocabulary to quickly read real words, nor proficient enough phonic decoding skills to rapidly blend letter sounds to quickly read nonsense words.

Table 12.2 Eugene—November of Grade 2 (2003)

	Standard/ Scaled Score	Percentile Rank	Grade Equivalent	Descriptive Level
Specific Cognitive Skills Testing				
Phonological Short-Term/Working Memory				
CTOPP Memory for Digits	11	63rd	3.7	average
Phonological Awareness Skills				
CTOPP Elision	7	16th	1.2	below average
CTOPP Segmenting Words	10	50th	<2.0	average
PAST	Level G		early 1	below average
Oral Blending Skills				
CTOPP Blending Words	10	50th	2.4	average
Rapid Automatized Naming				
CTOPP Rapid Digit Naming	10	50th	3.0	average
CTOPP Rapid Letter Naming	8	25th	2.0	low average
Background Information				
PIAT-R General Information	95	37th	1.8	average
Achievement Testing				
Word Identification				
TOWRE Sight Word Efficiency	75	5th	1.0	below average
WRAT-3 Reading	82	12th	1.3	below average
WRMT-R Word Identification	83	13th	1.4	below average
PIAT-R Reading Recognition	85	16th	1.2	below average
Phonics Skills/Nonsense Word Reading				
TOWRE Phonemic Decoding Efficiency	75	5th	1.0	below average
WRMT-R Word Attack	91	27th	1.3	average
Spelling				
WRAT-3 Spelling	78	7th	1.0	below average
PIAT-R Spelling	86	18th	1.1	low average

Difficulties with phonological short-term memory are very common among poor word-level readers, but this does not appear to be a problem for Eugene. His rapid automatized naming profile is not as clear. Typically, an individual student's performance on the CTOPP or CTOPP-2 rapid digits and rapid letters do not differ from one another by more than 1 scaled score point. It is less common to be off by 2 scaled score points, which represents two thirds of a standard deviation. Rapid digits and rapid letters equally correlate with word-reading skills, and they are highly correlated with each other, so Eugene should have done just as well on the rapid letters as he did on rapid digits. However, it likely means that he does not have a rapid automatized naming problem because his speed of access to the digits was at the 50th percentile.

The CTOPP Segmenting Words subtest suggests that Eugene is at the 50th percentile in phonological awareness. However, recall from earlier chapters that phoneme segmentation is not nearly as valid of an assessment of the phonological underpinnings of word-level reading as phonological manipulation tasks. His CTOPP Elision subtest and the PAST both suggest that he is at a beginning first-grade level in phonological awareness, so he is already a year behind his typically developing peers, which is consistent with his low reading scores. This evaluation was completed in 2003. Within a year or two of that, I stopped giving the Segmenting Words subtest because it usually demonstrated little or no correspondence to children's reading skills, except in the most severe cases. Indeed, the CTOPP manual reports that the correlation between Segmenting Words and reading is .29 (compared to .59 for Elision). It is thus unfortunate that our universal screeners rely on phoneme segmentation. Chapter 6 discusses the issue in detail.

Eugene displayed poor performance on two different types of spelling tasks. The WRAT-3 Spelling is a traditional dictation task, and the PIAT-R Spelling test is more like the orthography tasks described in Chapter 7. Eugene was presented with four different choices and he was instructed to point to the correct spelling based upon the word presented. Relative to normative samples, Eugene had more difficulty producing the spelling of a word than correctly guessing a spelling in a multiple-choice format. Spelling difficulties are very common among children with the dyslexic pattern, although there are exceptions.

SEVERE DYSLEXIC PATTERN

Karen's profile represents a more severe case than Eugene's, but with a few differences. Unlike Eugene, Karen had difficulties with both phonological short-term memory and rapid automatized naming (Table 12.3). These likely contributed to

Table 12.3 Karen—May of Grade 6 (2011)

	Standard/ Scaled Score	Percentile Rank	Grade Equivalent	Descriptive Level
Global Intelligence/Cognitive Testing				
WASI Verbal Scale	108	68th		average
WASI Performance Scale	96	39th		average
WASI Full Scale	102	53rd		average
Specific Cognitive Skills Testing				
Phonological Short-Term/Working Memory				
CTOPP Memory for Digits	7	16th	1.4	below average
WISC-III Digit Span	5	5th		below average
Phonological Awareness Skills				
CTOPP Elision	4	2nd	1.7	lower extreme
CTOPP Phoneme Reversal	6	9th	1.4	below average
PAST	highest correct level = K (but not E, I)		early 2nd	below average
PAST	highest automatic level = G (but not E)		early 1st	below average
Oral Blending Skills				
CTOPP Blending Words	12	75th	>9.7	high average
Rapid Automatized Naming				
CTOPP Rapid Digit Naming	5	5th	2.2	below average
CTOPP Rapid Letter Naming	4	2nd	2.0	lower extreme
Academic Achievement				
Word Identification				
TOWRE Sight Word Efficiency	64	<1st	1.8	lower extreme
WRAT-3 Reading	74	4th	2.7	below average
WRMT-R Word Identification	75	5th	2.4	below average
Phonics Skills/Nonsense Word Reading				
TOWRE Phonemic Decoding Efficiency	72	3rd	1.6	below average
WRMT-R Word Attack	86	17th	2.8	low average
Reading Comprehension				
WRMT-R Passage Comprehension	79	8th	2.8	below average
Spelling				
WRAT-3 Spelling	78	7th	2.4	below average

the severity of her reading difficulty. Like Eugene, Karen had higher word-reading and nonsense word reading scores when these tasks were untimed rather than timed. This suggests limited sight vocabulary and limited proficiency with phonic decoding. Karen's passage comprehension was significantly below average, despite her strong WASI verbal score. It can be easily surmised that her poor reading comprehension is solely the result of poor word-level reading skills.

Another observation is that Karen displayed strong performance on the CTOPP Blending Words subtest. Beyond about second grade, only the most severe phonological-core deficit students do poorly on this subtest. I do not routinely administer that subtest to older students, but I gave it to Karen because of her weaknesses on other phonological tasks. Yet even Karen, with a severe phonological-core deficit, had developed normal phonological blending skills. By contrast, her phonological analysis skills were poor. This illustrates why it is important to distinguish between phonological blending and phonological awareness/analysis (see Chapters 3, 4, and 6).

Karen's timed phonological awareness using the PAST demonstrated she is severely impaired. Her untimed phonological awareness was weak, but it was stronger than her timed performance. The PAST timed scoring appears to be a better index of phonological proficiency.

ELL STUDENT

Tim was born and raised in the Middle East and his native language was Arabic. His first formal schooling was when he arrived in the United States in grade 4. He never learned to read Arabic. From fourth to eighth grade, he received ELL services and English reading instruction, with very limited progress. The reason for this is likely that he had the phonological-core deficit; a combination of poor phonological short-term memory and phonological awareness (Table 12.4). His CTOPP Elision score is probably a better representation of his phonological skills than his Phoneme Reversal score, as the latter is dependent on phonological short-term memory. His extremely low score on Phoneme Reversal is likely the result of a combination of poor phonological awareness and poor phonological short-term memory. According to his ELL teacher and classroom teachers, his English oral comprehension skills were fairly strong, but below his eighth-grade peers (I had no language scores for him). One may argue that Tim's low score on the CTOPP Elision subtest is a byproduct of being a poor reader. However, given that he had four years of instruction in reading English, if he did not have the phonological-core deficit, his phonological awareness skills would be substantially stronger, as would his reading skills.

Table 12.4 Tim—June of Grade 8 (2010)

	Standard/ Scaled Score	Percentile Rank	Grade Equivalent	Descriptive Level
Specific Cognitive Skills Testing				
Phonological/Phonemic Awareness Skills				
CTOPP Elision	7	16th	4.4	below average
CTOPP Phoneme Reversal	3	1st	<2.0	lower extreme
Oral Blending				
CTOPP Blending Words	10	50th	>9.7	average
Phonological Short-Term/Working Memory				
CTOPP Memory for Digits	5	5th	<2.0	below average
Rapid Automatized Naming				
CTOPP Rapid Digit Naming	10	75th	>9.7	high average
CTOPP Rapid Letter Naming	11	63rd	>9.7	average
Academic Achievement				
Word Identification				
WRAT-3 Reading	65	1st	1.5	lower extreme
WRMT-R Word Identification	68	2nd	2.7	lower extreme
Phonics Skills/Nonsense Word Reading				
WRMT-R Word Attack	81	11th	3.2	below average
Reading Comprehension				
WRMT-R Passage Comprehension	78	7th	3.9	below average
Spelling				
WRAT-3 Spelling	66	2nd	1.4	lower extreme

COMPENSATOR PATTERN

More time and space are allotted to the compensator pattern because it is more difficult to detect. Jim was referred by his mother, not his teachers. His mother was an elementary school teacher and was concerned with his grades, his difficulty getting though all of his homework, and Jim's own complaints about his difficulties with school work.

Jim's profile is best understood by looking at the summary list of scores at the bottom of Table 12.5. He displays the prototypical compensating pattern: strong verbal skills; average reading comprehension that is substantially below his verbal skills; weaker word-level reading skills than reading comprehension, though still average; weaker phonic decoding than word-reading skills; and a mild to moderate weakness in phonemic awareness.

Jim's CTOPP Blending Words and Segmenting Words subtests were average. As already noted, these are not useful tests beyond about first grade; certainly

Table 12.5 Jim—December of Grade 6 (2010)

	Standard/ Scaled Score	Percentile Rank	Grade Equivalent	Descriptive Level
Specific Cognitive Skills Testing				
Phonological Short-Term/Working Memory				
CTOPP Memory for Digits	10	50th	7.4	average
WISC-III Digit Span	12	75th		high average
Listening/Language Comprehension				
WIAT Listening Comprehension	107	68th	7.9	average
WDRB Listening Comprehension	125	95th	>8.0	above average
WDRB Oral Vocabulary	115	84th	8.1	above average
Phonological Awareness Skills				
CTOPP Elision	10	50th	7.4	average
CTOPP Segmentation	12	75th	>8.0	high average
CTOPP Phoneme Reversal (Note: good WM)	8	25th	2.7	low average
PAST	highest correct level = K		early/mid 2	below average
PAST	highest automatic level = J		late 1/early 2	below average
Oral Blending Skills				
CTOPP Blending Words	11	63rd	>8.0	average
Rapid Automatized Naming				
CTOPP Rapid Digit Naming	9	37th	7.4	average
CTOPP Rapid Letter Naming	9	37th	6.7	average
Academic Achievement				
Reading Comprehension				
WIAT Reading Comprehension	100	50th	5.2	average
WDRB Passage Comprehension	101	53rd	6.2	average
WRMT-R Passage Comprehension	100	50th	5.9	average
PIAT-R Reading Comprehension	104	61st	6.7	average
TORC-3 Paragraph Reading	80	9th	3.2	below average

Table 12.5 (Continued)

	Standard/ Scaled Score	Percentile Rank	Grade Equivalent	Descriptive Level
Word Identification				
TOWRE Sight Word Efficiency	97	42nd	5.6	average
WRAT-3 Reading	93	32nd	4.1	average
WIAT Basic Reading	82	12th	3.2	below average
WRMT-R Word Identification	91	27th	3.9	average
WDRB Letter-Word Identification	90	25th	4.1	low average
PIAT-R Reading Recognition	93	32nd	4.3	average
Mean word recognition score = 91; Median = 93; 4.1 grade equivalent (both average)				
Phonics Skills/Nonsense Word Reading				
TOWRE Phonemic Decoding Efficiency	87	19th	3.4	low average
WRMT-R Word Attack	91	28th	3.7	average
WDRB Word Attack	81	10th	2.2	below average
Spelling				
WIAT Spelling	94	42nd	5.0	average
WRAT-3 Spelling	89	23rd	3.9	low average
Summary List of Jim's Scores Displaying the Compensator Pattern (based on median scores)				
Listening/Language Comprehension	115	84th	8.1	above average
Reading Comprehension	100	50th	5.9	average
Word Identification	91	27th	3.9	average
Phonics Skills/Nonsense Word Reading	87	19th	3.4	low average
Phonological Awareness Skills				
CTOPP Phoneme Reversal	8	25th	2.7	low average
PAST	highest automatic level = J		early 2	below average

not for detecting the subtle phonological awareness problems one might find in a compensator. However, the more sensitive Elision subtest was at the 50th percentile. As indicated in Chapter 6, many older students are able to obtain adequate scores on Elision via mental spelling, even if they have weak advanced phonemic awareness. For such students, a test of phonological awareness is needed that cannot be "worked around" via a mental spelling strategy that bypasses phonological awareness. The CTOPP Phoneme Reversal subtest is usually very sensitive to weaknesses in reading, but it also relies heavily on working memory. However, Jim's short-term memory performances ranged from the 50th to the 75th percentiles, so any weakness on Phoneme Reversal can be assumed to be the result of poor phonological awareness. Most of the items in Phoneme Reversal cannot be worked around through a mental spelling strategy, so it likely provides a better index of advanced phonological awareness skills in students with average or better phonological short-term memory. Jim's Phoneme Reversal score was at the 25th percentile. While considered average or low average by conventional descriptors (see Chapter 6), the 25th percentile is within the range of fourth- and eighth-grade students that the National Assessment of Educational Progress indicates read below a basic level. Jim clearly does not read below a basic level, but his phonological awareness, a key determinant of reading level, parallels that level of performance. He has so many strengths that his 25th percentile phonological awareness does not result in 25th percentile reading. To further support the interpretation of phonological awareness issues, Jim's PAST performance was weak. Most importantly, his automatic response to phonological awareness prompts was below what one would expect from a student older than second grade. The automatic score from the PAST is one of the few assessments of phonological manipulation that cannot be "faked" via a mental spelling strategy, because only instant, presumably nonstrategic responses make up that score. We can tentatively conclude that Jim's Phoneme Reversal subtest and the automatic score on the PAST both suggest he has weak advanced phonological awareness skills. These weaknesses are milder than the dyslexic cases already described. Yet it is likely problematic enough to make adding words to his sight vocabulary less efficient relative to his peers. His mild phonological awareness skills may also help us understand his relatively weak phonic decoding scores.

Compensators like Jim experience a cognitive "tug-of-war." Their strong verbal skills elevate their reading comprehension, while poor phonological awareness skills depress their word-level reading, which in turn limits their reading comprehension to a level substantially below their language comprehension. Because such students are bright, they are able to compensate their way through the early years of reading development. In the later grades, the reading load and written vocabulary demands become overwhelming, so they display difficulties. These difficulties can play themselves out as discouragement, poor attitude or motivation, behavioral issues, avoidance of reading, or declining grades. The answer is to detect these students early using better phonological awareness tests than are currently used in universal screeners. Once detected, their phonological awareness difficulties can be corrected through an RTI service delivery model.

MIXED TYPE

Sean's profile is a textbook case of the mixed type of reading difficulty (Table 12.6). He displays difficulties in word-level reading and language comprehension. Thus,

Table 12.6 Sean—September of Grade 3 (2005)

	Standard/ Scaled Score	Percentile Rank	Grade Equivalent	Descriptive Level
Global Intelligence/Cognitive Testing				
WISC-III Verbal Comprehension	87	19th		low average
WISC-III Perceptual Organization	89	23rd		low average
Listening/Language Comprehension				
WDRB Listening Comprehension	84	14th	K.9	below average
WDRB Oral Vocabulary	80	9th	K.7	below average
Attention/Inattention Ratings (school form-resource teacher)				
ADDES-2 Inattentive Scale	75	5th		well below average
ADDES-2 Impulsivity/ Hyperactivity	65	1st		lower extreme
Specific Cognitive Skills Testing				
Phonological Short-Term/Working Memory				
CTOPP Memory for Digits	10	50th	2.4	average
WISC-III Digit Span	9	37th		average
Phonological Awareness Skills				
CTOPP Elision	8	25th	1.7	low average
PAST	highest correct level = G			
PAST	highest automatic level = G		early 1	below average
Oral Blending Skills				
CTOPP Blending Words	10	50th	2.7	average
Rapid Automatized Naming				
CTOPP Rapid Digit Naming	7	16th	1.2	below average
CTOPP Rapid Object Naming	7	16th	1.2	below average
Academic Achievement				
Reading Comprehension				
WDRB Passage Comprehension	75	5th	1.3	below average
WRMT-R Passage Comprehension	81	10th		below average
Word Identification				
WRMT-R Word Identification	76	5th	1.4	below average
WDRB Word Identification	69	2nd	1.1	lower extreme
Phonics Skills/Nonsense Word Reading				
WDRB Word Attack	92	30th	1.9	average
WRMT-R Word Attack	92	30th		average

his reading comprehension is significantly below average. In addition, he has difficulties with focusing and attention.

What is interesting is that Sean displays scores in the average range for phonic decoding. This is likely due to the fact that he had been receiving special education reading help with a phonic emphasis. These directly taught skills were above his other skill areas. Also, his CTOPP Blending Words score was average, and blending is needed for phonic decoding. But this has not translated into improved word identification skills. It should be clear by now that this is because Sean has weak phonemic awareness proficiency, as demonstrated by his very weak automatic (timed) PAST score. Sean also possesses weak phonological short-term memory and rapid automatized naming, so he has deficits in each phonological-core deficit area except phonic decoding (likely due to remedial instruction).

HYPERLEXIC TYPE

Norma represents a very clear case of hyperlexia. She has consistently low language scores and weak background knowledge. By contrast, she has strong phonological awareness and short-term memory and outstanding rapid automatized naming. Her word identification scores were solidly average and her phonics skills were above average (Table 12.7).

In Chapter 9, it was indicated that reading comprehension subtests with different formats can yield different levels of performance. I read Keenan, Betjemann, and Olson (2008), which studied this issue, shortly before Norma's evaluation. In an effort to align my practice with this emerging research, I administered three different reading comprehension subtests with three different formats. By contrast, Sean's evaluation, presented above, occurred before I read that, so word-reading he only received a single reading comprehension test. Like the hyperlexic type, students with the mixed type of reading difficulty (like Sean) would be best served by being administered reading comprehension subtests with multiple formats (see Chapter 9).

All of Norma's scores on the three different types of reading comprehension tests were below average. This cannot be attributed to her word-reading skills, nor to poor working memory, which is another common contributor to poor reading comprehension. Rather, the source of her poor reading comprehension can be identified as her poor language skills and weakness in background knowledge.

Table 12.7 Norma—May of Grade 6 (2009)

	Standard/ Scaled Score	Percentile Rank	Grade Equivalent	Descriptive Level
Specific Cognitive Skills Testing				
Language /Listening Comprehension				
WIAT Listening Comprehension	71	3rd	1.6	below average
WDRB Listening Comprehension	67	1st	K.8	lower extreme
WDRB Oral Vocabulary	70	2nd	1.5	lower extreme
Background Knowledge				
WISC-III Information	4	2nd		lower extreme
Phonological Awareness/Oral Blending				
CTOPP Elision	11	63rd	>9.7	average
CTOPP Phoneme Reversal	11	63rd	>9.7	average
CTOPP Blending Words	15	95th	>9.7	above average
Phonological Short-Term/Working Memory				
CTOPP Memory for Digits	12	75th	>9.7	high average
WISC-III Digit Span	12	75th		high average
Rapid Automatized Naming				
CTOPP Rapid Digit Naming	17	99th	>9.7	upper extreme
CTOPP Rapid Letter Naming	16	98th	>9.7	upper extreme
Academic Achievement				
Word Identification				
WRMT-R Word Identification	101	52nd	6.9	average
WIAT Basic Reading	102	55th	6.4	average
Phonics Skills/Nonsense Word Reading				
WRMT-R Word Attack	117	88th	>9.0	above average
Reading Comprehension				
WRMT-R Passage Comprehension	81	10th	3.1	below average
TORC-3 Paragraph Reading	85	16th	4.0	below average
WIAT Reading Comprehension	76	5th	2.8	below average

SUMMARY

It is hoped that these case examples help illustrate and clarify how one might interpret the profiles of students with various types of reading difficulties. Five different types of reading difficulties were portrayed: dyslexia, hyperlexia, mixed, compensating, and ELL. Each would require a different approach to remediation, and the best remedial approach for each would only become clear after an evaluation that reveals each student's particular skill pattern.

Thirteen

READING DIFFICULTIES AND LEARNING DISABILITY IDENTIFICATION

The focus of this book has been on applying the empirical research on reading acquisition and reading difficulties/disabilities to intervention-oriented assessment and to intervention, not to the identification of an educational disability under the Individuals with Disabilities Education Improvement Act (IDEA, 2004). In keeping with this focus, the purpose of this chapter is not to provide detailed procedures and criteria for identifying a specific learning disability (SLD) in reading under IDEA (see Flanagan, Ortiz, & Alfonso, 2013). Indeed, the reading research field upon which this book is based has not reached an empirically validated consensus on criteria for identifying reading disabilities. Besides, reading difficulties commonly cut across nearly all IDEA disabilities, particularly SLD, Speech or Language Impairment (SLI), Intellectual Disability (ID), and Emotional Disturbance (ED).

Despite this, some thoughts are provided in this chapter to assist evaluation teams with identifying reading disabilities. The long-standing IQ–achievement discrepancy approach has been shown to be inadequate on multiple levels (e.g., Gresham & Vellutino, 2010). Recent research has demonstrated significant psychometric problems with the use of Curriculum Based Measurement (CBM) progress monitoring, which appears to influence its validity for determining a learning disability (Ardoin, Christ, Morena, Cormier, & Klingbeil, 2013; Betts, Pickart, & Heistad, 2009; Christ, Zopluoglu, Long, & Monaghen, 2012; Jenkins,

> **DON'T FORGET**
> ....
> While the reading research field has not developed a consensus on SLD identification, there are numerous empirical findings that can assist evaluation teams in providing more valid determinations of reading disabilities.

Graff, & Miglioretti, 2009; Wayman, Wallace, Wiley, Tichá, & Espin, 2007; Yeo, Kim, Branum-Martin, Wayman, & Espin, 2012). Also, attempts at identification using the patterns of strengths and weaknesses (PSW) approaches have been met with significant diagnostic accuracy issues (Stuebing, Fletcher, Branum-Martin, & Francis, 2013). This makes identifying an SLD a challenge for evaluation teams.

While the reading research field has not developed a consensus on SLD identification, there are numerous empirical findings that can assist evaluation teams in providing more valid determinations of reading disabilities. It cannot be emphasized enough, however, that reading problems fall along a continuum, with no clear dividing line. Thus, clinical judgment will continue to play a role, and clinical judgment informed by reading research will likely yield more valid decisions.

FAR FEWER STUDENTS WITH SLD?

If the research presented in Chapters 10 and 11 were implemented in schools, there would be far fewer students who would be considered to have a reading disability. Researchers have estimated that the percentage of students who would continue to function below the 30th and 16th percentiles on current norm-referenced assessments after applying the most highly successful intervention approaches would be

> **CAUTION**
>
> It is assumed in the following discussion of reading-related SLD identification that the highly effective prevention and intervention approaches discussed in Chapters 10 and 11 are already in place, so the issue of SLD identification applies to a far smaller percentage of students than would traditionally be the case.

approximately one sixth of our current percentages (Foorman, & Al Otaiba, 2009; Vellutino et al., 1996; Torgesen, 2004a). Indeed, Torgesen (2004a) indicated that if these highly successful approaches to prevention and intervention were widespread, the national norms would change and some sort of "absolute" grade-based scale of improvement would be needed to determine reading growth (e.g., second graders can do thus-and-such by this point). Torgesen, Rashotte, Alexander, Alexander, and MacPhee (2003) found that when they returned to a school district in which they conducted a study a few years earlier, the number and nature of poor readers changed as a result of the adoption of the approaches used in the earlier studies in that school. In the following discussion of identifying SLD in reading, it is presumed that a school has *already adopted* the highly successful approaches described in Chapters 10 and 11, and thus the percentage of cases of students with SLD would be substantially smaller.

CHARACTERISTICS THAT SUGGEST AN EDUCATIONAL DISABILITY—PART I: SLD IN WORD-LEVEL READING

Severe Phonological-Core Deficit

If a school makes use of the highly effective approaches described in Chapters 10 and 11, most of the mild and moderate cases of the phonological-core deficit can be resolved via an RTI-based approach. Even some of the more severe cases may yield to well-implemented RTI efforts. However, even the research studies with the best outcomes found that some weak phonological-core deficit readers made less progress than others. Let us examine each element of the phonological-core deficit.

Phonemic Awareness

Phonological awareness difficulties can be relatively easily resolved using explicit and systematic phonological awareness training. Truch (2003), whose clinic produced highly successful gains using three different phonological awareness–based intervention programs said:

> We found that it is indeed quite easy to bring about changes on the phonological variables in a very short period of time. Twelve or 24 hours of remedial work (of which, about 4–8 hours would be directly related to phonological activities) can bring students excellent gains on areas like segmenting, blending and phoneme manipulation. (p. 16)

It was mentioned in Chapter 11 that Truch (1994) found that of the 281 participants in his study with phonologically based reading difficulties, only 1 did not progress in phonological awareness, and about 75% developed completely normal phonological skills. Bhat, Griffin, and Sindelar (2003) boosted the phonological awareness skills of sixth through eighth graders by nearly 2 standard deviations in 18 lessons across 4 weeks. Thus, we have reason to believe that most phonological awareness difficulties, including severe cases, can yield to explicit phonemic awareness intervention in Tier 2 or 3 of RTI.

When using a phonological awareness training program, students with limited growth may be hindered by other difficulties, such as poor working memory, rapid automatized naming, very low general intelligence, and/or poor attention. Nonetheless, for treatment resistors being considered as SLD, an evaluation team should have comprehensive data on the students' phonological awareness progress and demonstrate that a substantial phonological awareness deficit persists despite a systematic attempt to address it.

Phonic Decoding

Studies with highly successful reading outcomes indicate that phonic decoding displays average improvements of between 15 to 30 standard score points as measured on pseudoword reading tests. Recall from Chapter 11 that if a student is not showing much progress in phonics, it is almost always due to poor phonological awareness skills. It would be a rare circumstance that a student continues to struggle in phonic decoding despite systematic and explicit remedial instruction in phonemic awareness to the advanced level, alongside phonics intervention (Truch, 1994). However, not all large gains in phonics skills result in phonics skills that are truly "normalized." Consider a student with an initial Word Attack standard score of 65. If the student makes a full standard deviation of improvement, the student would still be performing at the 9th percentile (standard score of 80). Such a student might be a good candidate for an SLD designation.

Some students with the phonological-core deficit score substantially lower on Word Attack than Word Identification. For example, the likely presence of a reading disability may be minimal in a student with a Word Identification score of 84 and a Word Attack score of 90 compared to a student whose Word Identification score is 86 and Word Attack is 74. The second student is more likely to have a reading disability than the first.

Rapid Automatized Naming

RAN has been long associated with reading disabilities, including the most severe forms of reading disabilities. RAN problems alone are not likely to result in a reading disability, with the possible exception of an SLD in reading fluency. RAN deficits cannot be directly remediated, and such deficits are often associated with a lower trajectory for remedial outcomes. As such, very low RAN performance may be considered a "marker" of an SLD in reading. However, in some studies, RAN spontaneously improved when reading improved, even if to a lesser degree than the reading improvement.

Phonological Working Memory

Deficits in working memory are common in students with SLDs in reading, writing, and math. It is arguable that working memory deficits are the most common problem that cuts across all types of learning difficulties. WM problems cannot be directly "fixed" in a manner that benefits reading progress. Like RAN, studies have shown improvement in WM following increases in reading skills. Also like RAN, poor WM is associated with weaker intervention outcomes. As a result,

WM will be a significant characteristic to examine when one considers whether a student should be considered as having a reading disability. Recall that WM affects both word reading and reading comprehension.

A Mixture of Multiple Phonological Deficits

The students most likely to demonstrate limited progress, despite the best-practice approaches in prevention and intervention described in Chapters 10 and 11, are the students who display deficiencies in two, three, or all four of the phonological-core deficit areas. Those with multiple deficits are likely to be the ones who have more severe reading difficulties and require longer-term and more intensive intervention. Yet the presence of multiple aspects of the phonological-core deficit should not be taken as an automatic indicator of a reading disability. Some students with difficulties in all of these areas show phonic decoding improvement subsequent to improved phonemic awareness. It was already mentioned that improvements in RAN and phonological WM have been shown to occur after substantial reading improvements. Conversely, some students with severe difficulties in only one of these areas may become treatment resistors (e.g., some students with a RAN scaled score of 1, 2, or 3). Nonetheless, students with multiple phonological-core deficits are more likely to be considered SLD in reading because these factors can have a cumulative, negative effect on reading.

CHARACTERISTICS THAT SUGGEST AN EDUCATIONAL DISABILITY—PART 2: READING COMPREHENSION

Reading comprehension difficulties are not unique to SLD but are common in SLI, ID, ED, autism, and other disabilities. If a student has a reading comprehension difficulty independent of word-level reading skills, that student often has a language-related problem. Such a student should receive a speech–language evaluation and could be considered as SLI or SLD, depending on the outcome of that evaluation and other evaluation information. A student's language difficulties may not be severe enough to warrant an SLI designation, but they still may be the primary source of reading comprehension difficulties. In such cases, SLD in reading comprehension may be more appropriate.

One of the many problems with the traditional IQ–achievement discrepancy approach to SLD identification is that some students have reading comprehension difficulties due to weak language skills. Such students were often denied services because their language skills lowered their verbal IQ scores, which lowered their overall IQ, making it difficult to display a discrepancy between IQ and reading comprehension.

Some may raise the concern that if such "nondiscrepant" students could be designated as SLD, that would substantially increase the number of identified students. However, if the highly effective prevention and intervention approaches are used, the percentage of students who qualify as SLD in reading would be substantially reduced. As a result, only less responsive students with more severe needs would be identified.

There are certain characteristics to consider when attempting to determine whether a student has a reading comprehension disability. First, one must take account of the child's word-level reading skills. Second, one needs to evaluate attention, working memory, vocabulary, general language skills, and background knowledge. Students with substantial difficulties in one or more of these could potentially have an SLD, and deficiencies in multiple skills would increase the likelihood a student would require longer-term help and thus be a good candidate for SLD or SLI.

An additional consideration regarding identifying an SLD in reading comprehension is the selection of reading comprehension tests, given that different tests can yield different outcomes (see Chapter 9).

GENERAL GUIDELINES FOR IDENTIFYING A READING DISABILITY

The following are general guidelines based on findings that have emerged from the reading research. Given the lack of consensus in the reading field on identification criteria and the fact that reading difficulties and disability fall along a continuum, clinical judgment will be needed, so none of the general guidelines below can be rigidly applied. However, the research findings applied below should result in more valid reading-related SLD determinations than when such judgments are made in the absence of this information.

List of General Guidelines

The two key factors that appear to be the most relevant in determining the presence of a reading disability are (a) *severity* of reading problems and the severity of the problems with the component skills that underlie reading, and (b) *responsiveness* to highly successful interventions.

Lower extreme in Reading Skills

Even though the most severely reading-disabled students can make large gains using highly effective interventions, many of them will still perform in the bottom quartile, or even in the bottom 16th percentile. For example, a student who responds well to intervention by making a full standard deviation of improvement may go from a standard score of 70 to 85, which is still at the 16th percentile. Thus, any student in the bottom 5th percentile in reading skills, based on nationally normed assessments (i.e., a standard score of 76 or lower), should be considered a good candidate for having a reading disability. While it is possible that even students this low might develop normalized reading performance (Simos et al., 2002; Torgesen et al., 2001), this guideline recognizes that such improvement will most likely require longer-term remediation. A diagnosis of SLD in reading would allow for that opportunity without taxing RTI resources, given that students starting that low have extremely limited prospects for developing normalized reading ability within a time frame typically allotted for RTI intervention.

Severe Deficits in Skills Associated With Reading

Students who score in the bottom 5% of the population on one or more of the component skills needed for word reading or reading comprehension (e.g., phonological awareness, verbal comprehension) are good candidates for a reading disability classification. This is true even if their reading scores are above the 5th percentile. Very low scores (e.g., at or below the 10th percentile) in phonological awareness, rapid automatized naming, working memory, vocabulary, and general language skills suggest a weak foundation for future reading growth. Even though some of these skills (particularly those easier to remediate, such as phonological awareness) can and should be addressed through an RTI service delivery model, the fact remains that students with extremely low performance in one or more of these component skills are at high risk for a reading disability. An example would be a student who has a reading comprehension score of 84 and a language score of 76. The prognosis for reading comprehension development in this individual without addressing the low language skills is poor. Also, weak RAN and/or WM are indicators that reading progress is likely to be modest.

DON'T FORGET

....

Students whose reading skills are so low that an improvement of a standard deviation would still leave them in the bottom quartile may be good candidates for an SLD designation.

The groundbreaking study by Vellutino et al. (1996), which was a major impetus to the development of RTI, is informative here. These researchers found that the students who made the least progress were the ones with the lowest initial scores on the reading-related assessments. Other studies have confirmed this pattern. As a result, it seems reasonable to use initial skill level as a general guide to a student's likely trajectory. This may assist in determining the likely presence of an SLD in reading.

The Presence of Multiple Weak Components Underlying Reading

If students are weak in multiple factors critical for skilled reading, research suggests they have a higher likelihood of being treatment resistors. Also, multiple "milder" weak areas can have a cumulative effect. So, if a student has phonological awareness, WM, RAN, and phonic decoding all in the 80 to 89 range, the cumulative effect of these weak skills can limit reading growth. However, a fairly large proportion of such students may see significant gains via an RTI service delivery model. It is only mentioned here because students with multiple low prerequisite skills are at greater risk of being treatment resistors.

Timed Reading Skills Significantly Below Untimed Performance

It is much harder for students to compensate on timed reading tasks than untimed ones, so the former is probably a better reflection of their skills and potential progress. Students with borderline untimed reading scores yet very low timed reading scores are good candidates for having a reading disability. For example, a student with untimed word identification and nonsense word reading of 86 and 84, but timed scores in those areas of 74 and 71, has a significant risk of an SLD in reading.

Response to Effective Interventions

Torgesen's (2005) review of intervention research provides guidance on how much intervention should be given before one decides a student is making adequate progress. Other studies have also addressed this question, particularly in the school psychology research literature (e.g., Christ, Zopluoglu, Monaghen, Pike-Balow, & Van Norman, 2013). However, Torgesen's (2005) review was different than most because it focused on the kind of progress found in studies using the highly effective intervention approaches described in Chapter 11, while the other studies and reviews did not.

Torgesen (2005) found that with the highly effective interventions, the largest reading gains occurred within the first 15 to 20 hours of instruction. After that, progress continued at a dramatically lower pace, but did not plateau. This suggests that when response to intervention is used as one of the criteria for determining the presence of an SLD in reading, 15 to 20 hours of instruction may be a good point of reference when using a highly effective intervention. By contrast, 15 to 20 hours of many of the conventional RTI intervention approaches (e.g., repeated readings, READ 180, Read Naturally, etc.; see Chapter 11) should not be expected to yield anything more than very limited results, based upon the research findings regarding these approaches. But if the highly effective approach to intervention described in Chapter 11 is used and there are not substantive gains in this 15- to 20-hour time frame, an SLD is very likely. This is a rigorous criterion given that even severely weak readers demonstrated important gains after 15 to 20 hours using these approaches. A major difference between the studies that Torgesen (2005) reviewed and the progress monitoring studies in the school psychology literature is that the former gauged progress with standard score point improvements on nationally normed tests, whereas the latter generally relied on CBM progress monitoring data. Standard score gains on nationally normed tests represent a very high criterion for demonstrating improvement. Such tests are not sensitive to smaller raw score gains like CBM assessment, so they require very substantial growth to see improvements (see Chapter 11 for a discussion of gauging reading progress).

What does 15 to 20 hours of instruction look like? If delivered daily, that would be one half hour a day for 6 weeks (15 hours) to 8 weeks (20 hours). If delivered three times a week, that would be one half hour a day for 10 weeks (15 hours) to 13 1/2 weeks (20 hours). It would also require pre- and post-tests using normed assessments. The reason for using standard scores over raw scores is because standard scores allow us to determine the degree to which students are "closing the gap" with their peers.

Special Education Reading Help Can Be Temporary for Most Poor Readers

DON'T FORGET

....

If schools' special educational remedial reading programs use the highly effective intervention approaches described in Chapter 11, then a special educational designation does not necessarily represent a long-term endeavor.

Because of the inadequacy of past attempts at reading remediation, we may have a tendency to think of an SLD "label" as something students will likely have for the remainder of their school careers. But with the effective remedial approaches described in Chapter 11, we see that a large portion of such students can improve to the point where SLD no longer applies. Torgesen et al. (2001) intervened with 60 third through fifth graders receiving special education who had average IQs, but their average word identification performances were in the second percentile. Following 65 hours of instruction, 40% of those students—who represented the most severely reading-disabled students—no longer required special educational help in reading. If one had a 30-minute daily 1:2 or 1:3 resource group for one half hour, such a group would reach 65 hours in about 26 weeks. There's nothing "magical" about 65 hours. The point here is that in less than one school year of instruction using a highly effective approach, even students with some of the most severe reading disabilities can "graduate" from special educational reading help. But because this level of intervention is well beyond what would be typically provided in a general educational RTI service, the traditional special educational context may be more appropriate in such cases. If the special education teachers are using the highly effective approaches that have been shown to dramatically improve reading progress, we should not have an aversion to designating a student as SLD.

Another idea is to consider "triaging" struggling readers to determine who is most likely to develop normalized reading performance in under half a school year or so via the available Tier 2 and Tier 3 RTI interventions and who may require more intensive (e.g., daily in a 1:2 or 1:3 group) and longer-term remediation. The former are students who would not be considered as having a reading disability (at least initially), whereas the latter would. The guidelines presented above could provide some assistance in that triaging process.

Al Otaiba et al. (2014) randomly assigned struggling first graders to one of two groups. One group went through Tier 2 then Tier 3 if they were unsuccessful with Tier 2. All of these students started with Tier 2, regardless of initial skill levels. Students in the second group were immediately placed in either Tier 2 or Tier 3 depending on the severity of their reading difficulty (i.e., there was no requirement to be in Tier 2 first). These researchers found that students in this second group outperformed the first group by the equivalent of 5 standard score points, even though they all received the same type of remedial instruction. This suggests that initial skill levels were a better guide to the level of RTI involvement then the traditional approach of starting at Tier 2 and only moving to Tier 3 if needed.

We may apply this finding to SLD identification in that students with lower skills should start in Tier 3, and if that level of intervention is insufficient, such a student could be considered for an SLD designation. Or, in more severe cases, it may be possible to bypass the RTI intervention process (see below).

The Key to Successful RTI

For RTI to be effective, we must first reduce the total number of struggling readers via our K–1 Tier 1 instruction combined with early Tier 2 supplemental instruction with at-risk K–1 students (see Chapter 10). This will result in far fewer students who are potential candidates for RTI *or* SLD in reading. That means we can avoid large, ineffective RTI group sizes, but can keep Tier 2 groups at a more manageable 1:3 to 1:4 (1:5 at the outer limit), and Tier 3 groups at 1:2 to 1:3. If we find ourselves with RTI group sizes of 8 or 10, that suggests that we need to examine the adequacy of our Tier 1 general education instruction and our K–1 Tier 2 early intervention.

As mentioned, Tier 1 and Tier 2 efforts should lead to far fewer students classified as SLD. For those who are classified for special educational services, we should be able to have small group sizes (1:2 to 1:3). This level of service would likely produce more "graduates" of resource room instruction and more "declassification" meetings than we currently have. Having fewer struggling readers does not mean we will decrease the need for RTI teachers or resource teachers. On the contrary, this whole scenario requires adequate personnel. The neurodevelopmental and environmental issues that produce struggling readers are not going away, so we will always need skilled instructors. However, the reduction in struggling readers means that we will be able to allocate those resources more intensively with the lower end of the reading continuum.

Must All Students Do RTI First?

> **CAUTION**
> ....
> Expecting all students to receive RTI before receiving an SLD classification does not appear to be an approach supported by research.

The research reviewed in Chapter 11 indicates that that we can get good results through small-group RTI interventions, even with students who have severe reading problems. The goal of RTI is to normalize reading as quickly as possible, not to keep students in RTI for multiple years. Yet if we try to serve the students who have little likelihood of "graduating" from RTI within 4 to 6 months or so, we make RTI service delivery less effective by having too many long-term participants making use of limited resources. As a result, requiring all students to participate in RTI prior to being designated as SLD in reading does not appear to be an effective approach. The research simply does not support this as being a wise use of available resources. Presuming that the special education instruction is of the highly effective sort described in Chapter 11, many individuals who begin their reading development in the bottom fifth percentile have a very reasonable likelihood of progressing out of the bottom quartile within 1 to 2 years. However, requiring that such students first be served via a general education RTI service for 3 to 6 months decreases the amount or intensity of services available for other students who could make more rapid progress during that time with RTI services. In the spirit of the Al Otaiba et al. (2014) study described above, it also suggests that requiring a student to progress through levels of RTI may delay a student from receiving the level of service he needs to begin making significant progress. If schools had unlimited funds for RTI, then special education services for reading would be unnecessary. Realistically, we need to work within the systems that we have. If a student is a strong candidate for having an SLD in reading based upon the guidelines discussed above, then spending a perfunctory time at each tier of RTI appears to be more a matter of checking off a box than a practice that is evidence-based or reasonable for either that student or for other students in unnecessarily large RTI groups.

When to Diagnose SLD and When to Use RTI

There is no hard rule for deciding when to start with an RTI approach and when to forgo that process and recommend an SLD designation. However, when students have multiple characteristics of a reading disability, such as those previously described (e.g., bottom fifth percentile in reading, very low on multiple component skills), it would appear that the best early intervention for these severe cases is a special education program using highly effective intervention approaches with daily small groups. Students not displaying this general pattern (the majority of weak readers) would be served under RTI.

Exclusionary Criteria for SLD Diagnosis

IDEA states: "Specific learning disability does not include learning problems that are primarily the result of visual, hearing, or motor disabilities, of intellectual disability, of emotional disturbance, or of environmental, cultural, or economic disadvantage" (§300.8 c 10 ii). The reading research field does not provide much guidance on some aspects of the exclusionary criteria, namely, visual, hearing, or motor disabilities, yet a few comments related to the other items may be in order.

Emotional Disturbance (ED)

All poor readers should be evaluated for the component skills needed for skilled reading, regardless of IDEA categorization. Many students with ED also have the phonological-core deficit. This is not to say they should be designated SLD rather than ED. Rather, it is to say that we must be careful not to dismiss their reading difficulties as being solely due to their emotional issues. While some students with ED have average reading skills, I have anecdotally found that nearly all weak readers with an ED designation whom I have evaluated performed poorly on one or more key phonological-core skills. This is important to determine because it directly affects intervention planning.

Educational Disadvantage

It is presumed that the solution to educational disadvantage is not an SLD classification but effective instruction and remediation.

Environmental, Cultural, or Economic Disadvantage

> **CAUTION**
> ....
> A major problem with the conventional exclusionary clause within the definition of SLD is that reading disabilities can be caused by environmental, economic, and cultural disadvantages, and the resulting reading levels and degree of responsiveness to intervention do not substantially differ from reading disabilities with a neurogenetic origin.

The SLD definition was developed long before there was much understanding of the causes of learning disabilities. We now know that they can be the result of genetic or environmental factors, or an interaction of the two (Metsala, 2011; Vellutino, Fletcher, Snowling, & Scanlon, 2004). For example, the phonological-core deficit can result from inadequate early language stimulation as well as from genetic factors. Reading comprehension difficulties resulting from higher-level language skill deficits can result from limited language opportunities due to environmental or cultural disadvantage, or it could be the result of a physical, developmental, or genetic factor that limits the growth rate of language. As a result, it seems unreasonable to exclude a student from qualifying as having an SLD because of a suspicion of environmental, cultural, or economic disadvantage because we now know these are key factors that can produce an SLD. However, the more recent RTI initiative (assuming the use of highly effective prevention and intervention approaches) can minimize the impact of these factors on early literacy development. This would mean that even if the learning problems were a result of such nongenetic factors, they might not lead to an SLD designation if a student is successful with the RTI intervention process. Word-level reading skills can typically be remediated more quickly and efficiently than language-based reading comprehension deficits. However, there will be cases in which weak language skills will affect reading comprehension and the student will potentially have an SLD in that area, and that language deficit is the result of insufficient early language stimulation. Thus, the student would qualify either as SLD in reading comprehension or SLI, regardless of the etiology of the problem. It appears that the general diagnostic considerations presented previously in this chapter (level of severity and responsiveness to effective interventions) should be more prominent in the decision process than deliberations about environmental, cultural, and economic disadvantages.

The original purpose of this aspect of the exclusionary clause was presumably to promote fairness. However, given our current understanding of the causes of reading difficulties, it seems this aspect of the exclusionary clause is quite unfair. One could argue that it is discriminatory to provide special educational services to a student who has a presumed neurogenetic etiology of their reading problem while denying such services to a student who is presumed to struggle in reading due to environmental factors, when both students display the same level of severity and have had the same degree of responsiveness to instruction. This aspect of the exclusionary clause needs revision in light of the evidence that significant and long-term learning difficulties can be the product of environmental disadvantage.

SUMMARY

There are no clear dividing lines between poor readers with and without reading disabilities. The two key factors that may help decide are the initial level of severity and a student's responsiveness to highly successful interventions. Students with very severe reading difficulties from the outset (perhaps in the bottom 5th percentile) display evidence of a reading disability because their prospects for normalized reading skills via a general educational remedial program are limited. Even a standard deviation gain using a highly effective program would result in below-average performance. Such students would be good candidates for an SLD in reading. Using valuable RTI resources with such students in order to follow a consistent process for all readers appears to be more of a doctrinaire decision rather than one that is consistent with the research on effective reading intervention. The presumption is that if such a student were to bypass the RTI interventions and be promptly identified as SLD, the student would immediately receive intensive remediation (daily instruction in 1:2 and 1:3 groups) using highly effective interventions with the prospect of normalized or nearly normalized reading performance within 1 to 2 years, resulting in an exit from the special educational system (at least for reading).

For students who have a higher starting level and do not display many of the other signs of a learning disability in reading, RTI should be commenced using the effective methods found in the studies presented in Chapter 11. If such approaches do not result in gap-closing improvements as measured on nationally normed tests, such students may be designated as SLD. What represents gap-closing improvements? We do not have sufficient research to guide us here. However, given that the most highly successful interventions yield about an average of a standard deviation of improvement in reading, one may want to consider a cutoff below that (for example, one half of a standard deviation or less) to be considered insufficient. This is something that each evaluation team would need to decide based upon initial starting level and normative progress made. However, modest gains with approaches that typically produce very large gains are strongly suggestive that a student needs more intensive intervention through special education.

AFTERWORD

I n the summer of 1999, I presented a 2-day workshop on reading for 85 teach-ers from about a dozen local school districts. At the time, orthographic map-ping was referred to in the research literature by multiple names, including *direct mapping* (Rack, Hulme, Snowling, & Wightman, 1994), the *representation hypothesis* (Perfetti, 1991), the *bonding* or *amalgamation* hypothesis (Ehri, 1992, 1998a), among others. It had just begun to receive independent experimental confirmation and a growing interest among reading researchers. Since that time, it has been considered "the most complete current theory of how children form sight word representations" (Torgesen, 2004b, p. 36).

I believed that this theory of how children remember words had the potential to transform how we approach reading difficulties. I told those 85 teachers that I could envision that in 20 years, we educators would be saying something like, "Do you remember years ago how we used to have all those reading problems? Now we have so very few." Given the value of this developing understanding of word learn-ing, coupled with the research on the highly effective intervention approaches that were consistent with orthographic mapping, I naively assumed that we were on the verge of a revolution in literacy education. Yet, for the next 16 years, I presented to teachers and school psychologists from dozens of school districts in several states, and this information seems to have remained the best kept secret in education. This is despite the fact that most of this research was the result of federal grant initiatives and was published in top educational, psychological, and even medical journals by researchers from top universities. In the 16 years since my 1999 "prediction" of a revolution in reading, we appear to be no further ahead than we were at that time. It is my hope that this book will function as a conduit between the scientific research on reading and our K–12 classrooms.

In the same year I made my prediction to that group of teachers, the Ameri-can Federation of Teachers stated there was a "chasm" between reading research and classroom practice (American Federation of Teachers, 1999). Four years later, Dr. Sally Shaywitz from Yale Medical School and the Yale Center for Dyslexia and Creativity wrote: "As a result of extraordinary scientific progress, reading and dyslexia are no longer a mystery; we now know what to do to ensure that each child becomes a good reader and how to help readers of all ages and at all levels" (Shaywitz, 2003, p. ix.). Shaywitz went on to say, "Alas, much of the time this new information appears to be a well-kept secret" (p. 6).

In my 27 years as a practicing school psychologist, I have sat across the table from hundreds of students from kindergarten to 12th grade who struggled with the skills needed to be good readers. For me, the content of this book does not represent an abstract set of research ideas and findings. It represents a reality I have been experiencing on a routine basis. As a member of the Society for the Scientific Study of Reading, I have had the fortunate opportunity to interact with a large number of reading researchers from around the world at our conferences. These are dedicated individuals who, like the teachers who are "in the trenches," want the very best for students who struggle in learning to read. But the disconnect between the two worlds I move in could not be more pronounced, and I hope this volume provides a way to bridge that great divide.

Changing people's perspectives regarding literacy practices that have been entrenched in our educational system for well over 100 years is a daunting task, no doubt. However, I think it can all be boiled down to one very simple set of questions. Do we continue with repackaged versions of the classic approaches that yield a high rate of struggling readers, supplemented by intervention approaches that produce an average of 2 to 5 standard score point gains on nationally normed assessments? Or, do we shift to scientifically validated approaches that can prevent 75% to 80% of the reading difficulties that we see as well as produce 12 to 20 standard score point gains among students with reading problems? It would seem that the choice is quite clear. The next step is to figure out a way to let the educational community know that this choice even exists.

GLOSSARY

his glossary contains many of the terms used in this book. Bold words within the definitions indicate an entry for that term elsewhere in this glossary.

Alphabetic principle The insight that the oral sounds in spoken words are represented by letters in print. It forms the basis of both **phonic decoding** and **orthographic mapping**.

Balanced instruction A viewpoint in literacy education that says that we should teach students using a combination of traditional **phonics**, **whole-word**, and **whole language** approaches. However, it tends to generally be the whole language approach re-named (Goodman, 2005) with some extra phonics.

Basal reader The conventional textbooks or reading series used to teach reading.

Blend A combination of two or three consonants in which the sounds of each consonant can be heard. Examples of beginning blends include: *br, gr, pl,* and *str*. Examples of ending blends include: *rt, st, rd, nd,* and *sk*. Compare with **digraph**.

Blending The process of combining sounds to pronounce a word. Blending skills are required for **phonic decoding**.

Compensators Students with strong verbal skills with a mild **phonological-core deficit** who compensate in their reading based upon strong language skills. They are often not recognized as having reading difficulties.

Decoding A term used in the broad sense to refer to correctly identifying words, whether familiar or unfamiliar. In a narrow sense, decoding refers to determining an unfamiliar word. Due to the inconsistent uses of the term, it was not used in this book except in the phrase *phonic decoding*.

Digraph A combination of two letters designed to represent a single sound. Common consonant digraphs include *ch, ph, sh,* and *th*, but also *gn-, kn-, wh-,* and *-mb*. Compare with **blend**. Common vowel digraphs include *ee, oa, ea*.

Diphthong   When two vowels are together and each vowel provides a contribution to the resulting sound (e.g., *oi* in *oil* and *oy* in *boy* [with *y* functioning as a vowel]).

Dyslexia   A condition in which an individual struggles with word reading despite adequate effort and instruction. There is no standard for precisely how weak the word-reading skills need to be in order to be considered dyslexic. Nearly all cases of dyslexia are caused by the **phonological-core deficit**. Dyslexia is a psychological and medical term, not an educational term. For this condition, IDEA uses "SLD in basic reading." In our culture, dyslexia has a mystique about it and many misconceptions. It simply refers to poor word-level reading, and speculations about visual-spatial-perceptual deficits have been inconsistent with research findings.

Grapheme   A single or multiletter unit that corresponds to a single phoneme. Most graphemes are a single letter (e.g., *t* = /t/), but some involve two or more letters (e.g., *sh, th, oo, oa*; the *-igh* in *high* and *-ough* in *though*).

Hyperlexia   A condition in which a student is proficient in word-level reading but displays poor reading comprehension due to weak language skills. Hyperlexics have been referred to as "word callers."

Letter-sound knowledge   The ability to recognize the phonic attributes of consonants, vowels, blends, digraphs, and vowel combinations. This is foundational to both **phonic decoding** and **orthographic mapping**.

Literacy-based approach   This term is often used interchangeably with **whole language**. It is an instructional approach using children's literature to teach literacy rather than **basal readers** or other traditional readers.

Nonsense words   Pronounceable letter patterns that are not real words (e.g., *blamp, vit, torg*). Nonsense word reading tasks estimate a student's **phonics** skills. Nonsense word spelling assesses letter-sound knowledge and phoneme awareness.

Onset   The consonant or consonants within a syllable that precede the vowel. In the words *hand, street*, and *tie*, the *h, st*, and *t* are the onsets, respectively. Not all syllables have onsets because many syllables begin with a vowel (e.g., *in, at, on*).

Onset-rime   A level of phonological awareness development typically more difficult than syllable-level awareness but less difficult than phoneme-level awareness. It involves separating syllables into two elements, the **onset** and the **rime**.

Orthographic mapping   The mental process used to store words for immediate, effortless retrieval. It is the mechanism for **sight-word** learning. It requires good **phonemic awareness**, **letter-sound knowledge**, and the **alphabetic principle**.

Orthography From the Greek "straight writing," this refers to the correct spellings of words. Orthographic skills are needed to read and spell. This term can also refer to a given writing system (e.g., English vs. German vs. Chinese orthography).

Phoneme The smallest unit of sound within spoken words. *Sat* has three phonemes (/s/ /a/ /t/), *shoe* has two (/sh/ /oo/), and *stake* has four (/s/ /t/ /A/ /k/). Phonemes typically match up to single letters but often do not, as these examples illustrate.

Phonemic awareness An awareness of individual sounds/phonemes in spoken words. It represents the most precise subcategory of **phonological awareness**. Because letters are designed to represent spoken phonemes, phonemic awareness is the type of phonological awareness that is essential for reading.

Phonics A system for approaching reading that focuses on the relationship between letters and sounds. Phonics helps with sounding out unfamiliar words.

Phonic decoding The process of sounding out unfamiliar words (or nonsense words) via a letter-sound conversion process combined with phonological blending.

Phonological While the term *auditory* refers to all sound input, the term *phono-logical* is limited to the sounds produced by spoken language. Poor readers typically have phonological difficulties, not broader auditory problems.

Phonological awareness Having an awareness of sounds in spoken words, whether syllables, **onsets**, **rimes**, or individual **phonemes**.

Phonological-core deficit A term used by researchers for problems with the phonological underpinnings of learning to read. This typically involves some combination of problems with **phonological awareness**, **rapid automatized naming**, **phonological short-term/working memory**, and/or **phonic decoding**. It can range from mild to severe and is the likely cause of most word-level reading problems. The phonological-core deficit can be caused by genetics, the environment (inadequate early language opportunities), or both.

Phonological proficiency Having a high degree of skill with awareness of sounds in spoken words and quick access to those sounds (**phonological awareness**. i.e., good **phonemic awareness** and **rapid automatized naming**). With adequate early literacy opportunities, those with phonological proficiency develop average or better word-reading skills. Those lacking phonological proficiency struggle in reading.

Phonological sensitivity Another term for **phonological awareness**.

Phonological short-term memory See **working memory**.

Pseudowords See **nonsense words**.

Psycholinguistic guessing game A theory of reading that proposes that guessing ability is central to skilled reading. This is the basis for the **three cueing systems** model and **whole language**.

Rapid automatized naming (RAN) Sometimes referred to as *rapid naming*, RAN refers to the skill of quickly accessing presumably rote information (numbers, letters, colors, or objects). Students slower than average with RAN typically struggle with word-level reading.

Rime An alternative spelling of *rhyme*. Reading researchers use this obscure spelling to refer to the part of a syllable that contains the vowel sound and any consonant sounds that follow the vowel in that syllable. In *most, bike,* and *you,* the rimes are *ost, ike,* and *ou.* The term can refer to oral or written forms.

Self-teaching hypothesis A view proposing that the process of sounding out unfamiliar words directs a student's attention to the word's spelling pattern and facilitates orthographic learning. When combined with **orthographic mapping**, we have a good understanding of how sight-word learning occurs.

Set for variability The ability to correctly determine a word based upon an incorrect pronunciation of that word.

Short-term memory See **working memory**.

Sight vocabulary The pool of words that a person can identify immediately and effortlessly, without the need to sound out the word or use context clues. It does not matter if these words are phonically regular or irregular, only that they are instantly familiar when encountered.

Sight words Any previously learned words that are part of a person's **sight vocabulary** and thus are immediately recognized "on sight," regardless of whether the word is phonically regular or irregular.

Three cueing systems model An approach to reading instruction based on the **psycholinguistic guessing game**. It assumes skilled reading involves gaining meaning from print using three types of cues: (1) semantic (word meanings and sentence context), (2) linguistic (grammatical features), and (3) grapho-phonic (letters and sounds). It is foundational to the **whole-language, literacy-based,** and **balanced instruction approaches**, as well as Reading Recovery and the Leveled Literacy Intervention.

Title I Federal funding for general educational remedial help. Services based on Title I have gone by different names at different times in different locations.

Vowel digraph When multiple letters form a single vowel sound (e.g., *ee, oa, igh*).

Whole language A **three-cueing systems**–based reading approach that emphasizes the integration of all aspects of language (reading, writing, speaking, and listening) and the use of authentic reading and writing activities (including children's literature). This is not the same as the **whole-word reading method**.

Whole-word reading method A traditional reading method in which children learn words as whole units, with little or no emphasis on phonetic analysis. It has also been called the *look–say method,* the *basal reading approach,* and the *sight-word method*. It is not the same as **whole language**.

Working memory The temporary memory buffer that holds the information we are thinking about at any given point in time. Working memory can be distinguished from **short-term memory**; the former involves a more active, central executive component, whereas the latter is more passive and phonological in nature. **Short-term memory** is slightly more affiliated with word reading and working memory is slightly more affiliated with reading comprehension. However, this distinction is based on large factor analyses. The overlap is so great that a distinction cannot be reliably made in individual evaluations. Poor working memory contributes to weaknesses in math, writing, but also word-level reading and reading comprehension.

FURTHER READING

A ll of the following resources provide the reader with additional opportunities to read about the findings from the interdisciplinary field of reading research. Items with an asterisk can be easily accessed via an Internet search using the author's name, the article title, and the publication.

NONTECHNICAL AND SEMITECHNICAL PRESENTATIONS OF READING RESEARCH

Aaron, P. G., Joshi, R., & Quatroche, D. (2008). *Becoming a professional reading teacher.* Baltimore, MD: Brookes.

Beck, I. L., McKeown, M. G., & Kucan, L. (2013). *Bringing words to life: Robust vocabulary instruction* (2nd ed.). New York, NY: Guilford Press.

*Beck, I. L., McKeown, M. G., & Kucan, L. (2013). Taking delight in words: Using oral language to build young children's vocabularies. *American Educator, Winter,* 36–41, 45–47.

Brady, S. A., Braze, D., & Fowler, C. A. (Eds.). (2011). *Explaining individual differences in reading: Theory and evidence.* New York, NY: Psychology Press.

Carroll, J. M., Bowyer-Crane, C., Duff, F., Hulme, C., & Snowling, M. J. (2011). *Developing language and literacy: Effective interventions in the early years.* Chichester, UK: Wiley.

Clarke, P. J., Truelove, E., Hulme, C., & Snowling, M. J. (2014). *Developing reading comprehension.* Chichester, UK: Wiley.

Foorman, B. R. (Ed.) (2003). *Preventing and remediating reading difficulties: Bringing science to scale.* Baltimore, MD: York Press.

Geva, E., & Wiener, J. (2014). *Psychological assessment of culturally and linguistically diverse children and adolescents: A practitioner's guide.* New York, NY: Springer.

*Hempenstall, K. (2006, April 14). The three-cueing model: Down for the count? *Education News.*

Kamhi, A. G., & Catts, H. W. (Eds.). (2011). *Language and reading disabilities* (3rd ed.). Boston, MA: Pearson.

Kilpatrick, D. A. (2015). *Equipped for reading success: A comprehensive, step-by-step program for developing phonemic awareness and fluent word recognition.* Syracuse, NY: Casey & Kirsch.

McCardle, P., & Chhabra V. (Eds.). (2004). *The voice of evidence in reading research.* Baltimore, MD: Brookes.

Moats, L. C. (2010). *Speech to print: Language essentials for teachers* (2nd ed.). Baltimore, MD: Brookes.

Oakhill, J., Cain, K., & Elbro, C. (2015). *Understanding and teaching reading comprehension: A handbook*. New York, NY: Routledge.

Shaywitz, S. (2003). *Overcoming dyslexia: A new and complete science-based program for reading problems at any level*. New York, NY: Alfred A. Knopf.

*Torgesen, J. K. (2004). Avoiding the devastating downward spiral: The evidence that early intervention prevents reading failure. *American Educator, Fall*, 6–19.

*Torgesen, J. K., Foorman, B. R., & Wagner, R. K. (2008). *Dyslexia: A brief for educators, parents, and legislators in Florida* (Technical report no. 8). Tallahassee, FL: FCRR.

Wolf, M. (2007). *Proust and the squid: The story and science of the reading brain*. New York, NY: HarperCollins.

MORE TECHNICAL AND EXTENSIVE OVERVIEWS OF THE FIELD OF READING RESEARCH

Rayner, K., Pollatsek, A., Ashby, J., & Clifton, C. (2011). *The psychology of reading* (2nd ed.). New York, NY: Psychology Press.

Snowling, M. J., & Hulme, C. (Eds.). (2005). *The science of reading: A handbook*. Oxford, UK: Blackwell.

OLDER/DATED RESOURCES THAT CONTINUE TO PROVIDE EXCELLENT INFORMATION

Adams, M. J. (1990). *Beginning to read: Thinking and learning about print*. Cambridge, MA: MIT Press.

*American Federation for Teachers. (1999). *Teaching reading IS rocket science*. Washington, DC: Author.

Blachman, B. A. (Ed.). (1997). *Foundations of reading acquisition and dyslexia*. Mahwah, NJ: Erlbaum.

Metsala, J. L., & Ehri, L. C. (Eds.). (1998). *Word recognition in beginning literacy*. Mahwah, NJ: Erlbaum.

School Psychology Review *special issue* in 1995, volume 3. (Free online to members of the National Association of School Psychologists.)

*Stahl, S. A. (1999). Different strokes for different folks: A critique of Learning Styles. *American Educator, Fall*, 1–5.

*Torgesen, J. K. (1998). Catch them before they fall: Identification and assessment to prevent reading failure in young children. *American Educator, Spring/Summer*, 1–8.

REFERENCES

Aaron, P. G. (1989). Qualitative and quantitative differences among dyslexic, normal and nondyslexic poor readers. *Reading and Writing: An Interdisciplinary Journal, 1,* 291–308. doi:10.1007/BF00386263

Aaron, P. G., Joshi, R. M., Gooden, R., & Bentum, K. E. (2008). Diagnosis and treatment of reading disabilities based on the component model of reading: An alternative to the discrepancy model of LD. *Journal of Learning Disabilities, 41*(1), 67–84.

Aaron, P. G., Joshi, R. M., Palmer, H., Smith, N., & Kirby, E. (2002). Separating genuine cases of reading disability from reading deficits caused by predominantly inattentive ADHD behavior. *Journal of Learning Disabilities, 35*(5), 425–436.

Adams, M. J. (1979). Models of word recognition. *Cognitive Psychology, 11,* 133–176.

Adams, M. J. (1990). *Beginning to read: Thinking and learning about print.* Cambridge, MA: MIT Press.

Adams, M. J., Foorman, B. R., Lundberg, I., & Beeler, T. (1998). *Phonemic awareness in young children.* Baltimore, MD: Brookes.

Adams, M. J., & Huggins, A. W. F. (1985). The growth of children's sight vocabulary: A quick test with educational and theoretical implications. *Reading Research Quarterly, 20*(3), 262–281.

Adelman, J. (Ed.) (2012a). *Visual word recognition: Vol. 1. Models and methods, orthography and phonology.* New York, NY: Psychology Press.

Adelman, J. (Ed.) (2012b). *Visual word recognition: Vol. 2. Meaning and context, individuals and development.* New York, NY: Psychology Press.

Adelman, J. S., & Brown, G. D. A. (2007). Phonographic neighbors, not orthographic neighbors, determine word naming latencies. *Psychonomic Bulletin & Review, 14,* 455–459.

Adesope, O. O., Lavin, T., Thompson, T., & Ungerleider, C. (2011). Pedagogical strategies for teaching literacy to ESL immigrant students: A meta-analysis. *British Journal of Educational Psychology, 81,* 629–653.

Adlof, S. M., Catts, H. W., & Lee, J. (2010). Kindergarten predictors of second versus eighth grade reading comprehension impairments. *Journal of Learning Disabilities, 43*(4), 332–345.

Agramonte, V., & Belfiore, P. J. (2002). Using mnemonics to increase early literacy skills in urban kindergarten students. *Journal of Behavioral Education, 11*(3), 181–190.

Ahmed, Y., Wagner, R. K., & Kantor, P. T. (2012). How visual word recognition is affected by developmental dyslexia. In J. S. Adelman (Ed.), *Visual word recognition: Vol. 2. Meaning and context, individuals and development* (pp. 196–215). New York, NY: Psychology Press.

Alexander, A. W., Andersen, H. G., Heilman, P. C., Voeller, K. K. S., & Torgesen, J. K. (1991). Phonological awareness training and remediation of analytic decoding deficits in a group of severe dyslexics. *Annals of Dyslexia, 41,* 193–206.

Algozzine, B., & Lockavith, J. F. (1998). Effects of the failure free reading program on students at-risk for reading failure. *Special Services in the Schools*, *13*(1–2), 95–105.

Algozzine, B., Lockavith, J. F., & Audette, R. (1997). Implementing Failure-Free Reading with students seriously at-risk for failure. *Australian Journal of Learning Disabilities*, *2*(3), 14–17.

Allor, J. H., Mathes, P. G., Roberts, J. K., Cheatham, J. P., & Champlin, T. M. (2010). Comprehensive reading instruction for students with intellectual disabilities: Findings from the first three years of a longitudinal study. *Psychology in the Schools*, *47*(5), 445–466. doi:10.1002/pits.20482

Alloway, T. P., Gathercole, S. E., Adams, A., & Willis, C., (2005). Working memory abilities in children with special educational needs. *Educational and Child Psychology*, *22*(4), 56–67.

Al Otaiba, S., Connor, C. M., Folsom, J. S., Wanzek, J., Greulich, L., Schatschneider, S., & Wagner, R. K. (2014). To wait in Tier 1 or intervene immediately: A randomized experiment examining first-grade response to intervention in reading. *Exceptional Children*, *81*(1) 11–27. DOI: 10.1177/0014402914532234

Al Otaiba, S., & Fuchs, D. (2002). Characteristics of children who are unresponsive to early literacy intervention: A review of the literature. *Remedial and Special Education*, *23*(5), 300–316.

Al Otaiba, S., & Fuchs, D. (2006). Who are the young children for whom best practices in reading are ineffective? An experimental and longitudinal study. *Journal of Learning Disabilities*, *39*(5), 414–431.

American Academy of Pediatrics. (2009). Learning disabilities, dyslexia, and vision. *Pediatrics*, *124*, 837–844. doi:10.1542/peds.2009-1445

American Federation for Teachers. (1999). *Teaching reading IS rocket science*. Washington, DC: Author.

Anderson, R. C., Hiebert, E. H., Scott, J. A., & Wilkinson, I. A. G. (1985). *Becoming a nation of readers: Report of the Commission on Reading*. Washington, DC: National Academy of Education.

Andrews, S. (1992). Frequency and neighborhood effects on lexical access: Lexical similarity or orthographic redundancy? *Journal of Experimental Psychology: Learning, Memory, and Cognition*, *18*, 234–254.

Anthony, J. L., Lonigan, C. J., Driscoll, K., Phillips, B. M., & Burgess, S. R. (2003). Phonological sensitivity: A quasi-parallel progression of word structure units and cognitive operations. *Reading Research Quarterly*, *38*, 470–487.

Archer, N., & Bryant, P. (2001). Investigating the role of context in learning to read: A direct test of Goodman's model. *British Journal of Psychology*, *92*, 579–591.

Ardoin, S. A., Christ, T. J., Morena, L. S., Cormier, D. C., & Klingbeil, D. A. (2013). A systematic review and summarization of the recommendations and research surrounding Curriculum-Based Measurement of oral reading fluency (CBM-R) decision rules. *Journal of School Psychology*, *51*, 1–18.

Ardoin, S. P., Witt, J. W., Suldo, S. M., Connell, J. E., Koenig, J. L., Resetar, J. L., … Williams, K. L. (2004). Examining the incremental benefits of administering a Maze and three versus one Curriculum-Based Measurement reading probes when conducting universal screening. *School Psychology Review*, *33*(2), 218–233.

Ashby, J., Dix, H., Bontrager, M., Dey, R., & Archer, A. (2013). Phonemic awareness contributes to text reading fluency: Evidence from eye movements. *School Psychology Review*, *42*(2), 157–170.

Australian Government (2005). *Teaching reading: Report and recommendations: National inquiry into the teaching of literacy*. Canberra, ACT: Department of Education Science and Training.

Backman, J. (1983). The role of psycholinguistic skills in reading acquisition: A look at early readers. *Reading Research Quarterly, 18*, 466–479.

Ball, E., & Blachman, B. A. (1991). Does phoneme awareness training in kindergarten make a difference in early word recognition and developmental spelling? *Reading Research Quarterly, 26*, 49–66.

Ball, E. W., & Blachman, B. A. (1988). Phoneme segmentation training: Effect on reading readiness. *Annals of Dyslexia, 38*, 208–225.

Barker, T. A., & Torgesen, J. K. (1995). An evaluation of computer-assisted instruction in phonological awareness with below average readers. *Journal of Educational Computing Research, 13*(1), 89–103.

Barkley, R. A. (1991). *Attention-deficit hyperactivity disorder: A clinical workbook*. New York, NY: Guilford Press.

Beck, I. L., McKeown, M. G., & Kucan, L. (2002). *Bringing words to life: Robust vocabulary instruction*. New York, NY: Guilford Press.

Beck, I. L., McKeown, M. G., & Kucan, L. (2013). *Bringing words to life: Robust vocabulary instruction* (2nd ed.). New York, NY: Guilford Press.

Begeny, J. C., Laugle, K. M., Krouse, H. E., Lynn, A. E., Tayrose, M. P., & Stage, S. A. (2010). A control-group comparison of two reading fluency programs: The Helping Early Literacy with Practice Strategies (HELPS) program and the Great Leaps K–2 reading program. *School Psychology Review, 39*, 137–155.

Bentum, K. E., & Aaron, P. G. (2003). Does reading instruction in learning disability resource rooms really work? A longitudinal study. *Reading Psychology, 24*, 361–382. doi:10.1080/02702710390227387

Berninger, V. W., & Abbott, R. D. (2013). Differences between children with dyslexia who are and are not gifted in verbal reasoning. *Gifted Child Quarterly, 57*(4), 223–233.

Berninger, V. W., Vermeulen, K., Abbott, R. D., McCutchen, D., Cotton, S., Cude, J., Dorn, S., & Sharon, T. (2003). Comparison of three approaches to supplementary reading instruction for low-achieving second-grade readers. *Language, Speech, and Hearing Services in Schools, 34*, 101–116.

Betts, J., Pickart, M., & Heistad, D. (2009). An investigation of the psychometric evidence of CBM-R passage equivalence: Utility of readability statistics and equating for alternate forms. *Journal of School Psychology 47*, 1–17.

Betts, J., Reschly, A., Pickart, M., Heistad, D., Sheran, C., & Marston, D. (2008). An examination of predictive bias for second grade reading outcomes from measures of early literacy skills in kindergarten with respect to English-language learners and ethnic subgroups. *School Psychology Quarterly, 23*(4), 553–570. doi:10.1037/1045-3830.23.4.553

Bhat, P., Griffin, C. C., & Sindelar, P. T. (2003). Phonological awareness instruction for middle school students with learning disabilities. *Learning Disabilities Quarterly, 26*, 73–87.

Bishop, D. V. M., Hayiou-Thomas, M. E., McDonald, D., & Bird, S. (2009). Children who read words accurately despite language impairment: Who are they and how do they do it? *Child Development, 80*(2), 593–605.

Bitana, T., & Karni, A. (2003). Alphabetical knowledge from whole words training: Effects of explicit instruction and implicit experience on learning script segmentation. *Cognitive Brain Research 16*, 323–337.

Blachman, B. A., Ball, E. W., Black, R. S., & Tangel, D. M. (1994). Kindergarten teachers develop phoneme awareness in low-income, inner-city classrooms: Does it make a difference? *Reading and Writing: An Interdisciplinary Journal, 6*, 1–18.

Blachman, B. A., Ball, E. W., Black, R. S., & Tangel, D. M. (2000). *Road to the code: A phonological awareness program for young children*. Baltimore, MD: Brookes.

Blachman, B. A., Schatschneider, C., Fletcher, J. M., Francis, D. J., Clonan, S. M., Shaywitz, B. A., & Shaywitz, S. E. (2004). Effects of intensive reading remediation for second and third graders and a 1-year follow-up. *Journal of Educational Psychology*, *96*, 444–461. doi:10.1037/0022-0663.96.3.444

Blachman, B. A., Schatschneider, C., Fletcher, J. M., Murray, M. S., Munger, K. A., & Vaughn, M. G. (2014). Intensive reading remediation in grade 2 or 3: Are there effects a decade later? *Journal of Educational Psychology*, *106*(1), 46–57. doi:10.1037/a0033663

Blachman, B. A., Tangel, D. M., Ball, E. W., Black, R., & McGraw, C. K. (1999). Developing phonological awareness and word recognition skills: A two-year intervention with low-income, inner-city children. *Reading and Writing: An Interdisciplinary Journal*, *11*, 239–273.

Boardman, A. G., Argüelles, M. E., Vaughn, S., Hughes, M. T., & Klingner, J. (2005). Special education teachers' views of research-based practices. *Journal of Special Education*, *39*(3), 168–180.

Bond, G. L., & Dykstra, R. (1967). The cooperative research program in first-grade reading instruction. *Reading Research Quarterly*, *2*(4), 5–142.

Booth, J. R., Mehdiratta, N., Burman, D. D., & Bitan, T. (2008). Developmental increases in effective connectivity to brain regions involved in phonological processing during tasks with orthographic demands. *Brain Research*, *1189*, 78–89.

Bowers, J. S. (2000). In defense of abstractionist theories of repetition priming and word identification. *Psychonomic Bulletin & Review*, *7*(1), 83–99.

Bowey, J. A., & Hansen, J. (1994). The development of orthographic rimes as units of word recognition. *Journal of Experimental Child Psychology*, *58*, 465–488.

Bowey, J. A., & Miller, R. (2007). Correlates of orthographic learning in third-grade children's silent reading, *Journal of Research in Reading*, *30*(2), 115–128. doi:10.1111/j.1467-9817.2007.00335.x

Bowey, J. A., & Muller, D. (2005). Phonological recoding and rapid orthographic learning in third-graders' silent reading: A critical test of the self-teaching hypothesis. *Journal of Experimental Child Psychology*, *92*, 203–219.

Bowey, J. A., & Underwood, N. (1996). Further evidence that orthographic rime usage in nonwords reading increases with word-level reading proficiency. *Journal of Experimental Child Psychology*, *63*, 526–562.

Bradley, L., & Bryant, P. E. (1983). Categorizing sounds and learning to read–A causal connection. *Nature*, *301*, 419–421.

Brady, S. A. (2011). Efficacy of phonics teaching for reading outcomes: Indications from post-NRP research. In S. A. Brady, D. Braze, & C. A. Fowler (Eds.), *Explaining individual differences in reading: Theory and evidence* (pp. 69–96). New York, NY: Psychology Press.

Brady, S. A., & Shankweiler, D. P. (1991). *Phonological processes in literacy: A tribute to Isabelle Y. Liberman*. Hillsdale, NJ: Erlbaum.

Bransford, J. D., & Johnson, M. K. (1972). Contextual prerequisites for understanding: Some investigations of comprehension and recall. *Journal of Verbal Learning and Verbal Behavior*, *11*, 717–726.

Bridges, M. S., & Catts, H. W. (2011). The use of a dynamic screening of phonological awareness to predict risk for reading disabilities in kindergarten children. *Journal of Learning Disabilities*, *44*, 330–338. doi:10.1177/0022219411407863

Bruck, M. (1992). Persistence of dyslexics' phonological awareness deficits. *Developmental Psychology*, *28*, 874–886.

Bryant, P., Nunes, T., & Barros, R. (2014). The connection between children's knowledge and use of grapho-phonic and morphemic units in written text and their learning at school. *British Journal of Educational Psychology*, *84*, 211–225.

Burgess, S. R., Hecht, S. A., & Lonigan, C. J. (2002). Relations of the home literacy environment (HLE) to the development of reading-related abilities: A one-year longitudinal study. *Reading Research Quarterly*, *37*(4), 408–426.

Burt, J. S. (2006). What is orthographic processing skill and how does it relate to word identification in reading? *Journal of Research in Reading*, *29*(4), 400–417. doi:10.1111/j.1467-9817.2006.00315.x

Byrne, B., Fielding-Barnsley, R., & Ashley, L. (2000). Effects of preschool phoneme identity training after six years: Outcome level distinguished from rate of response. *Journal of Educational Psychology*, *92*, 659–667.

Cain, K., & Bignell, S. (2014). Reading and listening comprehension and their relation to inattention and hyperactivity. *British Journal of Educational Psychology*, *84*, 108–124.

Cain, K., Oakhill, J., & Bryant, P. (2004). Children's reading comprehension ability: Concurrent prediction by working memory, verbal ability, and component skills. *Journal of Educational Psychology*, *96*(1), 31–42.

Cain, K., Oakhill, J., & Lemmon, K. (2004). Individual differences in the inference of word meanings from context: The influence of reading comprehension, vocabulary knowledge, and memory capacity. *Journal of Educational Psychology 96*(4), 671–681.

Calderón, M., Slavin, R., & Sánchez, M. (2011). Effective instruction for English Learners. *The Future of Children*, *21*(1), 104–127.

Caravolas, M. (2005). The nature and causes of dyslexia in different languages. In M. J. Snowling & C. Hulme (Eds.), *The science of reading: A handbook* (pp. 336–355). Malden, MA: Wiley-Blackwell.

Caravolas, M., Volín, J., & Hulme, C. (2005). Phoneme awareness is a key component of alphabetic literacy skills in consistent and inconsistent orthographies: Evidence from Czech and English children. *Journal Experimental Child Psychology*, *92*, 107–139. doi:10.1016/j.jecp.2005.04.003

Cardoso-Martins, C., Mamede Resende, S., & Assunção Rodrigues, L. (2002). Letter name knowledge and the ability to learn to read by processing letter-phoneme relations in words: Evidence from Brazilian Portuguese-speaking children. *Reading and Writing: An Interdisciplinary Journal*, *15*(3–4), 409–432.

Cardoso-Martins, C., Mesquita, T. C. L., & Ehri, L. (2011). Letter names and phonological awareness help children to learn letter-sound relations. *Journal of Experimental Child Psychology*, *109*, 25–38. doi:10.1016/j.jecp.2010.12.006

Carroll, D. (2008). *The psychology of language* (5th ed). Belmont, CA: Thompson/Wadsworth.

Carroll, J. B. (1956). The case of Dr. Flesch. *American Psychologist*, *11*(3), 158–163.

Carroll, J. M., Bowyer-Crane, C., Duff, F., Hulme, C., & Snowling, M. J. (2011). *Developing language and literacy: Effective interventions in the early years*. Chichester, UK: Wiley.

Carver, R. P. (2003). The highly lawful relationships among pseudoword decoding, word identification, spelling, listening, and reading. *Scientific Studies of Reading*, *7*(2), 127–154.

Casalis, S., Cole, P., & Sopo, D. (2004). Morphological awareness in developmental dyslexia. *Annals of Dyslexia*, *54*(1), 114–138.

Cassady, J. C., Smith, L. L., & Putman, S. M. (2008). Phonological awareness development as a discrete process: Evidence for an integrative model. *Reading Psychology*, *29*, 508–533. DOI: 10.1080/02702710802271966

Castiglioni-Spalten, M. L., & Ehri, L. C. (2003). Phonemic awareness instruction: Contribution of articulatory segmentation to novice beginners' reading and spelling. *Scientific Studies of Reading*, *7*(1), 25–52.

Castles, A., & Nation, K. (2006). How does orthographic learning happen? In S. Andrews (Ed.), *From inkmarks to ideas: Challenges and controversies about word recognition and reading* (pp. 151–179). Hove, UK: Psychology Press.

Cattell, J. M. (1886). The time taken up by cerebral operations. *Mind*, *44*, 524–538.

Catts, H. W. (2009). The Narrow view of reading promotes a broad view of comprehension. *Language, Speech and Hearing Services in Schools*, *40*, 178–183.

Catts, H. W., Adlof, S. M., & Weismer, S. E. (2006). Language deficits in poor comprehenders: A case for the simple view of reading. *Journal of Speech, Language, and Hearing Research*, *49*, 278–293.

Catts, H. W., Fey, M. E., Zhang, X., & Tomblin, J. B. (1999). Language basis of reading and reading disabilities: Evidence from a longitudinal investigation. *Scientific Studies of Reading*, *3*(4), 331–361.

Catts, H. W., Fey, M. E., Zhang, Z., & Tomblin, J. B. (2001). Estimating the risk of future reading difficulties in kindergarten children: A research-based model and its clinical implementation. *Language, Speech, and Hearing Services in Schools*, *32*, 38–50.

Catts, H. W., Hogan, T. P., & Fey, M. E. (2003). Subgrouping poor readers on the basis of individual differences in reading-related abilities. *Journal of Learning Disabilities*, *36*(2), 151–164.

Catts, H. W., Tomblin, J. B., Compton, D., & Sittner Bridges, M. (2012). Prevalence and nature of late-emerging poor readers. *Journal of Educational Psychology*, *104*(1) 166–181.

Center, Y., Freeman, L., Robertson, G., & Outhred, L. (1999). The effect of visual imagery training on the reading and listening comprehension of low listening comprehenders in year 2. *Journal of Research in Reading*, *22*(3), 241–256.

Chafouleas, S. M., Lewandowski, L. J., Smith, C. R., & Blachman, B. A. (1997). Phonological awareness skills in children: Examining performance across tasks and ages. *Journal of Psychoeducational Assessment*, *19*, 216–226.

Chapman, J. W., Tunmer, W. E., & Prochnow, J. E. (2001). Does success in the Reading Recovery program depend on developing proficiency in phonological-processing skills? A longitudinal study in a whole language instructional context. *Scientific Studies of Reading*, *5*(2), 141–176.

Chard, D. J., Ketterlin-Geller, L. R., Baker, S. K., Doabler, C., & Apichatabutra, C. (2009). Repeated reading interventions for students with learning disabilities: Status of the evidence. *Exceptional Children*, *75*(3), 263–281.

Christ, T. J., Zopluoglu, C., Long, J. D., & Monaghen, B. D. (2012). Curriculum-based measurement of oral reading: Quality of progress monitoring outcomes. *Exceptional Children*, *78*(3), 356–373.

Christ, T. J., Zopluoglu, C., Monaghen, B., Pike-Balow, A., & Van Norman, E. R. (2013). Curriculum-based measurement of oral reading: Multi-study evaluation of schedule, duration, and dataset quality on progress monitoring outcomes. *Journal of School Psychology*, *51*(1), 19–57.

Christensen, C. A., & Bowey, J. A. (2005). The efficacy of orthographic rime, grapheme–phoneme correspondence, and implicit phonics approaches to teaching decoding skills. *Scientific Studies of Reading*, *9*(4), 327–349.

Clarke, P. J., Truelove, E., Hulme, C., & Snowling, M. J. (2014). *Developing reading comprehension*. Chichester, UK: Wiley.

Clemens, N. H., Shapiro, E. S., & Thoemmes, F. (2011). Improving the efficacy of first grade reading screening: An investigation of word identification fluency with other early literacy indicators. *School Psychology Quarterly*, *26*(3), 231–244. doi:10.1037/a0025173

Compton, D. L., & Carlisle, J. F. (1994). Speed of word recognition as a distinguishing characteristic of reading disabilities. *Educational Psychology Review*, *6*(2), 115–140.

Compton, D. L., Miller, A. C., Elleman, A. M., & Steacy, L. M. (2014) Have we forsaken reading theory in the name of "quick fix" interventions for children with reading disability? *Scientific Studies of Reading*, *18*(1), 55–73. doi:10.1080/10888438.2013.836200

Constantinidou, M., & Stainthorp, R. (2009). Phonological awareness and reading speed deficits in reading disabled Greek-speaking children. *Educational Psychology*, *29*(2), 171–186.

Corkett, J. K., & Parrila, R. (2008). Use of context in the word recognition process by adults with a significant history of reading difficulties. *Annals of Dyslexia, 58*, 139–161. doi:10.1007/s11881-008-0018-1

Crowder, R. G., & Wagner, R. K. (1992). *The psychology of reading: An introduction.* New York, NY: Oxford University Press.

Cunningham, A. (1990). Explicit versus implicit instruction in phonemic awareness. *Journal of Experimental Child Psychology, 50*, 429–444.

Cunningham, A. (2006). Accounting for children's orthographic learning while reading text: Do children self-teach? *Journal of Experimental Child Psychology, 95*, 56–77.

Cunningham, A. E., Perry, K. E., Stanovich, K. E., & Share, D. L. (2002). Orthographic learning during reading: Examining the role of self-teaching. *Journal of Experimental Child Psychology, 82*, 185–199.

Cunningham, A. E., Perry, K. E., Stanovich, K. E., & Stanovich, P. J. (2004). Knowledge of K-3 teachers and their knowledge calibration in the domain of early literacy. *Annals of Dyslexia, 54*, 139–167.

Cunningham, A. E., & Stanovich, K. E. (1990) Assessing print exposure and orthographic processing skill in children: A quick measure of reading experience. *Journal of Educational Psychology, 82*(4), 733–740.

Cunnings, I., & Clahsen, H. (2007). The time-course of morphological constraints: Evidence from eye-movements during reading. *Cognition, 104*, 476–494.

Cutting, L. E., & Scarborough, H. S. (2006). Prediction of reading comprehension: Relative contributions of word recognition, language proficiency, and other cognitive skills can depend on how comprehension is measured. *Scientific Studies of Reading, 10*(3), 277–299.

Dahlin, K. I. E. (2013). Working memory training and the effect on mathematical achievement in children with attention deficits and special needs. *Journal of Education and Learning, 2*(1), 118–133.

Davis, C. J. (2012). The orthographic similarity of printed words. In J. S. Adelman (Ed.), *Visual word recognition: Vol. 1. Models and methods, orthography and phonology* (pp. 185–206). New York, NY: Psychology Press.

de Abreu, M. D., & Cardoso-Martins, C. (1998). Alphabetic access route in beginning reading acquisition in Portuguese: The role of letter-name knowledge. *Reading and Writing: An Interdisciplinary Journal 10*, 85–104.

Deacon, S. H., Benere, J., & Castles, A. (2012). Chicken or egg? Untangling the relationship between orthographic processing skill and reading accuracy. *Cognition, 122*, 110–117. doi:10.1016/j.cognition.2011.09.003

Deacon, S. H., & Kirby, J. R. (2004). Morphological awareness: Just "more phonological"? The roles of morphological and phonological awareness in reading development. *Applied Psycholinguistics, 25*, 223–238.

Deacon, S. H., Parrila, R., & Kirby, J. R. (2006). Processing of derived forms in high-functioning dyslexics. *Annals of Dyslexia, 56*(1), 103–128.

Deane, P., Sheehan, K. M., Sabatini, J., Futagi, Y., & Kostin, I. (2006). Differences in text structure and its implications for assessment of struggling readers. *Scientific Studies of Reading, 10*(3), 257–275.

Dehaene, S., & Cohen, L. (2011). The unique role of the visual word form area in reading. *Trends in Cognitive Sciences, 15*(6), 254–262.

de Jong, P. F. (2011). What discrete and serial rapid automatized naming can reveal about reading. *Scientific Studies of Reading, 15*(4), 314–337.

de Jong, P. F., Seveke, M-J., & van Veen, M. (2000). Phonological sensitivity and the acquisition of new words in children. *Journal of Experimental Child Psychology, 76*, 275–301.

de Jong, P. F., & Share, D. L. (2007). Orthographic learning during oral and silent reading. *Scientific Studies of Reading, 11*(1), 55–71. doi.10.1080/10888430709336634 de Jong, P. F., & van der Leij, A. (2002). Effects of phonological abilities and linguistic comprehension on the development of reading. *Scientific Studies of Reading, 6*, 51–77.

de Jong, P. F., & Vrielink, L. O. (2004). Rapid automatic naming: Easy to measure, hard to improve (quickly). *Annals of Dyslexia, 54*(1), 65–88.

Denkla, M. B., & Rudel, R. G. (1976). Rapid "automatized" naming (R.A.N.): Dyslexia differentiated from other learning disabilities. *Neuropsychologia, 14*, 471–479.

Department for Education and Skills. (2006). *Independent review of the teaching of early reading*. Nottingham, UK: Author. Retrieved from http://www.teachernet.gov.uk/publications

Desimoni, M., Scalisi, T. G., & Orsolini, M. (2012). Predictive and concurrent relations between literacy skills in grades 1 and 3: A longitudinal study of Italian children. *Learning and Instruction, 22*, 340–353.

Diakidoy, I. N., Stylianou, P., Karefillidou, C., & Papageorgiou, P. (2005). The relationship between listening and reading comprehension of different types of text at increasing grade levels. *Reading Psychology, 26*, 55–80.

DiLorenzo, K. E., Rody, C. A., Bucholz, J. L., & Brady, M. P. (2011). Teaching letter-sound connections with picture mnemonics: Itchy's Alphabet and early decoding. *Preventing School Failure: Alternative Education for Children and Youth, 55*(1), 28–34. doi:10.1080/10459880903286763

Dixon, L. Q. (2011). Singaporean kindergartners' phonological awareness and English writing skills. *Journal of Applied Developmental Psychology, 32*, 98–108. doi:10.1016/j.appdev.2011.02.008

Dixon, M., Stuart, M., & Masterson, J. (2002). The relationship between phonological awareness and the development of orthographic representations. *Reading and Writing: An Interdisciplinary Journal, 15*(3–4), 295–316.

Downey, D. M., Snyder, L. E., & Hill, B. (2000). College students with dyslexia: Persistent linguistic deficits and foreign language learning. *Dyslexia, 6*, 101–111.

Duff, F. J., & Hulme, C. (2012). The role of children's phonological and semantic knowledge in learning to read words. *Scientific Studies of Reading, 16*(6), 504–525. doi:10.1080/10888438.2011.598199

Dukleth Johnson, D. E., & Swanson, H. L. (2011). Cognitive characteristics of treatment-resistant children with reading disabilities: A retrospective study. *Journal of Psychoeducational Assessment, 29*(2), 137–149. doi:10.1177/0734282910380189

Dunning, D. L., Holmes, J., & Gathercole, S. E. (2013). Does working memory training lead to generalized improvements in children with low working memory? A randomized controlled trial. *Developmental Science, 16*(6), 915–925.

Eason, S. H., Sabatini, J., Goldberg, L., Bruce, K., & Cutting, L. E. (2013). Examining the relationship between word reading efficiency and oral reading rate in predicting comprehension among different types of readers. *Scientific Studies of Reading, 17*, 199–223. doi:10.1080/10888438.2011.652722

Ehri, L. C. (1992). Reconceptualizing the development of sight word reading and its relationship to recoding. In P .B. Gough, L. C. Ehri, & R. Treiman (Eds.), *Reading acquisition*. Hillsdale, NJ: Erlbaum.

Ehri, L. C. (1998a). Grapheme-phoneme knowledge is essential for learning to read words in English. In J. L. Metsala & L . C. Ehri (Eds.) *Word recognition in beginning literacy* (pp. 3–40). Mahwah, NJ: Erlbaum.

Ehri, L. C. (1998b). Research on learning to read and spell: A personal-historical perspective. *Scientific Studies of Reading, 2*(2), 97–114.

Ehri, L. C. (2005a). Learning to read words: Theory, findings, and issues. *Scientific Studies of Reading, 9*(2), 167–188.

Ehri, L. C. (2005b). Development of sight word reading: Phases and findings. In M. J. Snowling & C. Hulme (Eds.), *The science of reading: A handbook* (pp. 135–154). Oxford, UK: Blackwell.

Ehri, L. C. (2014). Orthographic mapping in the acquisition of sight word reading, spelling memory, and vocabulary learning, *Scientific Studies of Reading*, *18*(1), 5–21.

Ehri, L. C., Deffner, N. D., & Wilce, L. S. (1984). Pictorial mnemonics for phonics. *Journal of Educational Psychology*, *76*(5), 880–893.

Ehri, L. C., Nunes, S. R., Stahl, S. A., & Willows, D. M. (2001). Systematic phonics instruction helps students learn to read: Evidence from the National Reading Panel's meta-analysis. *Review of Educational Research*, *71*(3), 393–447.

Ehri, L. C., & Saltmarsh, J. (1995). Beginning readers outperform older disabled readers in learning to read words by sight. *Reading and Writing: An Interdisciplinary Journal*, *7*, 295–326.

Ehri, L. C., & Wilce, L. S. (1985). Movement into reading: Is the first stage of printed word learning visual or phonetic? *Reading Research Quarterly*, *20*, 163–179.

Ehri, L. C., & Wilce, L. S. (1987). Cipher versus cue reading: An experiment in decoding acquisition. *Journal of Educational Psychology*, *79*, 3–13.

Elbaum, B., Vaughn, S., Hughes, M. T., & Moody, S. W. (2000). How effective are one-to-one tutoring programs in reading for elementary students at risk for reading failure? A meta-analysis of the intervention research. *Journal of Educational Psychology*, *92*(4), 605–619.

Elbro, C., & Klint Petersen, D. (2004). Long-term effects of phoneme awareness and letter sound training: An intervention study with children at risk for dyslexia. *Journal of Educational Psychology*, *96*, 660–670.

Eldredge, J. L. (2005). Foundations of fluency: An exploration. *Reading Psychology*, *26*, 161–181. doi:10.1080/02702710590930519

Farnia, F., & Geva, E. (2013). Growth and predictors of change in English language learners' reading comprehension. *Journal of Research in Reading*, *36*(4), 389–421. doi:10.1111/jrir.12003

Fernald, A., Swingley, D., & Pinto, J. P. (2001). When half a word is enough: Infants can recognize spoken words using partial phonetic information. *Child Development*, *72*(4), 1003–1015.

Fernandes, T., Kolinsky, R., & Ventura, P. (2009). The metamorphosis of the statistical segmentation output: Lexicalization during artificial language learning. *Cognition*, *112*, 349–366.

Fitzgerald, J. (1995). English-as-a-second-language learners' cognitive reading processes: A review of research in the United States. *Review of Educational Research*, *65*(2), 145–190.

Flanagan, D. P., Ortiz, S. O., & Alfonso, V. C. (2013). *Essentials of cross-battery assessment* (3rd ed.). Hoboken, NJ: Wiley.

Fletcher, J. M., Lyon, G. R., Fuchs, L. S., & Barnes, M. A. (2007). *Learning disabilities: From identification to intervention*. New York, NY: Guilford Press.

Fletcher, J. M., Shaywitz, S. E., Shankweiler, D. P., Katz, L., Liberman, I. Y., Steubing, K. K., … Shaywitz, B. A. (1994). Cognitive profiles of reading disability: Comparisons of discrepancy and low achievement definitions. *Journal of Educational Psychology*, *86*, 6–23.

Flynn, L. J., Zheng, X., & Swanson, H. L. (2012). Instructing struggling older readers: A selective meta-analysis of intervention research. *Learning Disabilities Research & Practice*, *27*(1), 21–32.

Foorman, B., & Al Otaiba, S. (2009). Reading remediation: State of the art. In K. Pugh & P. McCardle (Eds.), *How children learn to read: Current issues and new directions in the integration of cognition, neurobiology and genetics of reading and dyslexia research and practice* (pp. 257–274). New York, NY: Psychology Press.

Foorman, B. R. (1995). Research on "the great debate": Code-oriented versus whole language approaches to reading instruction. *School Psychology Review, 24*(3), 376–392.

Foorman, B. R., Chen, D. T., Carlson, C., Moats, L., Francis, D. J., & Fletcher, J. M. (2001). The necessity of the alphabetic principle to phonemic awareness instruction. *Reading and Writing: An Interdisciplinary Journal, 16*, 289–324.

Foorman, B. R., Francis, D. J., Fletcher, J. M., Schatschneider, C., & Mehta, P. (1998). The role of instruction in learning to read: Preventing reading failure in at-risk children. *Journal of Educational Psychology, 90*(1), 37–55.

Foorman, B. R., & Torgesen, J. K. (2001). Critical elements of classroom and small-group instruction promote reading success in all children. *Learning Disabilities Research & Practice, 16*(4), 203–212.

Forster, K. I. (2012). A parallel activation model with a sequential twist. In J. S. Adelman (Ed.), *Visual word recognition: Vol. 1. Models and methods, orthography and phonology* (pp. 52–69). New York, NY: Psychology Press.

Fox, B., & Routh, D. K. (1976). Phonemic analysis and synthesis as word-attack skills. *Journal of Educational Psychology, 68*, 70–74.

Fox, B., & Routh, D. K. (1983). Reading disability, phonemic analysis, and dysphonetic spelling: A follow-up study. *Journal of Clinical Child Psychology, 12*(1), 28–32.

Fox, B., & Routh, D. K. (1984). Phonemic analysis and synthesis as word-attack skills: Revisited. *Journal of Educational Psychology, 76*, 1059–1064.

Frijters, J. C., Lovett, M. W., Sevcik, R. A., & Morris, R. D. (2013). Four methods of identifying change in the context of a multiple component reading intervention for struggling middle school readers. *Reading and Writing: An Interdisciplinary Journal, 26*, 539–563. doi:10.1007/s11145-012-9418-z

Frost, R. (1998). Toward a strong phonological theory of visual word recognition: True issues and false trails. *Psychological Bulletin, 123*(1), 71–99.

Frost, R. (2005). Orthographic systems and skilled word recognition processes in reading. In M. J. Snowling & C. Hulme (Eds.), *The science of reading: A handbook* (pp. 272–295). Malden, MA: Wiley-Blackwell.

Frost, S. J., Sandak, R., Mencl, W. E., Landi, N., Moore, D., Porta, G. D., … Pugh, K. R. (2009). Neurobiological and behavioral studies of skilled and impaired word reading. In E. L. Grigorenko & A. J. Naples (Eds.), *Single word reading: Behavioral and biological perspectives* (pp. 355–376). New York, NY: Psychology Press.

Froyen, D. J. W., Bonte, M. L., van Atteveldt, N., & Blomert, L. (2009). The long road to automation: Neurocognitive development of letter–speech sound processing. *Journal of Cognitive Neuroscience, 21*(3), 567–580.

Fuchs, D., Compton, D. L., Fuchs, L. S., Bryant, V. J., Hamlett, C. L., & Lambert, W. (2012). First-grade cognitive abilities as long-term predictors of reading comprehension and disability status. *Journal of Learning Disabilities, 45*(3), 217–231. doi:10.1177/0022219412442154

Fuchs, D., Fuchs, L. S., Thompson, A., Svenson, E., Yen, L., Al Otaiba, S., … Saenz, L. (2001). Peer-assisted learning strategies in reading: Extensions for kindergarten, first grade, and high school. *Remedial and Special Education, 22*(1), 15–21.

Fuchs, L. S., Fuchs, D., & Maxwell, L. (1988). The validity of informal reading comprehension measures. *Remedial and Special Education, 9*(2), 20–28.

Fulk, B. M., Lohman, D., & Belfiore, P. J. (1997). Effects of integrated picture mnemonics on the letter recognition and letter-sound acquisition of transitional first-grade students with special needs. *Learning Disability Quarterly, 20*, 33–42.

Gaskins, I.W., Ehri, L.C., Cress, C., O'Hara, C., & Donnelly, K. (1996/1997). Procedures for word learning: Making discoveries about words. *The Reading Teacher, 50*, 312–327.

Gathercole, S., & Galloway, T. P. (2008). *Working memory and learning: A practical guide for teachers*. London: Sage.

Gaultney, J. F. (1995). The effect of prior knowledge and metacognition on the acquisition of a reading comprehension strategy. *Journal of Experimental Child Psychology, 59,* 142–163.

Gellert, A. S., & Elbro, C. (2013). Cloze tests may be quick, but are they dirty? Development and preliminary validation of a cloze test of reading comprehension. *Journal of Psychoeducational Assessment, 31*(1), 16–28. doi:10.1177/0734282912451971

Georgiou, G. K., Parrila, R., Manolitsis, G., & Kirby, J. R. (2011). Examining the importance of assessing rapid automatized naming (RAN) for the identification of children with reading difficulties. *Learning Disabilities: A Contemporary Journal 9*(2), 5–26.

Gillam, R. B., Loeb, D. F., Hoffman, L. M., Bohman, T., Champlin, C. A., Thibodeau, L., ... Friel-Patti, S. (2008). The efficacy of Fast ForWord language intervention in school-age children with language impairment: A randomized controlled trial. *Journal of Speech, Language, and Hearing Research, 51,* 97– 119.

Glezer, L. S., Kim, J., Rule, J., Jiang, X., & Riesenhuber, M. (2015). Adding words to the brain's visual dictionary: Novel word learning selectively sharpens orthographic representations in the VWFA. *Journal of Neuroscience, 35*(12):4965–4972. doi:10.1S23/JNEUROSCI.4031-14.2015

Goff, D. A., Pratt, C., & Ong, B. (2005). The relations between children's reading comprehension, working memory, language skills and components of reading decoding in a normal sample. *Reading and Writing: An Interdisciplinary Journal, 18,* 583–616.

Goldfus, C. (2012). Knowledge foundations for beginning reading teachers in EFL. *Annals of Dyslexia, 62,* 204–221. doi:10.1007/s11881-012-0073-5

Goodman, K. S. (1976). Reading: A psycholinguistic guessing game. In H. Singer & R. B. Ruddell (Eds.), *Theoretical models and processes of reading* (2nd ed., pp. 497–508). Newark, DE: International Reading Association.

Goodman, K. S. (1981). Response to Stanovich. *Reading Research Quarterly, 16*(3), 477–478.

Goodman, K. S. (1989). Whole Language research: Foundations and development. *Elementary School Journal, 90*(2), 207–221.

Goodman, K. S. (1996). *On reading*. Portsmouth, NH: Heinemann.

Goodman, K. S. (2005). Making sense of written language: A lifelong journey. *Journal of Literacy Research, 37,* 1–24.

Goodwin, A. P., & Ahn, S. (2010). A meta-analysis of morphological interventions: Effects on literacy achievement of children with literacy difficulties. *Annals of Dyslexia, 60,* 183–208.

Gough, P. B., & Tunmer, W. E. (1986). Decoding, reading, and reading disability. *Remedial and Special Education, 7,* 6–10.

Gough, P. B., & Walsh, M. A. (1991). Chinese, Phoenicians, and the orthographic cipher of English. In S. A. Brady & D. P. Shankweiler (Eds.), *Phonological processes in literacy: A tribute to Isabelle Y. Liberman* (pp. 199–209). Hillsdale, NJ: Erlbaum.

Graham, S., & Santangelo, T. (2014). Does spelling instruction make students better spellers, readers, and writers? A meta-analytic review. *Reading and Writing: An Interdisciplinary Journal, 27*(9), 1703–1743. doi:10.1007/s11145-014-9517-0

Grainger, J., & Whitney, C. (2004). Does the huamn mnid raed wrods as a wlohe? *Trends in Cognitive Sciences 8*(2), 58–59. doi:10.1016/j.tics.2003.11.006

Gray, E. S. (2008). Understanding dyslexia and its instructional implications: A case to support intense intervention. *Literacy Research and Instruction, 47,* 116–123. doi:10.1080/19388070701878790

Gray, S. A., Chaban, P., Martinussen, R., Goldberg, R., Gotlieb, H., Kronitz, R., Hockenberry, M., & Tannock, R. (2012). Effects of a computerized working memory training program on working memory, attention, and academics in adolescents with severe

LD and comorbid ADHD: A randomized controlled trial. *Journal of Child Psychology and Psychiatry, 53*(12), 1277–1284. doi:10.1111/j.1469-7610.2012.02592.x

Greenway, C. (2002). The process, pitfalls and benefits of implementing a reciprocal teaching intervention to improve the reading comprehension of a group of year 6 pupils. *Educational Psychology in Practice, 18*(2), 113–137.

Gresham, F. M., & Vellutino, F. R. (2010). What is the role of intelligence in the identification of specific learning disabilities? Issues and clarifications. *Learning Disabilities Research & Practice, 25*(4), 194–206.

Grigorenko, E., L., & Naples, A. J. (Eds.). (2008). *Single-word reading: Behavioral and biological perspectives*. New York, NY: Erlbaum.

Haddock, M. (1976). Effects of an auditory and an auditory-visual method of blending instruction on the ability of prereaders to decode synthetic words. *Journal of Educational Psychology, 68*, 825–831.

Halderman, L. K., Ashby, J., & Perfetti, C. A. (2012). Phonology: An early and integral role in identifying words. In J. S. Adelman (Ed.), *Visual word recognition (Vol. 1): Models and methods, orthography and phonology* (pp. 207–228). New York, NY: Psychology Press.

Hanson, V. L. (1991). Phonological processing without sound. In S. A. Brady & D. P. Shankweiler (Eds.), *Phonological processes in literacy: A tribute to Isabelle Y. Liberman* (pp. 153–161). Hillsdale, NJ: Erlbaum.

Harlaar, N., Cutting, L., Deater-Deckard, K., DeThorne, L. S., Justice, L. M., Schatschneider, C., ... Petrill, S. A. (2010). Predicting individual differences in reading comprehension: A twin study. *Annals of Dyslexia, 60*, 265–288. doi:10.1007/s11881-010-0044-7

Harn, B. A., Stoolmiller, M., & Chard, D. J. (2008). Measuring the dimensions of alphabetic principle on the reading development of first graders: The role of automaticity and unitization. *Journal of Learning Disabilities, 41*, 143–157. doi:10.1177/0022219407313585

Hart, B., & Risley, T. R. (2003). The early catastrophe: The 30 million word gap by age 3. *American Educator, Spring*, 4–9.

Hatcher, P. J., Hulme, C., & Snowling, M. J. (2004). Explicit phoneme training combined with phonic reading instruction helps young children at risk of reading failure. *Journal of Child Psychology and Psychiatry, 45*(2), 338–358.

Hedrick, W. B., & Cunningham, J. W. (2002). Investigating the effect of wide reading on listening comprehension of written language. *Reading Psychology, 23*, 107–126.

Hempenstall, K. (2002). The three-cueing system: Help or hindrance? *Direct Instruction News, Fall*, 42–51.

Hernandez, D. J. (2012). *Double jeopardy overview: How third-grade reading skills and poverty influence high school graduation*. Baltimore, MD: Annie E. Casey Foundation.

Hindman, A. H., & Wasik, B. A. (2008). Head Start teachers' beliefs about language and literacy instruction. *Early Childhood Research Quarterly, 23*, 479–492.

Høien, T., Lundberg, I., Stanovich, K. E., & Bjaalid, I.-K. (1995). Components of phonological awareness. *Reading and Writing: An Interdisciplinary Journal, 7*, 171–188.

Holmes, J., Gathercole, S. E., & Dunning, D. L. (2009). Adaptive training leads to sustained enhancement of poor working memory in children. *Developmental Science 12*(4), F9–F15. doi:10.1111/j.1467-7687.2009.00848.x

Holmes, V. M. (1996). Skilled reading and orthographic processing. *Austsralian Journal of Psychology, 48*(3), 149–154.

Hoover, W. A., & Gough, P. B. (1990). The simple view of reading. *Reading and Writing: An Interdisciplinary Journal, 2*, 127–160.

Hua, A. N., & Keenan, J. M. (2014). The role of text memory in inferencing and in comprehension deficits. *Scientific Studies of Reading, 18*(6), 415–431. doi:10.1080/10888438.2014.926906

Hulme, C., Bowyer-Crane, C., Carroll, J. M., Duff, F. J., Snowling, M. J. (2012). The causal role of phoneme awareness and letter-sound knowledge in learning to read: Combining intervention studies with mediation analyses. *Psychological Science, 23*(6), 572–577.

Hulme, C., Goetz, K., Gooch, D., Adams, J., & Snowling, M. J. (2007). Paired-associate learning, phoneme awareness, and learning to read. *Journal of Experimental Child Psychology, 96*, 150–166. doi:10.1016/j.jecp.2006.09.002

Hulme, C., & Snowling, M. J. (2009). *Developmental disorders of language learning and cognition.* Malden, MA: Wiley-Blackwell.

Hulme, C., & Snowling, M. J. (2011). Children's reading comprehension difficulties: Nature, causes, and treatments. *Current Directions in Psychological Science, 20*(3), 139–142. doi:10.1177/0963721411408673

Individuals with Disabilities Education Act, 20 U.S.C. § 1400 (2004).

Jacobson, C. (1999). How persistent is reading disability? Individual growth curves in reading. *Dyslexia, 5*, 78–93.

Jaynes, W. S., & Littell, H. W. (2000). Meta-analysis of studies examining the effect of whole language instruction on the literacy of low-SES students. *Elementary School Journal, 101*(1), 21–33.

Jenkins, J. R., Fuchs, L. S., van den Broek, P., Espin, C., & Deno, S. L. (2003). Sources of individual differences in reading comprehension and reading fluency. *Journal of Educational Psychology, 95*(4), 719–729. doi:10.1037/0022-0663.95.4.719

Jenkins, J. R., Graff, J. J., & Miglioretti, D. L. (2009). Estimating reading growth using intermittent CBM progress monitoring. *Exceptional Children, 75*(2), 151–165.

Jitendra, A. K., & Gajria, M. (2011). Main idea and summarization instruction to improve reading comprehension. In R. E. O'Connor & P. F. Vadasy (Eds.), *Handbook of reading interventions* (pp. 198–219). New York, NY: Guilford.

Joffe, V. L., Cain, K., & Marić, N. (2007). Comprehension problems in children with specific language impairment: Does mental imagery training help? *International Journal of Language and Communication Disorders, 42*(6), 648–664.

Johnson-Glenberg, M. C. (2000). Training reading comprehension in adequate decoders/poor comprehenders: Verbal versus visual strategies. *Journal of Educational Psychology, 92*(4), 772–782. doi:10.1037//O022-O663.92.4.772

Johnston, A. M., Barnes, M. A., & Desrochers, A. (2008). Reading comprehension: Developmental processes, individual differences, and interventions. *Canadian Psychology, 49*(2), 125–132. doi:10.1037/0708-5591.49.2.125

Joshi, R. M., & Aaron, P. G. (2000). The component model of reading: Simple view of reading made a little more complex. *Reading Psychology, 21*, 85–97.

Joshi, R. M., Binks, E., Graham, L., Ocker-Dean, E., Smith, D. L., & Boulware-Gooden, R. (2009). Do textbooks used in university reading education courses conform to the instructional recommendations of the National Reading Panel? *Journal of Learning Disabilities, 42*(5), 458–463. doi:10.1177/0022219409338739

Joshi, R. M., Binks, E., Hougen, M., Dahlgren, M. E., Ocker-Dean, E., & Smith, D. L. (2009). Why elementary teachers might be inadequately prepared to teach reading. *Journal of Learning Disabilities, 42*(5), 392–402. doi:10.1177/0022219409338736

Juel, C., Griffith, P. L., & Gough, P. B. (1986). Acquisition of literacy: A longitudinal study of children in first and second grade. *Journal of Educational Psychology, 78*, 243–255.

Juel, C., & Minden-Cupp, C. (2000). Learning to read words: Linguistic units and instructional strategies. *Reading Research Quarterly, 35*, 458–492.

Kamhi, A. G. (2009). The case for the narrow view of reading. *Language, Speech, and Hearing Services in the Schools, 40*, 174–177.

Kamhi, A. G. (2012). Perspectives on assessing and improving reading comprehension. In A. G. Kamhi & H. W. Catts (Eds.), *Language and reading disabilities* (3rd ed., pp. 146–162). Boston, MA: Pearson.

Kamhi, A. G. (2014). Improving clinical practices for children with language and learning disorders. *Language, Speech, and Hearing Services in Schools, 45*, 92–103. doi:10.1044/2014_LSHSS-13-0063

Kamhi, A. G., & Catts, H. W. (Eds.). (2011). *Language and reading disabilities* (3rd ed.). Boston, MA: Pearson.

Katz, L., & Frost, S. J. (2001). Phonology constrains the internal orthographic representation. *Reading & Writing: An Interdisciplinary Journal, 14*, 297–332.

Kavale, K. A., & Forness, S. R. (1987). Substance over style: Assessing the efficacy of modality testing and teaching. *Exceptional Children, 54*(3), 228–239.

Keenan, J. M., & Betjemann, R. S. (2006). Comprehending the Gray Oral Reading Test without reading it: Why comprehension tests should not include passage-independent items. *Scientific Studies of Reading, 10*(4), 363–380.

Keenan, J. M., Betjemann, R. S., & Olson, R. K. (2008). Reading comprehension tests vary in the skills they assess: Differential dependence on decoding and oral comprehension. *Scientific Studies of Reading, 12*(3), 281–300. doi:10.1080/10888430802132279

Keller, T. A., & Just, M. A. (2009). Altering cortical connectivity: Remediation-induced changes in the white matter of poor readers. *Neuron, 64*, 624–631. doi:10.1016/j.neuron.2009.10.018

Kendeou, P., Savage, R., & van den Broek, P. (2009). Revisiting the simple view of reading. *British Journal of Educational Psychology, 79*, 353–370.

Kendeou, P., van den Broek, P., Helder, A., & Karlsson, J. (2014). A cognitive view of reading comprehension: Implications for reading difficulties. *Learning Disabilities Research and Practice, 29*(1), 10–16.

Kerins, M. (2006). The effects of systematic reading instruction on three classifications of readers. *Reading Research and Instruction, 45*(3), 243–260.

Kieffer, M. J., Vukovic, R. K., & Berry, D. (2013). Roles of attention shifting and inhibitory control in fourth-grade reading comprehension. *Reading Research Quarterly, 48*(4), 333–348.

Kilpatrick, D. A. (2012a). Phonological segmentation assessment is not enough: A comparison of three phonological awareness tests with first and second graders. *Canadian Journal of School Psychology, 27*(2), 150–165.

Kilpatrick, D. A. (2012b). Not all phonological awareness tests are created equal: Considering the practical validity of phonological manipulation vs. segmentation. *Communiqué: Newspaper of the National Association of School Psychologists, 40*(6), 31–33.

Kilpatrick, D. A. (2014a). Tailoring interventions in reading based on emerging research on the development of word recognition skills. In J. T. Mascolo, D. P. Flanagan, & V. C. Alfonso (Eds.), *Essentials of planning, selecting and tailoring intervention: Addressing the needs of the unique learner* (pp. 123–150). Hoboken, NJ: Wiley.

Kilpatrick, D. A. (2014b, July). *The compensating dyslexics we never hear about: A multiple case study approach.* Paper presented at the Society for the Scientific Study of Reading International Conference, Santa Fe, NM.

Kilpatrick, D. A. (2015a). *Equipped for reading success: A comprehensive, step-by-step program for developing phonemic awareness and fluent word recognition.* Syracuse, NY: Casey & Kirsch.

Kilpatrick, D. A. (2015b). *The compensating dyslexics we never hear about: A multiple case study approach.* Manuscript submitted for publication.

Kilpatrick, D. A., & Song, M. S. (2015c). *The phonemic proficiency hypothesis of orthographic learning: An examination of how phonemic skills influence orthographic memory.* Manuscript submitted for publication.

Kilpatrick, D. A., Byrnes, C., Randall, D., & Isler, L. (2015). *How much can the simple view of reading explain about typical reading development*. Manuscript in preparation.

Kilpatrick, D. A., & Cole, L. A. (2015). Exploring the development of sight-word learning in second and fifth graders using rimes, pseudorimes, and real-word rimes. Manuscript submitted for publication.

Kilpatrick, D. A., & McInnis, P. J. (2015). The Phonological Awareness Screening Test (PAST): An initial report. Manuscript submitted for publication.

Kim, A.-H., Vaughn, S., Wanzek, J., & Wei, S. (2004). Graphic organizers and their effects on the reading comprehension of students with LD: A synthesis of research. *Journal of Learning Disabilities, 37*(2), 105–118.

Kim, J. S., Samson, J. F., Fitzgerald, R., & Hartry, A., (2010). A randomized experiment of a mixed-methods literacy intervention for struggling readers in grades 4–6: Effects on word reading efficiency, reading comprehension and vocabulary, and oral reading fluency. *Reading and Writing: An Interdisciplinary Journal, 23*, 1109–1129. doi:10.1007/s11145-009-9198-2

Kim, Y.-S., Petscher, Y., Foorman, B. R., & Zhou, C. (2010). The contributions of phonological awareness and letter-name knowledge to letter-sound acquisition—A cross-classified multilevel model approach. *Journal of Educational Psychology, 102*(2). doi:10.1037/a0018449

Kintsch, W., & Rawson, K. A. (2005). Comprehension. In M. J. Snowling & C. Hulme (Eds.), *The science of reading: A handbook* (pp. 209–226). Oxford, UK: Blackwell.

Kirk, C., & Gillon, G. T. (2007). Longitudinal effects of phonological awareness intervention on morphological awareness in children with speech impairment. *Language, Speech, and Hearing Services in Schools, 38*, 342–352.

Kjeldsen, A.-C., Kärnä, A., Niemi, P., Olofsson, A., & Witting, K. (2014). Gains from training in phonological awareness in kindergarten predict reading comprehension in grade 9. *Scientific Studies of Reading, 18*(6), 452–467. doi:10.1080/10888438.2014.940080

Klingner, J., & Artiles, A. J. (2006). English language learners struggling to learn to read: Emergent scholarship on linguistic differences and learning disabilities. *Journal of Learning Disabilities, 39*(5), 386–389.

Klingner, J. K., Morrison, A., & Eppolito, A. (2011). Metacognition to improve reading comprehension. In R. E. O'Connor & P. F. Vadasy (Eds.), *Handbook of reading interventions* (pp. 220–253). New York, NY: Guilford Press.

Krafnick, A. J., Flowers, D. L., Napoliello, E. M., & Eden, G. F. (2011). Gray matter volume changes following reading intervention in dyslexic children. *NeuroImage, 57*, 733–741.

Krieger, V. K. (1981). Hierarchy of "confusable" high-frequency words in isolation and context. *Learning Disabilities Quarterly, 4*, 131–138.

Kroese, J. M., Hynd, G. E., Knight, D. F., Hiemenz, J. R., & Hall, J. (2000). Clinical appraisal of spelling ability and its relationship to phonemic awareness (blending, segmenting, elision, and reversal), phonological memory, and reading in reading disabled, ADHD, and normal children. *Reading & Writing: An Interdisciplinary Journal, 13*, 105–131.

Kucer, S. B. (2011). Revisiting the contextual information available to readers reading. *Literacy Research and Instruction, 50*, 216–228. doi:10.1080/19388071.2010.512378

Kuder, S. J. (1990). Effectiveness of DISTAR reading program for children with learning disabilities. *Journal of Learning Disabilities, 23*(1), 69–71.

LaBerge, D., & Samuels, S. J. (1974). Toward a theory of automatic information processing in reading. *Cognitive Psychology 6*, 293–323.

Laing, E., & Hulme, C. (1999). Phonological and semantic processes influence beginning readers' ability to learn to read words. *Journal of Experimental Child Psychology, 73*, 183–207.

Landerl, K., Ramus, K., Moll, K., Lyytinen, H., Leppänen, P. H., Lohvansuu, K., ... Schulte-Körne, G. (2013). Predictors of developmental dyslexia in European orthographies with varying complexity. *Journal of Child Psychology and Psychiatry, 54*(6), 686–694. doi:10.1111/jcpp.12029

Landi, N., Perfetti, C. A., Bolger, D. J., Dunlap, S., & Foorman, B. R. (2006). The role of discourse context in developing word form representations: A paradoxical relation between reading and learning. *Journal of Experimental Child Psychology, 94*, 114–133.

Leach, J. M., Scarborough, H. S., & Rescorla, L. (2003). Late-emerging reading disabilities. *Journal of Educational Psychology, 95*(2), 211–224.

Lederberg, A. R., Schick, B., & Spencer, P. E. (2013). Language and literacy development of deaf and hard-of-hearing children: Successes and challenges. *Developmental Psychology, 49*(1), 15–30. doi:10.1037/a0029558

Lenchner, O., Gerber, M. M., & Routh, D. K. (1990). Phonological awareness tasks as predictors of decoding ability: Beyond segmentation. *Journal of Learning Disabilities, 23*(4), 240–247.

Lennon, J. E., & Slesinski, C. (1999). Early intervention in reading: Results of a screening and intervention program for kindergarten students. *School Psychology Review, 28*(3), 353–364.

Lervåg, A., & Aukrust, V. G., (2010). Vocabulary knowledge is a critical determinant of the difference in reading comprehension growth between first and second language learners. *Journal of Child Psychology and Psychiatry 51*(5), 612–620. doi:10.1111/j.1469-7610.2009.02185.x

Lervåg, A., Bråten, I., & Hulme, C. (2009). The cognitive and linguistic foundations of early reading development: A Norwegian latent variable longitudinal study. *Developmental Psychology, 45*(3), 764–781.

Lervåg, A., & Hulme, C. (2009). Rapid Automatized Naming (RAN) taps a mechanism that places constraints on the development of early reading fluency. *Psychological Science, 20*(8), 1040–1047.

Lesaux, N. K., & Siegel, L. S. (2003). The development of reading in children who speak English as a second language. *Developmental Psychology, 39*(6), 1005–1019. doi:10.1037/0012-1649.39.6.1005

Levine, A. (1994). The great debate revisited. *Atlantic Monthly, December,* 38–44.

Levy, B. A., & Lysynchuk, L. (1997). Beginning word recognition: Benefits of training by segmentation and whole word methods. *Scientific Studies of Reading, 1*(4), 359–387.

Lewkowicz, N. K. (1980). Phonemic awareness training: What to teach and how to teach it. *Journal of Educational Psychology, 72*(5), 686–700.

Leybaert, J. (2000). Phonology acquired through the eyes and spelling in deaf children. *Journal of Experimental Child Psychology, 75*, 291–318.

Li, M., & Kirby, J. R. (2014). Unexpected poor comprehenders among adolescent ESL students. *Scientific Studies of Reading, 18*(2), 75–93. doi:10.1080/10888438.2013.775130

Liberman, I. Y., & Liberman, A. M. (1990). Whole language vs. code emphasis: Understanding assumptions and their implications for reading instruction. *Annals of Dyslexia, 40*, 51–76.

Lindamood, P. C., & Lindamood, P. (2004). *Lindamood Auditory Conceptualization Test-Third Edition (LAC-3)*. Austin, TX: PRO-ED.

Lipka, O., Lesaux, N. K., & Siegel, L. S. (2006). Retrospective analyses of the reading development of grade 4 students with reading disabilities: Risk status and profiles over 5 years. *Journal of Learning Disabilities, 39*(4), 364–378.

Litt, R., & Nation, K. (2014). The nature and specificity of paired associate learning deficits in children with dyslexia. *Journal of Memory and Language, 71*, 71–88.

Litt, R. A., de Jong, P. F., van Bergen, E., & Nation, K. (2013). Dissociating crossmodal and verbal demands in paired associate learning (PAL): What drives the PAL–reading relationship? *Journal of Experimental Child Psychology, 115*, 137–149.

Lovett, M. W., Borden, S. L., DeLuca, T., Lacerenza, L., Benson, N. J., & Brackstone, D. (1994). Treating the core deficits of developmental dyslexia: Evidence of transfer of learning after phonologically- and strategy-based reading training programs. *Developmental Psychology, 30*(6), 805–822.

Lovett, M. W., Lacerenza, L., & Borden, S. L. (2000). Putting struggling readers on the PHAST track: A program to integrate phonological and strategy-based remedial reading instruction and maximize outcomes. *Journal of Learning Disabilities, 33*(5), 458–476.

Lovett, M. W., Lacerenza, L., Borden, S. L., Frijters, J. C., Steinbach, K. A., & De Palma, M. (2000). Components of effective remediation for developmental reading disabilities: Combining phonological and strategy-based instruction to improve outcomes. *Journal of Educational Psychology, 92*(2), 263–283.

Lovett, M. W., Lacerenza, L., De Palma, M., & Frijters, J. C. (2012). Evaluating the efficacy of remediation for struggling readers in high school. *Journal of Learning Disabilities, 45*(2), 151–169.

Lundberg, I., Frost, J., & Petersen, O. (1988). Effects of an extensive program for stimulating phonological awareness in preschool children. *Reading Research Quarterly, 23*, 263–284.

Lundberg, I., Olofsson, Å., & Wall, S. (1980). Reading and spelling skills in the first school years predicted from phonemic awareness skills in kindergarten. *Scandinavian Journal of Psychology, 21*(3), 159–173.

Lupker, S. J. (2005). Word recognition: Theories and findings. In M. J. Snowling & C. Hulme (Eds.), *The science of reading: A handbook* (pp. 39–60). Malden, MA: Wiley-Blackwell.

Macaruso, P., & Shankweiler, D. (2010). Expanding the simple view of reading in accounting for reading skills in community college students. *Reading Psychology, 31*, 454–471.

Maclean, M., Bryant, P. E., & Bradley, L. (1987). Rhymes, nursery rhymes and reading in early childhood. *Merrill-Palmer Quarterly, 33*, 255–282.

Mancilla-Martinez, J., Kieffer, M. J., Biancarosa, G., Christodoulou, J. A., & Snow, C. E. (2011). Investigating English reading comprehension growth in adolescent language minority learners: some insights from the simple view. *Reading and Writing: An Interdisciplinary Journal, 24*, 339–354. doi:10.1007/s11145-009-9215-5

Manis, F. R., Custodio, R., & Szeszulski, P. A. (1993). Development of phonological and orthographic skill: A 2-year longitudinal study of dyslexic children. *Journal of Experimental Child Psychology, 56*, 64–86.

Marley, S. C., Levin, J. R., & Glenberg, A. M. (2007). Improving Native American children's listening comprehension through concrete representations. *Contemporary Educational Psychology, 32*, 537–550.

Marr, M., & Gormley, K., (1982). Children's recall of familiar and unfamiliar text. *Reading Research Quarterly, 18*(1), 89–104.

Marshall, D., Christo, C., & Davis, J. (2013). Performance of school age reading disabled students on the phonological awareness subtests of the Comprehensive Test of Phonological Processing (CTOPP). *Contemporary School Psychology, 17*(1), 93–101.

Martens, V. E. G., & de Jong, P. F. (2008). Effects of repeated reading on the length effect in word and pseudoword reading. *Journal of Research in Reading, 31*(1), 40–54. doi:10.1111/j.1467-9817.2007.00360.x

Masonheimer, P. E., Drum, P. A., & Ehri, L. C. (1984). Does environmental print identification lead children into word reading? *Journal of Reading Behavior, 16*, 257–271. doi:10.1080/10862968409547520

Mather, N., Roberts, R., Hammill, D. D., & Allen, E. A. (2008). *Test of orthographic competence*. Austin, TX: PRO-ED.

Mather, N., & Wendling, B. J. (2014). Examiner's manual. *Woodcock-Johnson IV Tests of Achievement*. Rolling Meadows, IL: Riverside.

Maughan, B., Hagell, H., Rutter, M., & Yule, W. (1994). Poor readers in secondary school. *Reading and Writing: An Interdisciplinary Journal*, *6*, 125–150.

Maughan, B., Rowe, R., Loeber, R., & Stouthamer-Loeber, M. (2003). Reading problems and depressed mood. *Journal of Abnormal Child Psychology*, *31*(2), 219–229.

Maurer, U., & McCandliss, B. D. (2008). The development of visual expertise for words: The contribution of electrophysiology. In E. L. Grigorenko & A. J. Naples (Eds.), *Single word reading: Behavioral and biological perspectives* (pp. 43–63). New York, NY: Psychology Press.

McCallum, R. D., & Moore, S. (1999). Not all imagery is created equal: The role of imagery in the comprehension of main ideas in exposition. *Reading Psychology*, *20*, 21–60.

McClelland, J. L. (1976). Preliminary letter identification in the perception of words and nonwords. *Journal of Experimental Psychology: Human Perception and Performance*, *2*(1), 80–91.

McGee, R., Prior, M., Williams, S., Smart, D., & Sanson, A. (2002). The long-term significance of teacher-rated hyperactivity and reading ability in childhood: Findings from two longitudinal studies. *Journal of Child Psychology and Psychiatry*, *43*(8), 1004–1017.

McGeown, S. P., Medford, E., & Moxon, G. (2013). Individual differences in children's reading and spelling strategies and the skills supporting strategy use. *Learning and Individual Differences*, *28*, 75–81.

McGrew, K. S., & Flanagan, D. P. (1998). *Intelligence test desk reference: Gf-Gc Cross-Battery Assessment*. Boston: Allyn & Bacon.

McGuinness, D. (1997). Strategies as predictors of reading skill: A follow-on study. *Annals of Dyslexia*, *47*, 117–150.

McGuinness, C., McGuinness, D., & McGuinness, G. (1996). Phono-Graphix: A new method for remediating reading difficulties. *Annals of Dyslexia*, *46*, 73–96.

McInnis, P. J. (1981). *Decoding keys for reading success*. New York, NY: Walker Educational.

McInnis, P. J. (1999). *A guide to readiness and reading: Phonemic awareness and blending* (3rd ed.). Penn Yan, NY: ARL.

McKague, M., Davis, C., Pratt, C., & Johnston, M. B. (2008). The role of feedback from phonology to orthography in orthographic learning: An extension of item-based accounts. *Journal of Research in Reading*, *31*(1), 55–76.

McKague, M., Pratt, C., & Johnston, M. B. (2001). The effect of oral vocabulary on reading visually novel words: A comparison of the dual-route- cascaded and triangle frameworks. *Cognition*, *80*, 231–262.

McKeown, M. G., & Beck I. L. (2011). Making vocabulary interventions engaging and effective. In R. E. O'Connor, & P. F. Vadasy (Eds.), *Handbook of reading interventions* (pp. 138–168). New York, NY: Guilford Press.

McKeown, M. G., & Beck I. L. (2014). Effects of vocabulary instruction on measures of language processing: Comparing two approaches. *Early Childhood Research Quarterly*, *29*, 520–530.

McLaughlin, M. J., Speirs, K., & Shenassa, E. D. (2014). Reading disability and adult attained education and income: Evidence from a 30-year longitudinal study of a population-based sample. *Journal of Learning Disabilities*, *47*(4), 374–386.

Melby-Lervåg, M., Hulme, C., & Halaas Lyster, S.-A. (2012). Phonological skills and their role in learning to read: A meta-analytic review. *Psychological Bulletin*, *138*(2), 322–352.

Messbauer, V. C. S., & de Jong, P. F. (2003). Word, nonword, and visual paired associate learning in Dutch dyslexic children. *Journal of Experimental Child Psychology*, *84*, 77–96.

Metsala, J. L. (2011). Lexical reorganization and the emergence of phonological awareness. In S. B. Neuman & D. K. Dickinson (Eds.), *Handbook of early literacy research* (Vol. *3*, pp. 66–82). New York, NY: Guilford Press.

Miller, A. C., & Keenan, J. M. (2009). How word decoding skill impacts text memory: The centrality deficit and how domain knowledge can compensate. *Annals of Dyslexia*, *59*, 99–113. doi:10.1007/s11881-009-0025-x

Miller, A. C., Keenan, J. M., Betjemann, R. S., Willcutt, E. G., Pennington, B. F., & Olson R. K. (2013). Reading comprehension in children with ADHD: Cognitive underpinnings of the centrality deficit. *Journal of Abnormal Child Psychology*, *41*, 473–483.

Miller, B., McCardle, P., & Hernandez, R. (2010). Advances and remaining challenges in adult literacy research. *Journal of Learning Disabilities*, *43*(2), 101–107.

Mitchell, C., & Begeny, J. C. (2014). Improving student reading through parents' implementation of a structured reading program. *School Psychology Review*, *43*(1), 41–58.

Moats, L. (2009). Still wanted: Teachers with knowledge of language. Introduction to special issue. *Journal of Learning Disabilities*, *42*(5), 387–391.

Moats, L. C. (1994). Missing foundation in teacher education: Knowledge of the structure of spoken and written language. *Annals of Dyslexia*, *44*, 81–102.

Mol, S. E., & Bus, A. G. (2011). To read or not to read: A meta-analysis of print exposure from infancy to early adulthood. *Psychological Bulletin*, *137*(2), 267–296. doi:10.1037/a0021890

Moll, K., Ramus, F., Bartling, J., Bruder, J., Kunze, S., Neuhoff, N., … Landerl, K. (2014). Cognitive mechanisms underlying reading and spelling development in five European orthographies. *Learning and Instruction*, *29*, 65–77. doi:10.1016/j.learninstruc.2013.09.003

Moody, S. W., Vaughn, S., Hughes, M. T., & Fischer, M. (2000). Reading instruction in the resource room: Set up for failure. *Exceptional Children*, *66*(3), 305–316.

Morgan, P. L., Farkas, G., Tufis, P. A., & Sperling, R. A. (2008). Are reading and behavior problems risk factors for each other? *Journal of Learning Disabilities*, *41*(5), 417–436.

Munger, K. A., & Blachman, B. A. (2013). Taking a "simple view" of the Dynamic Indicators of Basic Early Literacy skills as a predictor of multiple measures of third-grade reading comprehension. *Psychology in the Schools*, *50*(7). doi:10.1002/pits.21699

Nation, K. (2005). Children's reading comprehension difficulties. In M. J. Snowling & C. Hulme (Eds.), *The science of reading: A handbook* (pp. 248–265). Oxford, UK: Blackwell.

Nation, K., Angell, P., & Castles, A. (2007). Orthographic learning via self-teaching in children learning to read English: Effects of exposure, durability, and context. *Journal of Experimental Child Psychology*, *96*, 71–84.

Nation, K., Clarke, P., Marshall, C. M., & Durand, M. (2004). Hidden language impairments in children: Parallels between poor reading comprehension and specific language impairment? *Journal of Speech, Language, and Hearing Research*, *47*, 199–211.

Nation, K., Clarke, P., & Snowling, M. J. (2002). General cognitive ability in children with reading comprehension difficulties. *British Journal of Educational Psychology*, *72*, 549–560.

Nation, K., & Cocksey, J. (2009a). The relationship between knowing a word and reading it aloud in children's word reading development. *Journal of Experimental Child Psychology*, *103*, 296–308.

Nation, K., & Cocksey, J. (2009b). Beginning readers activate semantics from sub-word orthography. *Cognition*, *110*, 273–278.

Nation, K., & Snowling, M. J. (1997). Assessing reading difficulties: The validity and utility of current measures of reading skill. *British Journal of Educational Psychology*, *67*, 359–370.

Nation, K., & Snowling, M. J. (1998). Individual differences in contextual facilitation: Evidence from dyslexia and poor reading comprehension. *Child Development, 69*(4), 996–1011.

Nation, K., Snowling, M. J., & Clarke, P. J. (2007). Dissecting the relationship between language skills and learning to read. Semantic and phonological contributions to new vocabulary learning in children with poor reading comprehension. *Advances in Speech-Language Pathology, 9,* 131–139.

National Early Literacy Panel (NELP). (2008). *Developing early literacy: Report of the National Early Literacy Panel*. Washington, DC: National Institute for Literacy.

National Institute of Child Health and Human Development. (2000). *Report of the National Reading Panel. Teaching children to read: An evidence-based assessment of the scientific research literature on reading and its implications for reading instruction: Reports of the subgroups* (NIH Publication No. 00-4754). Washington, DC: U.S. Government Printing Office.

Nelson, J. M., & Machek, G. R. (2007). A survey of training, practice, and competence in reading assessment and intervention. *School Psychology Review, 36*(2), 311–327.

Ness, M. K., & Southall, G. (2010). Preservice teachers' knowledge of and beliefs about dyslexia. *Journal of Reading Education, 36*(1), 36–43.

Nevo, E., & Breznitz, Z. (2011). Assessment of working memory components at 6 years of age as predictors of reading achievements a year later. *Journal of Experimental Child Psychology, 109,* 73–90.

Nicholson, T. (1997). Closing the gap on reading failure: Social background, phonemic awareness, and learning to read. In B. A. Blachman (Ed.), *Foundations of reading acquisition and dyslexia* (pp. 381–407). Mahwah, NJ: Erlbaum.

Norton, E. S., & Wolf, M. (2012). Rapid Automatized Naming (RAN) and reading fluency: Implications for understanding and treatment of reading disabilities. *Annual Review of Psychology, 63,* 427–452. doi:10.1146/annurev-psych-120710-100431

Oakhill, J., Cain, K., & Elbro, C. (2015). *Understanding and teaching reading comprehension: A handbook*. New York: Routledge.

Oakhill, J. V., & Patel, S. (1991). Can imagery training help children who have comprehension problems? *Journal of Research in Reading, 14,* 106–115.

O'Connor, R. E. (2011). Teaching older students to read. In R. E. O'Connor & P. F. Vadasy (Eds.), *Handbook of reading interventions* (pp. 380–404). New York, NY: Guilford Press.

O'Connor, R. E., Jenkins, J. R., & Slocum, T. A. (1995). Transfer among phonological tasks in kindergarten: Essential instructional content. *Journal of Educational Psychology, 87*(2), 202–217.

O'Connor, R., Notari-Syverson, A., & Vadasy, P. (1998a). First-grade effects of teacher-led phonological activities in kindergarten for children with mild disabilities: A follow-up study. *Learning Disabilities Research and Practice, 13,* 43–52.

O'Connor, R. E., Notari-Syverson, A., & Vadasy, P. F. (1998b). *Ladders to literacy: A kindergarten activity book*. Baltimore, MD: Brookes.

O'Connor, R. E., Notari-Syverson, A., & Vadasy, P. F. (2005). *Ladders to literacy: A kindergarten activity book* (2nd ed.). Baltimore, MD: Brookes.

O'Connor, R. E., & Vadasy, P. F. (Eds.) (2011). *Handbook of reading interventions*. New York, NY: Guilford.

O'Connor, R. E., White, A., & Swanson, H. L. (2007). Repeated reading versus continuous reading: Influences on reading fluency and comprehension. *Exceptional Children, 74*(1), 31–46.

O'Leary, P. M., Cockburn, M. K., Powell, D. R., & Diamond, K. E. (2010). Head Start teachers' views of phonological awareness and vocabulary knowledge instruction. *Early Childhood Education Journal, 38,* 187–195. doi:10.1007/s10643-010-0394-0

Olofsson, Å., & Lundberg, I. (1983). Can phonemic awareness be trained in kindergarten? *Scandinavian Journal of Psychology*, *24*, 35–44.

Olofsson, Å., & Lundberg, I. (1985). Evaluation of long term effects of phonemic awareness training in kindergarten: Illustrations of some methodological problems in evaluation research. *Scandinavian Journal of Psychology*, *26*, 21–34.

Ontario Ministry of Education (2003). Early reading strategy: The report of the expert panel on early reading in Ontario. Ontario, Canada. Ontario Ministry of Education.

Ozuru, Y., Dempsey, K., & McNamara, D. S. (2009). Prior knowledge, reading skill, and text cohesion in the comprehension of science texts. *Learning and Instruction*, *19*, 228–242.

Palinscar, A. S., & Brown, A. L. (1984). Reciprocal teaching of comprehension-monitoring activities. *Cognition and Instruction*, *1*(2), 117–175.

Papalewis, R. (2004). Struggling middle school readers: Successful, accelerating intervention. *Reading Improvement*, *41*(1), 24–37.

Pennington, B. F., Cardoso-Martins, C., Green, P. A., & Lefly, D. L. (2001). Comparing the phonological and double deficit hypotheses for developmental dyslexia. *Reading and Writing: An Interdisciplinary Journal*, *14*, 707–755.

Pennington, B. F., & Olson, R. K. (2005). Genetics of dyslexia. In M. J. Snowling & C. Hulme (Eds.), *The science of reading: A handbook* (pp. 453–472). Oxford, UK: Blackwell.

Peereman, R., & Content, A. (1997). Orthographic and phonological neighborhoods in naming: Not all neighbors are equally influential in orthographic space. *Journal of Memory and Language*, *37*, 382–410.

Perfetti, C. A. (1985). *Reading ability*. New York, NY: Oxford University Press.

Perfetti, C. A. (1991). Representations and awareness in the acquisition of reading competence. In L. Rieben & C. A. Perfetti (Eds.), *Learning to read: Basic research and its implications* (pp. 33–44). Hillsdale, NJ: Erlbaum.

Perfetti, C. A. (2011). Phonology is critical in reading: But a phonological deficit is not the only source of low reading skill. In S. A. Brady, D. Braze, & C. A. Fowler (Eds.), *Explaining individual differences in reading: Theory and evidence* (pp. 153–171). New York, NY: Psychology Press.

Perfetti, C. A., Beck, I., Bell, L., & Hughes, C. (1987). Phonemic knowledge and learning to read are reciprocal: A longitudinal study of first grade children. *Merrill-Palmer Quarterly*, *33*, 283–319.

Perfetti, C. A., & Hogaboam, T. (1975). Relationship between single word decoding and reading comprehension skill. *Journal of Educational Psychology*, *67*(4), 461–469.

Perfetti, C. A., Landi, N., & Oakhill, J. (2005). The acquisition of reading comprehension skill. In M. J. Snowling & C. Hulme (Eds.), *The science of reading: A handbook* (pp. 227–247). Malden, MA: Wiley-Blackwell.

Piasta, S. B., & Wagner, R. K. (2010). Developing early literacy skills: A meta-analysis of alphabet learning and instruction. *Reading Research Quarterly*, *45*(1), 8–38. doi:10.1598/RRQ.45.1.2

Powell, D., Stainthorp, R., Stuart, M., Garwood, H., & Quinlan, P. (2007). An experimental comparison between rival theories of rapid automatized naming performance and its relationship to reading. *Journal of Experimental Child Psychology*, *98*, 46–68.

Preßler, A.-L., Könen, T., Hasselhorn, M., & Krajewski, K. (2014). Cognitive preconditions of early reading and spelling: A latent-variable approach with longitudinal data. *Reading and Writing: An Interdisciplinary Journal*, *27*, 383–406. doi:10.1007/s11145-013-9449-0

Prochnow, J. E., Tunmer, W. E., & Chapman, J. W. (2013). A longitudinal investigation of the influence of literacy-related skills, reading self-perceptions, and inattentive behaviours on the development of literacy learning difficulties. *International Journal of Disability, Development and Education*, *60*(3), 185–207.

Protopapas, A., Sideridis, G. D., Mouzaki, A., & Simos, P. G. (2011). Matthew effects in reading comprehension: Myth or reality? *Journal of Learning Disability, 44*(5), 402–420.

Pugh, K., & McCardle, P. (Eds.). (2009). *How children learn to read: Current issues and new directions in the integration of cognition, neurobiology and genetics of reading and dyslexia research and practice.* New York, NY: Psychology Press.

Rack, J., Hulme, C., Snowling, M., & Wightman, J. (1994). The role of phonology in young children's learning of sight words: The direct mapping hypothesis. *Journal of Experimental Child Psychology, 57*, 42–71.

Rack, J. P., Snowling, M. J., & Olson, R. K. (1992). The nonword reading deficit in developmental dyslexia: A review. *Reading Research Quarterly, 27*, 28–53.

Rapp, D. N., van den Broek, P., McMaster, K. L., Kendeou, P., & Espin, C. A. (2007). Higher-order comprehension processes in struggling readers: A perspective for research and intervention. *Scientific Studies of Reading, 11*(4), 289–312.

Rashotte, C. A., MacPhee, K., & Torgesen, J. K. (2001). Effectiveness of a group reading instruction program with poor readers in multiple grades. *Learning Disabilities Quarterly, 24*, 119–134.

Rayner, K., & Pollatsek, A. (1989). *The psychology of reading.* Hillsdale, NJ: Erlbaum.

Rayner, K., Pollatsek, A., Ashby, J., & Clifton, C. (2011). *The psychology of reading* (2nd ed.). New York, NY: Psychology Press.

Reed, D. K. (2011). A review of the psychometric properties of retell instruments. *Educational Assessment, 16*, 123–144. doi:10.1080/10627197.2011.604238

Reed, D. K., & Vaughn, S. (2012). Retell as an indicator of reading comprehension. *Scientific Studies of Reading, 16*(3), 187–217. doi:10.1080/10888438.2010.538780

Reitsma, P. (1983). Printed word learning in beginning readers. *Journal of Experimental Child Psychology, 36*, 321–339.

Reynolds, C. R., & Kamphaus, R. W. (2007). *Test of irregular word reading efficiency.* Lutz, FL: PAR.

Ricketts, J. (2011). Research review: Reading comprehension in developmental disorders of language and communication. *Journal of Child Psychology and Psychiatry, 52*(11), 1111–1123. doi:10.1111/j.1469-7610.2011.02438.x

Ricketts, J., Jones, C. R. G., Happé, F., & Charman, T. (2013). Reading comprehension in autism spectrum disorders: The role of oral language and social functioning. *Journal of Autism and Developmental Disorders, 43*, 807–816. doi:10.1007/s10803-012-1619-4

Ripoll Salceda, J. C., Alonso, G. A., & Castilla-Earls, A. P. (2014). The simple view of reading in elementary school: A systematic review. *Revista de Logopedia, Foniatría y Audiología, 34*(1), 17–31.

Ritchey, K. D., & Goeke, J. L. (2006). Orton-Gillingham and Orton-Gillingham-based reading instruction: A review of the literature. *Journal of Special Education, 40*(3), 171–183.

Roberts, G., Good, R., & Corcoran, S. (2005) Story Retell: A fluency-based indicator of reading comprehension. *School Psychology Quarterly, 20*(3), 304–317.

Roberts, T. A. (2003). Effects of alphabet-letter instruction on young children's word recognition. *Journal of Educational Psychology, 95*(1), 41–51. doi:10.1037/0022-0663.95.1.41

Robertson, C., & Salter, W. (2007). *The phonological awareness test-2.* Austin, TX: Linguisystems/PRO-ED.

Rosner, J. (1971). Phonic analysis training and beginning reading skills. *Proceedings of the Annual Convention of the American Psychological Association, 6*(2), 533–534.

Rosner, J. (1999). *PASP: Phonological awareness skills program.* Austin, TX: PRO-ED.

Rosner, J., & Simon, D. P. (1971). The auditory analysis test: An initial report. *Journal of Learning Disabilities, 4*(7), 384–392.

Sabatini, J. P., Sawaki, Y., Shore, J. R., & Scarborough, H. S. (2010). Relationships among reading skills of adults with low literacy. *Journal of Learning Disabilities, 43*, 122–138. doi:10.1177/0022219409359343

Sadoski, M., McTigue, R. M., & Paivio, A. (2012). A dual coding theoretical model of decoding in reading: Subsuming the LaBerge and Samuels model. *Reading Psychology, 33*, 465–496. doi:10.1080/02702711.2011.557330

Sáenz, L. M., Fuchs, L. S., & Fuchs, D. (2005). Peer-assisted learning strategies for English language learners with learning disabilities. *Exceptional Children, 71*(3), 231–247.

Scanlon, D. M., Anderson, K. L., & Sweeney, J. M. (2010). *Early intervention for reading difficulties: The interactive strategies approach.* New York, NY: Guilford Press.

Scanlon, D. M., Gelzheiser, L. M., Vellutino, F. R., Schatschneider, C., & Sweeney, J. M. (2008). Reducing the incidence of early reading difficulties: Professional development for classroom teachers vs. direct interventions for children. *Learning and Individual Differences, 18*, 346–359.

Scanlon, D. M., Vellutino, F. R., Small, S. G., Fanuele, D. P., & Sweeney, J. M. (2005). Severe reading difficulties—Can they be prevented? A comparison of prevention and intervention approaches. *Exceptionality, 13*(4), 209–227.

Scarborough, H. S., & Brady, S. A. (2002). Toward a common terminology for talking about speech and reading: A glossary of the "phon" words and some related terms. *Journal of Literacy Research, 34*(3), 299–336.

Scarborough, H. S., & Dobrich, W. (1994). On the efficacy of reading to preschoolers. *Developmental Review, 14*, 245–302.

Schatschneider, C., Fletcher, J. M., Francis, D. J., Carlson, C. D., & Foorman, B. R. (2004). Kindergarten prediction of reading skills: A longitudinal comparative analysis. *Journal of Educational Psychology, 96*(2), 265–282.

Schatschneider, C., Francis, D. J., Foorman, B. R., Fletcher, J. M., & Mehta, P. (1999). The dimensionality of phonological awareness: An application of item response theory. *Journal of Educational Psychology, 91*(3), 439–449.

Schneider, W., Ennemoser, M., Roth, E., & Küspert, P. (1999). Prevention of dyslexia: Does training in phonological awareness work for everybody? *Journal of Learning Disabilities, 32*(5), 429–436.

Schneider, W., Kuspert, P., Roth, E., Vise, M., & Marx, H. (1997). Short- and long-term effects of training phonological awareness in kindergarten: Evidence from two German studies. *Journal of Experimental Child Psychology, 66*, 311–340.

Schwanenflugel, P. J., & Ruston, H. P. (2008). Becoming a fluent reader: From theory to practice. In M. R. Kuhn & P. J. Schwanenflugel (Eds.), *Fluency in the classroom* (pp. 1–16). New York, NY: Guilford Press.

Scott, J., & Ehri, L. (1990). Sight word reading in prereaders: Use of logographic vs. alphabetic access routes. *Journal of Reading Behavior, 22*, 149–166.

Seymour, P. H. K. (2009). Continuity and discontinuity in the development of single-word reading: Theoretical speculations. In E. L. Grigorenko & A. J. Naples (Eds.), *Single word reading: Behavioral and biological perspectives* (pp. 1–24). New York, NY: Psychology Press.

Seymour, P. H. K., & Evans, H. M. (1994). Levels of phonological awareness and learning to read. *Reading and Writing: An Interdisciplinary Journal, 6*, 221–250.

Seymour, P. K., Aro, M., & Erskine, J. M. (2003). Foundation literacy acquisition in European orthographies. *British Journal of Psychology, 94*, 143–174.

Shankweiler, D., Crain, S., Katz, L., Fowler, A. E., Liberman, A. M., Brady, S. A., … Shaywitz, B. A. (1995). Cognitive profiles of reading-disabled children: Comparison of language skills in phonology, morphology, and syntax. *Psychological Science, 6*(3), 149–156.

Shapiro, A. (2004). How including prior knowledge as a subject variable may change outcomes of learning research. *American Educational Research Journal, 41*(1), 159–189.

Shapiro, L. R., & Solity, J. (2008). Delivering phonological and phonics training within whole-class teaching. *British Journal of Educational Psychology, 78*, 597–620.

Share, D. L. (1995). Phonological recoding and self-teaching: Sine qua non of reading acquisition. *Cognition, 55*, 151–218.

Share, D. L. (1999). Phonological recoding and orthographic learning: A direct test of the self-teaching hypothesis. *Journal of Experimental Child Psychology 72*, 95–129.

Share, D. L. (2004a). Orthographic learning at a glance: On the time course and developmental onset of self-teaching. *Journal of Experimental Child Psychology, 87*, 267–298.

Share, D. L. (2004b). Knowing letter names and learning letter sounds: A causal connection. *Journal of Experimental Child Psychology, 88*, 213–233.

Share, D. (2011). On the role of phonology in reading acquisition: The self-teaching hypothesis. In S. A. Brady, D. Braze, & C. A. Fowler (Eds.), *Explaining individual differences in reading: Theory and evidence* (pp. 45–68). New York, NY: Psychology Press.

Share, D., Jorm, A. F., MacLean, R., & Matthews, R. (2002). Temporal processing and reading disability. *Reading and Writing: An Interdisciplinary Journal, 15*(1–2), 151–178.

Shaywitz, S. (2003). *Overcoming dyslexia: A new and complete science-based program for reading problems at any level*. New York, NY: Alfred A. Knopf.

Shmidman, A., & Ehri, L. C. (2010). Embedded picture mnemonics to learn letters. *Scientific Studies of Reading, 14*(2), 159–182. doi:10.1080/10888430903117492

Short, E., J., Feagans, L., McKinney, J. D., & Appelbaum, M. I. (1986). Longitudinaly stability of LD subtypes based on age- and IQ-achievement discrepancies. *Learning Disability Quarterly, 9*, 214–225.

Simos, P. G., Fletcher, J. M., Bergman, E., Breier, J. I., Foorman, B. R., Castillo, E. M., ... Papanicolau, A. C. (2002). Dyslexia-specific brain activation profile becomes normal following successful remedial training. *Neurology, 58*, 1203–1213.

Simos, P. G., Rezaie, R., Fletcher, J. M., & Papanicolaou, A. C. (2013). Time-constrained functional connectivity analysis of cortical networks underlying phonological decoding in typically developing school-aged children: A magnetoencephalography study. *Brain & Language 125*, 156–164.

Slate, J., Algozzine, B., & Lockavith, J. F. (1998). Effects of intensive remedial reading instruction. *Journal of At-Risk Issues, 5*(1), 30–35.

Slavin, R. E., Cheung, A., Groff, C., & Lake, C. (2008). Effective reading programs for middle and high schools: A best evidence synthesis. *Reading Research Quarterly, 43*(3), 290–322.

Slavin, R. E., Lake, C., Davis, S., & Madden, N. A. (2011). Effective programs for struggling readers: A best-evidence synthesis. *Educational Research Review, 6*, 1–26. doi:10.1016/j.edurev.2010.07.002

Smith, F. (1999). Why systematic phonics and phonemic awareness instruction constitute an educational hazard. *Language Arts, 77*(2), 150–155.

Smith, F., & Goodman, K. S. (1971). On the psycholinguistic method of teaching reading. *Elementary School Journal, 17*, 177–181.

Smith, N. B. (1965). *American reading instruction*. Newark, DE: International Reading Association.

Snow, C. E., Burns, M. S., & Griffin, P. (1998). *Preventing reading difficulties in young children*. Washington, DC: National Academy Press.

Snowling, M. J., & Hulme, C. (2011). Evidence-based interventions for reading and language difficulties: Creating a virtuous circle. *British Journal of Educational Psychology, 81*, 1–23.

Sparks, R., Patton, J., & Murdoch, A. (2014). Early reading success and its relationship to reading achievement and reading volume: replication of "10 years later." *Reading and Writing: An Interdisciplinary Journal, 27*, 189–211. doi:10.1007/s11145-013-9439-2

Sparks, R. L., Patton, J., Ganschow, L., & Humbach, N. (2012). Relationships among L1 print exposure and early L1 literacy skills, L2 aptitude, and L2 proficiency. *Reading and Writing: An Interdisciplinary Journal, 25*, 1599–1634. doi:10.1007/s11145-011-9335-6

Spear-Swerling, L. (2004). Fourth graders' performance on a state-mandated assessment involving two different measures of reading comprehension. *Reading Psychology*, *25*, 121–148. doi:10.1080/02702710490435727

Spencer, S. A., & Manis, F. R. (2010). The effects of a fluency intervention program on the fluency and comprehension outcomes of middle-school students with severe reading deficits. *Learning Disabilities Research & Practice*, *25*(2), 76–86.

Spörer, N., & Brunstein, J. C. (2009). Fostering the reading comprehension of secondary school students through peer-assisted learning: Effects on strategy knowledge, strategy use, and task performance. *Contemporary Educational Psychology 34*, 289–297.

Sprenger-Charolles, L., Siegel, L. S., & Bonnet, P. (1998). Reading and spelling acquisition in French: The role of phonological mediation and orthographic factors. *Journal of Experimental Child Psychology*, *68*, 134–165.

Staels, E., & van den Broeck, W. (2014). Orthographic learning and the role of text-to-speech software in Dutch disabled readers. *Journal of Learning Disabilities*, *48*(1), 39–50.

Stage, S. A., Abbott, R. D., Jenkins, J. R., & Berninger, V. W. (2003). Predicting response to early reading intervention from verbal IQ, reading-related language abilities, attention ratings, and verbal IQ–word reading discrepancy: Failure to validate discrepancy method. *Journal of Learning Disabilities*, *36*(1), 24–33.

Stahl, S. A. (1999). Different strokes for different folks: A critique of Learning Styles. *American Educator, Fall*, 1–5.

Stahl, S. A., & Kuhn, M. R. (1995). Does whole language or instruction matched to learning styles help children learn to read? *School Psychology Review*, *24*(3), 393–404.

Stahl, S. A., & Miller, P. D. (1989). Whole Language and Language Experience approaches for beginning reading: A quantitative research synthesis. *Review of Educational Research*, *59*(1), 87–116.

Stahl, S. A., & Murray, B. A. (1994). Defining phonological awareness and its relationship to early reading. *Journal of Educational Psychology*, *86*(2), 221–234.

Stanovich, K. E. (1980). Toward an interactive-compensatory model of individual differences in the development of reading fluency. *Reading Research Quarterly*, *16*(1), 32–71.

Stanovich, K. E. (1993). Romance and reality. *The Reading Teacher*, *47*(4), 280–291.

Stanovich, K. E., Cunningham, A. E., & Cramer, B. B. (1984). Assessing phonological awareness in kindergarten children: Issues of task comparability. *Journal of Experimental Child Psychology*, *38*, 175–190.

Stanovich, K. E., Nathan, R. G., West, R. F., & Vala-Rossi, M. (1985). Word recognition in context: Spreading activation, expectancy, and modularity. *Child Development*, *56*, 1418–1428.

Stanovich, K. E., & Siegel, L. S. (1994). Phenotypic performance profile of children with reading disabilities: A regression-based test of the phonological-core variable-difference model. *Journal of Educational Psychology*, *86*(1), 24–53.

Steacy, L. M., Kirby, J. R., Parrila, R., & Compton, D. L. (2014). Classification of double deficit groups across time: an analysis of group stability from kindergarten to second grade. *Scientific Studies of Reading*, *18*, 255–273. doi: 10.1080/10888438.2013.873936

Stebbins, M. S., Stormont, M., Lembke, E. S., Wilson, D. J., & Clippard, D. (2012) Monitoring the effectiveness of the Wilson reading system for students with disabilities: One district's example. *Exceptionality: A Special Education Journal*, *20*(1), 58–70. doi:10.1080/09362835.2012.640908

Stothers, M., & Klein, P. D. (2010). Perceptual organization, phonological awareness, and reading comprehension in adults with and without learning disabilities. *Annals of Dyslexia*, *60*, 209–237. Doi: 10.1007/s11881-010-0042-9

Strong, J. K., Torgerson, C. J., Torgerson, D., & Hulme, C. (2011). A systematic meta-analytic review of evidence for the effectiveness of the "Fast ForWord" language intervention program. *Journal of Child Psychology and Psychiatry*, *52*(3), 224–235. doi:10.1111/j.1469-7610.2010.02329.x

Stroud, J. B., Blommers, P., & Lauber, M. (1957). Correlation analysis of WISC and achievement tests. *Journal of Educational Psychology*, *48*(1), 18–26.

Stuart, M., Stainthorp, R., & Snowling, M. (2008). Literacy as a complex activity: Deconstructing the simple view of reading. *Literacy*, *42*(2), 59–66.

Stuebing, K. K., Fletcher, J. M., Branum-Martin, L., & Francis, D. J. (2013). Evaluation of the technical adequacy of three methods for identifying specific learning disabilities based on cognitive discrepancies. *School Psychology Review*, *41*(1), 3–22.

Stuebing, K. K., Fletcher, J. M., LeDoux, J. M., Lyon, G. R., Shaywitz, S. E., & Shaywitz, B. A. (2002). Validity of IQ-discrepancy classifications of reading disabilities: A meta-analysis. *American Educational Research Journal*, *39*(2), 469–518.

Swank, L. K., & Catts, H. W. (1994). Phonological awareness and written word decoding. *Language, Speech, and Hearing Services in Schools*, *25*, 9–14.

Swanson, E. A., & Vaughn, S. (2010). An observation study of reading instruction provided to elementary students with learning disabilities in the resource room. *Psychology in the Schools*, *47*(5), 481–492. doi:10.1002/pits.20484

Swanson, H. L., Zheng, X., & Jerman, O. (2009). Working memory, short-term memory, and reading disabilities: A selective meta-analysis of the literature. *Journal of Learning Disabilities*, *42*(3), 260–287. doi:10.1177/0022219409331958

Swanson, L. (1978). Verbal encoding effects on the visual short-term memory of learning disabled and normal readers. *Journal of Educational Psychology*, *70*(4), 539–544.

Tangel, D. M., & Blachman, B. A. (1992). Effect of phoneme awareness instruction on kindergarten children's invented spelling. *Journal of Literacy Research*, *24*, 233–261. doi:10.1080/10862969209547774

Taylor, W. (1953). Cloze procedure: A new tool for measuring readability. *Journalism Quarterly, Fall*, 415–433.

Thompkins, A. C., & Binder, K. S. (2003). A comparison of the factors affecting reading performance of functionally illiterate adults and children matched by reading level. *Reading Research Quarterly*, *38*(2), 236–258.

Thompson, G. B., Connelly, V., Fletcher-Flinn, C. M., & Hodson, S. J. (2009). The nature of skilled adult reading varies with type of instruction in childhood. *Memory & Cognition*, *37*(2), 223–234. doi:10.3758/MC.37.2.223

Thompson, G. B., McKay, M. F., Fletcher-Flinn, C. M., Connelly, V., Kaa, R. T., & Ewing, J. (2008). Do children who acquire word reading without explicit phonics employ compensatory learning? Issues of phonological recoding, lexical orthography, and fluency. *Reading and Writing: An Interdisciplinary Journal*, *21*, 505–537. doi:10.1007/s11145-007-9075-9

Tiu, R. D., Thompson, L. A., & Lewis, B. A. (2003). The role of IQ in a component model of reading. *Journal of Learning Disabilities*, *36*(5), 424–436.

Tomblin, J. B., Zhang, X., Buckwalter, P., & Catts, H. (2000). The association of reading disability, behavioral disorders, and language impairment among second-grade children. *Journal of Child Psychology and Psychiatry*, *41*(4), 473–482.

Torgesen, J. K. (2000). Individual differences in response to early interventions in reading: The lingering problem of treatment registers. *Learning Disabilities Research and Practice*, *15*, 55–64. doi:10.1207/SLDRP1501 6

Torgesen, J. K. (2004a). Lessons learned from the last 20 years of research on interventions for students who experience difficulty learning to read. In P. McCardle & V. Chhabra (Eds.), *The voice of evidence in reading research* (pp. 355–382). Baltimore, MD: Brookes.

Torgesen, J. K. (2004b, March). Bringing it all together: From phonemic awareness to fluency. Paper presented at the CORE Literacy Leadership Summit. Retrieved from http://www.fcrr.org/science/pdf/torgesen/core_pafluency.pdf

Torgesen, J. K. (2005). Recent discoveries on remedial interventions for children with dyslexia. In M. J. Snowling & C. Hulme (Eds.), *The science of reading: A handbook* (pp. 521–537). Malden, MA: Wiley-Blackwell.

Torgesen, J. K., Alexander, A. W., Wagner, R. K., Rashotte, C. A., Voeller, K. K. S., & Conway, T. (2001). Intensive remedial instruction for children with severe reading, disabilities: Immediate and long-term outcomes from two instructional approaches. *Journal of Learning Disabilities, 34*(1), 33–58, 78.

Torgesen, J., Myers, D., Schirm, A., Stuart, E., Vartivarian, S., Mansfield, W., … Haan, C. (2007). National assessment of Title I interim report to Congress: Volume II: Closing the reading gap, first year findings from a randomized trial of four reading interventions for striving readers. Washington, DC: U.S. Department of Education, Institute of Education Sciences.

Torgesen, J. K., Rashotte, C. A., Alexander, A., Alexander, J., & MacPhee, K. (2003). Progress toward understanding the instructional conditions necessary for remediating reading difficulties in older children. In B. R. Foorman (Ed.), *Preventing and remediating reading difficulties: Bringing science to scale* (pp. 275–297). Baltimore, MD: York Press.

Torgesen, J. K., Wagner, R. K., & Rashotte, C. A. (1997). Prevention and remediation of severe reading disabilities: Keeping the end in mind. *Scientific Studies of Reading, 1*(3), 217–234.

Torgesen, J. K., Wagner, R. K., Rashotte, C. A., Herron, J., & Lindamood, P. (2010). Computer-assisted instruction to prevent early reading difficulties in students at risk for dyslexia: Outcomes from two instructional approaches. *Annals of Dyslexia, 60*, 40–56. doi:10.1007/s11881-009-0032-y

Torgesen, J. K., Wagner, R. K., Rashotte, C. A., Rose, E., Lindamood, P., Conway, T., & Garvan, C. (1999). Preventing reading failure in young children with phonological processing disabilities: Group and individual responses to instruction. *Journal of Educational Psychology, 91*, 579–593.

Treiman, R. (2006). Knowledge about letters as a foundation for reading and spelling. In R. M. Joshi & P. G. Aaron (Eds.), *Handbook of orthography and literacy* (pp. 581–599). Mahwah, NJ: Erlbaum.

Treiman, R., Goswami, U., & Bruck, M. (1990). Not all nonwords are alike: Implications for reading development and theory. *Memory & Cognition, 18*(6), 559–567.

Treiman, R., & Rodriquez, R. (1999). Young children use letter names in learning to read words. *Psychological Science, 10*(4), 334–338.

Treiman, R., Sotak, L., & Bowman, M. (2001). The roles of letter names and letter sounds in connecting print to speech. *Memory & Cognition, 29*(6), 860–873.

Treiman, R., Tincoff, R., & Richmond-Welty, E. D. (1996). Letter names help children to connect print and speech. *Developmental Psychology, 32*(3), 505–514.

Treiman, R., Weatherston, S., & Berch, D. (1994). The role of letter names in children's learning of phoneme-grapheme relations. *Applied Psycholinguistics 15*, 97–122.

Truch, S. (1994). Stimulating basic reading processes using auditory discrimination in depth. *Annals of Dyslexia, 44*, 60–80.

Truch, S. (2003). Comparing remedial outcomes using LIPS and Phono-graphix: An in-depth look from a clinical perspective. Unpublished manuscript, Reading Foundation, Calgary, Alberta, Canada. Retrieved from http://www.readingfoundation.com/uploads/documents/comparingRemedialOutcomes.pdf

Truch, S. (2004). Remedial outcomes with different reading programs. Paper presented at the International Dyslexia Association Conference, San Diego, CA. Retrieved from http://www.readingfoundation.com/uploads/documents/reading-outcomes.pdf

Tunmer, W. E. (2011). Forward. In S. A. Brady, D. Braze, & C. A. Fowler (Eds.), *Explaining individual differences in reading: Theory and evidence* (pp. ix–xiv). New York, NY: Psychology Press.

Tunmer, W. E., & Chapman, J. W. (1998). Language prediction skill, phonological recoding ability, and beginning reading. In C. Hulme & R. M. Joshi (Eds.), *Reading and spelling: Development and disorders* (pp. 33–67). Mahwah, NJ: Erlbaum.

Tunmer, W. E., & Chapman, J. W. (2002). The relation of beginning readers' reported word identification strategies to reading achievement, reading-related skills, and academic self-perceptions. *Reading and Writing: An Interdisciplinary Journal 15*, 341–358.

Tunmer, W. E., & Chapman, J. W. (2012). Does set for variability mediate the influence of vocabulary knowledge on the development of word recognition skills? *Scientific Studies of Reading, 16*(2), 122–140. doi:10.1080/10888438.2010.542527

Tunmer, W. E., Chapman, J. W., & Prochnow, J. E. (2002). Preventing negative Matthew Effects in at-risk readers: A retrospective study. In B. R. Foorman, (Ed.), *Preventing and remediating reading difficulties: Bringing science to scale* (pp. 121–163). Baltimore, MD: York Press.

Vaessen, A., Bertrand, D., Tóth, D., Csépe, V., Faísca, L., Reis, A., & Blomert, L. (2010). Cognitive development of fluent word reading does not qualitatively differ between transparent and opaque orthographies. *Journal of Educational Psychology, 102*(4), 827–842. DOI: 10.1037/a0019465

Vaessen, A., & Blomert, L. (2010). Long-term cognitive dynamics of fluent reading development. *Journal of Experimental Child Psychology, 105*, 213–231. doi:10.1016/j.jecp.2009.11.005

Van den Broeck, W., & Geudens, A. (2012). Old and new ways to study characteristics of reading disability: The case of the nonword-reading deficit. *Cognitive Psychology, 65*, 414–456.

Van den Broeck, W., Geudens, A., & van den Bos, K. P. (2010). The nonword-reading deficit of disabled readers: A developmental interpretation. *Developmental Psychology. 46*(3), 717–734.

van Orden, G. S., & Kloos, H. (2005). Question of phonology and reading. In M. J. Snowling & C. Hulme (Eds.), *The science of reading: A handbook* (pp. 61–78). Oxford, UK: Blackwell.

Vaughn, S., Cirino, P. T., Wanzek, J., Fletcher, J. M., … Francis, D. J. (2010). Response to intervention for middle school students with reading difficulties: effects of a primary and secondary intervention. *School Psychology Review, 39*(1), 3–21.

Vaughn, S., Linan-Thompson, S., & Hickman, P. (2003). Response to instruction as a means of identifying students with reading/learning disabilities. *Exceptional Children, 69*, 391–409.

Vaughn, S., Wexler, J., Leroux, A., Roberts, G., Denton, C., Barth, A., & Fletcher, J. (2012). Effects of intensive reading intervention for eighth-grade students with persistently inadequate response to intervention. *Journal of Learning Disabilities, 45*(6), 515–525.

Vaughn, S., Wexler, J., Roberts, G., Barth, A. A., … Denton, C. A. (2011). Effects of individualized and standardized interventions on middle school students with reading disabilities. *Exceptional Children, 77*(4), 391–407.

Vellutino, F. R. (1979). *Dyslexia: Theory and research*. Cambridge, MA: MIT Press.

Vellutino, F. R., Fletcher, J. M., Snowling, M. J., & Scanlon, D. M. (2004). Specific reading disability (dyslexia): What have we learned in the past four decades? *Journal of Child Psychology and Psychiatry 45*(1), 2–40.

Vellutino, F. R., & Scanlon, D. M. (2002). The interactive strategies approach to reading intervention. *Contemporary Educational Psychology, 27*, 573–635.

Vellutino, F. R., Scanlon, D. M., & Jaccard, J. J. (2003). Toward distinguishing between cognitive and experiential deficits as primary sources of difficulty in learning to read: A two year follow-up of difficult to remediate and readily remediated poor readers. In B. R. Foorman (Ed.), *Preventing and remediating reading difficulties: Bringing science to scale* (pp. 73–120). Baltimore, MD: York Press.

Vellutino, F. R., Scanlon, D. M., & Lyon, G. R. (2000). Differentiating between difficult-to-remediate and readily remediated poor readers: More evidence against the IQ–achievement discrepancy definition of reading disability. *Journal of Learning Disabilities, 33,* 223–238.

Vellutino, F. R., Scanlon, D. M., Sipay, E. R., Small, S. G., Pratt, A., Chen, R., & Denkla, M. B. (1996). Cognitive profiles of difficult-to-remediate and readily remediated poor readers: Early intervention as a vehicle for distinguishing between cognitive and experiential deficits as basic causes of specific reading disability. *Journal of Educational Psychology, 88,* 601–638.

Vellutino, F. R., Scanlon, D M., & Tanzman, M. S. (1994). Components of reading ability: Issues and problems in operationalizing word identification, phonological coding, and orthographic coding. In G. R. Lyon (Ed.), *Frames of reference for the assessment of learning disabilities: New views on measurement issues* (pp. 279–332). Baltimore, MD: Brookes.

Vellutino, F. R., Scanlon, D. M., Zhang, H., & Schatschneider, C. (2008). Using response to kindergarten and first grade intervention to identify children at-risk for long-term reading difficulties. *Reading and Writing: An Interdisciplinary Journal, 21,* 437–480. doi:10.1007/s11145-007-9098-2

Vellutino, F., Steger, J., DeSetto, L., & Phillips, F. (1975). Immediate and delayed recognition of visual stimuli in poor and normal readers. *Journal of Experimental Child Psychology, 19,* 223–232.

Verhoeven, L., & van Leeuwe, J. (2008). Prediction of the development of reading comprehension: A longitudinal study. *Applied Cognitive Psychology, 22,* 407–423. doi:10.1002/acp.1414

Vloedgraven, J., & Verhoeven, L. (2009). The nature of phonological awareness throughout the elementary grades: An item response theory perspective. *Learning and Individual Differences, 19,* 161–169.

Vukovic, R. K., & Siegel, L. S. (2006). The double-deficit hypothesis: A comprehensive analysis of the evidence. *Journal of Learning Disabilities, 39*(1), 25–47.

Wagner, R. K., & Torgesen, J. K. (1987). The nature of phonological processing and its causal role in the acquisition of reading skills. *Psychological Bulletin, 101,* 192–212.

Wagner, R. K., Torgesen, J. K., Laughon, P., Simmons, K., & Rashotte, C. A. (1993). Development of young readers' phonological processing abilities. *Journal of Educational Psychology, 85*(1), 83–103.

Wagner, R. K., Torgesen, J. K., & Rashotte, C. A. (1994). Development of reading-related phonological abilities: New evidence of bidirectional causality from a latent variable longitudinal study. *Developmental Psychology, 30*(1), 73–87.

Wagner, R. K., Torgesen, J. K., & Rashotte, C. A. (1999). *The comprehensive test of phonological processing.* Austin, TX: PRO-ED.

Wagner, R. K., Torgesen, J. K., Rashotte, C. A., & Pearson, N. A. (2013). *Comprehensive test of phonological processing* (2nd ed.). Austin, TX: PRO-ED.

Wallach, M. A., & Wallach, L. (1976). *Teaching all children to read.* Chicago, IL: University of Chicago Press.

Wanzek, J., Vaughn, S. K., Scammacca, N. K., Metz, K., Murray, C. S., Roberts, G., & Danielson, L. (2013). Extensive reading interventions for students with reading difficulties after grade 3. *Review of Educational Research, 83*(2), 163–195. doi:10.3102/0034654313477212

Wayman, M. M., Wallace, T., Wiley, H. I., Tichá, R., & Espin, C. A. (2007). Literature synthesis on curriculum-based measurement in reading. *Journal of Special Education, 41*(2), 85–120.

Weaver, P. A., & Rosner, J. (1979). Relationships between visual and auditory perceptual skills and comprehension in students with learning disabilities. *Journal of Learning Disabilities, 12*(9), 617–621.

Westby, C. E. (2012). Perspectives on assessing and improving reading comprehension. In A. G. Kamhi & H. W. Catts (Eds.), *Language and reading disabilities* (3rd ed., pp. 163–225). Boston, MA: Pearson.

Whalley, K., & Hansen, J. (2006). The role of prosodic sensitivity in children's reading development. *Journal of Research in Reading, 29*(3), 288–303.

Whiteley, H. E., & Smith, C. D. (2001). The use of tinted lenses to alleviate reading difficulties. *Journal of Research in Reading, 24*(1), 30–40.

Wilkins, A. J., Lewis, E., Smith, F., Rowland, E., & Tweedie, W. (2001). Coloured overlays and their benefit for reading. *Journal of Research in Reading, 24*(1), 41–64.

Willcutt, E. G., Betjemann, R. S., Pennington, B. F., Olson, R. K., DeFries, J. C., & Wadsworth, S. J. (2007). Longitudinal study of reading disability and attention-deficit/hyperactivity disorder: Implications for education. *Mind, Brain, and Education, 1*(4), 181–192.

Williams, J. P. (1980). Teaching decoding with an emphasis on phoneme analysis and phoneme blending. *Journal of Educational Psychology, 72*, 1–15.

Williams, J. P., & Pao, L. S. (2011). Teaching narrative and expository text structure to improve comprehension. In R. E. O'Connor & P. F. Vadasy (Eds.), *Handbook of reading interventions* (pp. 220–253). New York, NY: Guilford Press.

Wise, B. W., Ring, J., & Olson, R. K. (1999). Training phonological awareness with and without explicit attention to articulation. *Journal of Experimental Child Psychology 72*, 271–304.

Wolf, M., & Bowers, P.G. (1999). The double-deficit hypothesis for the developmental dyslexias. *Journal of Educational Psychology 91*, 415–438.

Wolff, U. (2014). RAN as a predictor of reading skills, and vice versa: Results from a randomised reading intervention. *Annals of Dyslexia, 64*, 151–165. doi:10.1007/s11881-014-0091-6

Woodcock, R. W. (1998). *The Woodcock reading mastery test-Revised-Normative update.*. Circle Pines, MN: AGS.

Woodcock, R. W. (2011). *The Woodcock reading mastery test* (3rd ed.). Boston, MA: Pearson.

Yeo, S., Kim, D.-I., Branum-Martin, L., Wayman, M. M., & Espin, C. A. (2012). Assessing the reliability of curriculum-based measurement: An application of latent growth modeling. *Journal of School Psychology, 50*, 275–292.

Yesil-Dagli, U. (2011). Predicting ELL students' beginning first grade English oral reading fluency from initial kindergarten vocabulary, letter naming, and phonological awareness skills. *Early Childhood Research Quarterly 26*, 15–29.

Yopp, H. K. (1988). The validity and reliability of phonemic awareness tests. *Reading Research Quarterly, 23*(3), 159–177.

Zeno, S. M., Ivens, S. H., Millard, R. T., & Duvvuri, R. (1995). *The educator's word frequency guide*. Minneapolis, MN: Questar Assessment.

Ziegler, J. C., & Goswami, U. (2005). Reading acquisition, developmental dyslexia, and skilled reading across languages: A psycholinguistic grain size theory. *Psychological Bulletin, 131*(1), 3–29.

ABOUT THE AUTHOR

David A. Kilpatrick, PhD, is an Assistant Professor of Psychology for the State University of New York, College at Cortland, and a New York State Certified School Psychologist with the East Syracuse-Minoa Central School District. He received his Bachelor of Arts in psychology from the State University of New York, College at Cortland, a Master of Arts in theological studies from Gordon-Conwell Theological Seminary near Boston, MA, and a PhD in school psychology from Syracuse University.

David has been a practicing school psychologist for 27 years and has conducted well over 1,000 evaluations of students with reading difficulties. He has presented reading workshops to teachers and school psychologists in several states. He conducts research on the component skills involved word-level reading development with a focus on reading difficulties. In addition to his interests in psychology, David is a part-time professional magician and has done over 2,000 magic shows since 1986.

David and his wife Andrea have five grown children and three grandchildren. They live near Syracuse, NY.

Other books by David Kilpatrick:

Equipped for Reading Success: A Comprehensive, Step-by-Step Program for Developing Phonemic Awareness and Fluent Word Recognition (2015).

Keys to Effective Discipline: A Parent's Guide to Dealing with Difficult Behavior (2000).

ABOUT THE ONLINE RESOURCES

Thank you for choosing the *Essentials of Psychological Assessment* series. *Essentials of Assessing, Preventing, and Overcoming Reading Difficulties* includes downloadable resources designed to enhance your education and practice.

To access your resources, please follow these steps:

Step 1 Go to www.wiley.com/go/psyessresources

Step 2 Enter your email address, the password provided below, and click "submit"

   Password: reading2015

Step 3 Select and download the listed resources

If you need any assistance, please contact Wiley Customer Care 800-762-2974 (U.S.), 317-572-3994 (International) or visit www.wiley.com.

CONTENT INCLUDED IN THE ONLINE RESOURCES

1. The Phonological Awareness Screening Test (PAST)
   - Standard version of the PAST
   - Four alternate versions of the PAST
   - PAST Short Form (for universal screening)
   - Instructions for the administration of the PAST
   - Validity and reliability data on the PAST
   - An audio file that demonstrates the administration of the PAST
2. An audio file that provides assistance on pronouncing phonemes in isolation to assist with assessment and instruction
3. A paper that provides assistance on pronouncing phonemes in isolation
4. A document that describes 22 word study activities that promote orthographic mapping

Index

Page numbers in italics refer to illustrations.